Speed Bump™

Speed Bump™

Cartoons for Idea People
by Dave Coverly

ECW Press

Published by ECW PRESS
2120 Queen Street East, Suite 200, Toronto, Ontario, Canada M4E 1E2

NATIONAL LIBRARY OF CANADA CATALOGUING IN PUBLICATION

Coverly, Dave
Speed Bump : cartoons for idea people / Dave Coverly.

ISBN 1-55022-658-4

1. Caricatures and cartoons — United States. 2. American wit and humor, Pictorial. I. Title.

NC1429.C68s64 2004   41.5 973   C2004-902597-X

Cover and Text Design: Tania Craan
Layout: Gail Nina
Production: Mary Bowness
Printing:

DISTRIBUTION

CANADA: Jaguar Book Group, 100 Armstrong Avenue, Georgetown, ON, L7G 5S4
UNITED STATES: Independent Publishers Group, 814 North Franklin Street,
Chicago, Illinois 60610

5 4 3 2 1

PRINTED AND BOUND IN CANADA

ECW PRESS
ecwpress.com

IDEAS IN THE MIST

What makes a Good Idea for a cartoon? Where do Ideas come from? Where do Ideas go when you're done with them? And why are Ideas so darn slippery and chameleon-like? One minute they're there, in your grasp; the next minute they're gone, blending in with the wallpaper of your everyday thoughts.

Everyone has Ideas. Most of us enjoy them for a fleeting moment, as though catching a glimpse of a strangely beautiful bird, and then forget them almost immediately. But a cartoonist's job is much like being a bird watcher. We take note of them. We process what we've seen through our mental binoculars and share it.

The very fact that we ALL have Ideas is what makes cartoons so fun to read. The best of them should tap into this common experience, should touch on something recognizable, should peel away the layers of the things most people take for granted.

A comic panel, unlike a comic strip, has one shot to get its Idea across to you. The set-up, the people or animals or both, the location, the punch line, all come at you at once. The trick for a panel cartoonist is to make the Idea decipherable in a matter of seconds, even though the cartoon itself may have taken all afternoon to create. And to make it decipherable, a cartoonist often uses things we all have in common, as well as clichés, idioms and metaphors. These are all important shortcuts to humor.

The final step toward getting a Good Idea Is taking these recognizable things . . . and mixing them up. The cartoon on this page is a perfect example of what I try to do with "Speed Bump". I was working on a panel about the witch and the candy house and coming up empty . . . later that same day I was working on a different panel about suburban sprawl, and again coming up empty (it was one of those days . . .). But then I turned my mental binoculars around and, seen from a distance, the Ideas merged . . .

The rest of this book is a catalogue of other Ideas I've had. Some you may like better than others, since humor is so subjective . . . but here's hoping you glimpse a strangely beautiful bird or two . . .

Dave Coverly
Summer 2004

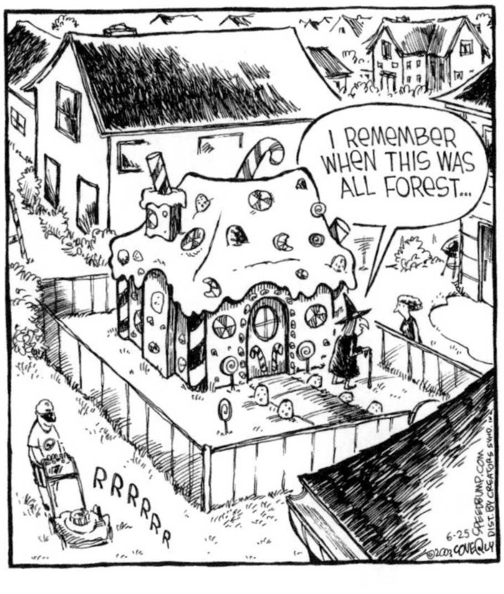
I REMEMBER WHEN THIS WAS ALL FOREST...
RRRRRRR
6-25
SPEEDBUMP.COM
DIST. BY CREATORS SYND. INC.
©2003 COVERLY

CHEERS/NA ZDRAVI/SALUD/KAMPAI/LECHYD DA/PROSIT...

... To family, friends, and anyone who's dropped me a nice note about the cartoons over the years . . . In particular, thanks to Kenny Zelnis, a former teacher, current muse, and constant source of positive encouragement for 25 years; and Jim Borgman, the world's greatest cartoonist and an even better human being . . .

FOREWORD

I remember it as a crisp April day when I first set eyes on young Meriwether Coverly. As I readied the paints for my palette and stoked the woodstove to stave off the chill of the morning, I heard the faint rapping of tiny knuckles on my studio door. Cracking it open I saw a waif not two feet tall, dressed in tattered knickers, a silly patchwork cap and leaning on a tiny crutch. To see him made me laugh and I invited him in for hot cider and a visit that would last, well, a lifetime.

He told me in a brave big-boy voice that he was an artist and would someday be "the greatest cartoonist the world had ever seen." He spread out a handful of crayon scrawls across my drawing table and studied my reaction. It was all I could do to keep a straight face as I rubbed my chin whiskers. The noses were much too big, the cross hatching all wrong, and his grasp of three-point perspective was tenuous at best. But in the end the lad won my heart and I adopted him as my own son. I renamed him David, Michelangelo's feisty young warrior.

Thus began our halcyon days. I would bounce little Dave on my knee, squeeze his fat little cheeks and prop him on a tall stool where he would squeal with delight and clap his pudgy hands as he watched me create a dozen or more cartoons before his wondering eyes. In those days I worked large, each cartoon covering a wall of my immense studio overlooking the river, and young Dave and I would watch the steamboats paddling up the river as my assistants photographed each finished cartoon for the newspaper's engravers and hurriedly applied a fresh layer of plaster to the wall awaiting my next creation.

At a quarter past noon, Dave and I would pause for lunch and amble hand in hand down the rows of lavender bushes and magnolia trees to the orchard. There I would hoist him onto my shoulders and he would disappear into the quivering pear tree branches, emerging minutes later with as much plump fruit as his little arms could carry. His eyes would twinkle as I lowered him to the ground, and there we would feast on cheeses, figs, pickled beets, mutton and merlot as we gazed out over the poppy fields and spotted in the clouds the images that would become that afternoon's cartoons.

All these years later I can hardly see a "Speed Bump" cartoon on a refrigerator door without smelling the sweet scent of lavender, tasting pear juice dribbling down my chin and hearing little Dave's merry laughter echoing in my soul. In these wretched days when newspaper comics are churned out by supercomputers randomly selecting characters, backgrounds and captions from an offshore database and edited by legions of humorless bureaucrats in suburban office parks, it is these memories that comfort me as I watch the clouds pass by my tenement window and wait another day by the phone for his call.

Jim Borgman
Co-creator of "Zits" and Pulitzer Prize-winning editorial cartoonist for the *Cincinnati Enquirer*

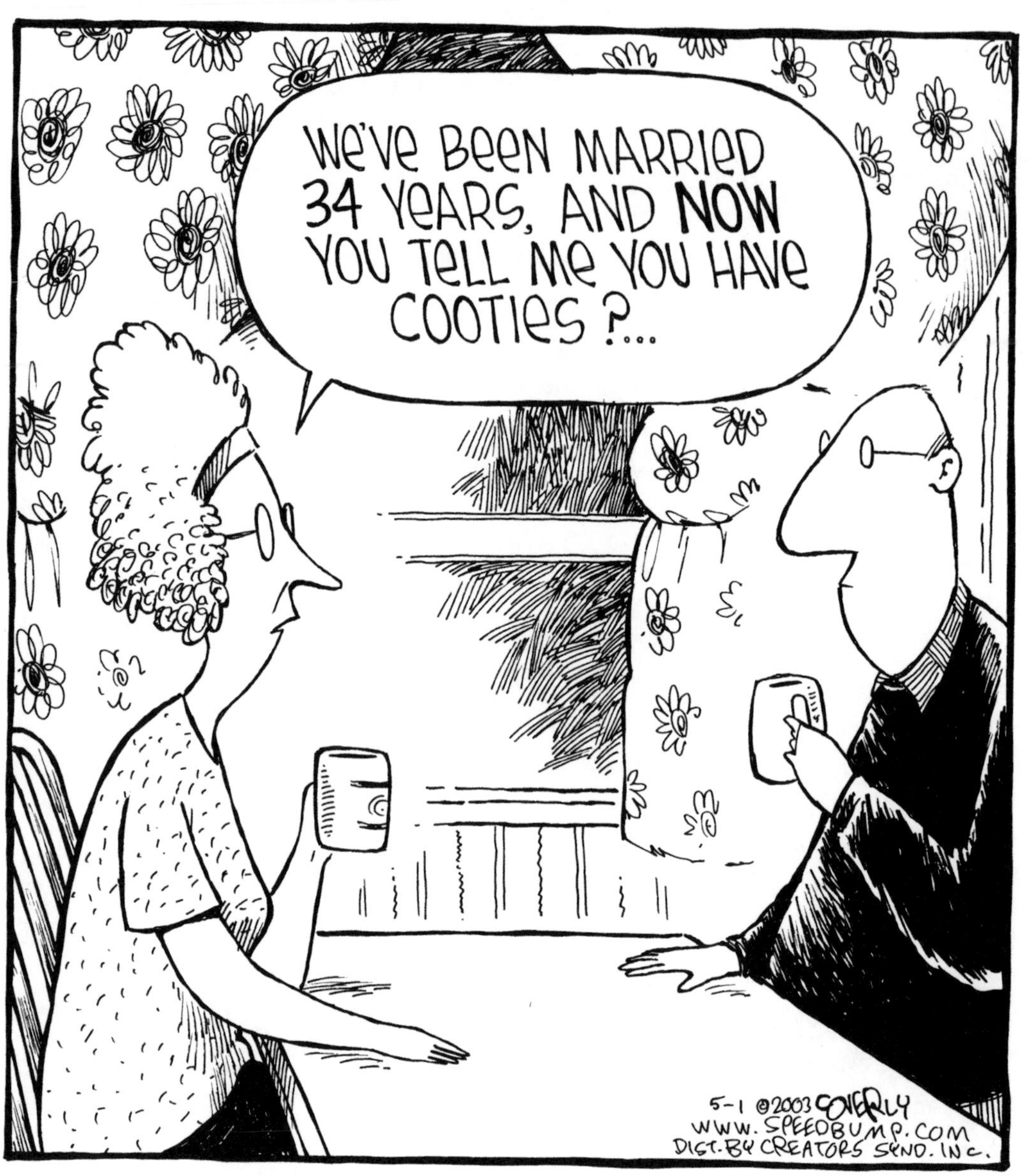
WE'VE BEEN MARRIED 34 YEARS, AND NOW YOU TELL ME YOU HAVE COOTIES ?...
5-1 ©2003 COVERLY
WWW.SPEEDBUMP.COM
DIST. BY CREATORS SYND. INC.

Relationships

Despite what you may have heard, love does not make the world go 'round.

Love makes the world laugh.

All you need to do is check out the comics page of your local newspaper to see how many cartoons are about the differences between husbands and wives, or boyfriends and girlfriends. Hey, "The Lockhorns" has had a nice, long run riffing on ONLY that. For a cartoon to be popular, it has to have some sort of universal appeal, and there's nothing more universal than love.

Also, I think laughing together is love's strongest bond.

So maybe it's really laughter that makes the world go 'round.

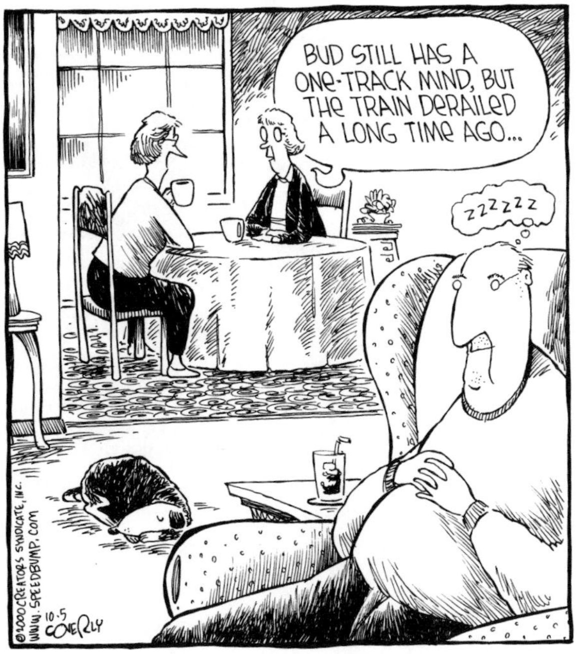
BUD STILL HAS A ONE-TRACK MIND, BUT THE TRAIN DERAILED A LONG TIME AGO...
ZZZZZZ
©2000 CREATORS SYNDICATE, INC.
WWW.SPEEDBUMP.COM
10-5
COVERLY

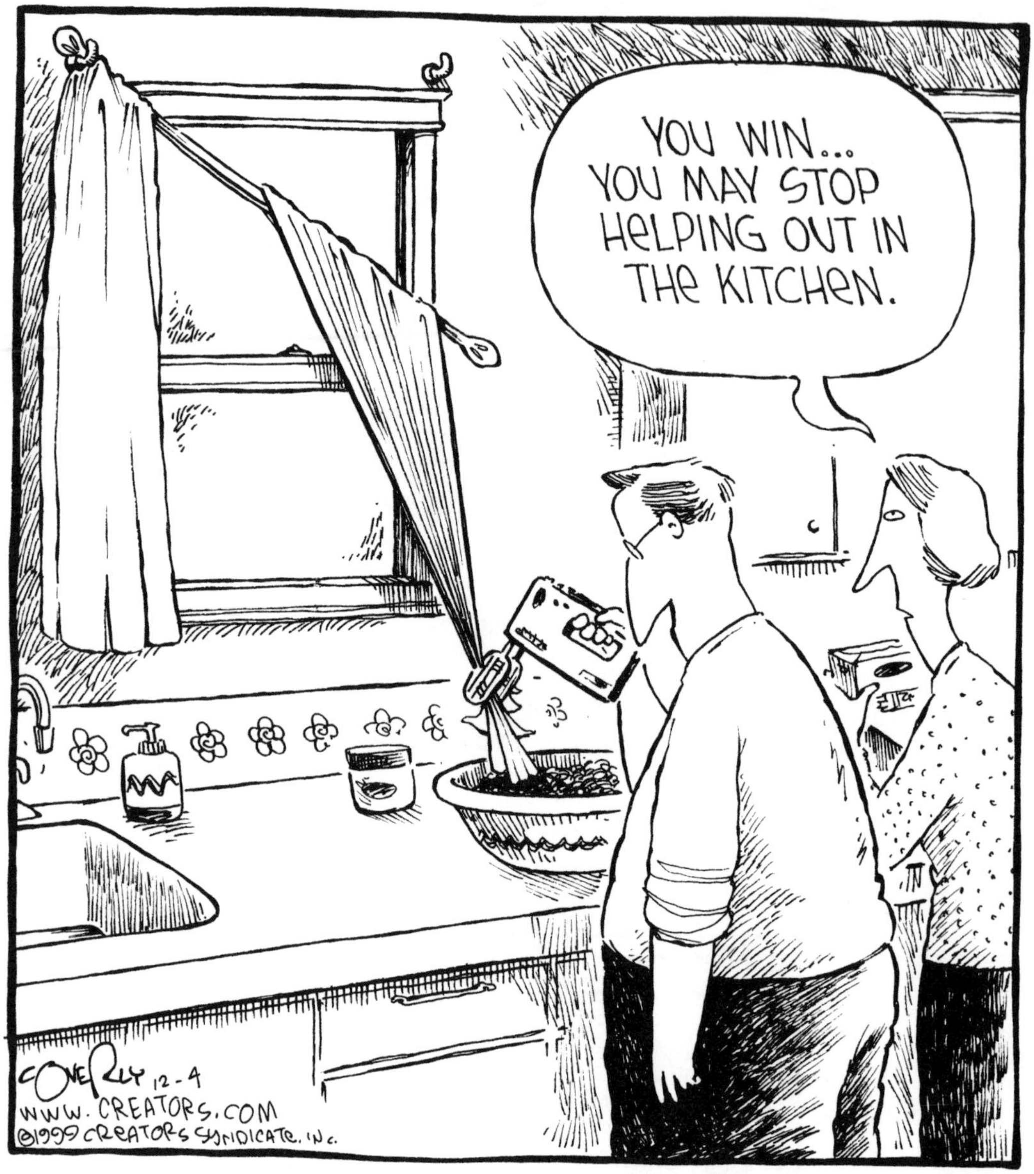
YOU WIN... YOU MAY STOP HELPING OUT IN THE KITCHEN.
CONERLY 12-4
WWW.CREATORS.COM
©1999 CREATORS SYNDICATE, INC.

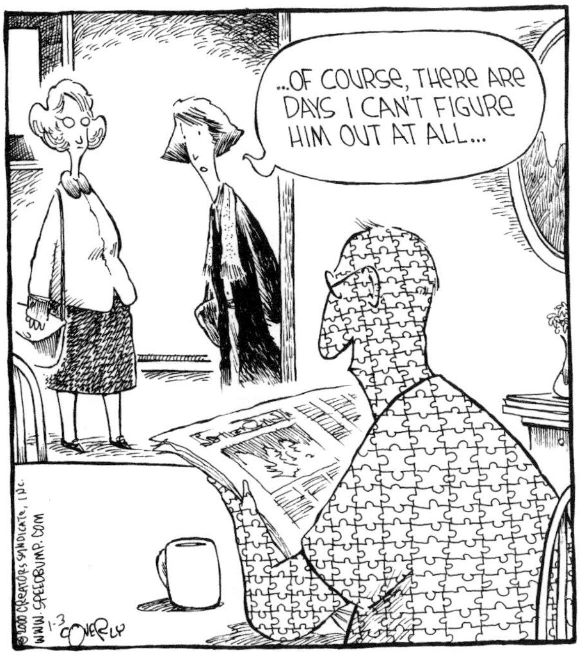
...OF COURSE, THERE ARE DAYS I CAN'T FIGURE HIM OUT AT ALL...
©2000 CREATORS SYNDICATE, INC.
WWW.SPEEDBUMP.COM
1-3 COVERLY

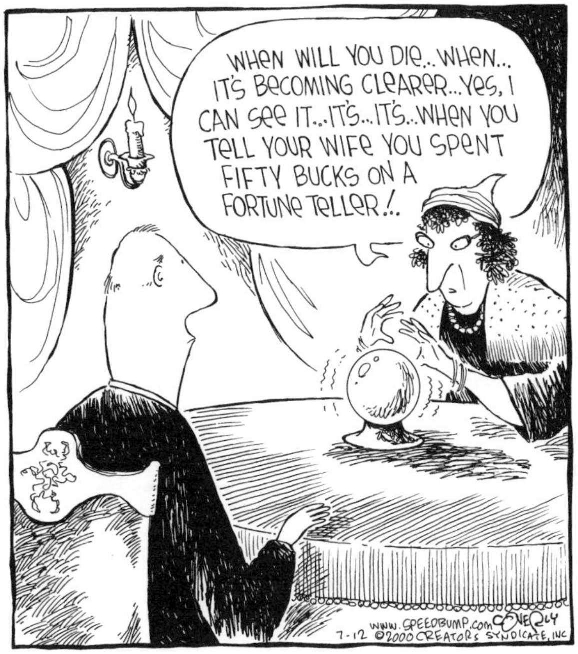
WHEN WILL YOU DIE..WHEN... IT'S BECOMING CLEARER...YES, I CAN SEE IT...IT'S...IT'S..WHEN YOU TELL YOUR WIFE YOU SPENT FIFTY BUCKS ON A FORTUNE TELLER!..
7-12 WWW.SPEEDBUMP.com COVERLY
©2000 CREATORS SYNDICATE, INC

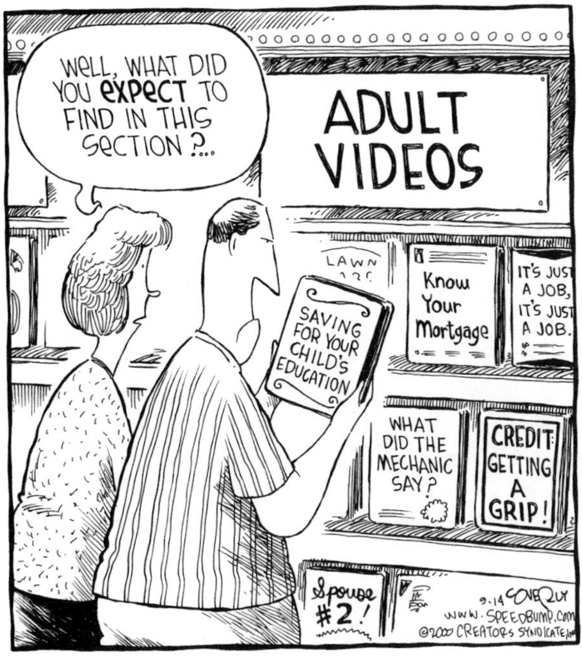
WELL, WHAT DID YOU EXPECT TO FIND IN THIS SECTION?...
ADULT VIDEOS
SAVING FOR YOUR CHILD'S EDUCATION
Know Your Mortgage
IT'S JUST A JOB, IT'S JUST A JOB.
WHAT DID THE MECHANIC SAY?
CREDIT: GETTING A GRIP!
Spouse #2!
9-14 COVERLY
WWW.SPEEDBUMP.com
©2000 CREATORS SYNDICATE, INC

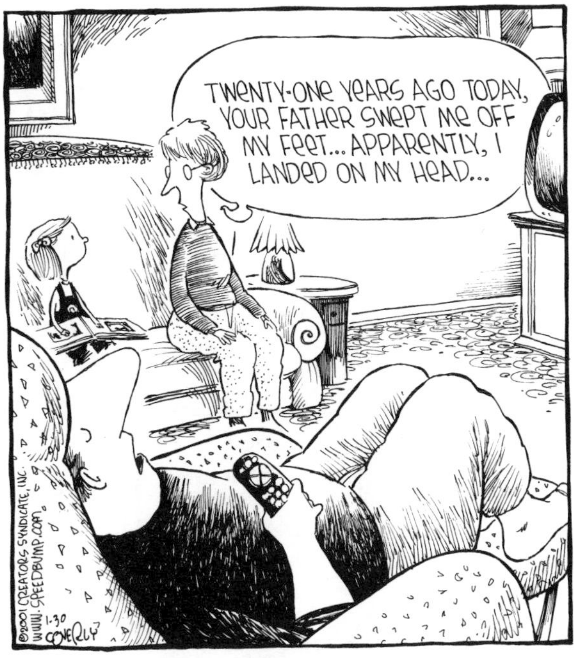
TWENTY-ONE YEARS AGO TODAY, YOUR FATHER SWEPT ME OFF MY FEET... APPARENTLY, I LANDED ON MY HEAD...
©2001 CREATORS SYNDICATE, INC.
WWW.SPEEDBUMP.com
1-30 COVERLY

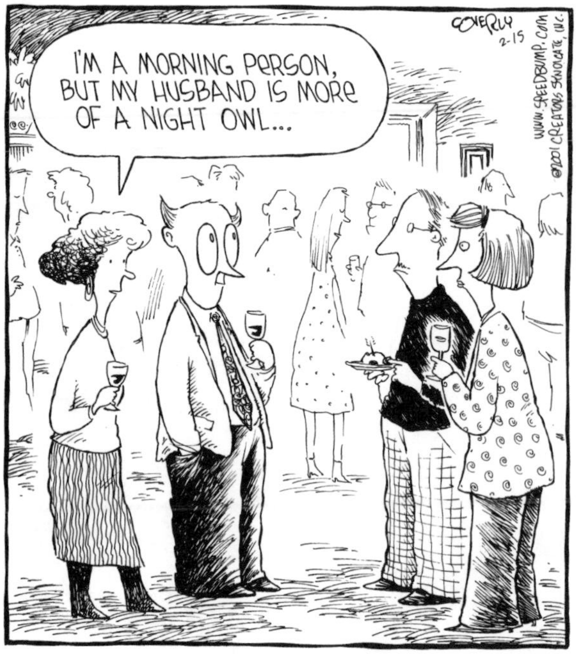
I'M A MORNING PERSON, BUT MY HUSBAND IS MORE OF A NIGHT OWL...
COVERLY 2-15
WWW.SPEEDBUMP.COM ©2001 CREATORS SYNDICATE, INC.

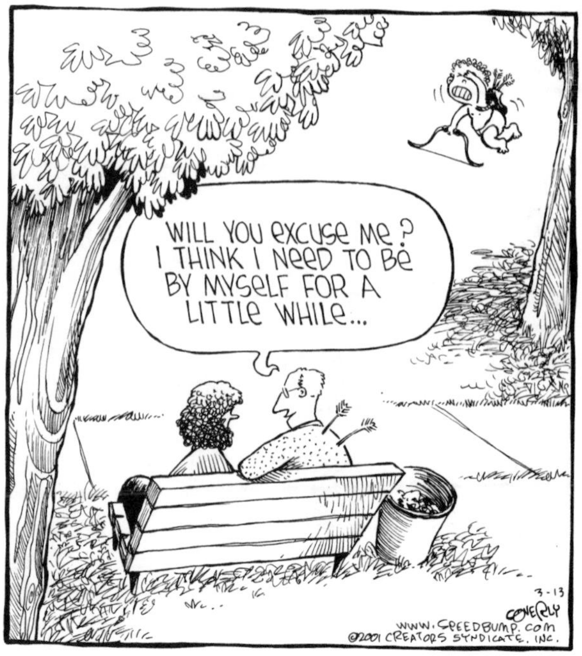
WILL YOU EXCUSE ME? I THINK I NEED TO BE BY MYSELF FOR A LITTLE WHILE...
3-13
COVERLY
WWW.SPEEDBUMP.COM
©2001 CREATORS SYNDICATE, INC.

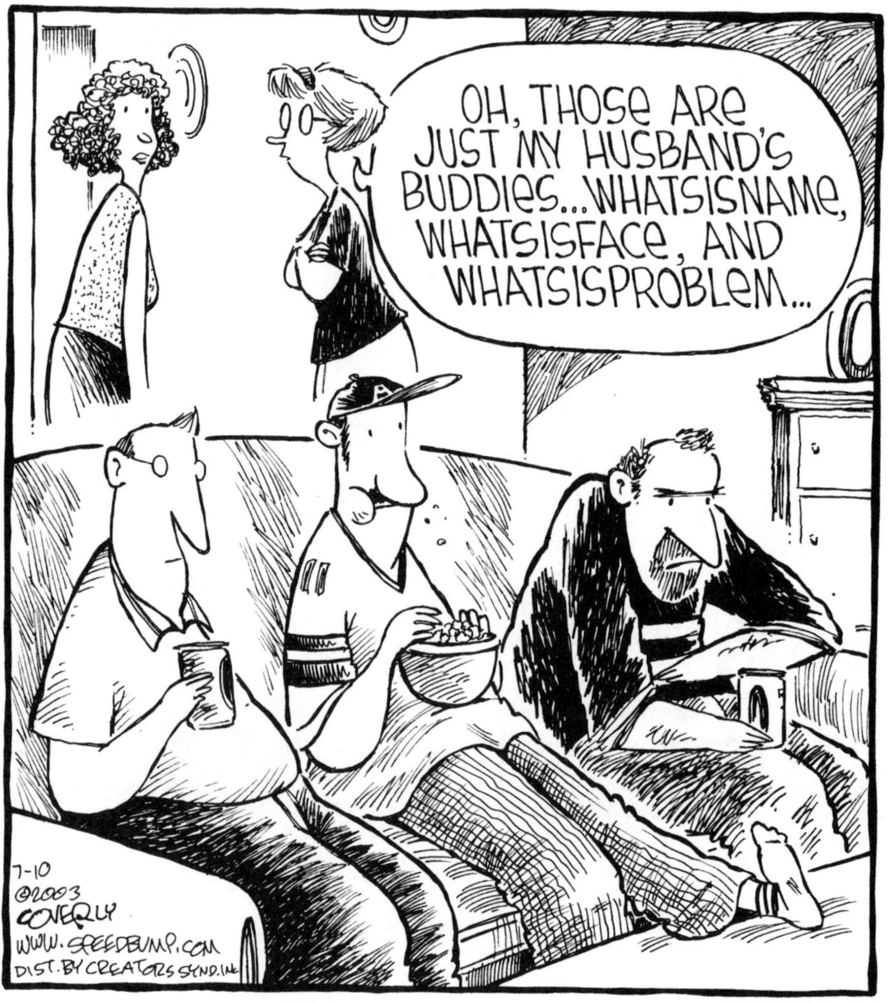
OH, THOSE ARE JUST MY HUSBAND'S BUDDIES...WHATSISNAME, WHATSISFACE, AND WHATSISPROBLEM...
7-10
©2003
COVERLY
WWW.SPEEDBUMP.COM
DIST. BY CREATORS SYND. INC.

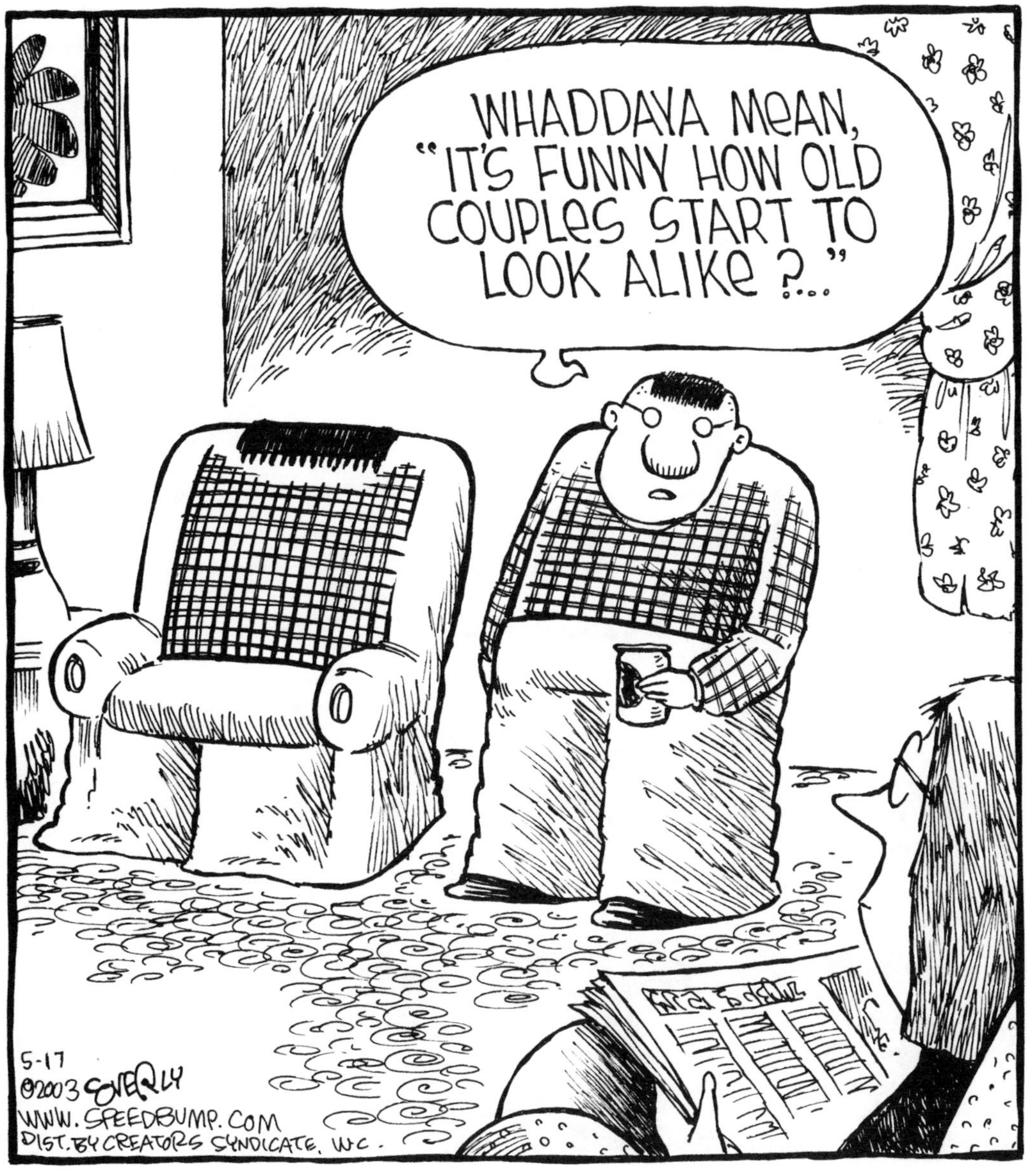
WHADDAYA MEAN, "IT'S FUNNY HOW OLD COUPLES START TO LOOK ALIKE ?..."
5-17
©2003 COVERLY
WWW.SPEEDBUMP.COM
DIST. BY CREATORS SYNDICATE, INC.

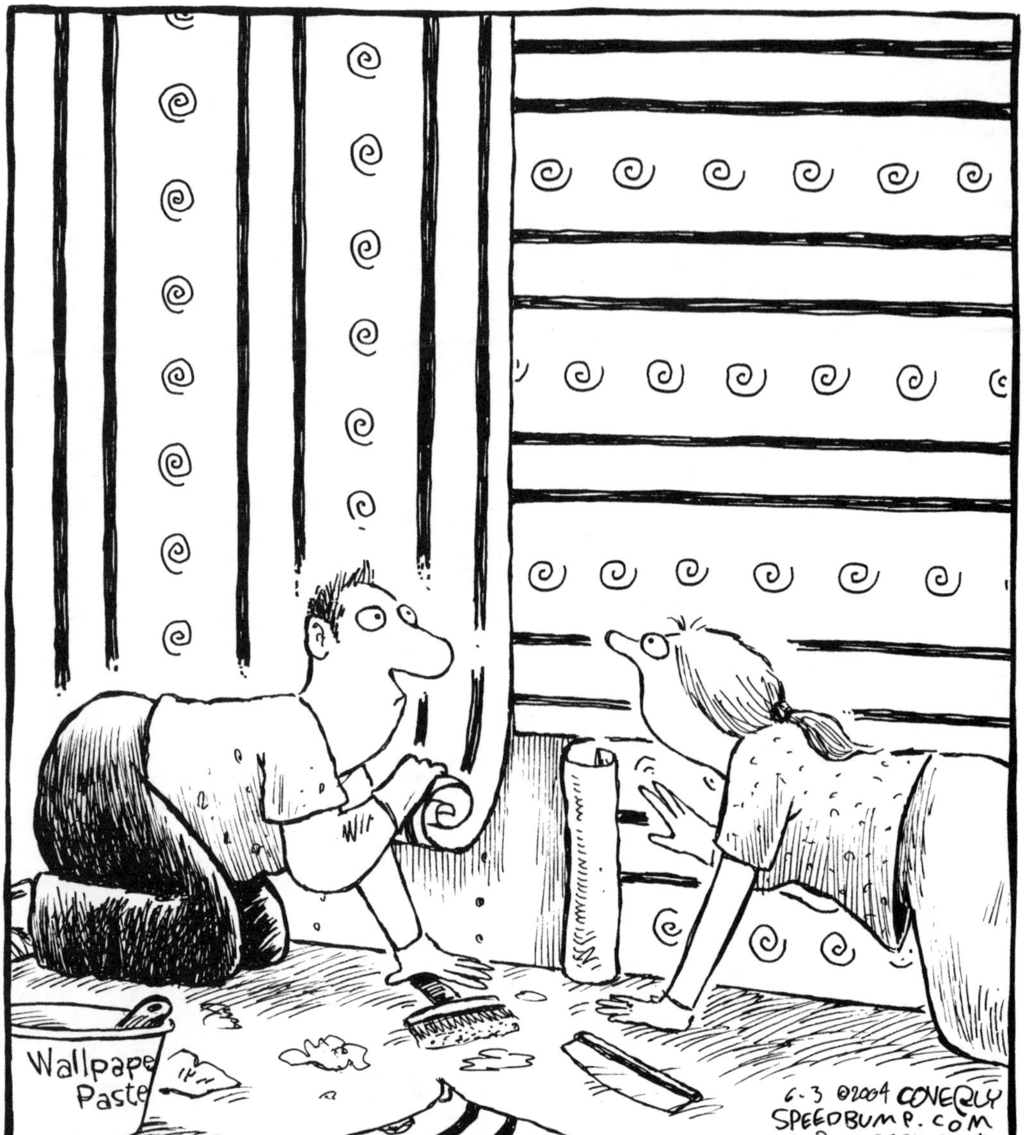
Wallpaper Paste
6-3 ©2004 COVERLY
SPEEDBUMP.COM
DIST. BY CREATORS SYND. INC.

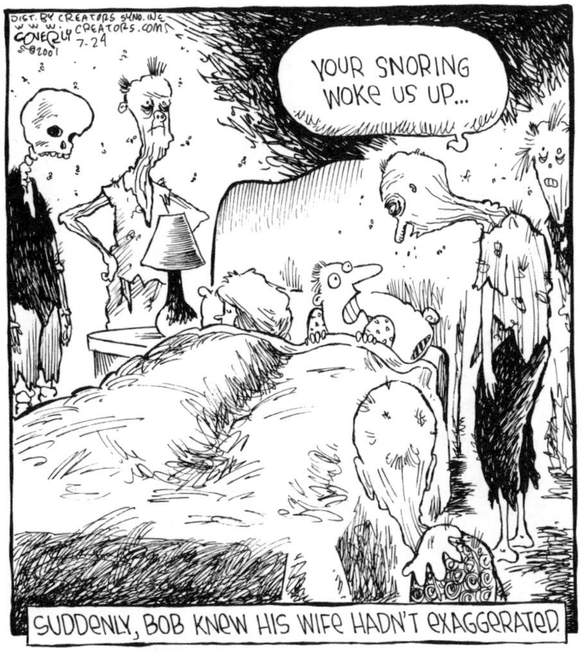
YOUR SNORING WOKE US UP...
SUDDENLY, BOB KNEW HIS WIFE HADN'T EXAGGERATED.

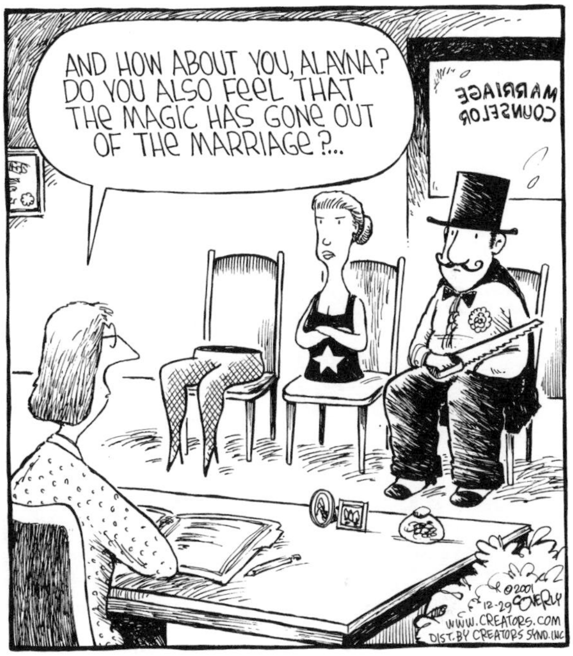
AND HOW ABOUT YOU, ALAYNA? DO YOU ALSO FEEL THAT THE MAGIC HAS GONE OUT OF THE MARRIAGE?...
WWW.CREATORS.COM
DIST. BY CREATORS SYND. INC

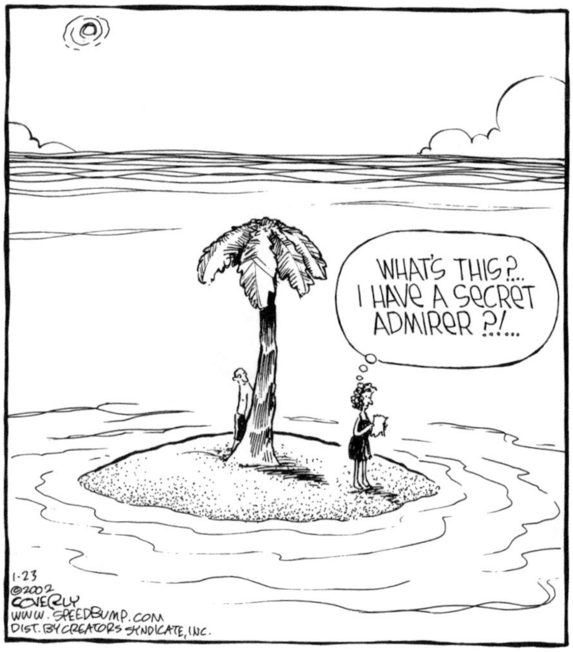
WHAT'S THIS?...
I HAVE A SECRET
ADMIRER ?!...
1-23
©2002
COVERLY
WWW.SPEEDBUMP.COM
DIST. BY CREATORS SYNDICATE, INC.

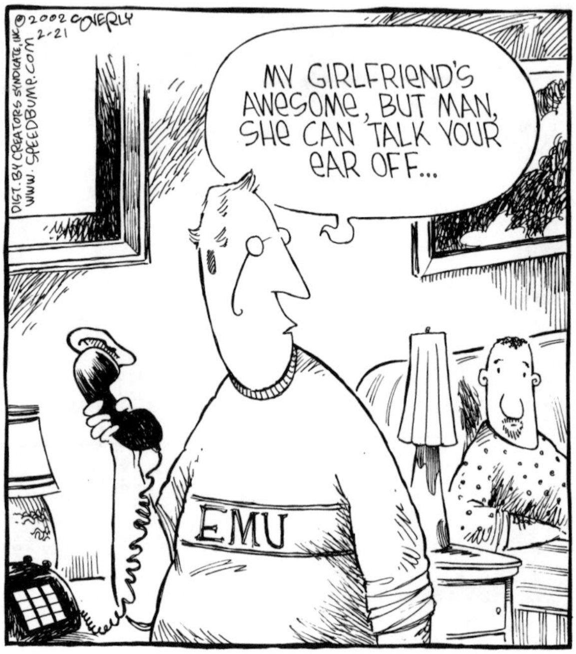
©2002 COVERLY
2-21
DIST. BY CREATORS SYNDICATE, INC.
WWW.SPEEDBUMP.COM
MY GIRLFRIEND'S
AWESOME, BUT MAN,
SHE CAN TALK YOUR
EAR OFF...
EMU

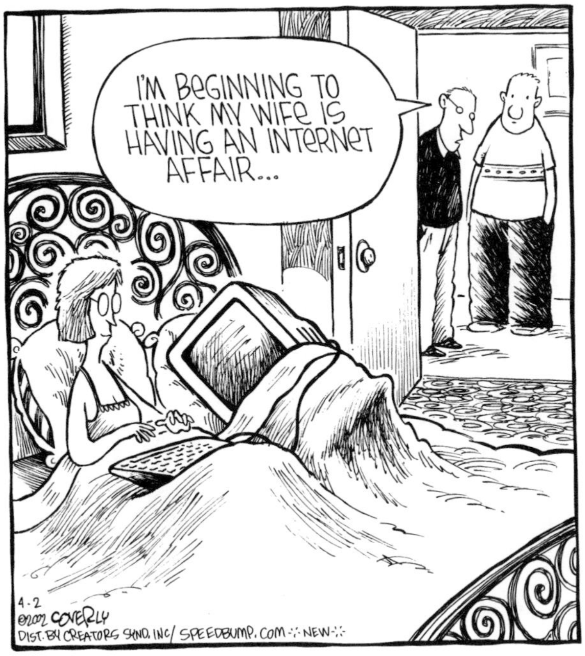
I'M BEGINNING TO THINK MY WIFE IS HAVING AN INTERNET AFFAIR...
4-2
©2002 COVERLY
DIST. BY CREATORS SYND. INC./ SPEEDBUMP.COM NEW

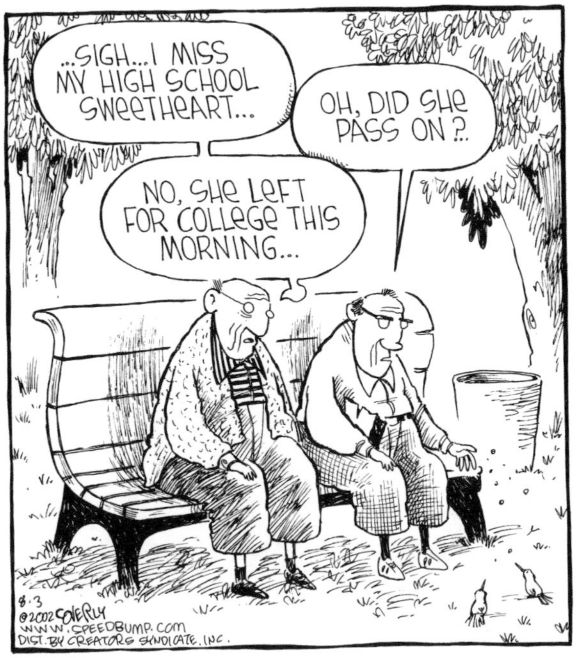
...SIGH...I MISS MY HIGH SCHOOL SWEETHEART...
OH, DID SHE PASS ON?..
NO, SHE LEFT FOR COLLEGE THIS MORNING...
8-3
©2002 COVERLY
WWW.SPEEDBUMP.COM
DIST. BY CREATORS SYNDICATE, INC.

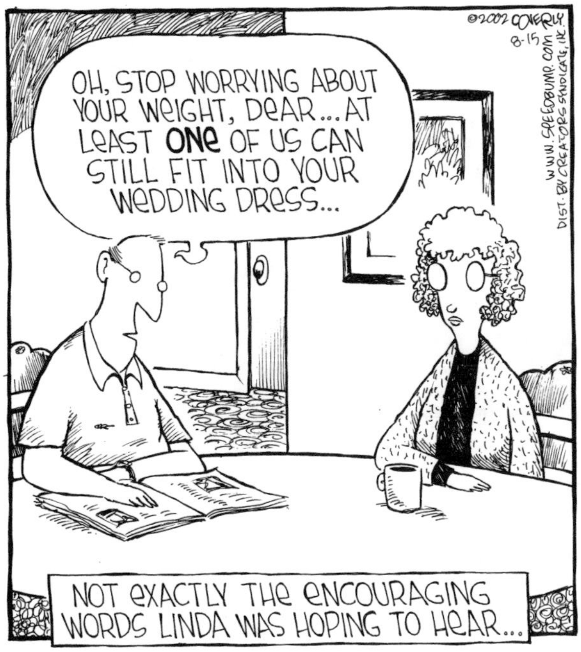
OH, STOP WORRYING ABOUT YOUR WEIGHT, DEAR...AT LEAST **ONE** OF US CAN STILL FIT INTO YOUR WEDDING DRESS...
©2002 COVERLY
8-15
WWW.SPEEDBUMP.COM
DIST. BY CREATORS SYNDICATE, INC.
NOT EXACTLY THE ENCOURAGING WORDS LINDA WAS HOPING TO HEAR...

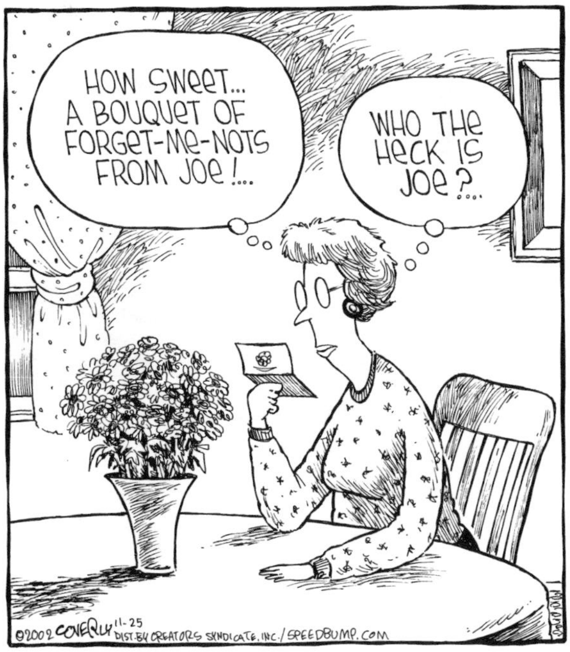
HOW SWEET... A BOUQUET OF FORGET-ME-NOTS FROM JOE!...
WHO THE HECK IS JOE?...
©2002 COVERLY 11-25
DIST. BY CREATORS SYNDICATE, INC./SPEEDBUMP.COM

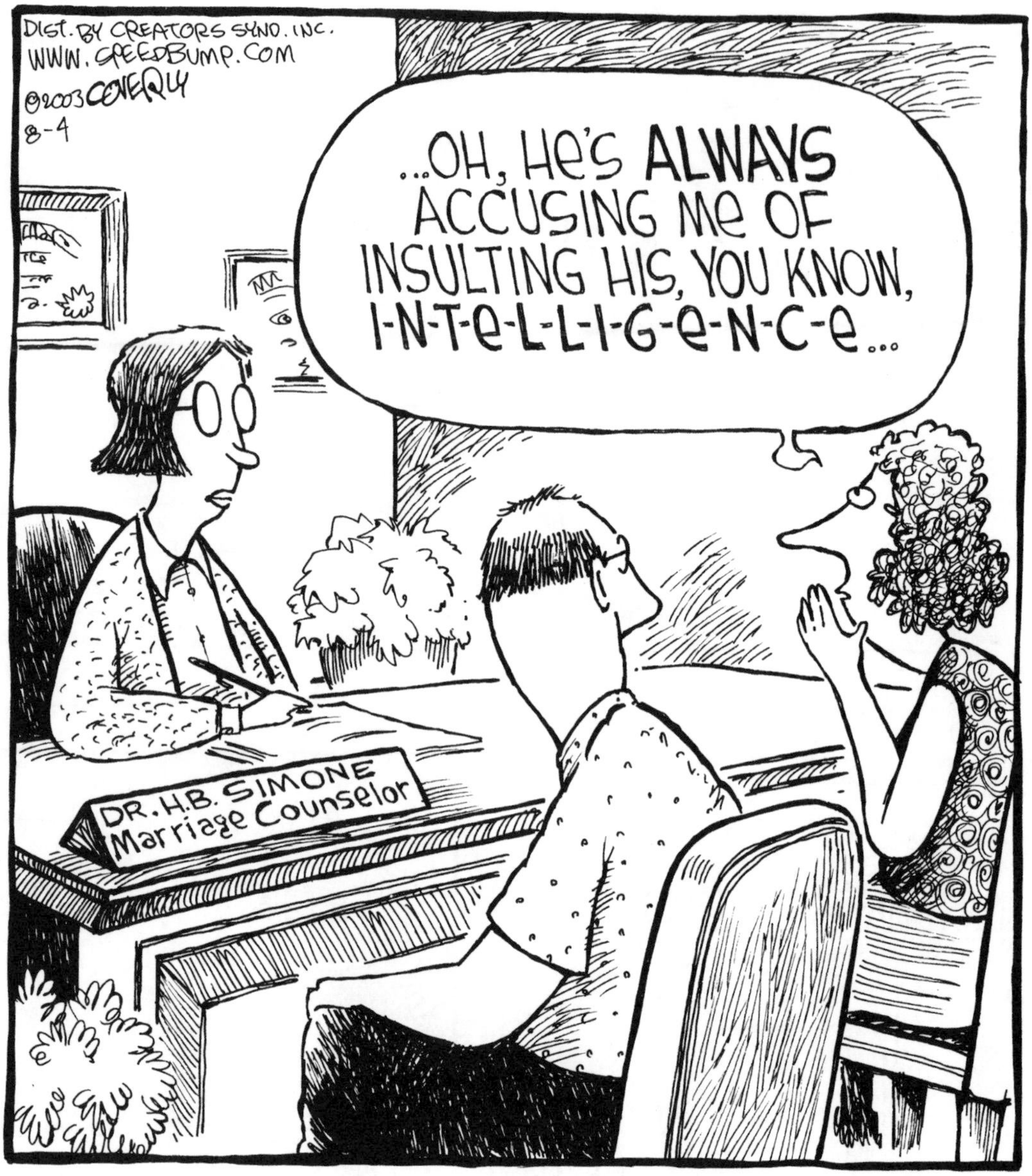
DIST. BY CREATORS SYND. INC.
WWW.SPEEDBUMP.COM
©2003 COVERLY
8-4
...OH, HE'S **ALWAYS** ACCUSING ME OF INSULTING HIS, YOU KNOW, I-N-T-E-L-L-I-G-E-N-C-E...
DR. H.B. SIMONE
Marriage Counselor

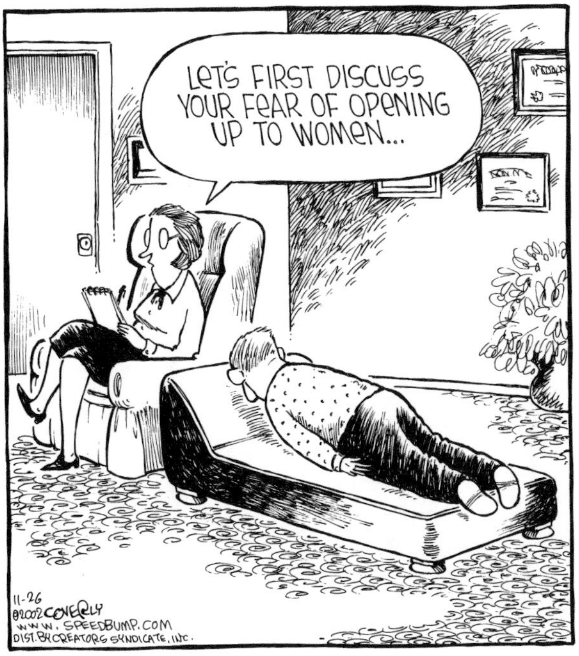
LET'S FIRST DISCUSS YOUR FEAR OF OPENING UP TO WOMEN...
11-26
©2002 COVERLY
WWW.SPEEDBUMP.COM
DIST. BY CREATORS SYNDICATE, INC.

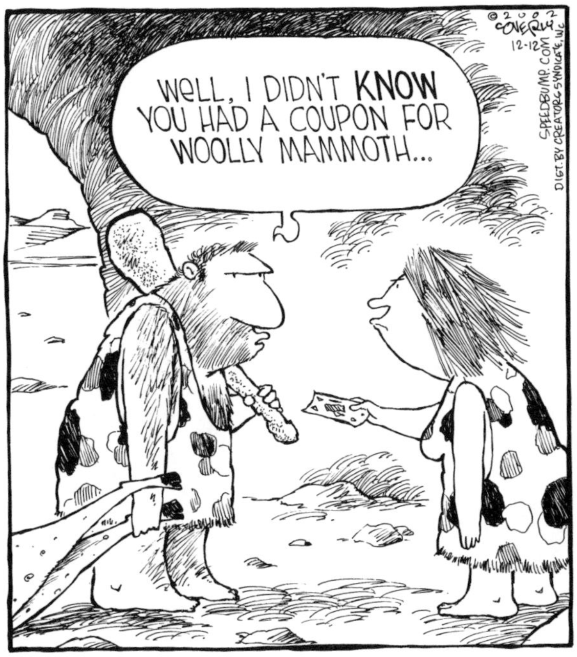
WELL, I DIDN'T KNOW YOU HAD A COUPON FOR WOOLLY MAMMOTH...
©2002 COVERLY
12-12
SPEEDBUMP.COM
DIST. BY CREATORS SYNDICATE, INC.

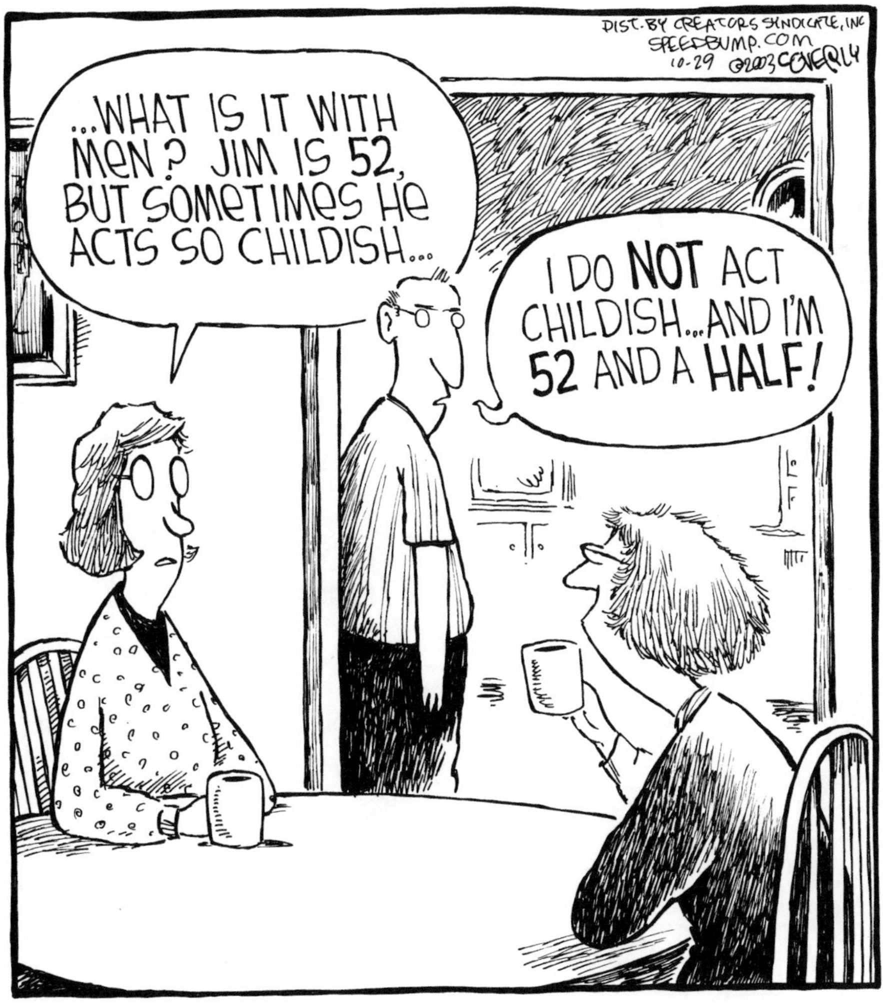
DIST. BY CREATORS SYNDICATE, INC
SPEEDBUMP.COM
10-29 ©2003 COVERLY
...WHAT IS IT WITH MEN? JIM IS 52, BUT SOMETIMES HE ACTS SO CHILDISH...
I DO NOT ACT CHILDISH...AND I'M 52 AND A HALF!

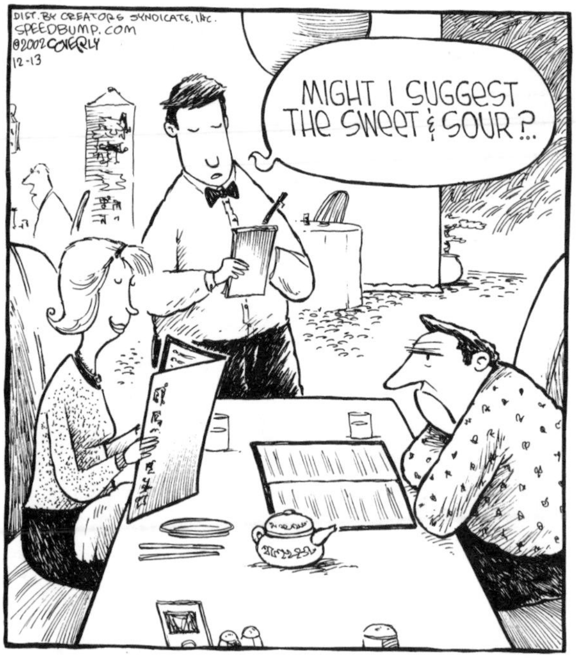
DIST. BY CREATORS SYNDICATE, INC.
SPEEDBUMP.COM
©2002 COVERLY
12-13
MIGHT I SUGGEST THE SWEET & SOUR?..

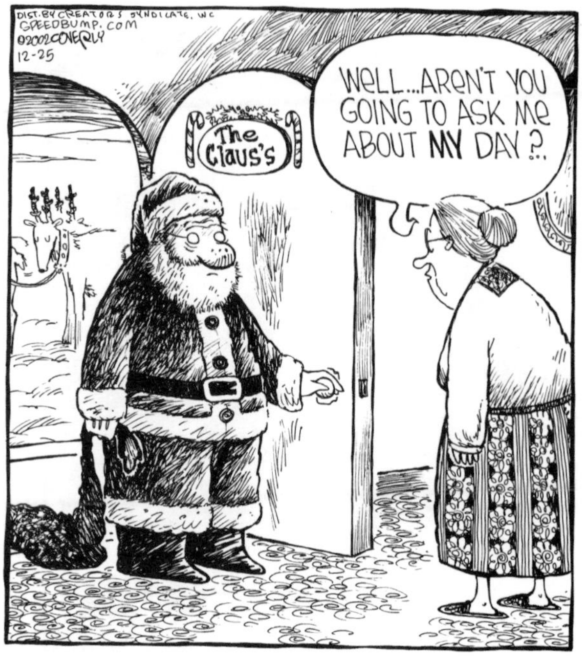
DIST. BY CREATORS SYNDICATE, INC
SPEEDBUMP.COM
©2002 COVERLY
12-25
The Claus's
WELL...AREN'T YOU GOING TO ASK ME ABOUT MY DAY?..

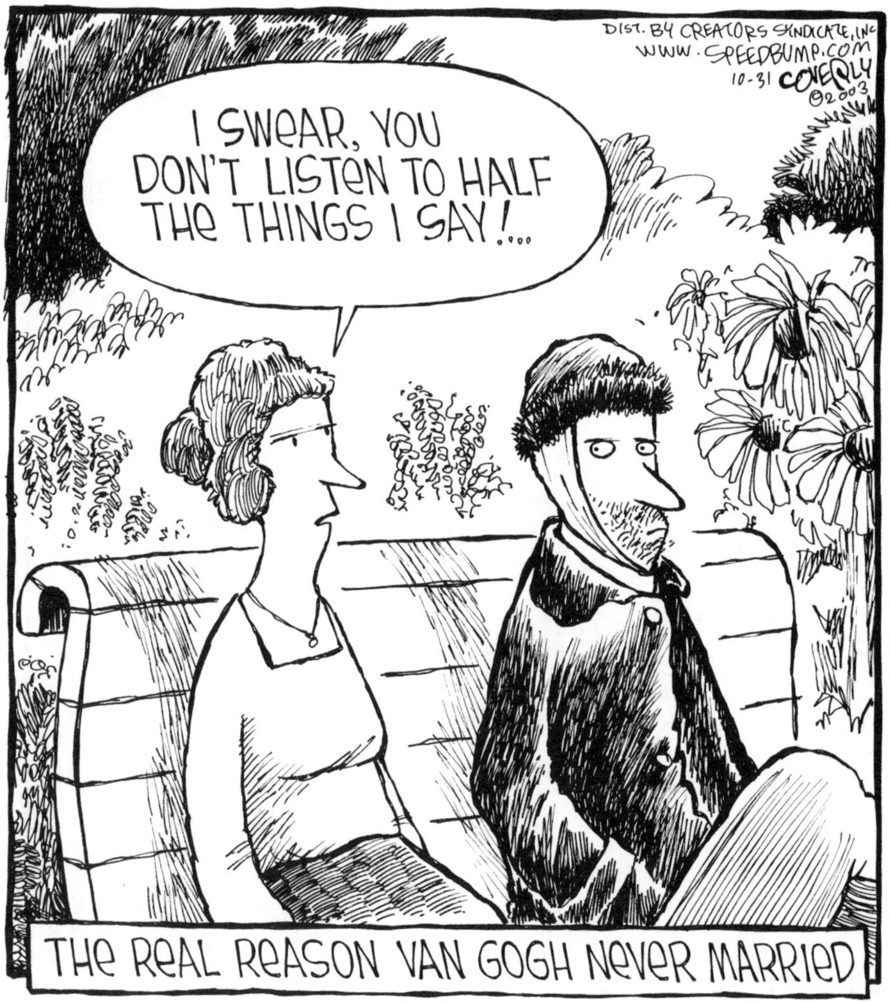
DIST. BY CREATORS SYNDICATE, INC
WWW.SPEEDBUMP.COM
10-31 COVERLY ©2003
I SWEAR, YOU DON'T LISTEN TO HALF THE THINGS I SAY!..
THE REAL REASON VAN GOGH NEVER MARRIED

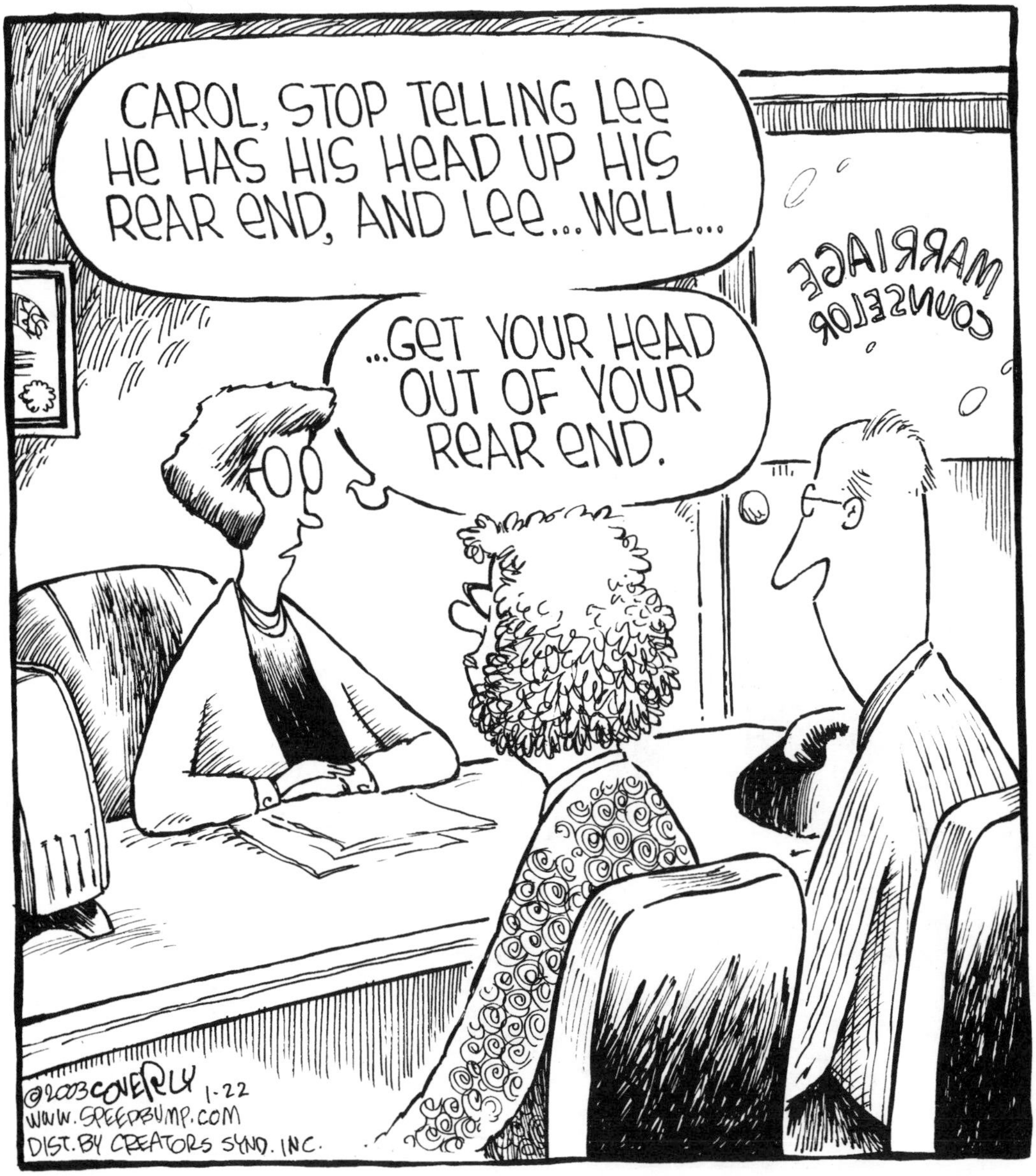
CAROL, STOP TELLING LEE HE HAS HIS HEAD UP HIS REAR END, AND LEE...WELL...
...GET YOUR HEAD OUT OF YOUR REAR END.
MARRIAGE COUNSELOR
©2003 COVERLY 1-22
WWW.SPEEDBUMP.COM
DIST. BY CREATORS SYND. INC.

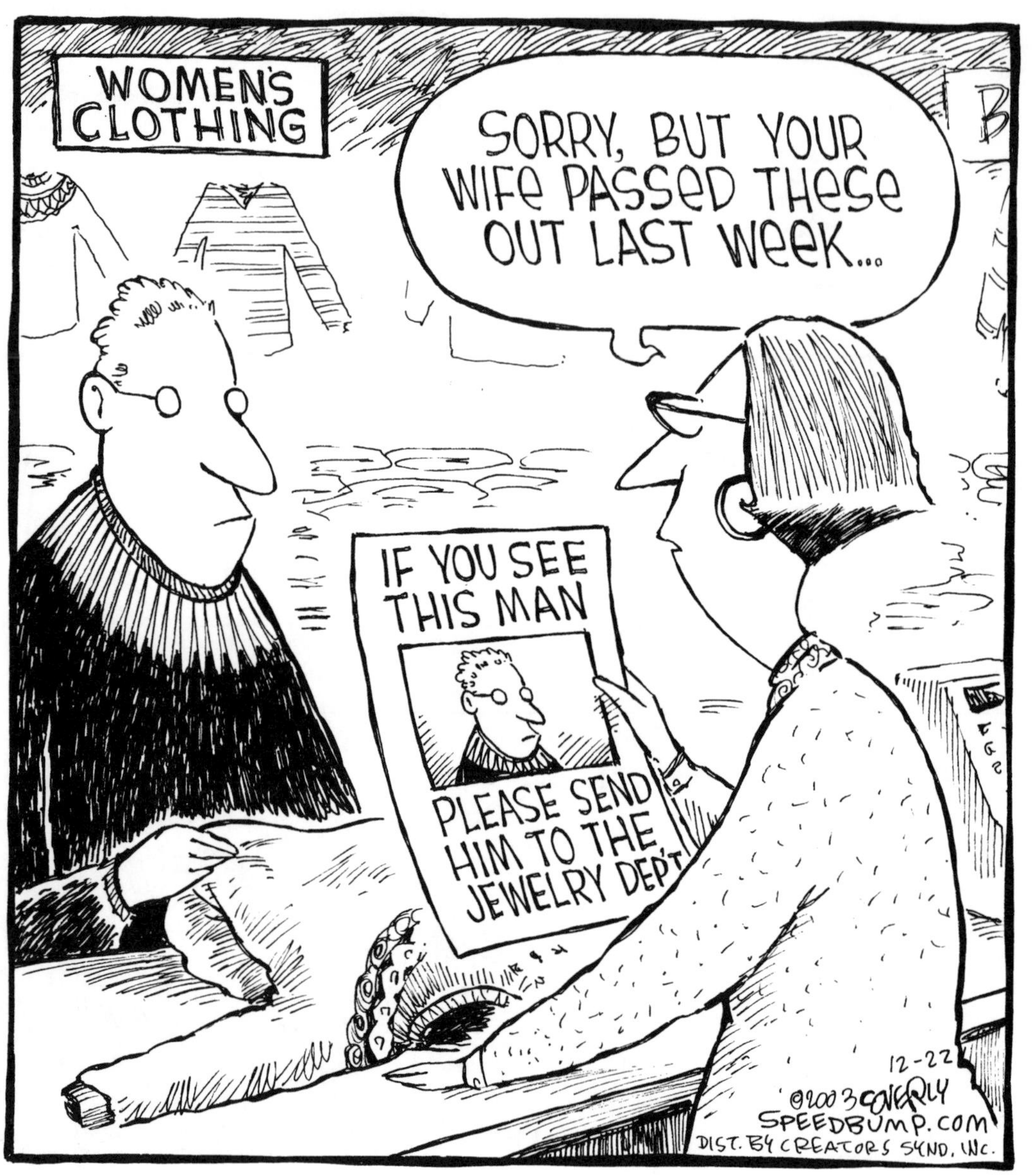
WOMEN'S CLOTHING
SORRY, BUT YOUR WIFE PASSED THESE OUT LAST WEEK...
IF YOU SEE THIS MAN
PLEASE SEND HIM TO THE JEWELRY DEP'T
12-22
©2003 COVERLY
SPEEDBUMP.COM
DIST. BY CREATORS SYND. INC.

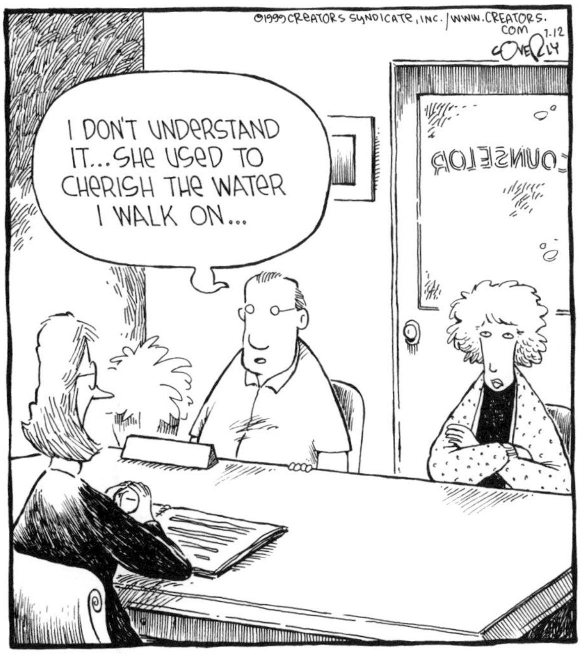
©1999 CREATORS SYNDICATE, INC. / WWW.CREATORS.COM
7-12 COVERLY
I DON'T UNDERSTAND IT... SHE USED TO CHERISH THE WATER I WALK ON...
COUNSELOR

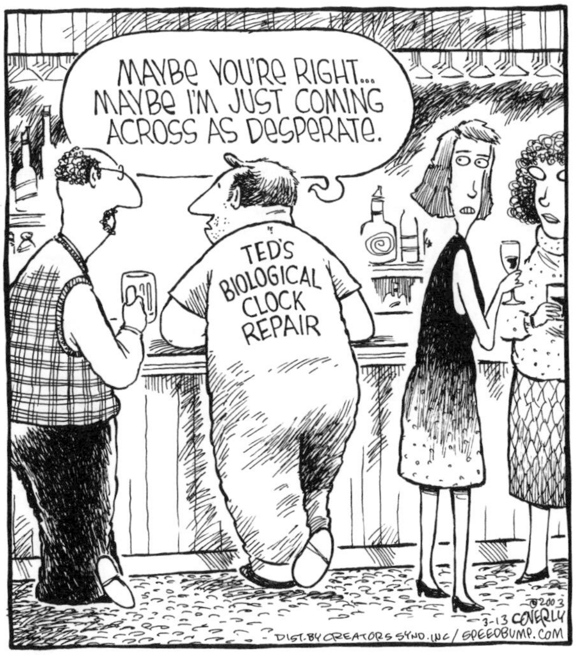
MAYBE YOU'RE RIGHT... MAYBE I'M JUST COMING ACROSS AS DESPERATE.
TED'S BIOLOGICAL CLOCK REPAIR
©2003 3-13 COVERLY
DIST. BY CREATORS SYND. INC / SPEEDBUMP.COM

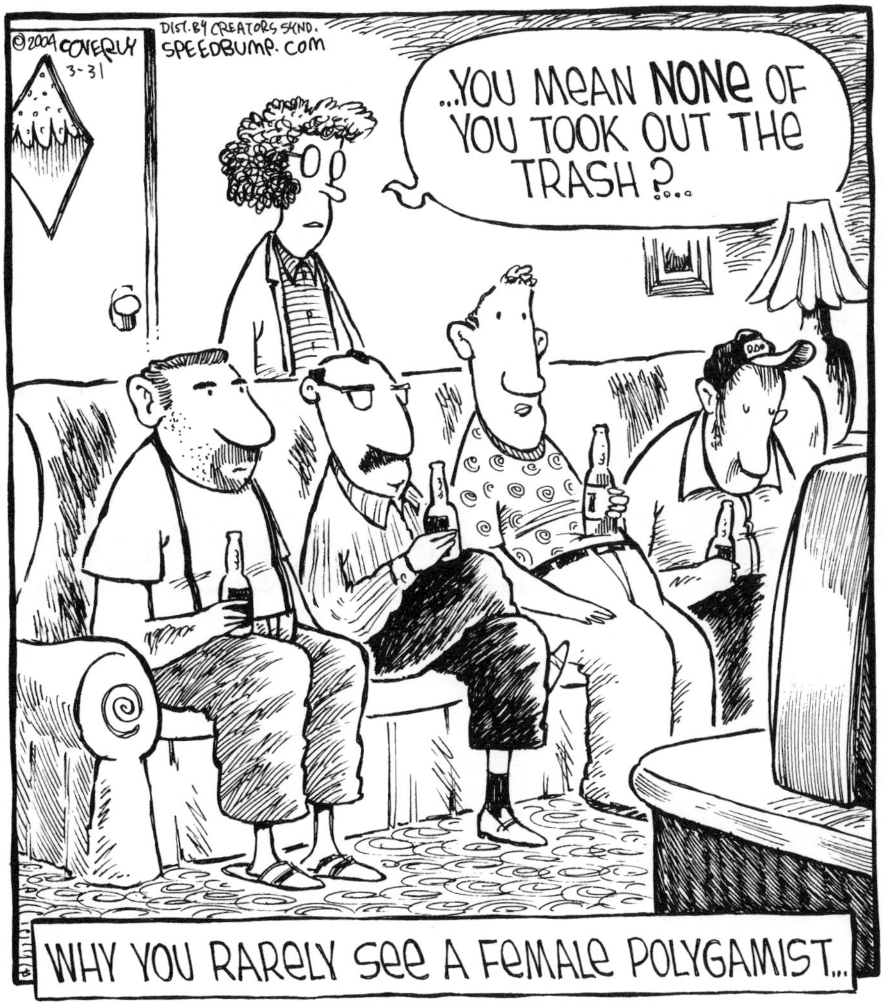
©2004 COVERLY 3-31
DIST. BY CREATORS SYND. SPEEDBUMP.COM
...YOU MEAN NONE OF YOU TOOK OUT THE TRASH ?...
WHY YOU RARELY SEE A FEMALE POLYGAMIST...

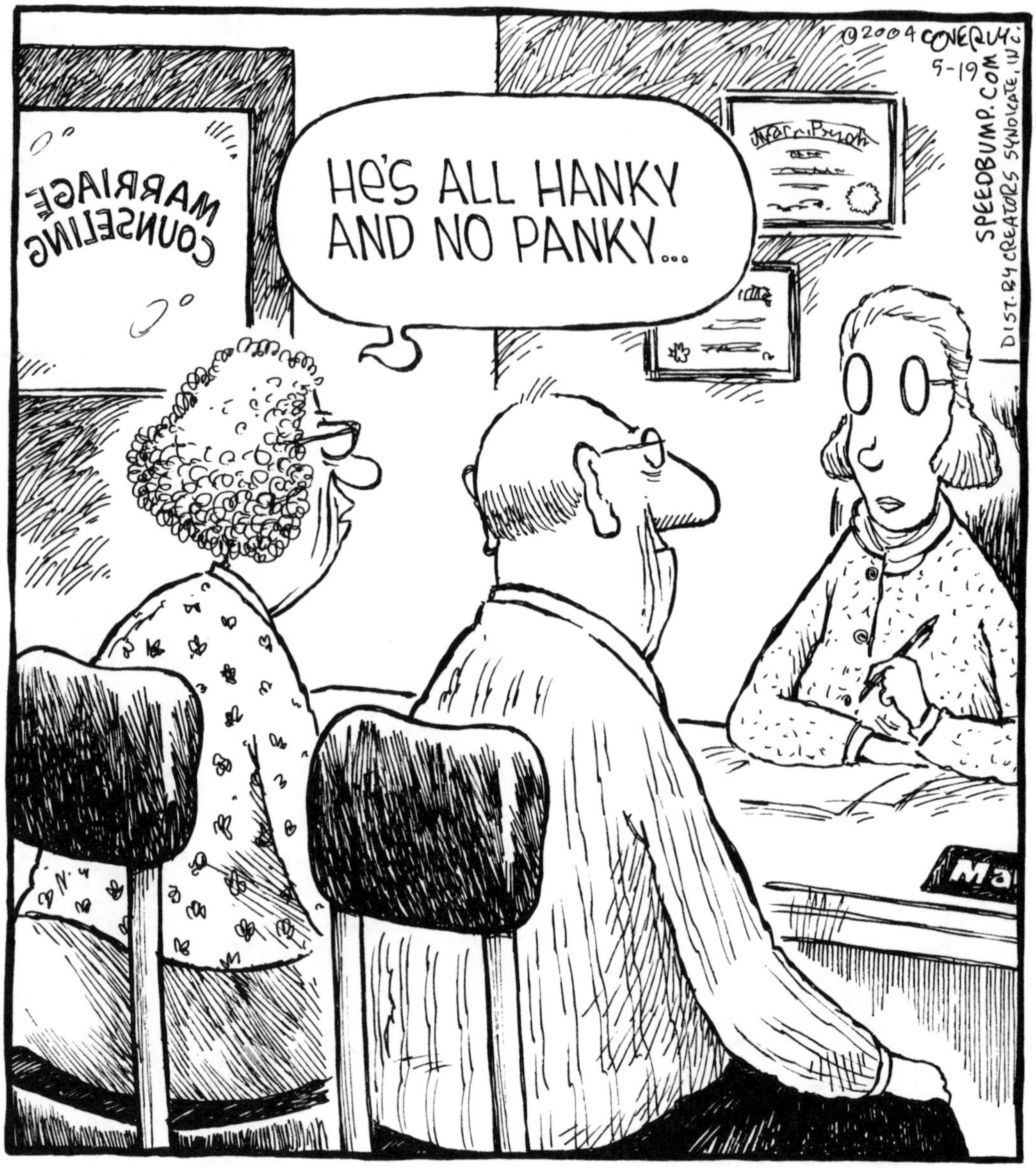
MARRIAGE COUNSELING
HE'S ALL HANKY AND NO PANKY...
©2004 COVERLY
5-19
SPEEDBUMP.COM
DIST. BY CREATORS SYNDICATE, INC.

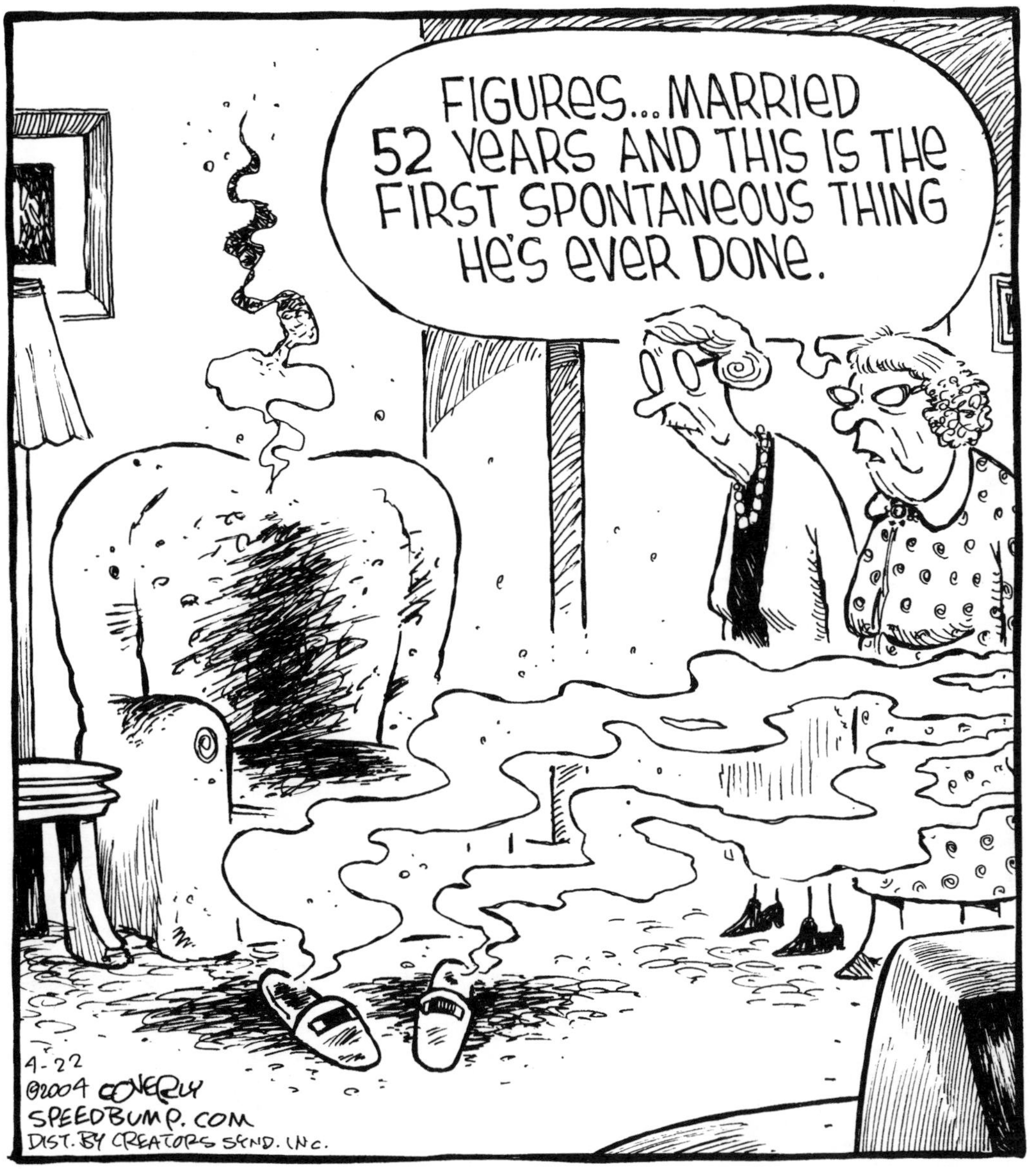

FIGURES...MARRIED 52 YEARS AND THIS IS THE FIRST SPONTANEOUS THING HE'S EVER DONE.
4-22
©2004 COVERLY
SPEEDBUMP.COM
DIST. BY CREATORS SYND. INC.

Kids Inspire the Darndest Ideas

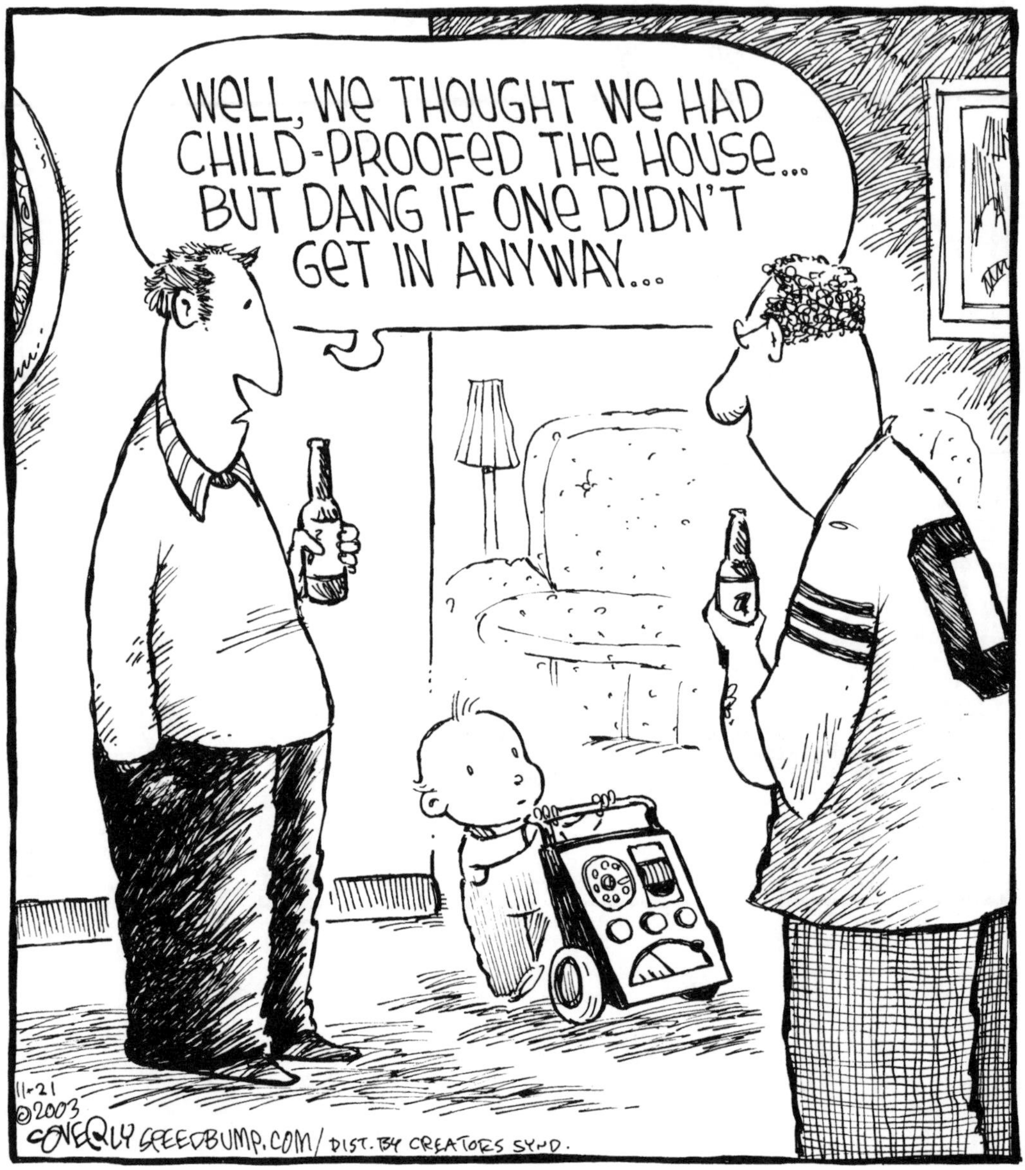
WELL, WE THOUGHT WE HAD CHILD-PROOFED THE HOUSE... BUT DANG IF ONE DIDN'T GET IN ANYWAY...
11-21 ©2003 COVERLY SPEEDBUMP.COM/ DIST. BY CREATORS SYND.

Anyone who works in a creative field knows that creativity is directly affected by one's personal life. This is especially true of humor. Even the smallest distraction can really bog down my ability to come up with cartoon ideas. The other side of this, however, is that Major Life Changes nearly always dish up new and interesting cartoon possibilities.

Having children qualifies as a Major Life Change.

And my two daughters have been quite an inspiration. For example:

A few years ago, I took Simone, 2, and Alayna, 6, to McDonald's. We were standing in line, waiting to order lunch, when I asked them what they wanted to drink. Simone was just learning to talk, and Alayna was just learning how much fun it was to help her talk correctly. At a decibel level only children find normal, the following conversation ensued between the two of them:

> "Simone, do you want milk or juice?"
> "DOUCHE!"
> "No, Simone, it's JUICE."
> "DOUCHE."
> "Simone! J . . . J . . . JUICE . . ."
> "DOUCHE!"
> "NOT DOUCHE! JUICE! . . . J . . . J . . . J . . . JUICE!"
> "AAAAAAAAA!!! DOUCHE, LAYNA! I . . . WANT . . . DOUCHE!"

Of course, Alayna had no idea that 'douche' is an actual word — she was just annoyed at the sheer wrongness of it. By this time, the two men in front of us were shaking with silent laughter. I gave Alayna 'the look' so that she would end her side of the conversation, but 'the look' only works when my wife does it. When I try, my face just takes on an 'I smell something foul' expression (it's interchangeable with my Diaper Changing Face). Wiping the beads of sweat forming on my upper lip, I changed tactics:

> "Why don't you two go pick out someplace to sit?"
> "I WANT DOUCHE!"
> "SIMONE!" Alayna screamed. "IT'S NOT DOUCHE!"

> McDonald's had gone eerily quiet. I changed my order "to go."

I'm often asked if I get a lot of specific ideas from my kids. I don't. There's not a lot of call for douche cartoons in newspapers these days. But I do get a lot of inspiration from them, and can honestly say that most of the cartoons in this chapter would never have occurred to me 10 years ago . . .

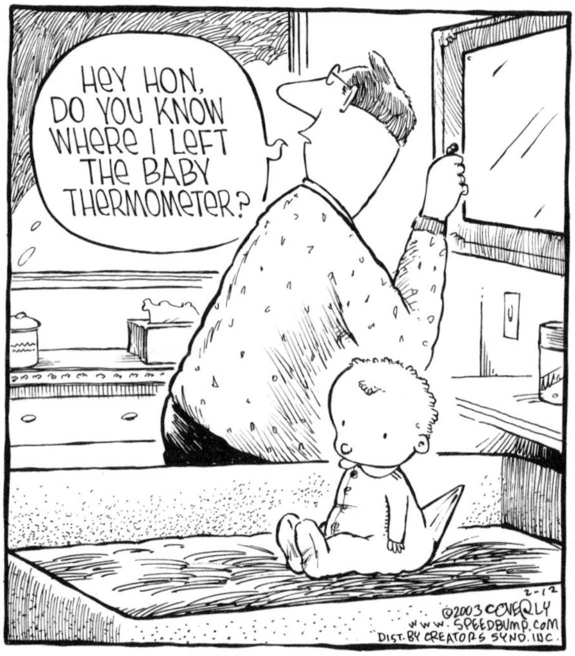
HEY HON, DO YOU KNOW WHERE I LEFT THE BABY THERMOMETER?
2-12
©2003 COVERLY
WWW.SPEEDBUMP.COM
DIST. BY CREATORS SYND. INC.

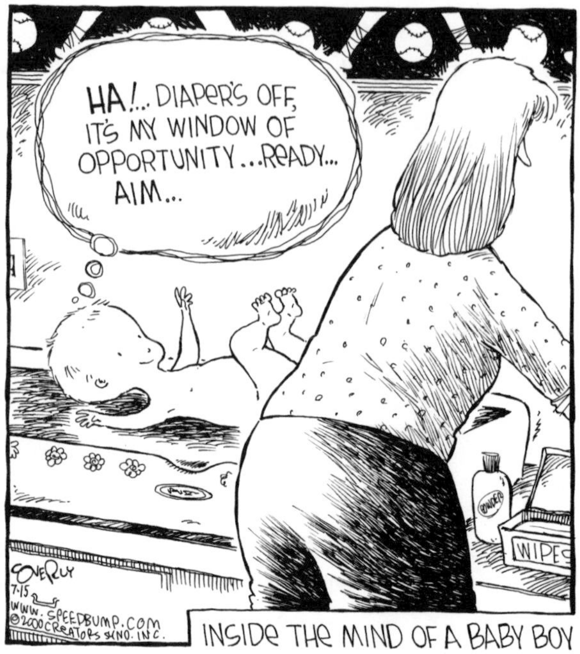
HA!... DIAPER'S OFF, IT'S MY WINDOW OF OPPORTUNITY...READY... AIM...
WIPES
COVERLY
7-15
WWW.SPEEDBUMP.COM
©2000 CREATORS SYND. INC.

INSIDE THE MIND OF A BABY BOY

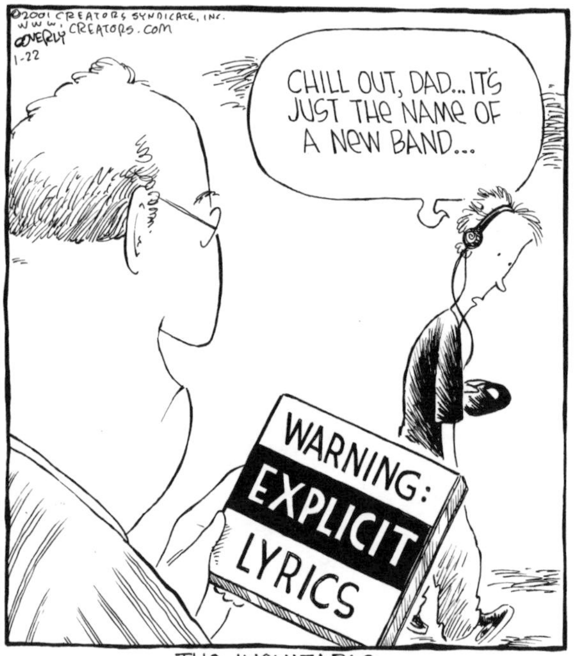
©2001 CREATORS SYNDICATE, INC.
WWW.CREATORS.COM
COVERLY
1-22
CHILL OUT, DAD... IT'S JUST THE NAME OF A NEW BAND...
WARNING:
EXPLICIT
LYRICS

THE INEVITABLE

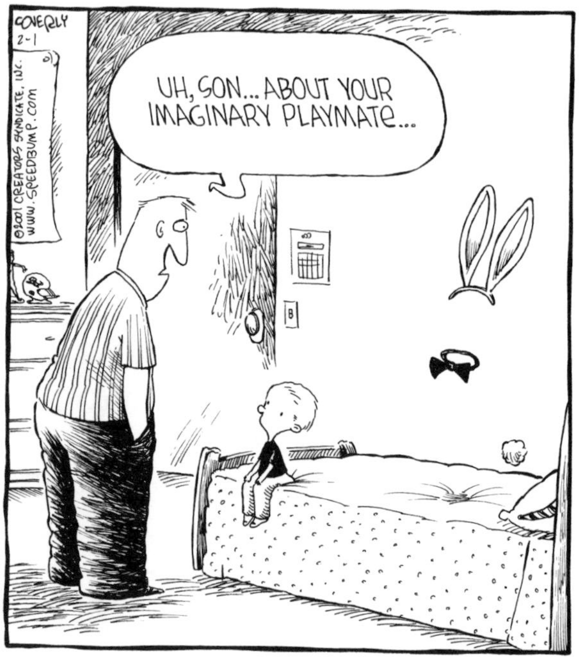
COVERLY
2-1
©2001 CREATORS SYNDICATE, INC.
WWW.SPEEDBUMP.COM
UH, SON... ABOUT YOUR IMAGINARY PLAYMATE...

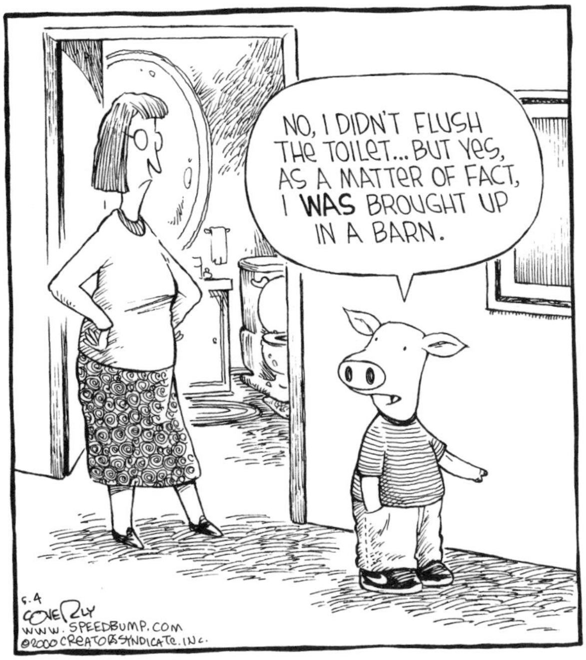
NO, I DIDN'T FLUSH THE TOILET... BUT YES, AS A MATTER OF FACT, I WAS BROUGHT UP IN A BARN.
5-4
COVERLY
WWW.SPEEDBUMP.COM
©2000 CREATORS SYNDICATE, INC.

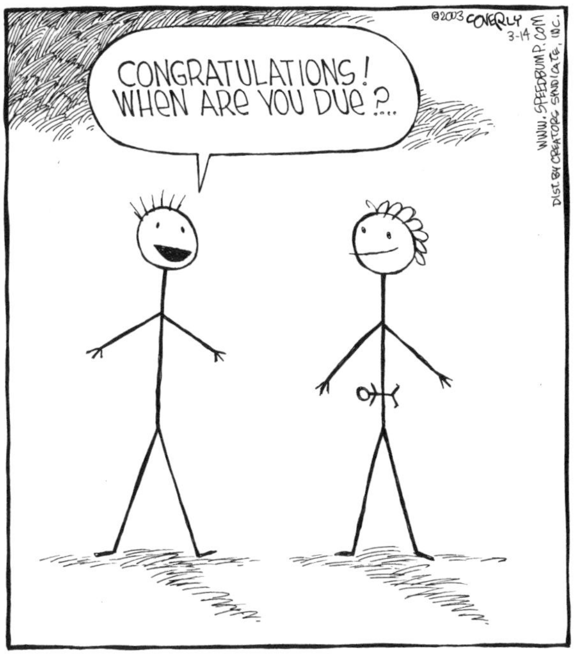
©2003 COVERLY
3-14
WWW.SPEEDBUMP.COM
DIST. BY CREATORS SYNDICATE, INC.
CONGRATULATIONS! WHEN ARE YOU DUE?...

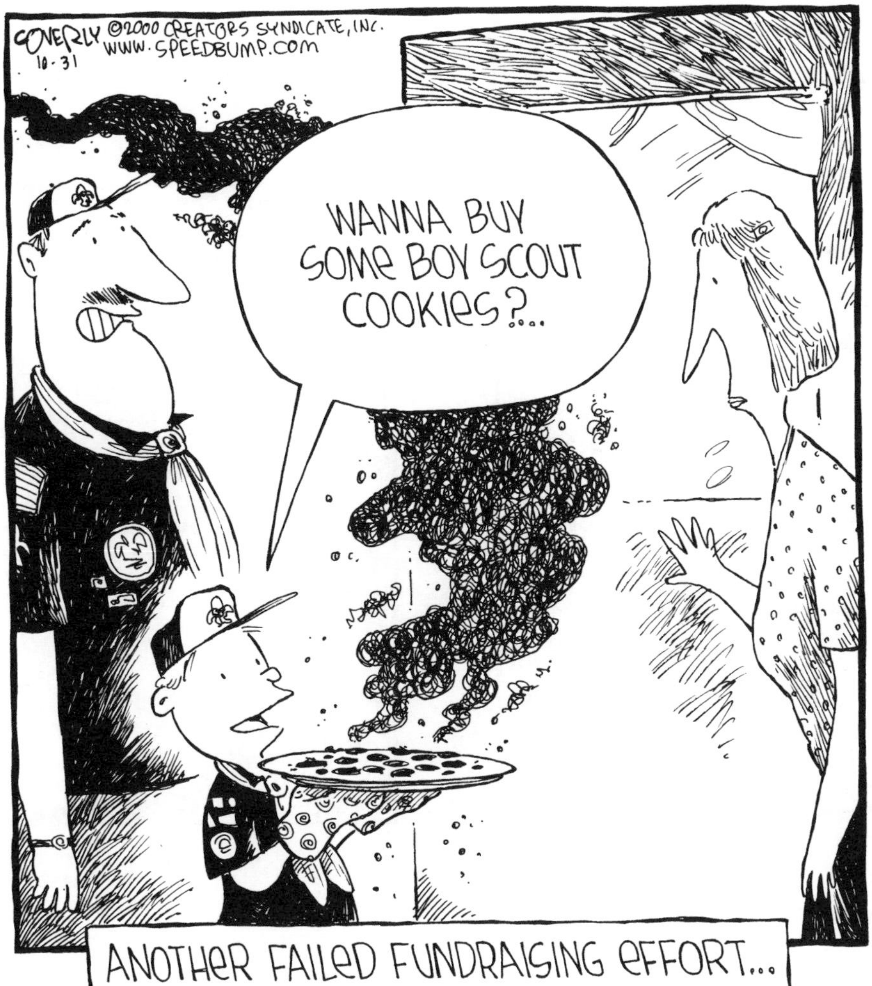
COVERLY ©2000 CREATORS SYNDICATE, INC.
WWW.SPEEDBUMP.COM
10-31
WANNA BUY SOME BOY SCOUT COOKIES?...
ANOTHER FAILED FUNDRAISING EFFORT...

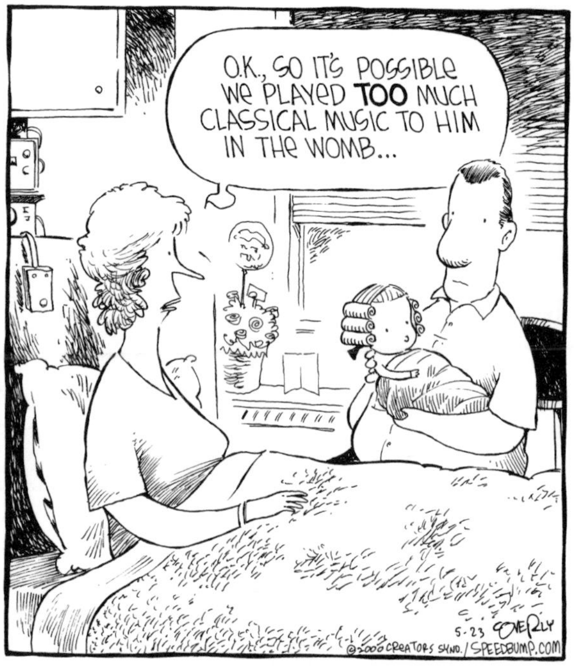
O.K., SO IT'S POSSIBLE WE PLAYED **TOO** MUCH CLASSICAL MUSIC TO HIM IN THE WOMB...

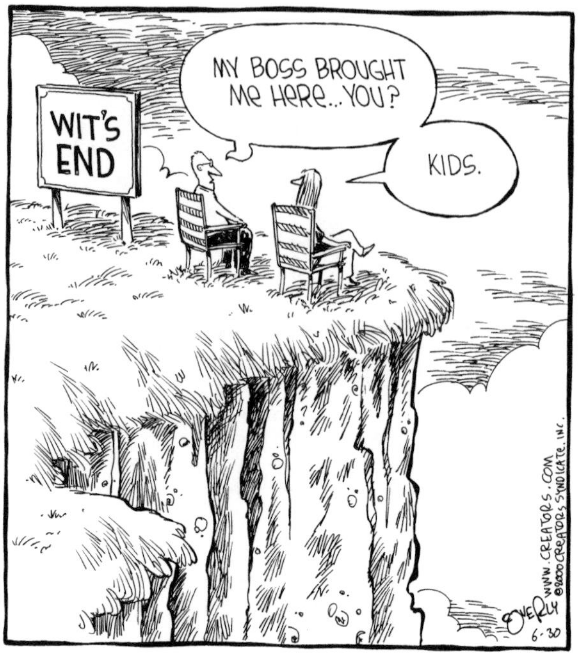
WIT'S END
MY BOSS BROUGHT ME HERE... YOU?
KIDS.

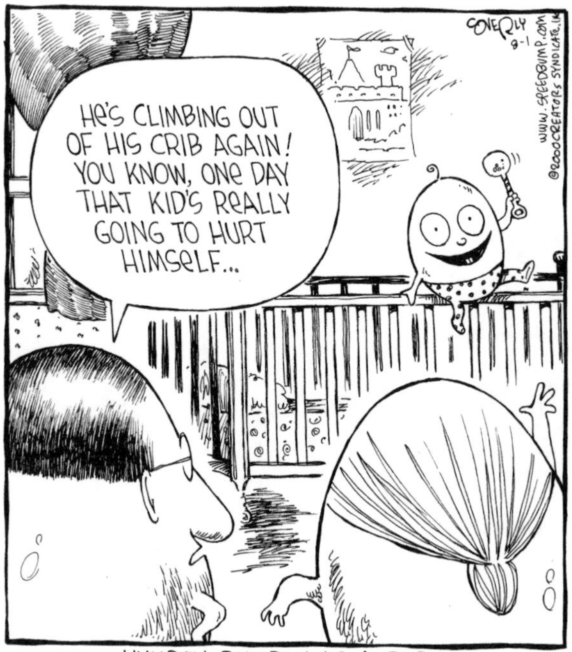
HE'S CLIMBING OUT OF HIS CRIB AGAIN! YOU KNOW, ONE DAY THAT KID'S REALLY GOING TO HURT HIMSELF...

HUMPTY DUMPTY AS A BABY

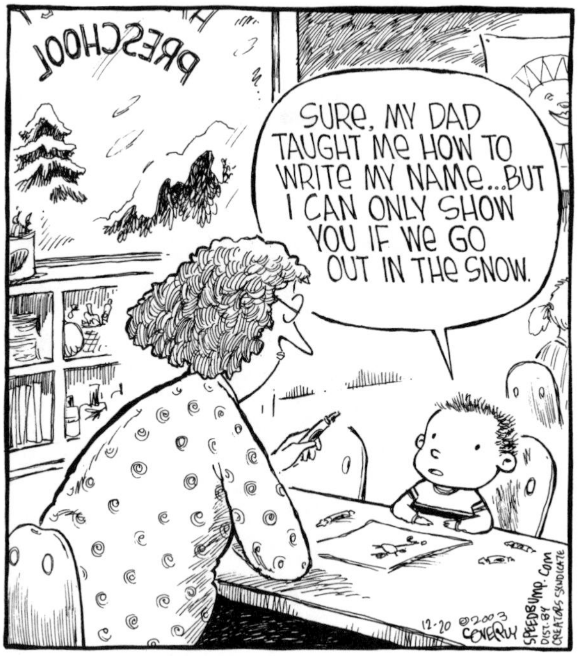
PRESCHOOL
SURE, MY DAD TAUGHT ME HOW TO WRITE MY NAME...BUT I CAN ONLY SHOW YOU IF WE GO OUT IN THE SNOW.

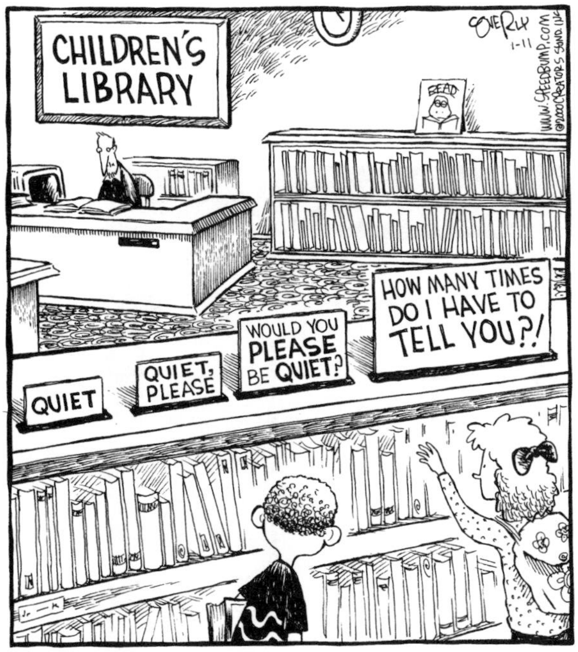
CHILDREN'S LIBRARY
COVERLY 1-11
READ
HOW MANY TIMES DO I HAVE TO TELL YOU?!
WOULD YOU PLEASE BE QUIET?
QUIET, PLEASE
QUIET

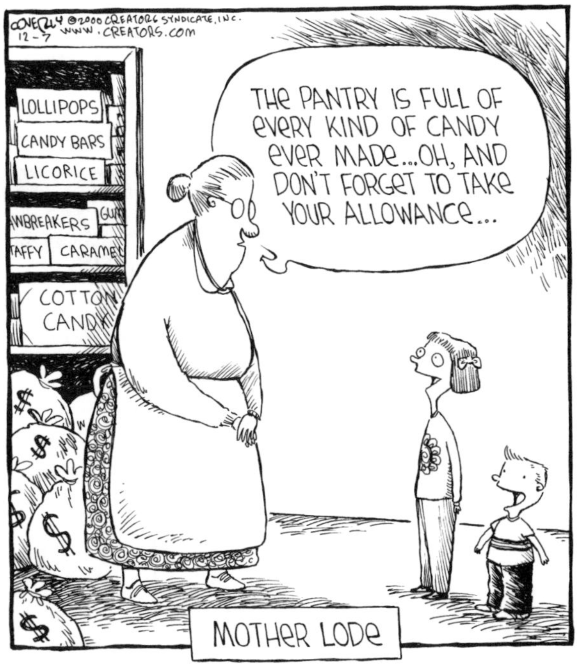
COVERLY ©2000 CREATORS SYNDICATE, INC. 12-7 WWW.CREATORS.COM
LOLLIPOPS
CANDY BARS
LICORICE
TAFFY
THE PANTRY IS FULL OF EVERY KIND OF CANDY EVER MADE...OH, AND DON'T FORGET TO TAKE YOUR ALLOWANCE...

MOTHER LODE

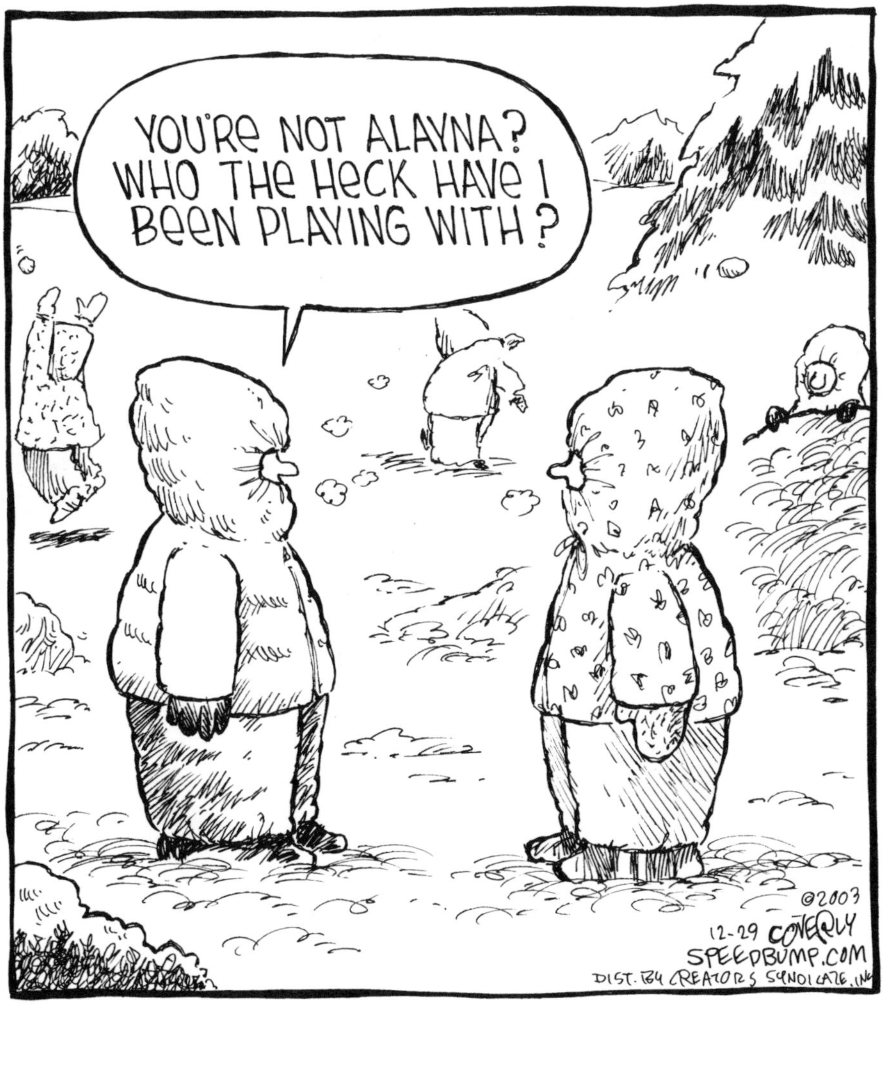
YOU'RE NOT ALAYNA? WHO THE HECK HAVE I BEEN PLAYING WITH?
©2003 12-29 COVERLY
SPEEDBUMP.COM
DIST. BY CREATORS SYNDICATE, INC.

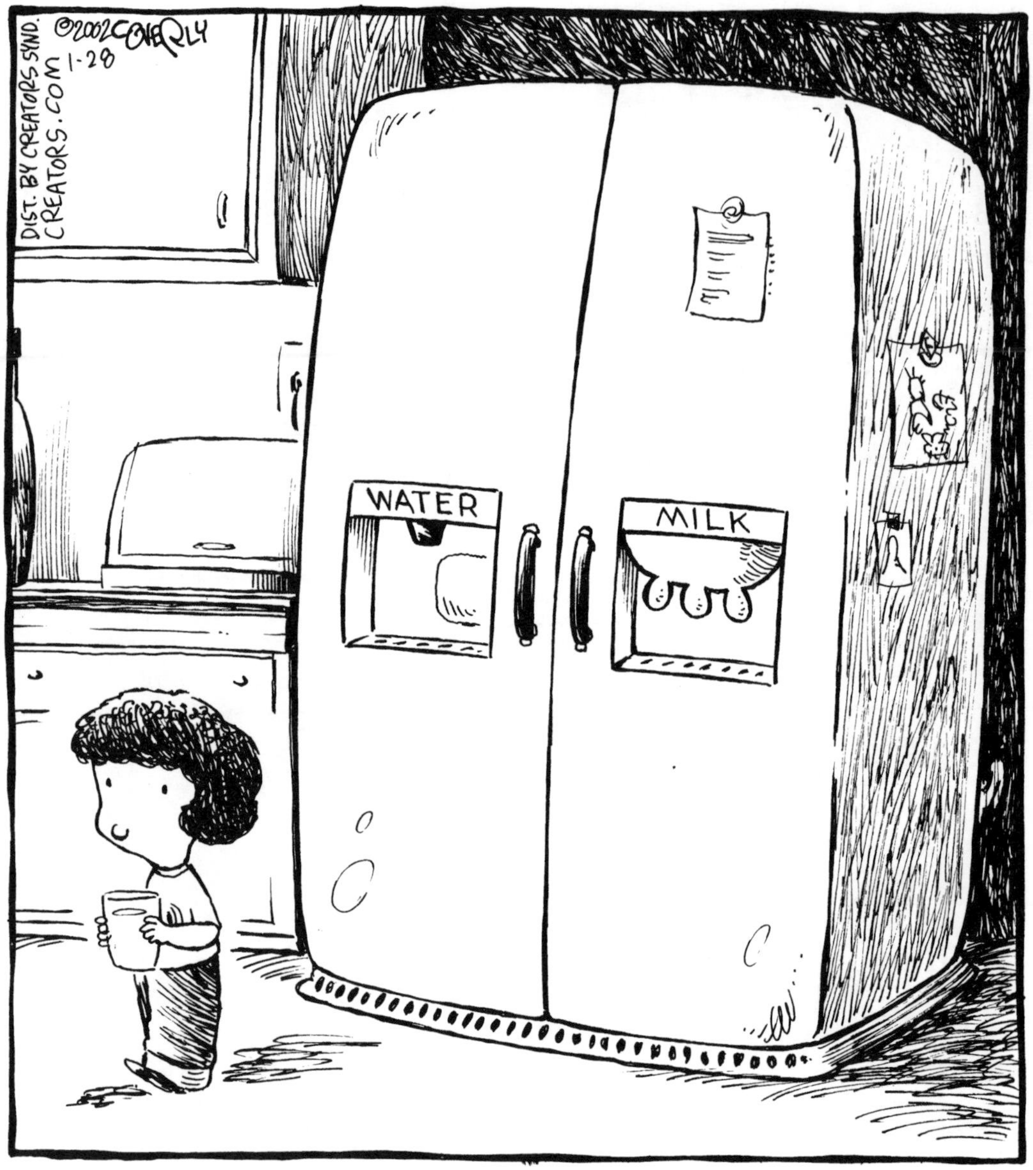
DIST. BY CREATORS SYND.
CREATORS.COM
©2002 COVERLY
1-28
WATER
MILK

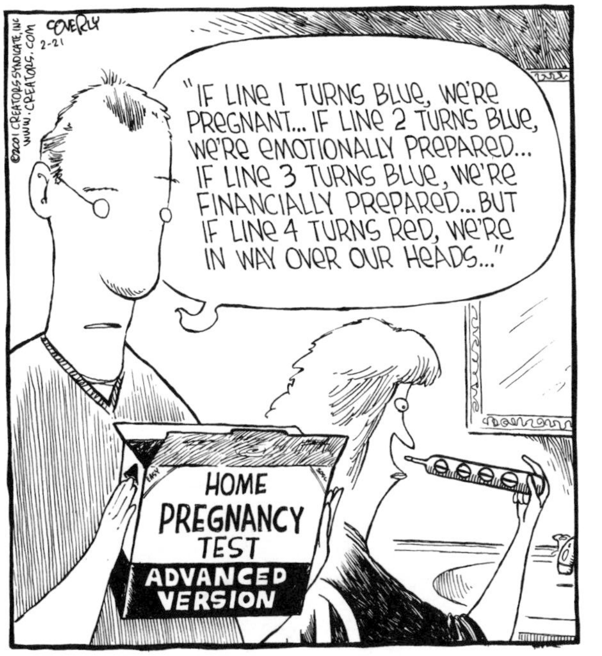
"IF LINE 1 TURNS BLUE, WE'RE PREGNANT... IF LINE 2 TURNS BLUE, WE'RE EMOTIONALLY PREPARED... IF LINE 3 TURNS BLUE, WE'RE FINANCIALLY PREPARED... BUT IF LINE 4 TURNS RED, WE'RE IN WAY OVER OUR HEADS..."
HOME PREGNANCY TEST
ADVANCED VERSION

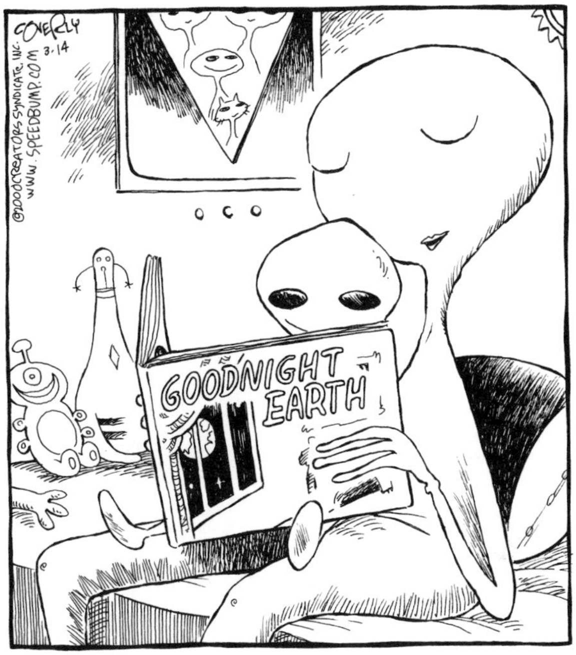
GOODNIGHT EARTH

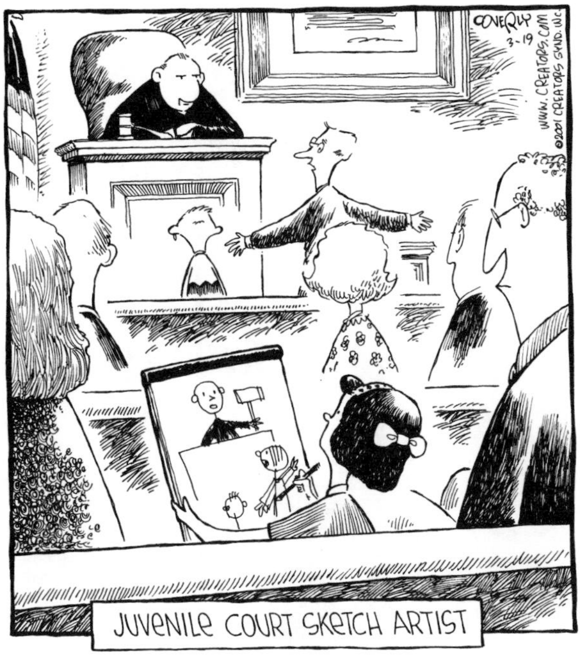

JUVENILE COURT SKETCH ARTIST

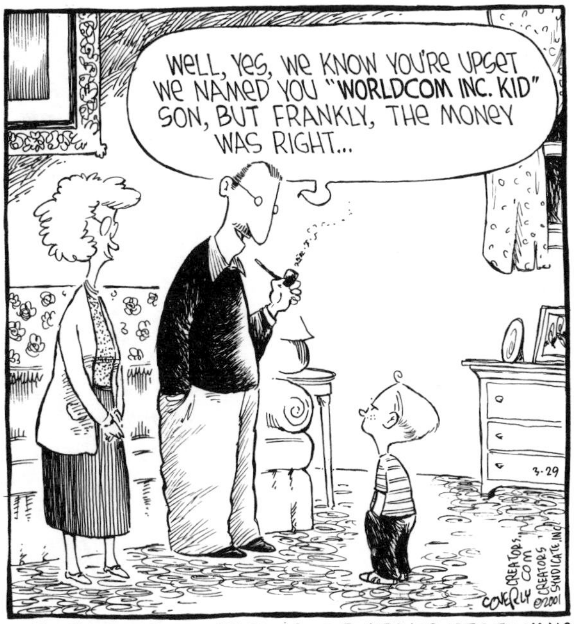
WELL, YES, WE KNOW YOU'RE UPSET WE NAMED YOU "WORLDCOM INC. KID" SON, BUT FRANKLY, THE MONEY WAS RIGHT...

WHEN THERE ARE NO STADIUMS OR BUILDINGS LEFT TO NAME

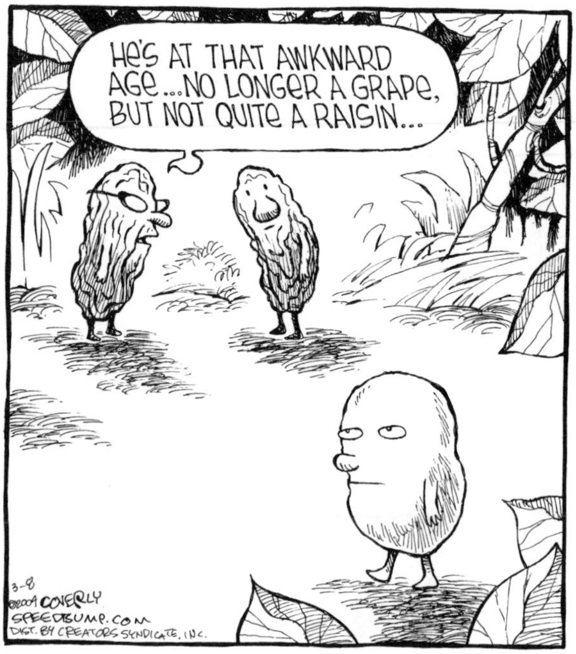
HE'S AT THAT AWKWARD AGE...NO LONGER A GRAPE, BUT NOT QUITE A RAISIN...
3-8
©2004 COVERLY
SPEEDBUMP.COM
DIST. BY CREATORS SYNDICATE, INC.

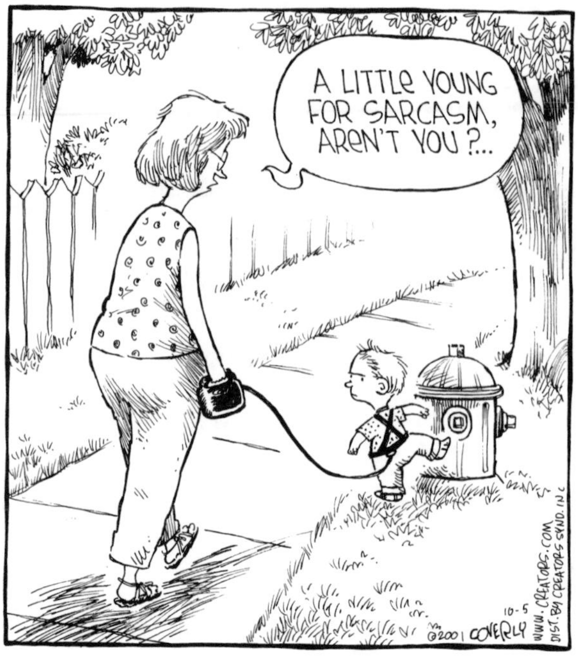
A LITTLE YOUNG FOR SARCASM, AREN'T YOU ?...
10-5
©2001 COVERLY
WWW.CREATORS.COM
DIST. BY CREATORS SYND. INC

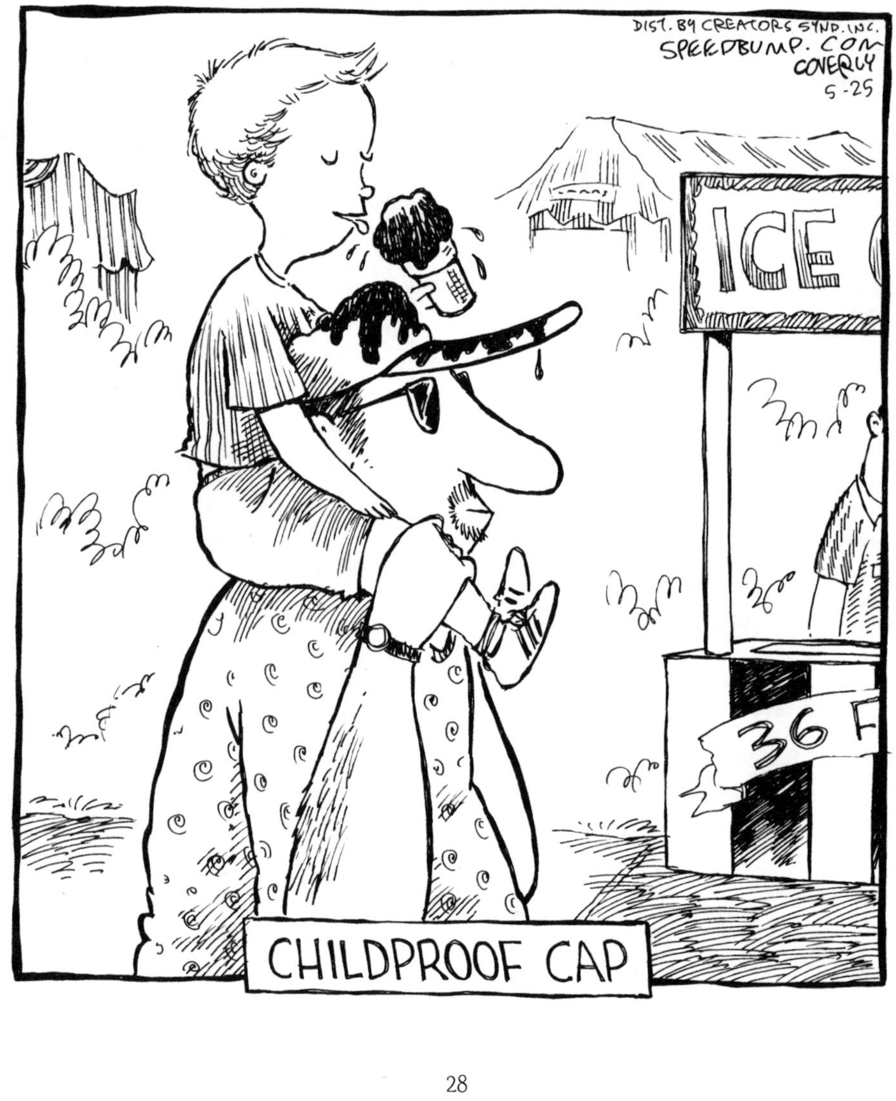
DIST. BY CREATORS SYND. INC.
SPEEDBUMP.COM
COVERLY
5-25
ICE
36
CHILDPROOF CAP

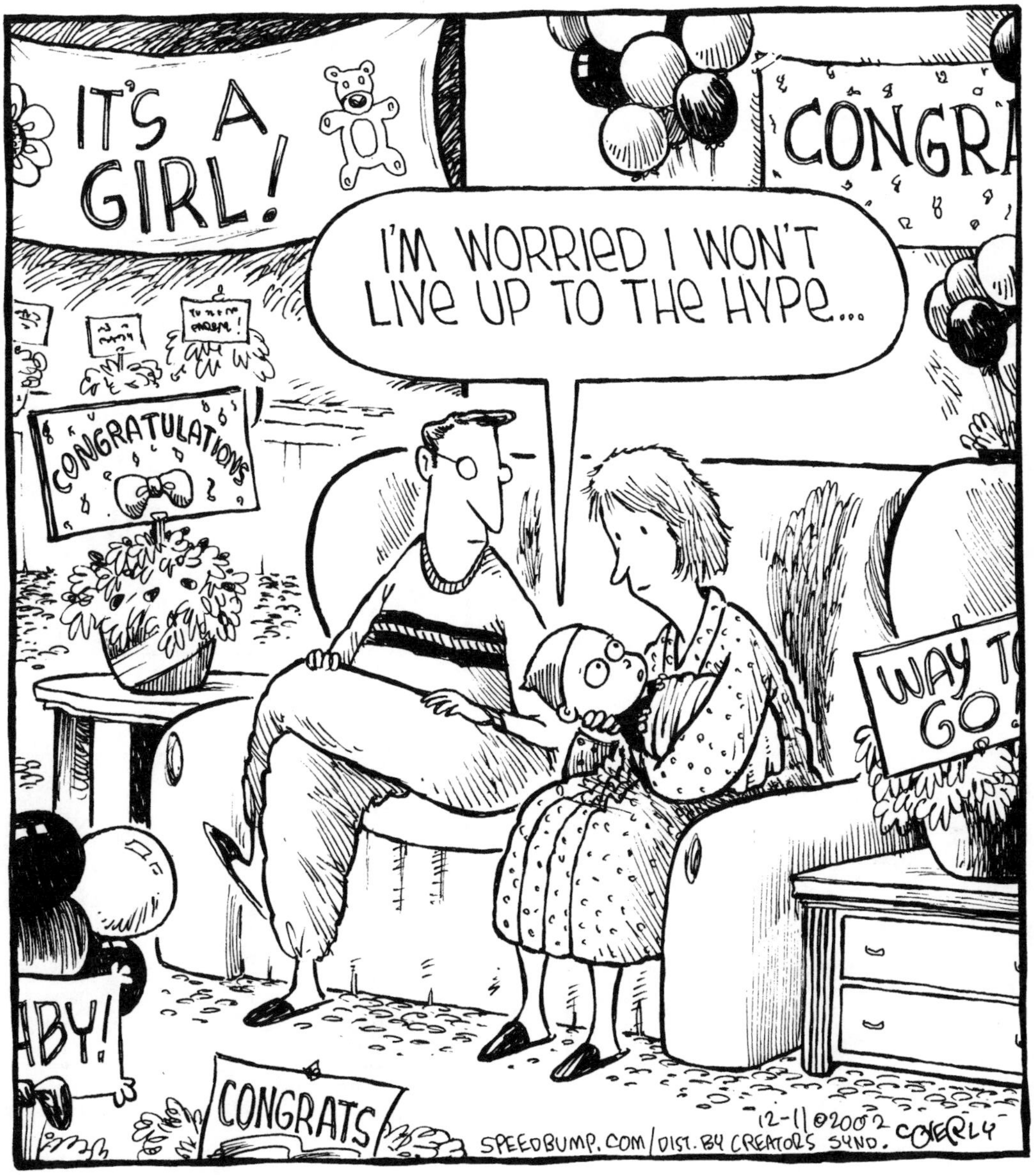
IT'S A GIRL!
CONGRA
I'M WORRIED I WON'T LIVE UP TO THE HYPE...
CONGRATULATIONS
WAY TO GO
ABY!
CONGRATS
12-11 ©2002
SPEEDBUMP.COM/DIST. BY CREATORS SYND.

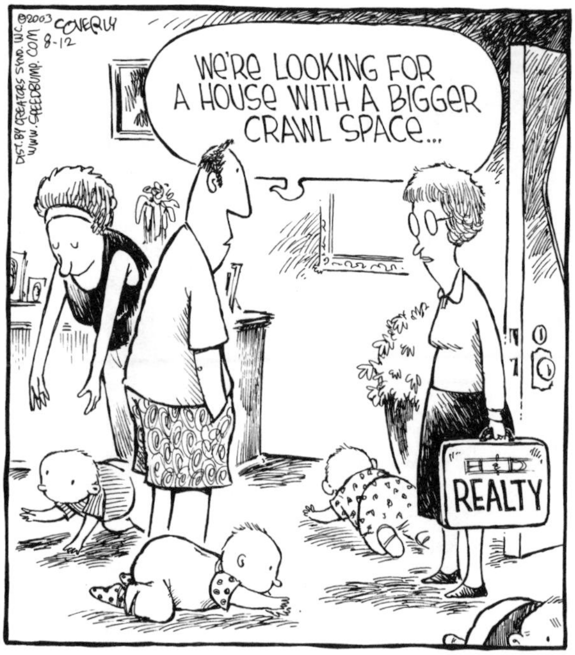
WE'RE LOOKING FOR A HOUSE WITH A BIGGER CRAWL SPACE...
REALTY
©2003 COVERLY 8-12
DIST. BY CREATORS SYND. INC.
WWW.SPEEDBUMP.COM

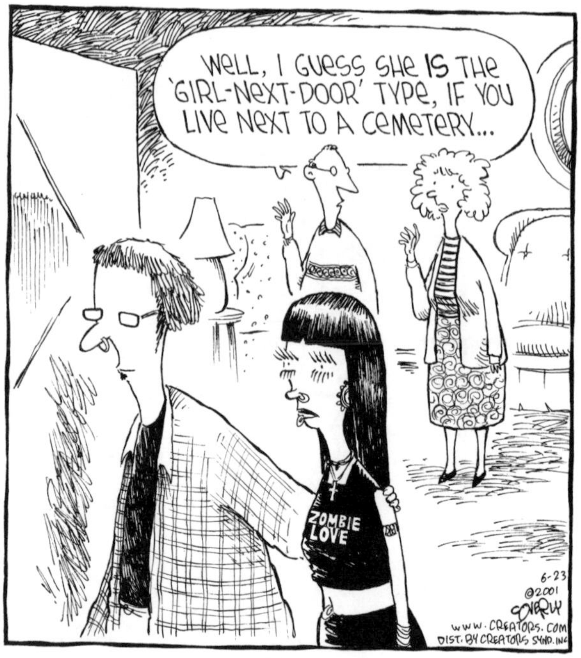
WELL, I GUESS SHE IS THE 'GIRL-NEXT-DOOR' TYPE, IF YOU LIVE NEXT TO A CEMETERY...
ZOMBIE LOVE
6-23
©2001
COVERLY
WWW.CREATORS.COM
DIST. BY CREATORS SYND. INC.

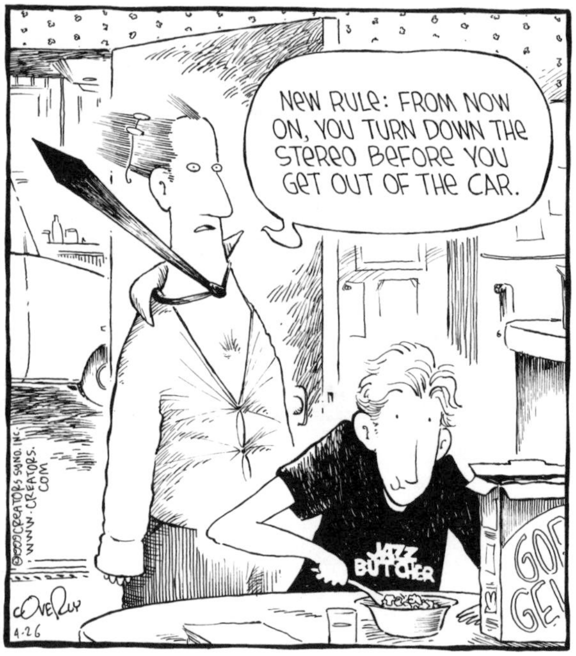
NEW RULE: FROM NOW ON, YOU TURN DOWN THE STEREO BEFORE YOU GET OUT OF THE CAR.
JAZZ BUTCHER
COVERLY
4-26

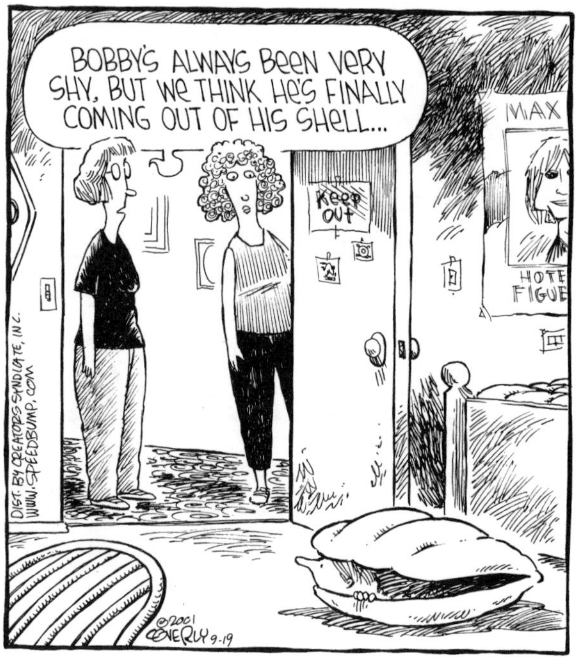
BOBBY'S ALWAYS BEEN VERY SHY, BUT WE THINK HE'S FINALLY COMING OUT OF HIS SHELL...
KEEP OUT
MAX
DIST. BY CREATORS SYNDICATE, INC.
WWW.SPEEDBUMP.COM
©2001
COVERLY 9-19

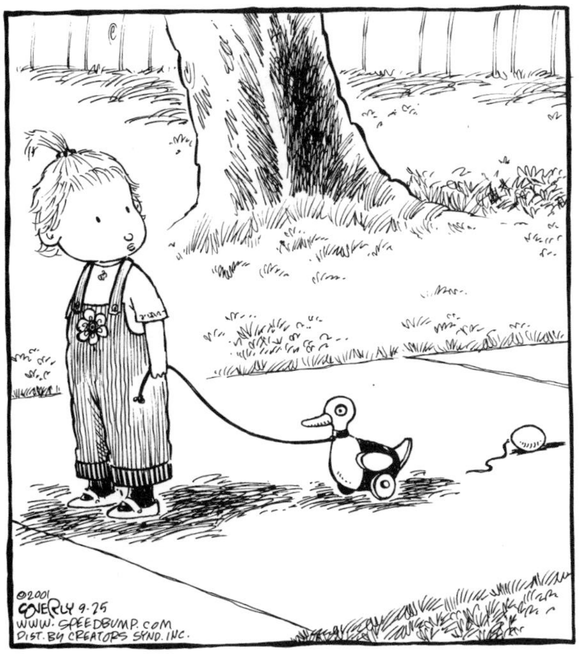
©2001 COVERLY 9-25
WWW.SPEEDBUMP.COM
DIST. BY CREATORS SYND. INC.

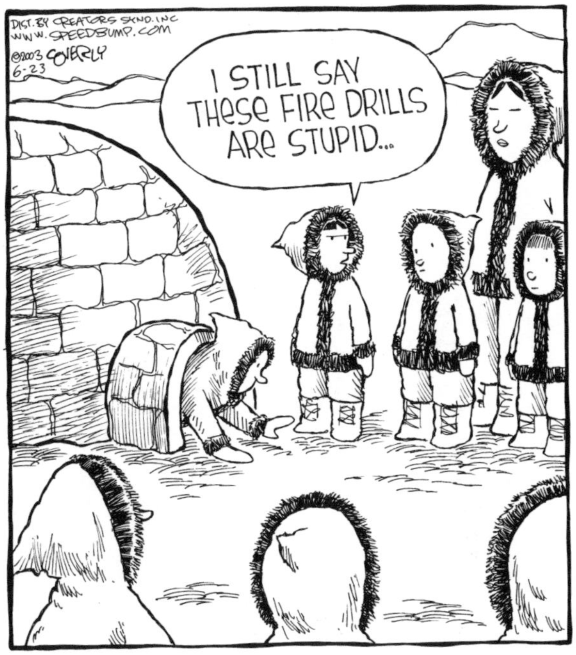
DIST. BY CREATORS SYND. INC
WWW.SPEEDBUMP.COM
©2003 COVERLY 6-23
I STILL SAY THESE FIRE DRILLS ARE STUPID...

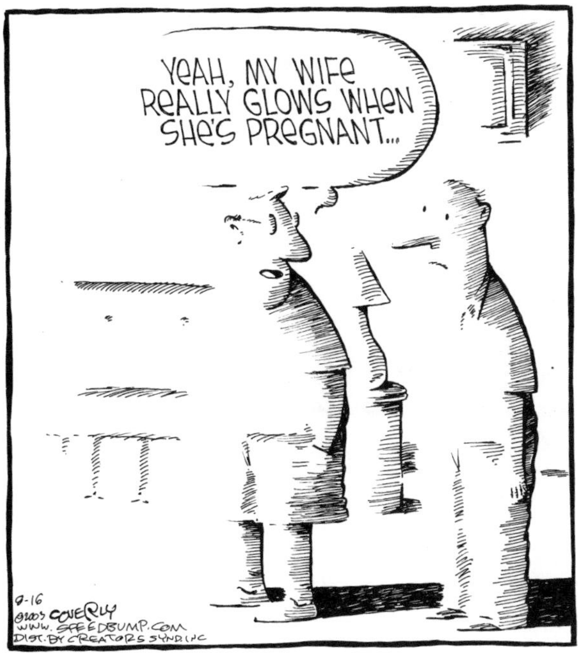
YEAH, MY WIFE REALLY GLOWS WHEN SHE'S PREGNANT...
©2003 COVERLY
WWW.SPEEDBUMP.COM
DIST. BY CREATORS SYND. INC

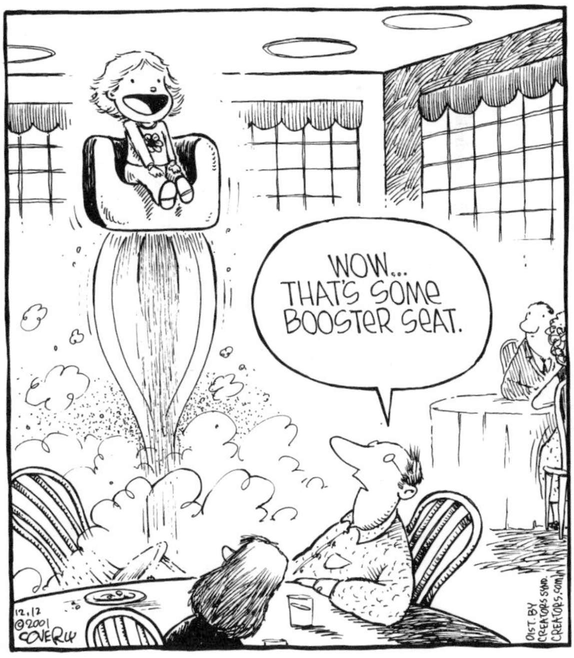
WOW... THAT'S SOME BOOSTER SEAT.
12.12 ©2001 COVERLY
DIST. BY CREATORS SYND.
CREATORS.COM

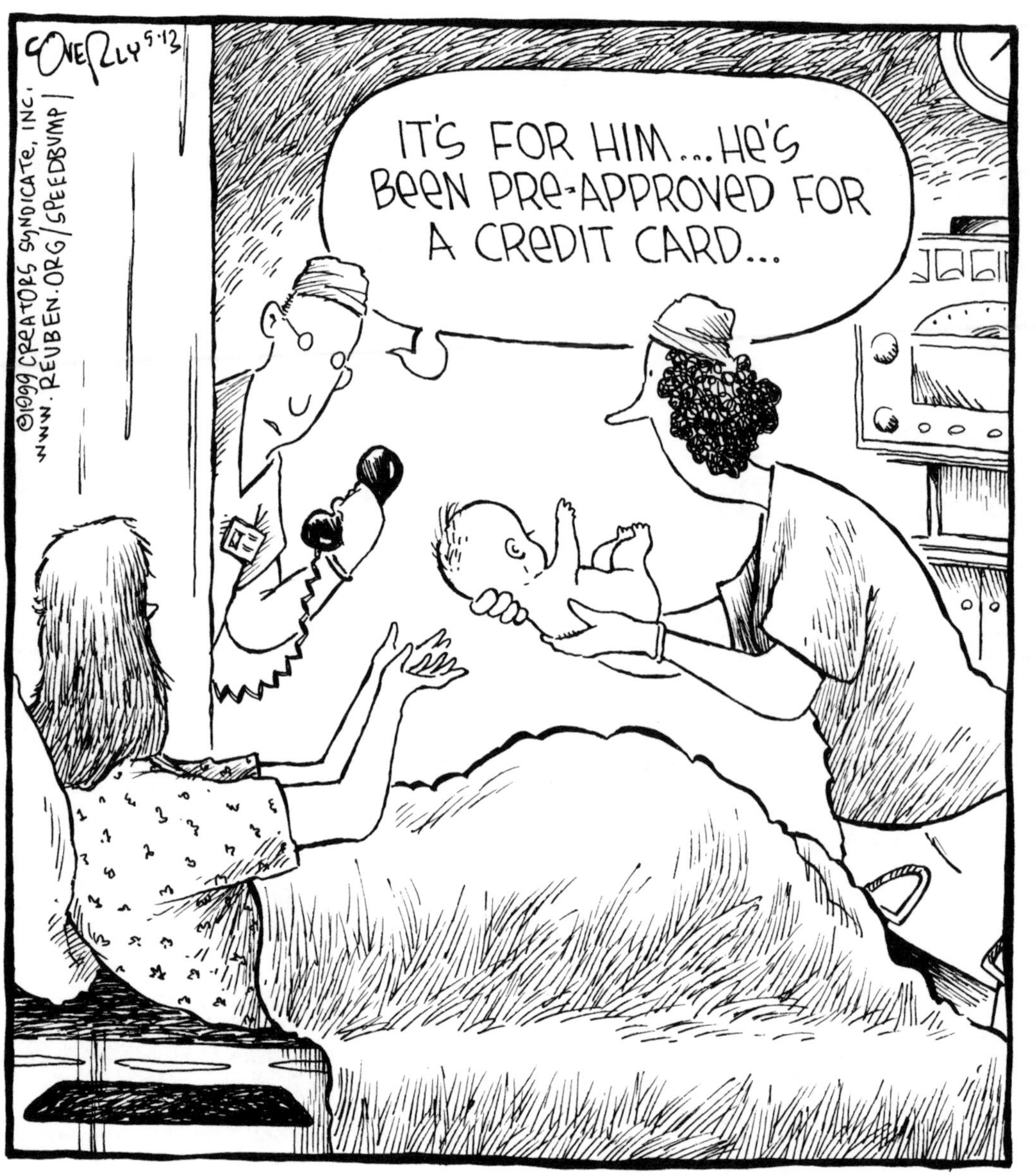
IT'S FOR HIM....HE'S BEEN PRE-APPROVED FOR A CREDIT CARD...
COVERLY 5-13
©1999 CREATORS SYNDICATE, INC.
WWW.REUBEN.ORG/SPEEDBUMP

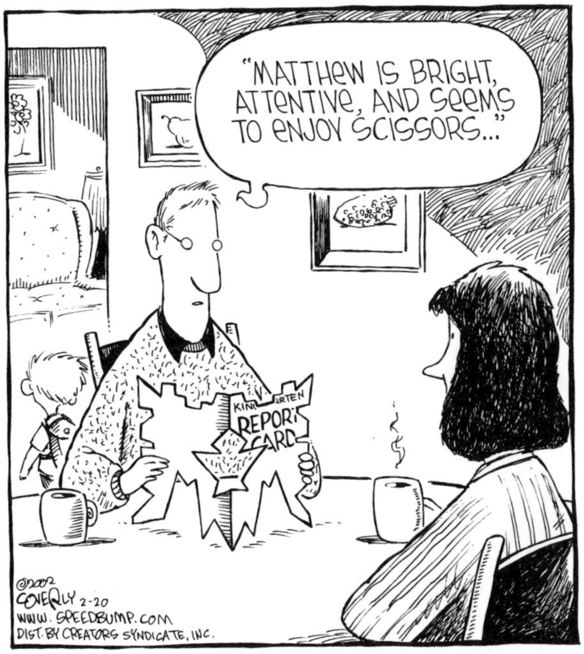
"MATTHEW IS BRIGHT, ATTENTIVE, AND SEEMS TO ENJOY SCISSORS..."
©2002 COVERLY 2-20
WWW.SPEEDBUMP.COM
DIST. BY CREATORS SYNDICATE, INC.

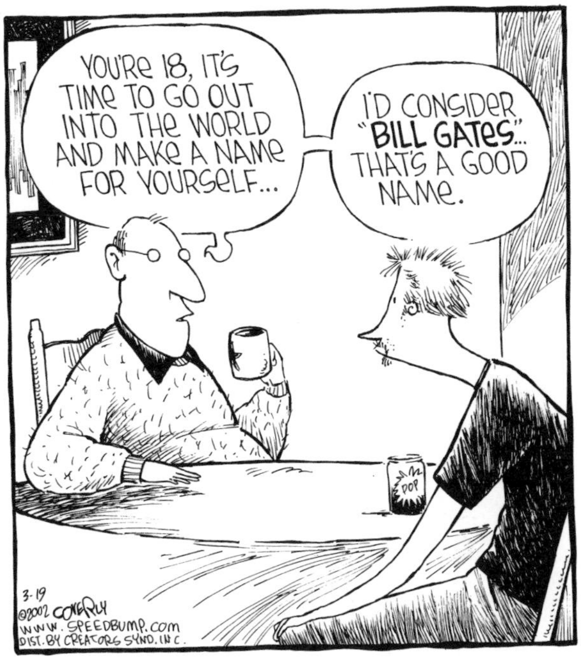
YOU'RE 18, IT'S TIME TO GO OUT INTO THE WORLD AND MAKE A NAME FOR YOURSELF...
I'D CONSIDER "BILL GATES"... THAT'S A GOOD NAME.
POP
3-19
©2002 COVERLY
WWW.SPEEDBUMP.COM
DIST. BY CREATORS SYND. INC.

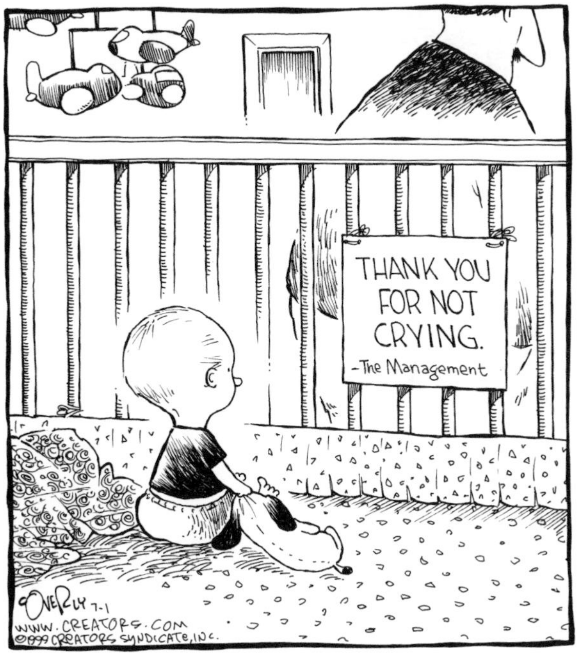
THANK YOU FOR NOT CRYING.
-The Management
COVERLY 7-1
WWW.CREATORS.COM
©1999 CREATORS SYNDICATE, INC.

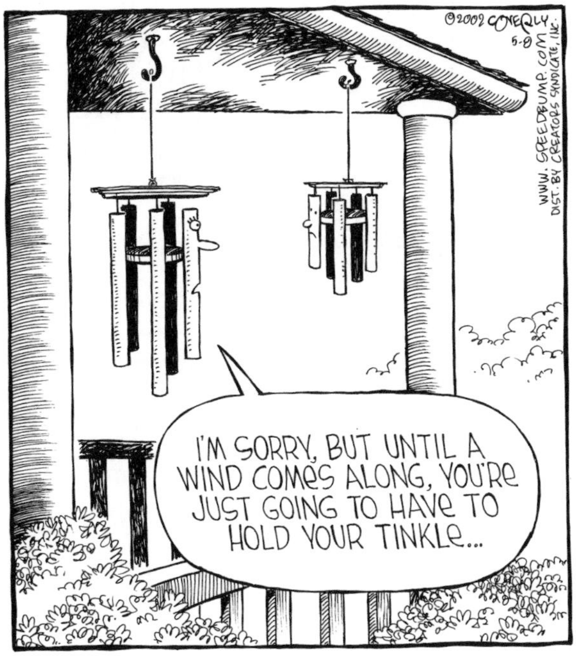
©2002 COVERLY 5-8
WWW.SPEEDBUMP.COM
DIST. BY CREATORS SYNDICATE, INC.
I'M SORRY, BUT UNTIL A WIND COMES ALONG, YOU'RE JUST GOING TO HAVE TO HOLD YOUR TINKLE...

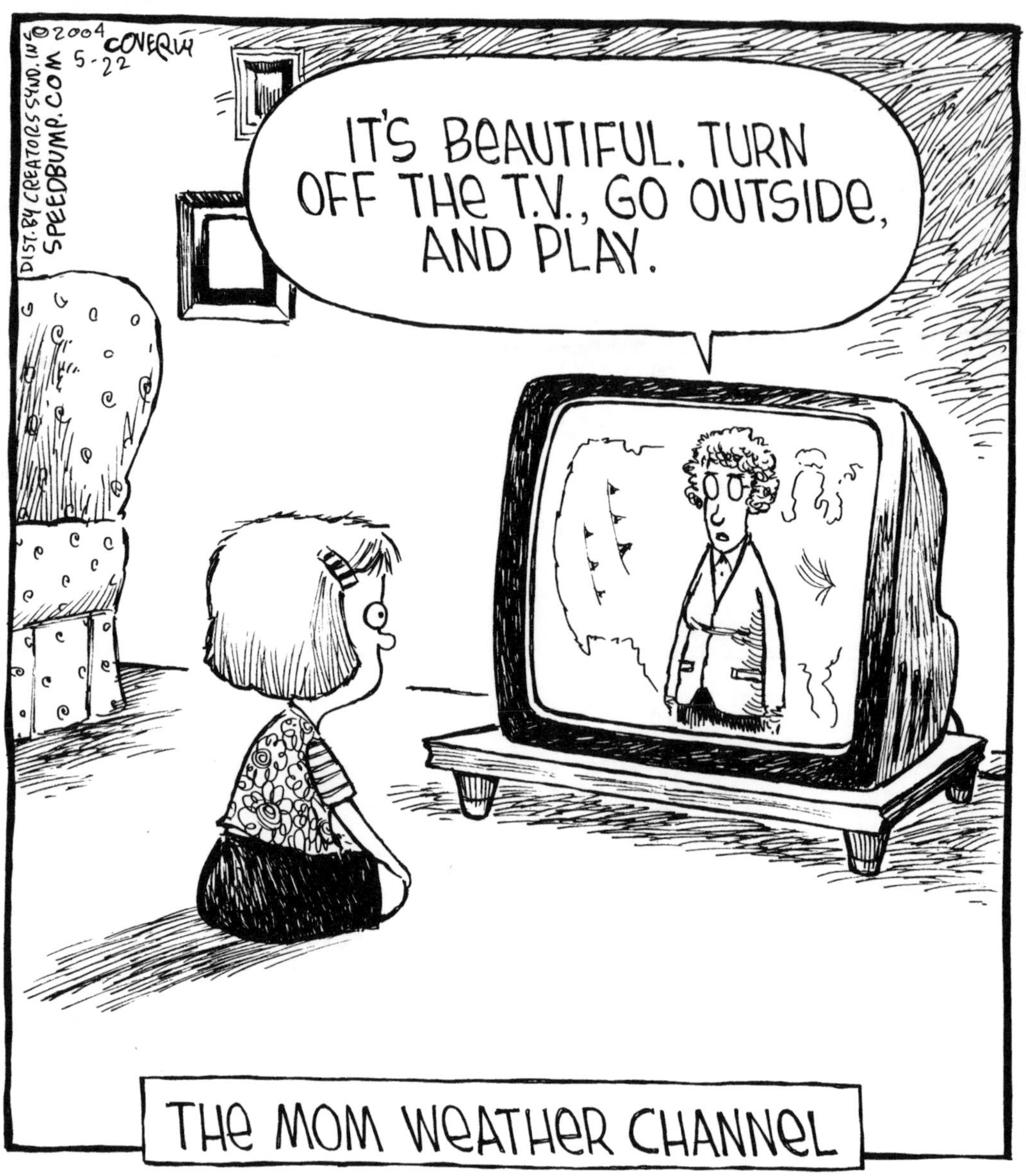
©2004 COVERLY 5-22
DIST. BY CREATORS SYND. INC
SPEEDBUMP.COM
IT'S BEAUTIFUL. TURN OFF THE T.V., GO OUTSIDE, AND PLAY.

THE MOM WEATHER CHANNEL

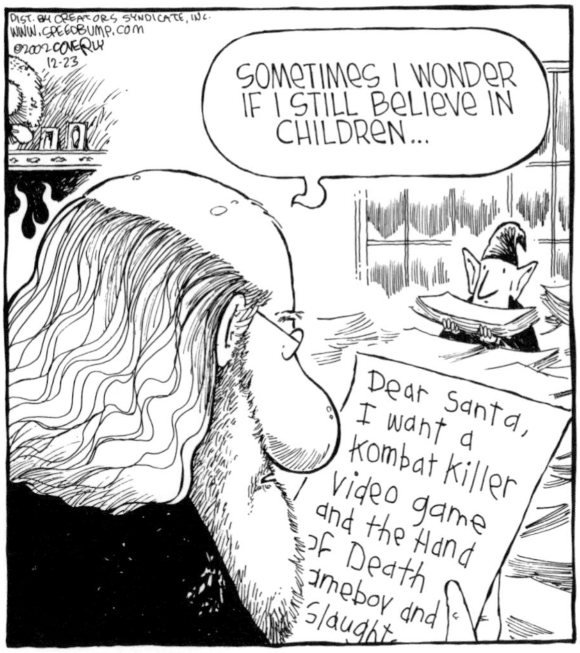
DIST. BY CREATORS SYNDICATE, INC.
WWW.SPEEDBUMP.COM
©2002 COVERLY
12-23
SOMETIMES I WONDER IF I STILL BELIEVE IN CHILDREN...
Dear Santa, I want a Kombat Killer video game and the Hand of Death
ameboy and
slaught

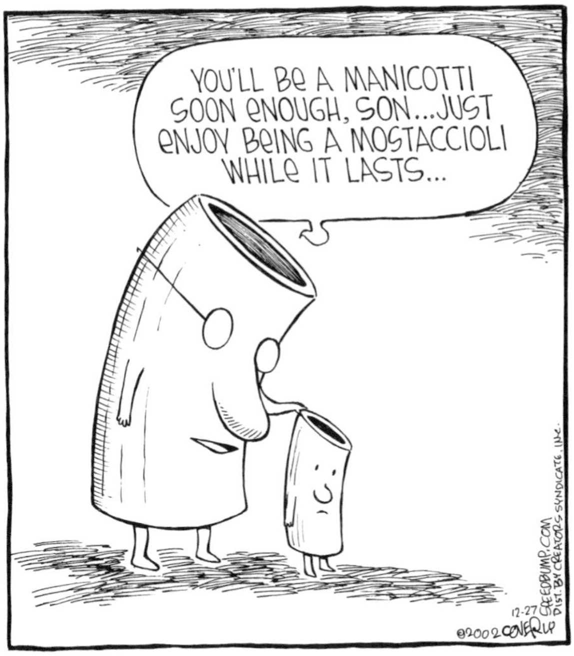
YOU'LL BE A MANICOTTI SOON ENOUGH, SON...JUST ENJOY BEING A MOSTACCIOLI WHILE IT LASTS...
12-27
SPEEDBUMP.COM
DIST. BY CREATORS SYNDICATE, INC.
©2002 COVERLY

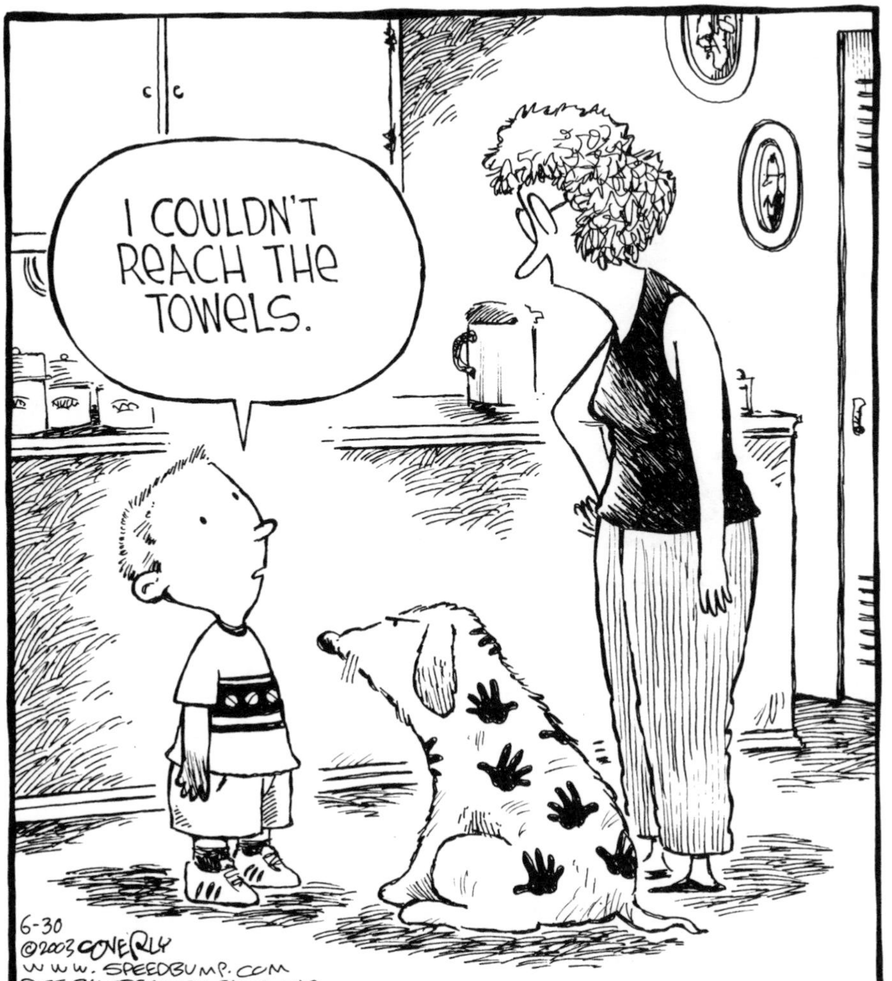
I COULDN'T REACH THE TOWELS.
6-30
©2003 COVERLY
WWW.SPEEDBUMP.COM
DIST. BY CREATORS SYND. INC.

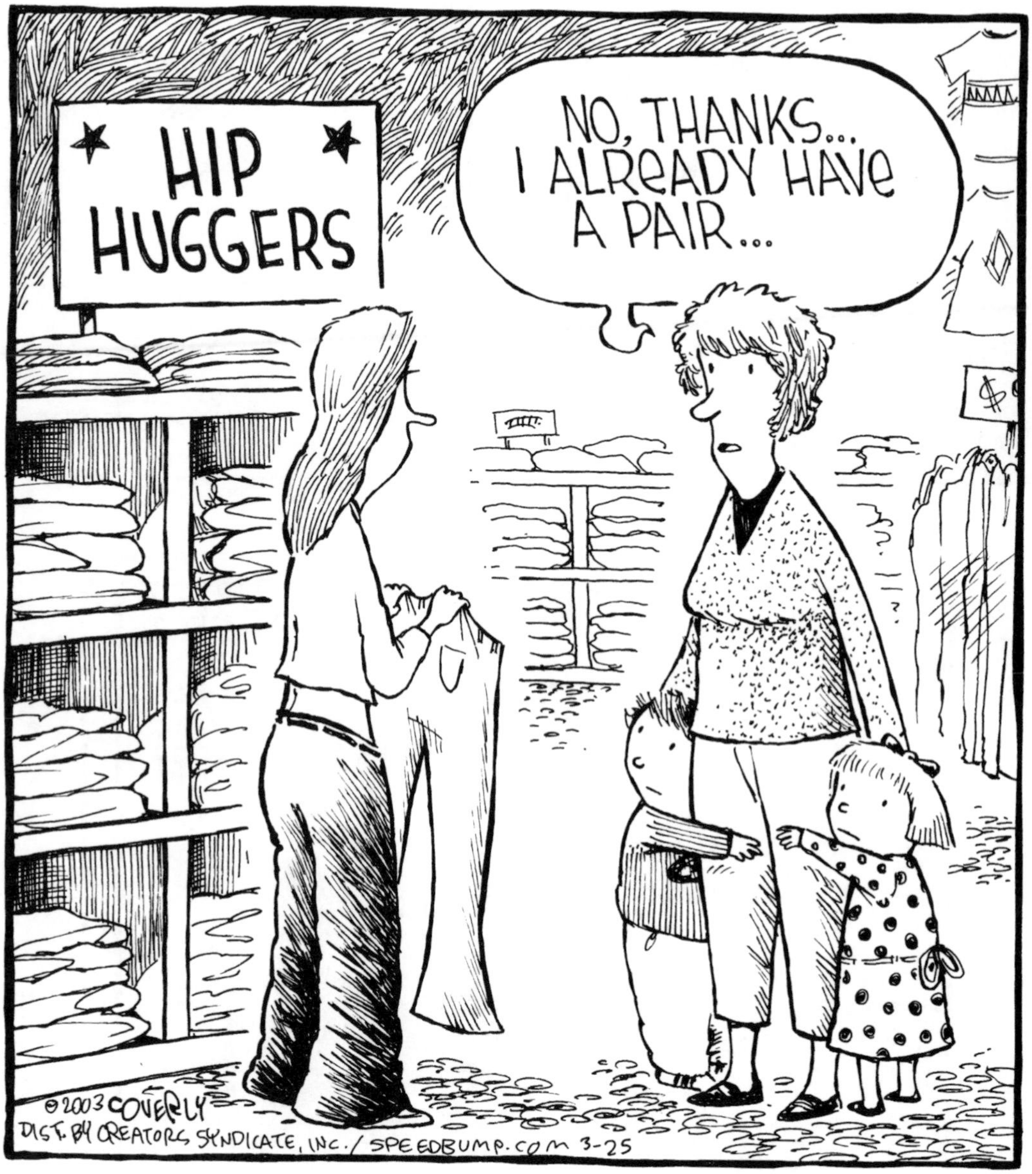
HIP HUGGERS
NO, THANKS... I ALREADY HAVE A PAIR...
©2003 COVERLY
DIST. BY CREATORS SYNDICATE, INC. / SPEEDBUMP.COM 3-25

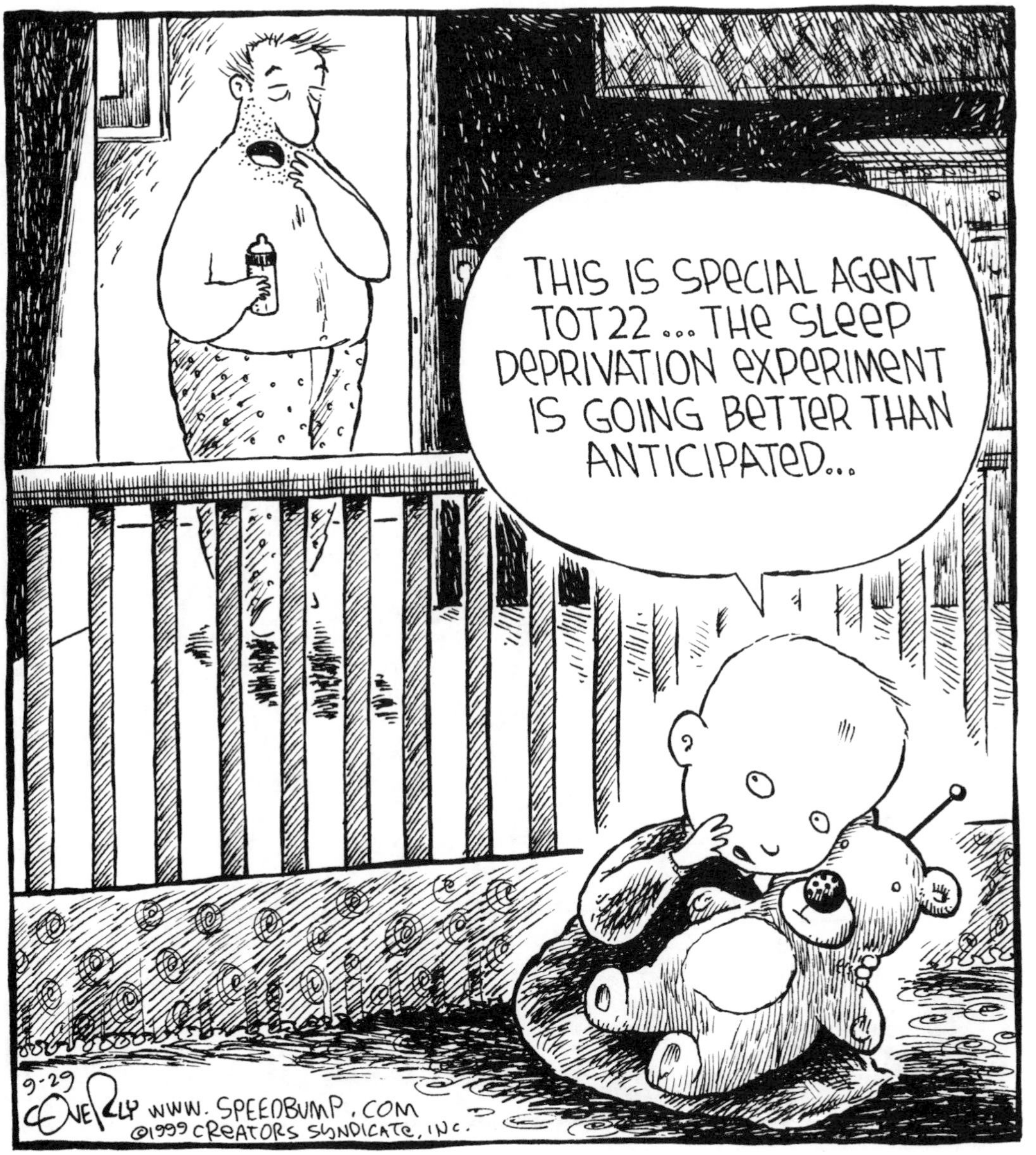
THIS IS SPECIAL AGENT TOT22 ... THE SLEEP DEPRIVATION EXPERIMENT IS GOING BETTER THAN ANTICIPATED...
9-29
COVERLY WWW.SPEEDBUMP.COM
©1999 CREATORS SYNDICATE, INC.

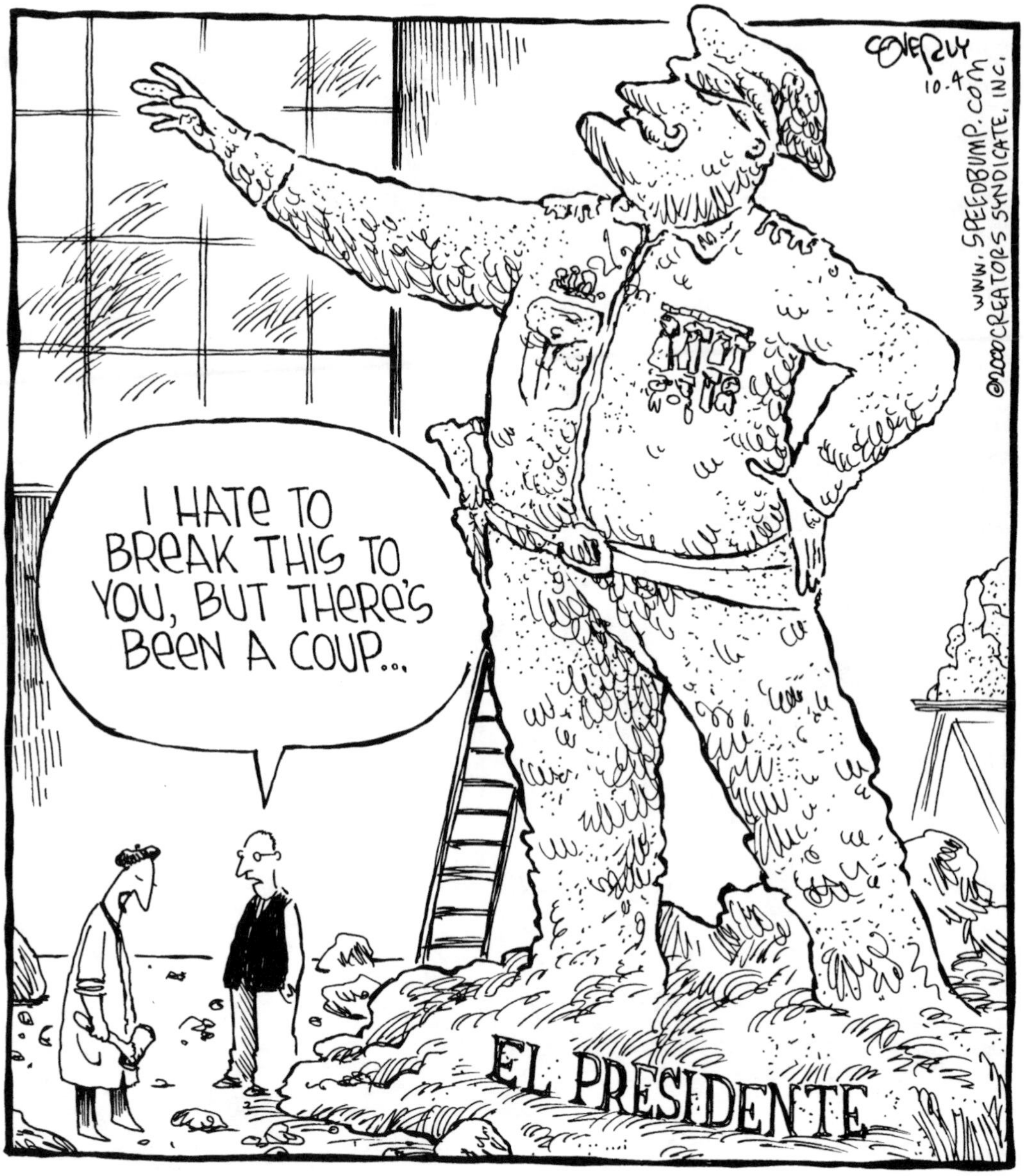
I HATE TO BREAK THIS TO YOU, BUT THERE'S BEEN A COUP...
EL PRESIDENTE
COVERLY 10.4
WWW.SPEEDBUMP.COM
©2000 CREATORS SYNDICATE, INC.

On the Job

My personal job history is pathetic, really: golf course groundskeeper, tennis instructor, pizza delivery boy, and bookstore clerk. My last job, before diving into cartooning full-time, was as an artist for a public relations firm. It didn't go well. I wasn't big on suits and normal person hours. The head of the firm finally fired me, telling me I had a "freelance personality." In hindsight, this was a very insightful comment.

In other words, none of the cartoons in this chapter is based on experience. But they seem sort of universal in their themes.

For the record, the best job was the pizza delivery gig. I spent the evening picking up tips and driving like a maniac while listening to Detroit Tigers baseball games on the car radio. It was nearly as fun as the job I have now.

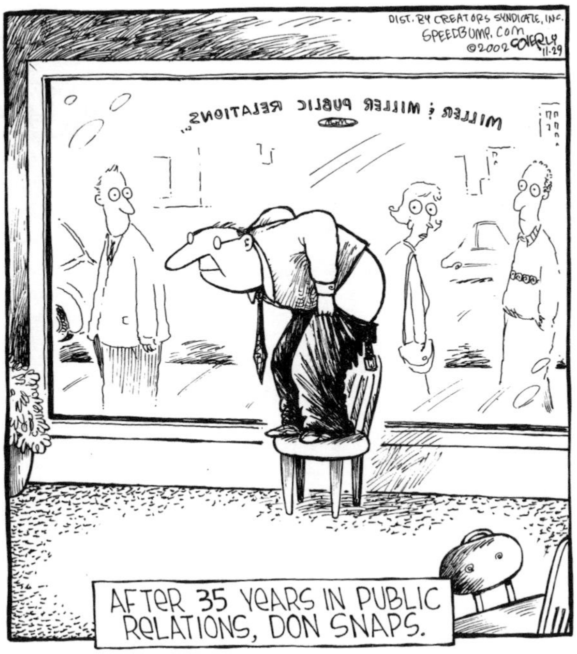
DIST. BY CREATORS SYNDICATE, INC.
SPEEDBUMP.COM
©2002 COVERLY
11-29
MILLER & MILLER PUBLIC RELATIONS
AFTER 35 YEARS IN PUBLIC RELATIONS, DON SNAPS.

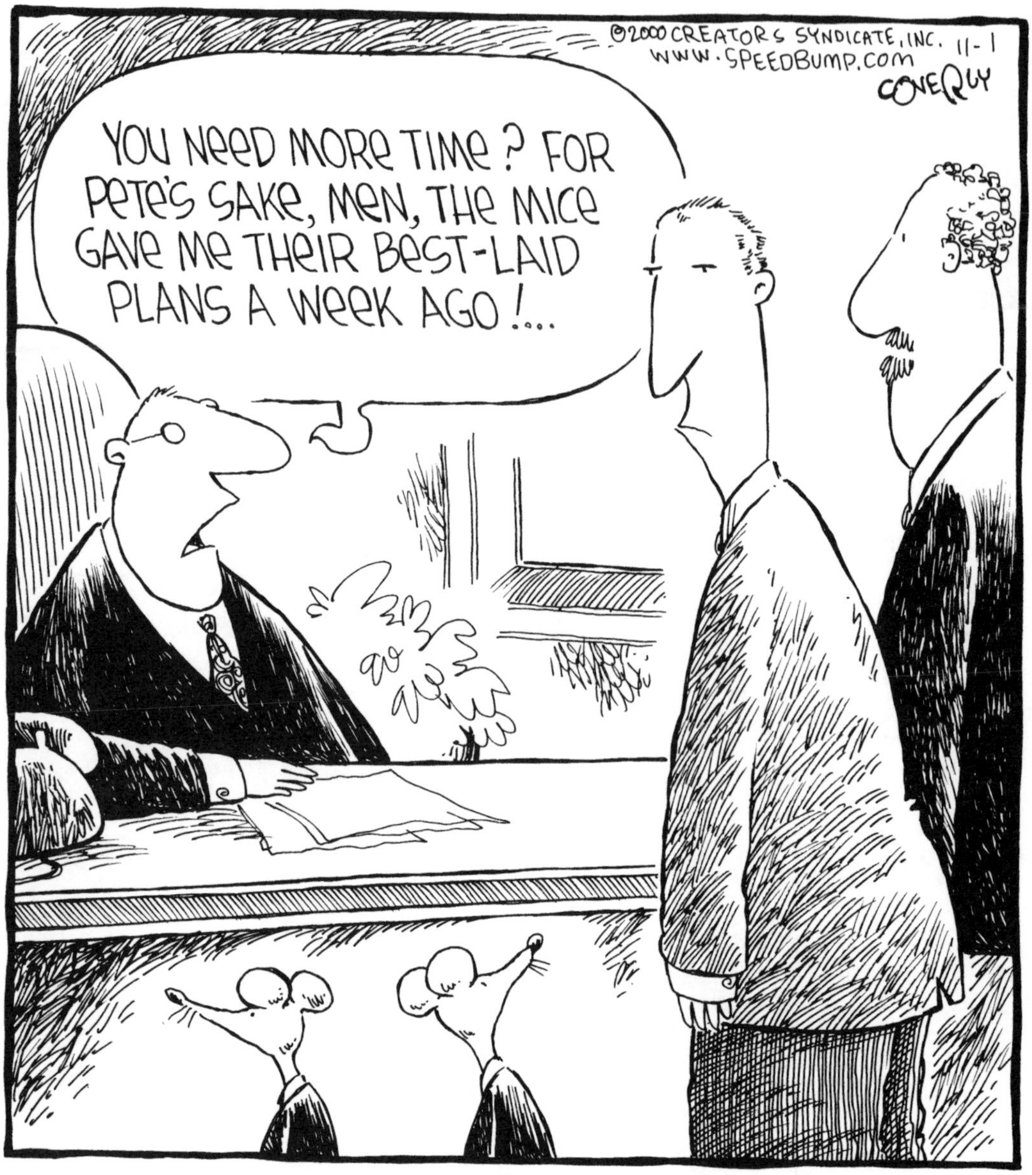
©2000 CREATORS SYNDICATE, INC. 11-1
WWW.SPEEDBUMP.COM
COVERLY
YOU NEED MORE TIME? FOR PETE'S SAKE, MEN, THE MICE GAVE ME THEIR BEST-LAID PLANS A WEEK AGO!...

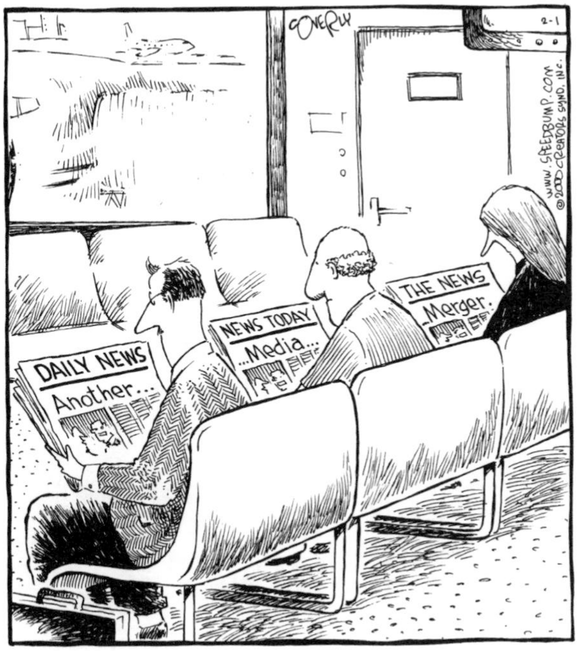
DAILY NEWS
Another...
NEWS TODAY
...Media...
THE NEWS
Merger...
CONERLY
2-1
WWW.SPEEDBUMP.COM
©2000 CREATORS SYND. INC.

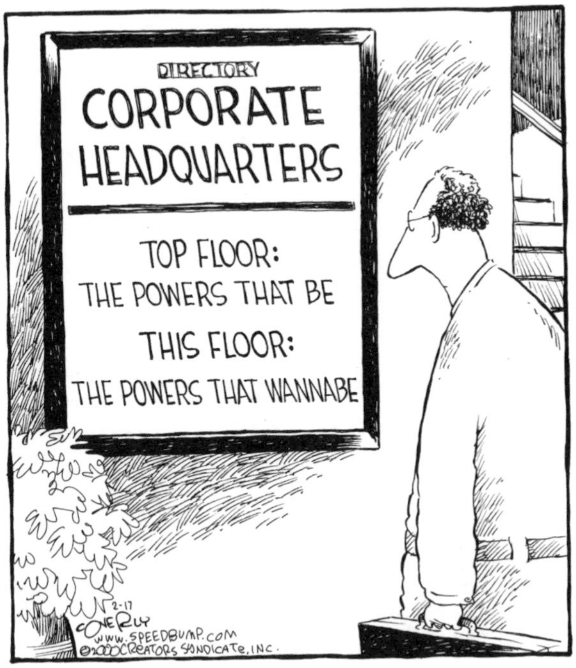
DIRECTORY
CORPORATE HEADQUARTERS
TOP FLOOR:
THE POWERS THAT BE
THIS FLOOR:
THE POWERS THAT WANNABE
2-17
CONERLY
www.SPEEDBUMP.COM
©2000 CREATORS SYNDICATE, INC.

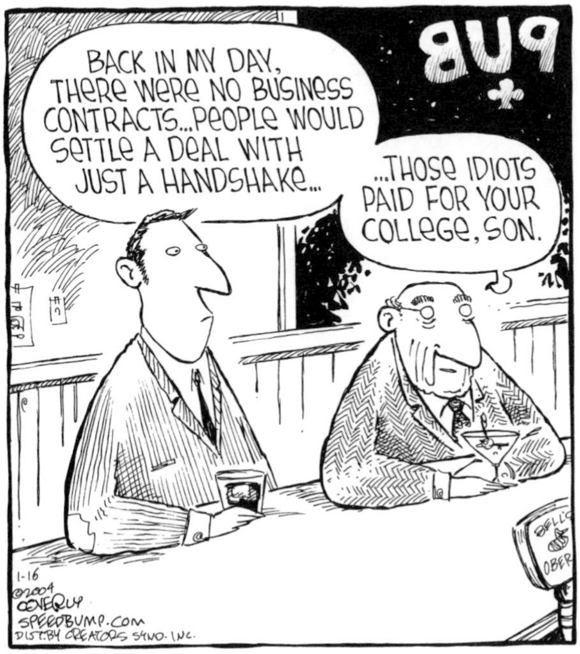
BACK IN MY DAY, THERE WERE NO BUSINESS CONTRACTS...PEOPLE WOULD SETTLE A DEAL WITH JUST A HANDSHAKE...
...THOSE IDIOTS PAID FOR YOUR COLLEGE, SON.
1-16
©2004
CONERLY
SPEEDBUMP.COM
DIST. BY CREATORS SYND. INC.

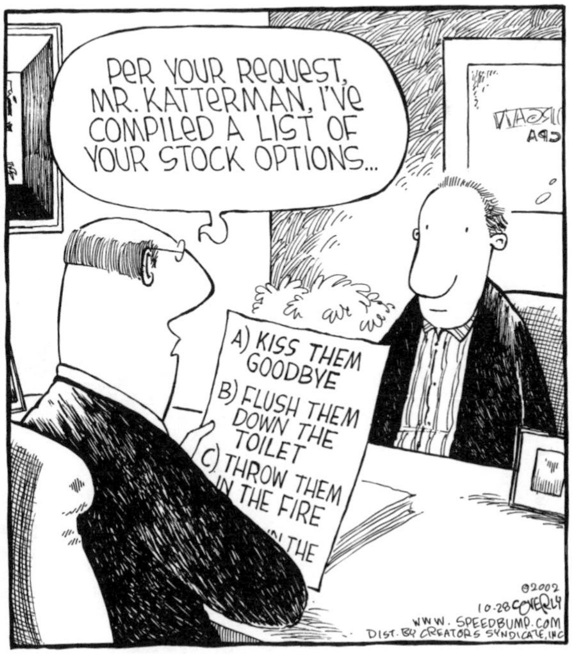
PER YOUR REQUEST, MR. KATTERMAN, I'VE COMPILED A LIST OF YOUR STOCK OPTIONS...
A) KISS THEM GOODBYE
B) FLUSH THEM DOWN THE TOILET
C) THROW THEM IN THE FIRE
©2002
10-28 CONERLY
WWW. SPEEDBUMP.COM
DIST. BY CREATORS SYNDICATE, INC

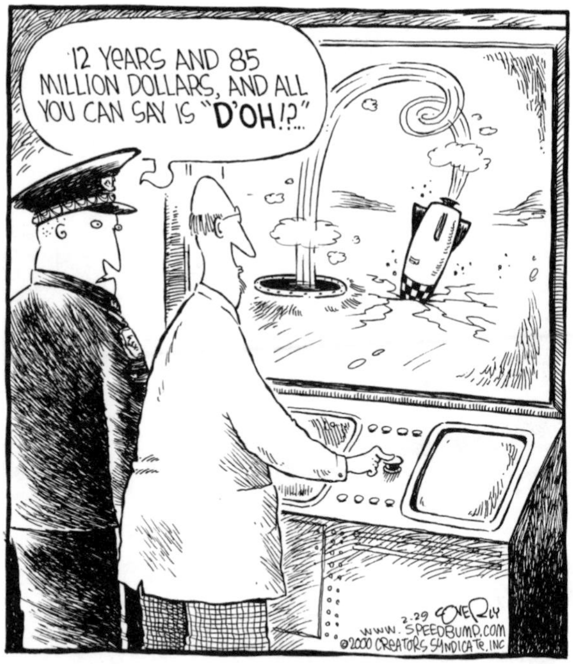
12 YEARS AND 85 MILLION DOLLARS, AND ALL YOU CAN SAY IS "D'OH!?"...
2-29
COVERLY
WWW.SPEEDBUMP.COM
©2000 CREATORS SYNDICATE, INC

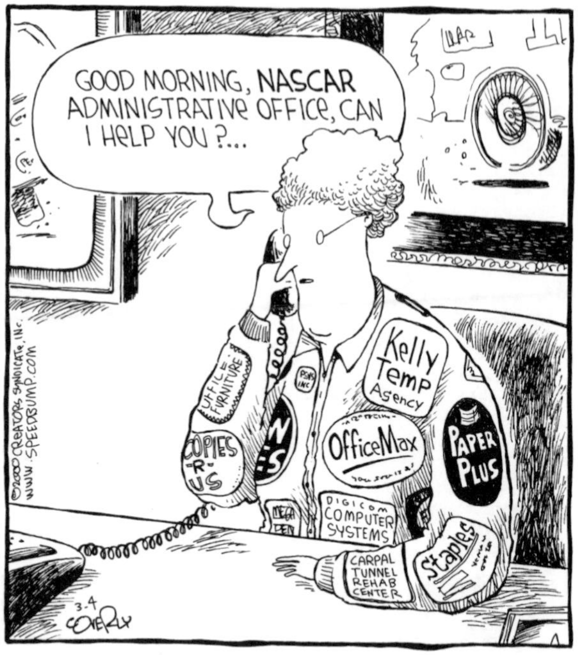
GOOD MORNING, NASCAR ADMINISTRATIVE OFFICE, CAN I HELP YOU?...
Kelly Temp Agency
OFFICE FURNITURE
COPIES -R- US
OfficeMax
PAPER PLUS
DIGICOM COMPUTER SYSTEMS
CARPAL TUNNEL REHAB CENTER
Staples
©2000 CREATORS SYNDICATE, INC.
WWW.SPEEDBUMP.COM
3-4
COVERLY

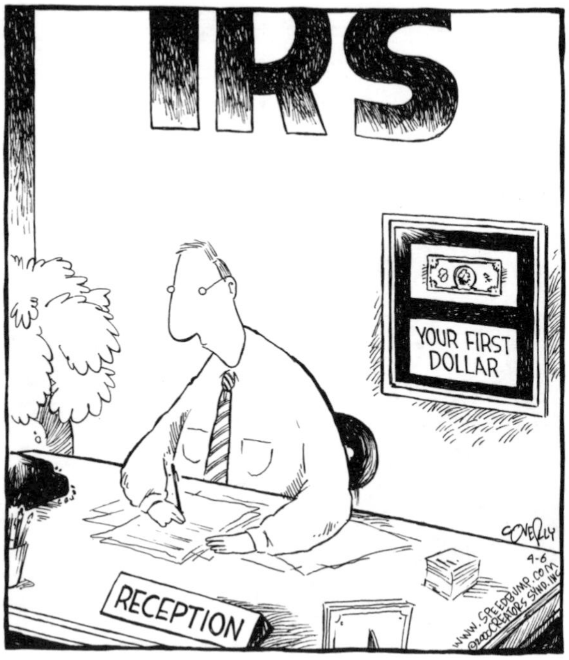
IRS
YOUR FIRST DOLLAR
RECEPTION
COVERLY
4-6
WWW.SPEEDBUMP.COM
©2000 CREATORS SYND. INC

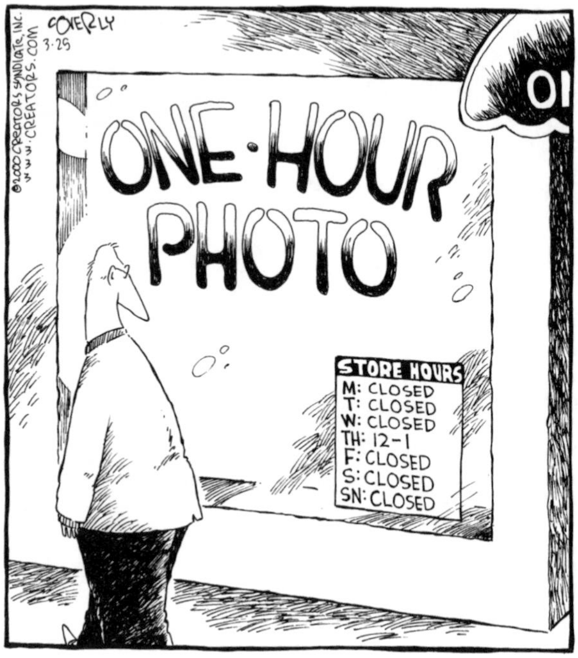
COVERLY
3-25
©2000 CREATORS SYNDICATE, INC.
WWW.CREATORS.COM
ONE-HOUR PHOTO
STORE HOURS
M: CLOSED
T: CLOSED
W: CLOSED
TH: 12-1
F: CLOSED
S: CLOSED
SN: CLOSED

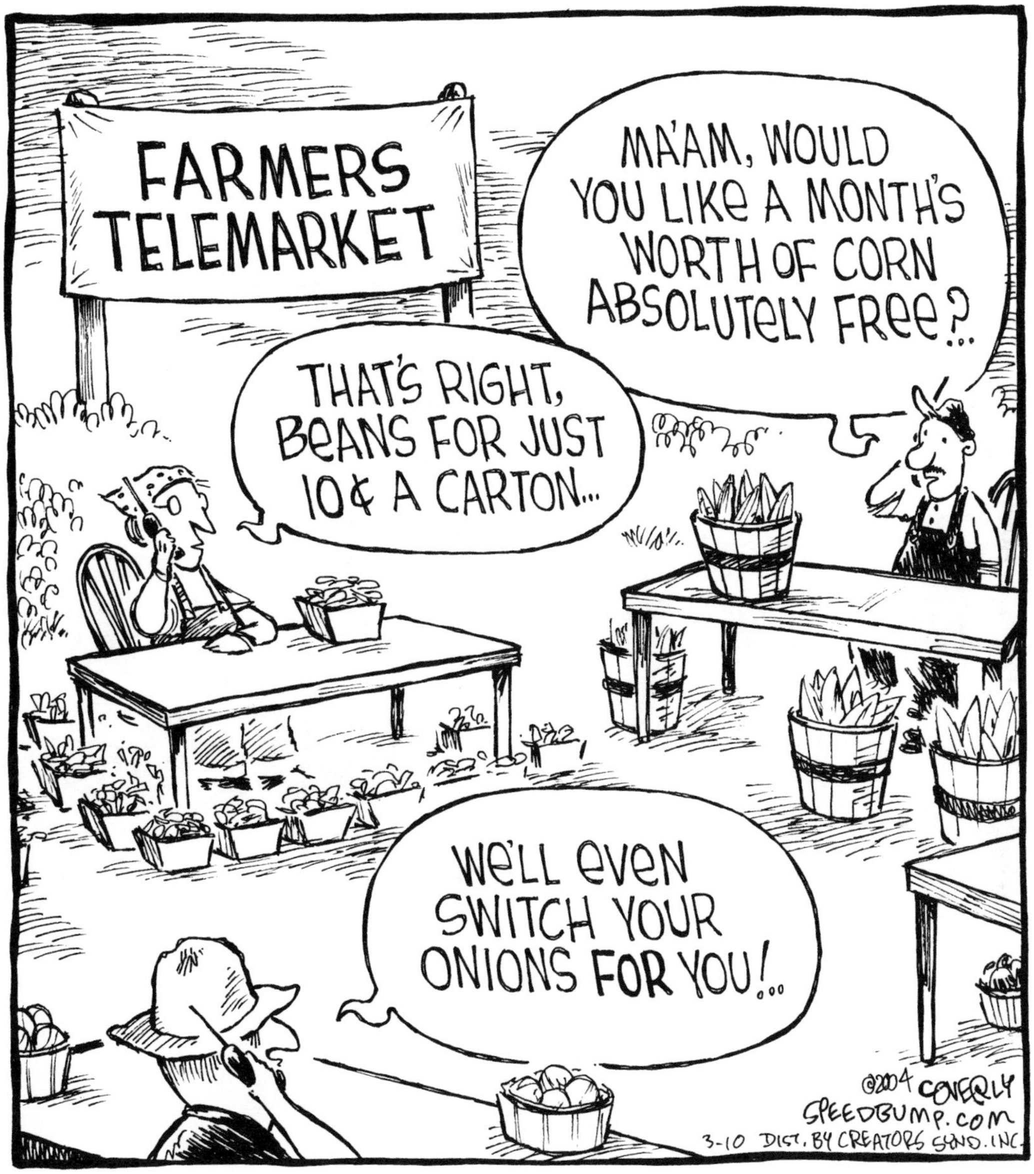
FARMERS TELEMARKET
MA'AM, WOULD YOU LIKE A MONTH'S WORTH OF CORN ABSOLUTELY FREE?...
THAT'S RIGHT, BEANS FOR JUST 10¢ A CARTON...
WE'LL EVEN SWITCH YOUR ONIONS FOR YOU!...
©2004 COVERLY
SPEEDBUMP.COM
3-10 DIST. BY CREATORS SYND. INC.

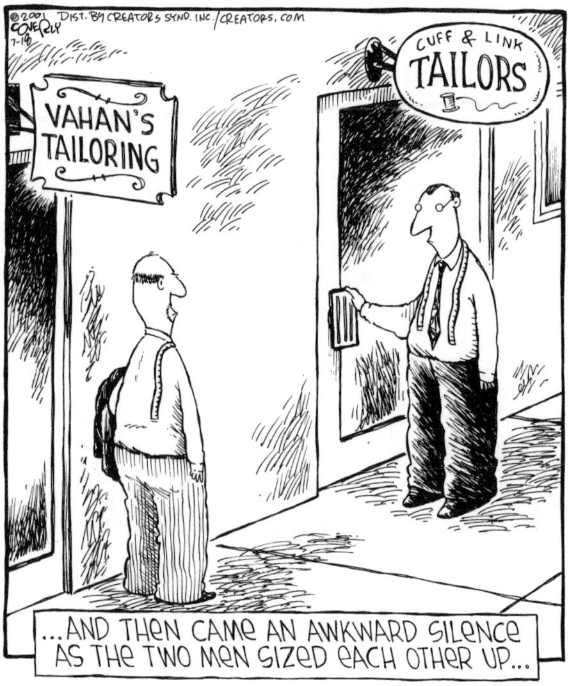
©2001 COVERLY 7-19 DIST. BY CREATORS SYND. INC./CREATORS.COM
VAHAN'S TAILORING
CUFF & LINK TAILORS
...AND THEN CAME AN AWKWARD SILENCE AS THE TWO MEN SIZED EACH OTHER UP...

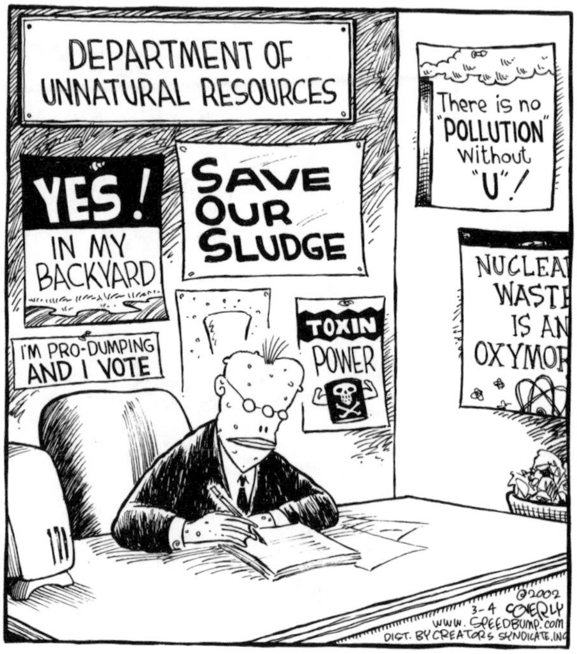
DEPARTMENT OF UNNATURAL RESOURCES
YES! IN MY BACKYARD
SAVE OUR SLUDGE
There is no "POLLUTION" without "U"!
I'M PRO-DUMPING AND I VOTE
TOXIN POWER
NUCLEA WASTE IS AN OXYMOR
©2002 3-4 COVERLY WWW.SPEEDBUMP.COM DIST. BY CREATORS SYNDICATE, INC.

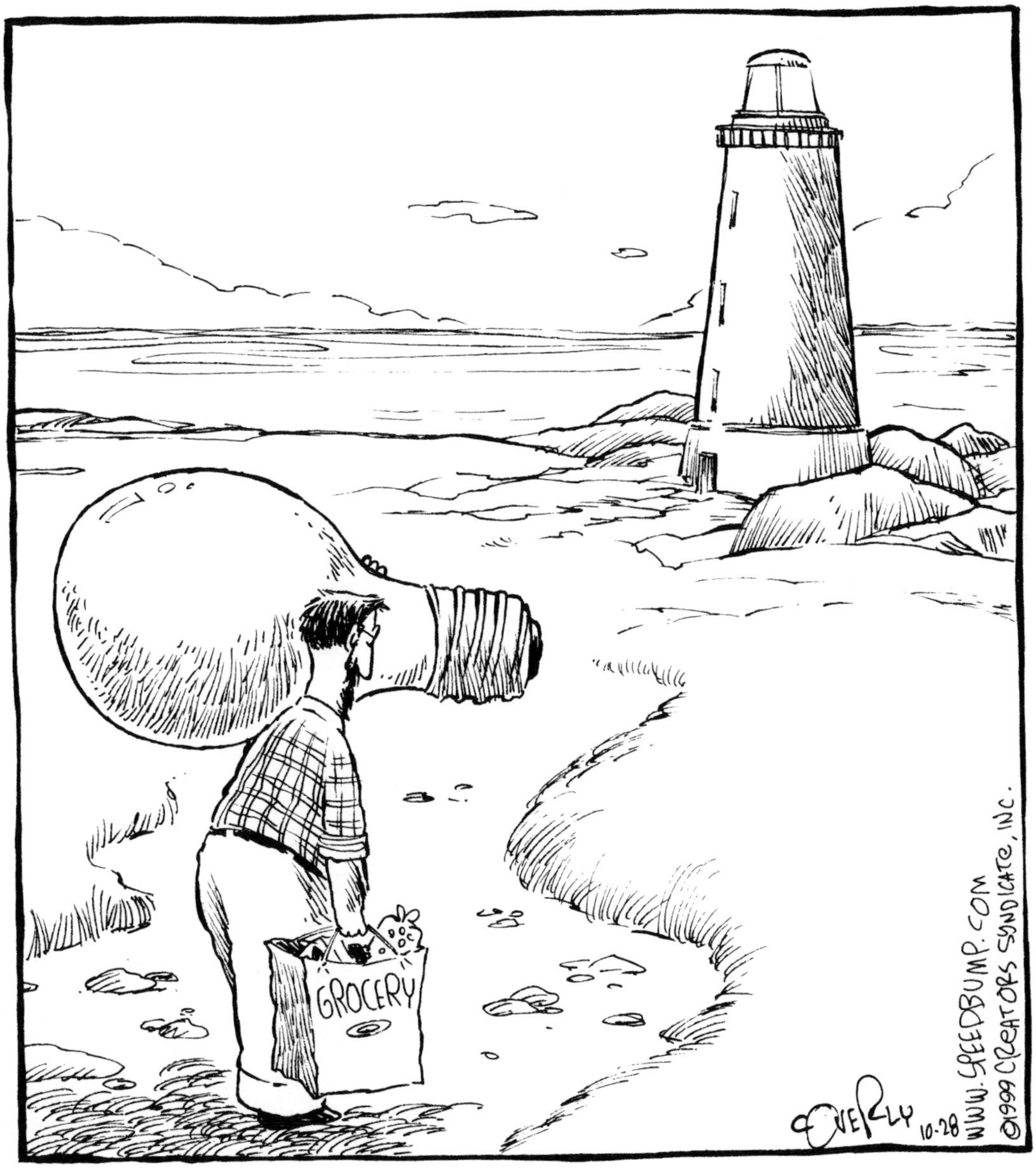
GROCERY
WWW.SPEEDBUMP.COM
©1999 CREATORS SYNDICATE, INC.
10-28

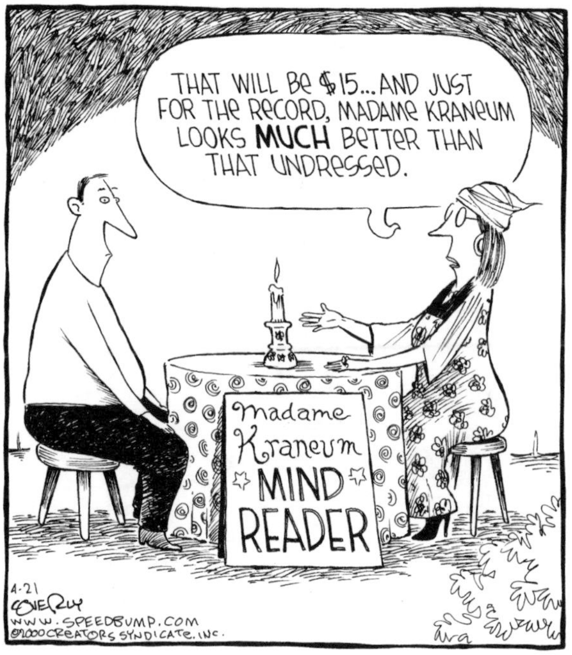
THAT WILL BE $15... AND JUST FOR THE RECORD, MADAME KRANEUM LOOKS **MUCH** BETTER THAN THAT UNDRESSED.
Madame Kraneum MIND READER
4-21
COVERLY
WWW.SPEEDBUMP.COM
©2000 CREATORS SYNDICATE, INC.

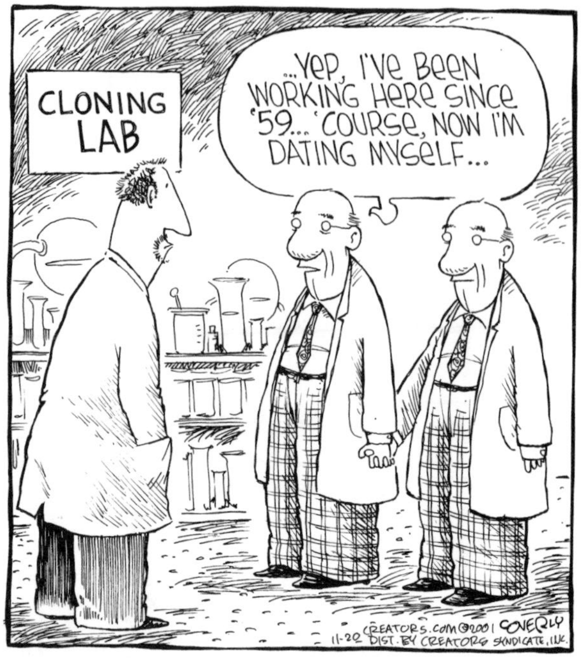
CLONING LAB
...YEP, I'VE BEEN WORKING HERE SINCE '59... 'COURSE, NOW I'M DATING MYSELF...
CREATORS.COM ©2001 COVERLY
11-22 DIST. BY CREATORS SYNDICATE, INC.

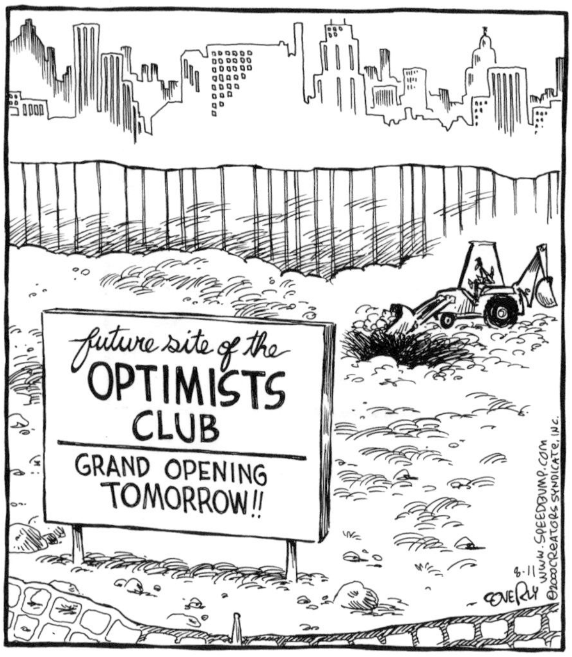
future site of the
OPTIMISTS CLUB
GRAND OPENING TOMORROW!!
8-11
COVERLY
WWW.SPEEDBUMP.COM
©2000 CREATORS SYNDICATE, INC.

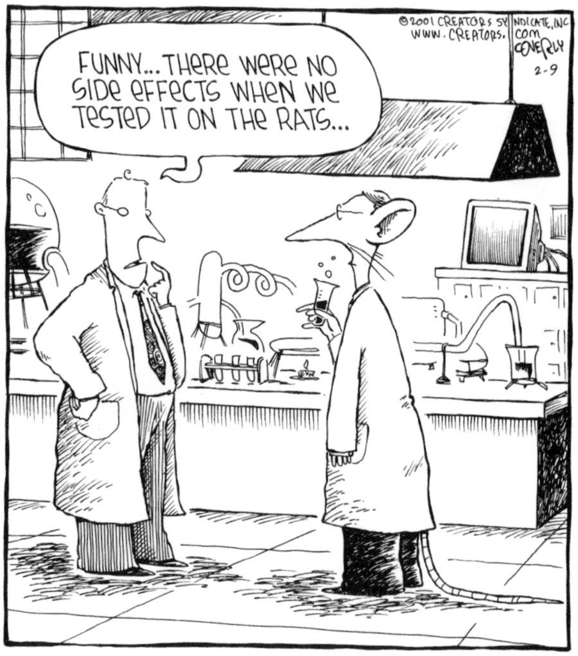
©2001 CREATORS SYNDICATE, INC.
WWW.CREATORS.COM
COVERLY
2-9
FUNNY... THERE WERE NO SIDE EFFECTS WHEN WE TESTED IT ON THE RATS...

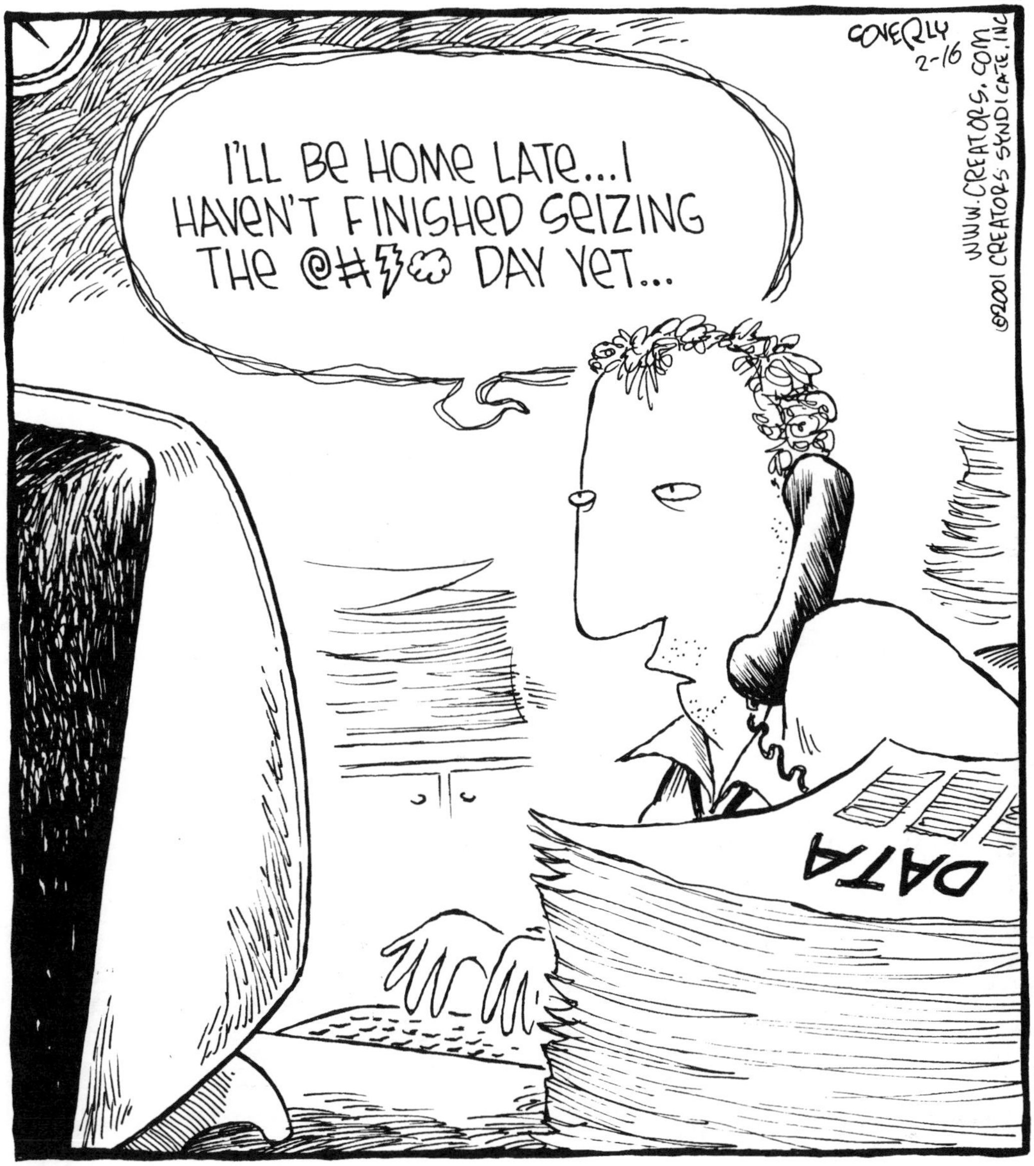
I'LL BE HOME LATE...I HAVEN'T FINISHED SEIZING THE @#⚡☁ DAY YET...
DATA
COVERLY 2-16
WWW.CREATORS.COM
©2001 CREATORS SYNDICATE, INC

HOLD ON, REX... IT'S THE OFFICE AGAIN...
RING RING RING... RING RING RING...
©2001 COVERLY 10-15 www.SPEEDBUMP.COM DIST. BY CREATORS SYNDICATE, INC.

©2001 CREATORS SYNDICATE, INC. www.SPEEDBUMP.COM COVERLY 2-27
MISFORTUNE 500 COMPANIES
DEAD GUY & NO SONS, INC. ▼1¾
BLACK CAT INDUSTRIES, INC.
ACCIDENT-PRONE ROOFERS, INC
BUBONIC STUDIES, INC.
ALL THUMBS ELECTRIC CO.
THIN ICE, INC.
LOOK-AFTER-YOU-LEAP,
LEAD BALLOON INVESTORS ▼7¼

OH, DANNY BOY, THE PIPES, THE PIPES ARE CALLING...!
EVERY @$#% MORNING...
O'REILLY & SON PLUMBING
3-1 COVERLY www.SPEEDBUMP.COM ©2001 CREATORS SYNDICATE, INC.

©2001 CREATORS SYNDICATE, INC. www.CREATORS.COM COVERLY 3-26

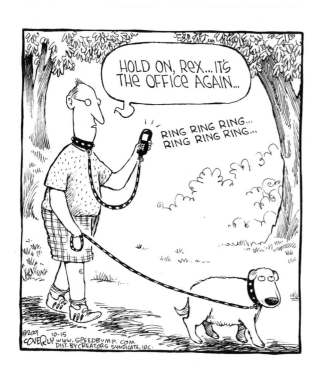

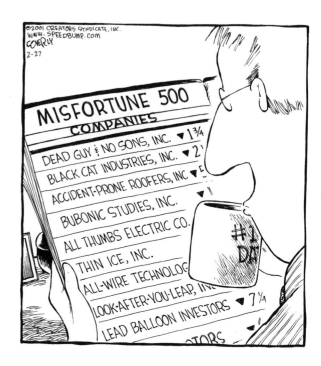

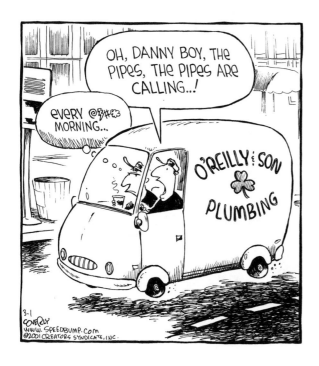

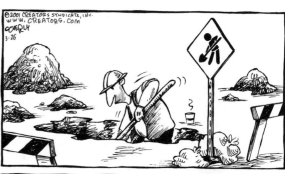

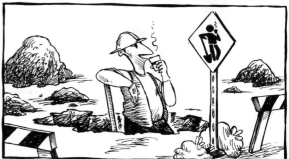

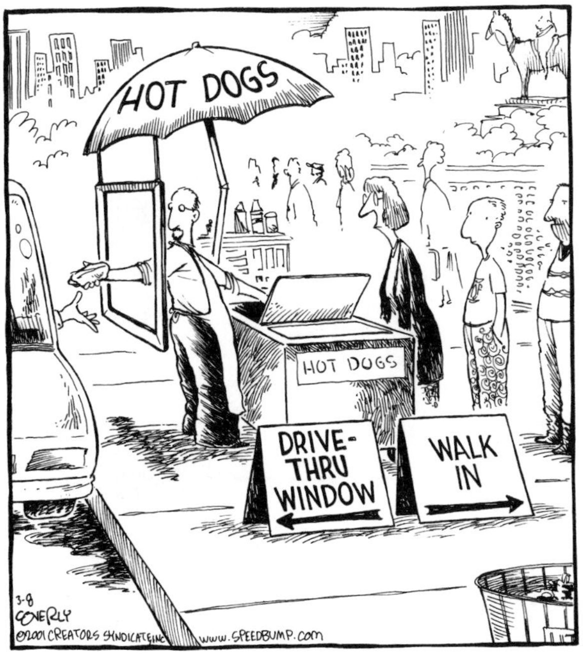
HOT DOGS
HOT DOGS
DRIVE-THRU WINDOW
WALK IN
3-8
COVERLY
©2001 CREATORS SYNDICATE INC
www.SPEEDBUMP.com

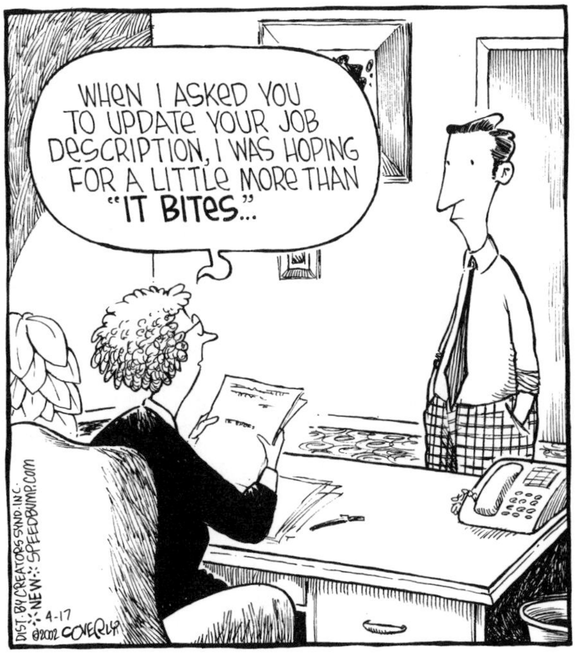
WHEN I ASKED YOU TO UPDATE YOUR JOB DESCRIPTION, I WAS HOPING FOR A LITTLE MORE THAN "IT BITES"...
DIST. BY CREATORS SYND. INC.
NEW: WWW.SPEEDBUMP.com
4-17
©2002 COVERLY

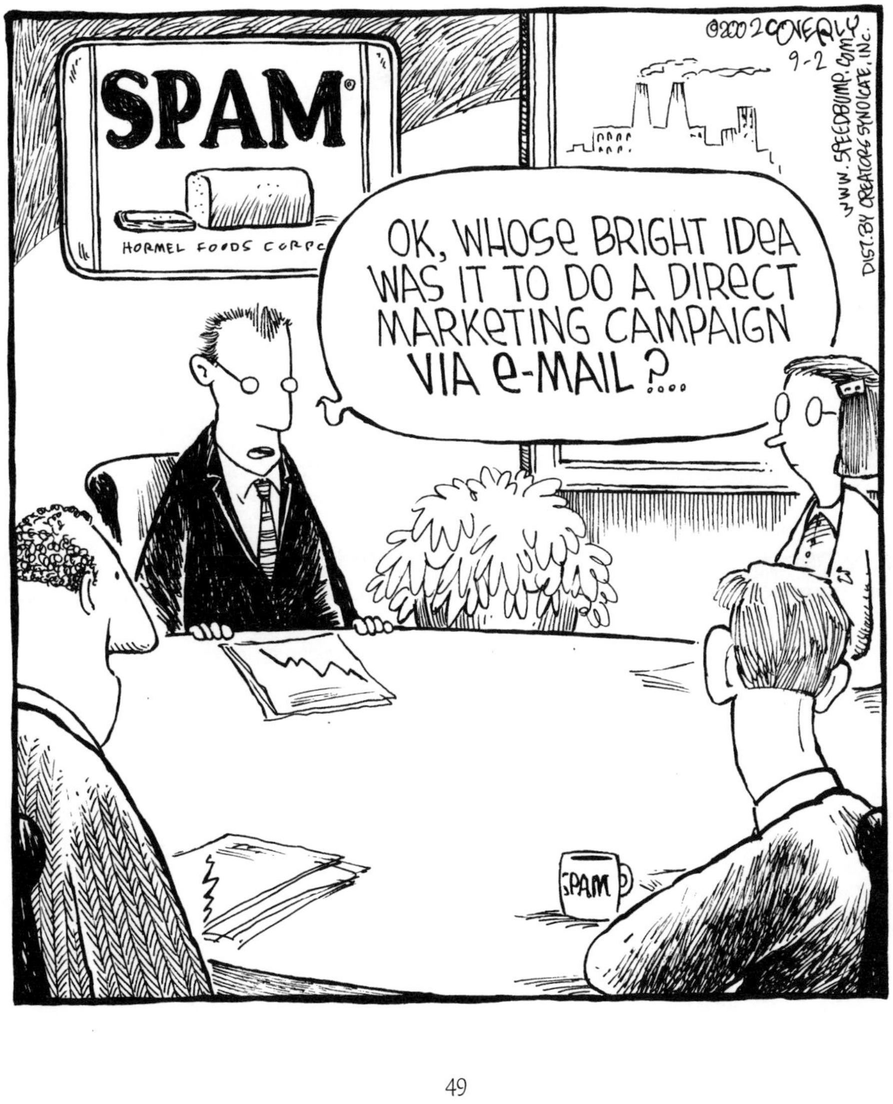
SPAM®
HORMEL FOODS CORP
OK, WHOSE BRIGHT IDEA WAS IT TO DO A DIRECT MARKETING CAMPAIGN VIA E-MAIL?...
SPAM
©2002 COVERLY
9-2
WWW.SPEEDBUMP.COM
DIST. BY CREATORS SYNDICATE, INC.

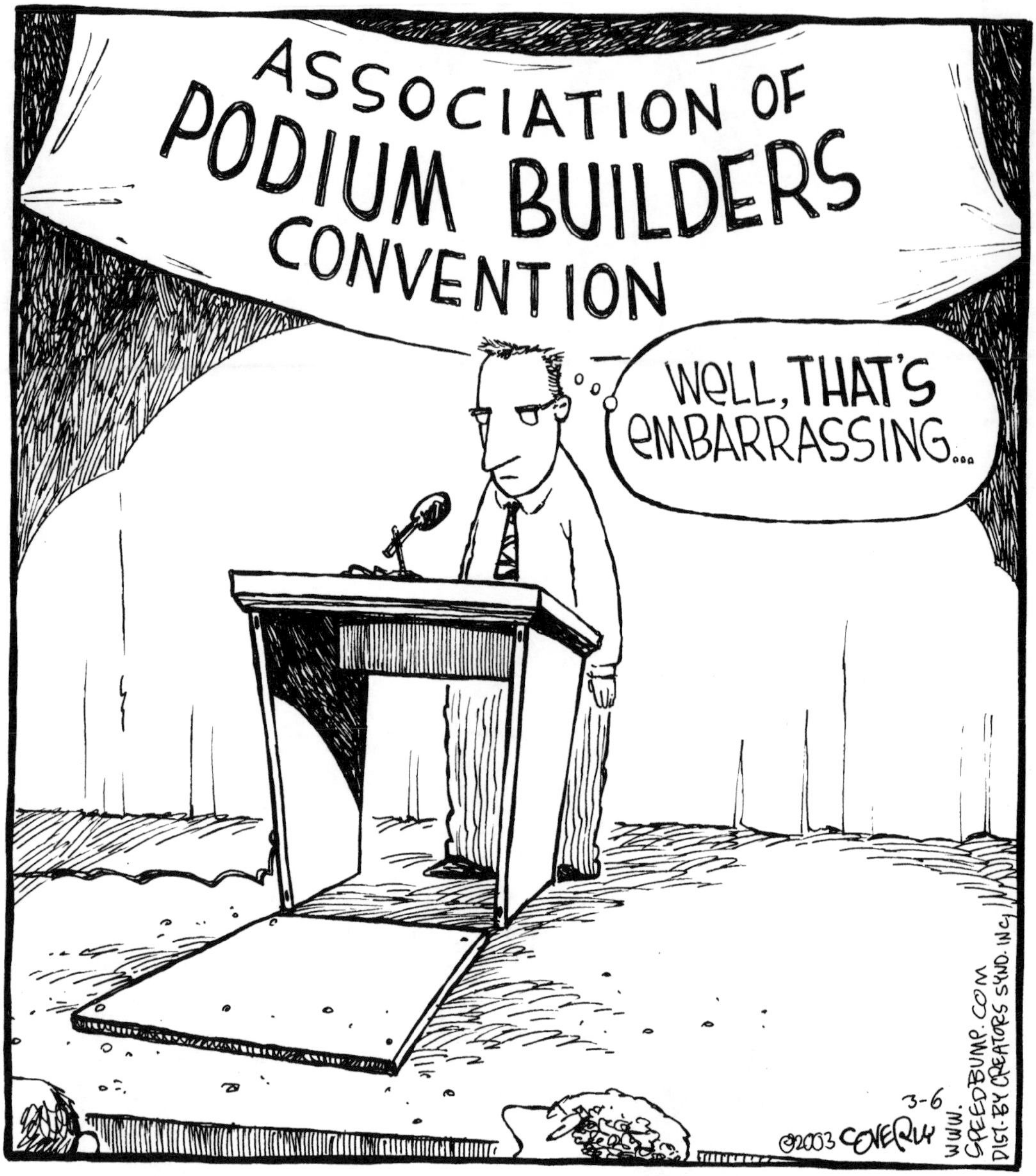
ASSOCIATION OF PODIUM BUILDERS CONVENTION
WELL, THAT'S EMBARRASSING...
3-6
©2003 COVERLY
WWW.SPEEDBUMP.COM
DIST. BY CREATORS SYND. INC.

"(Can you spot the mistake? Yep, as many readers were quick to point out when this ran in the paper, that's not a podium, it's a lectern . . . oops . . .)"

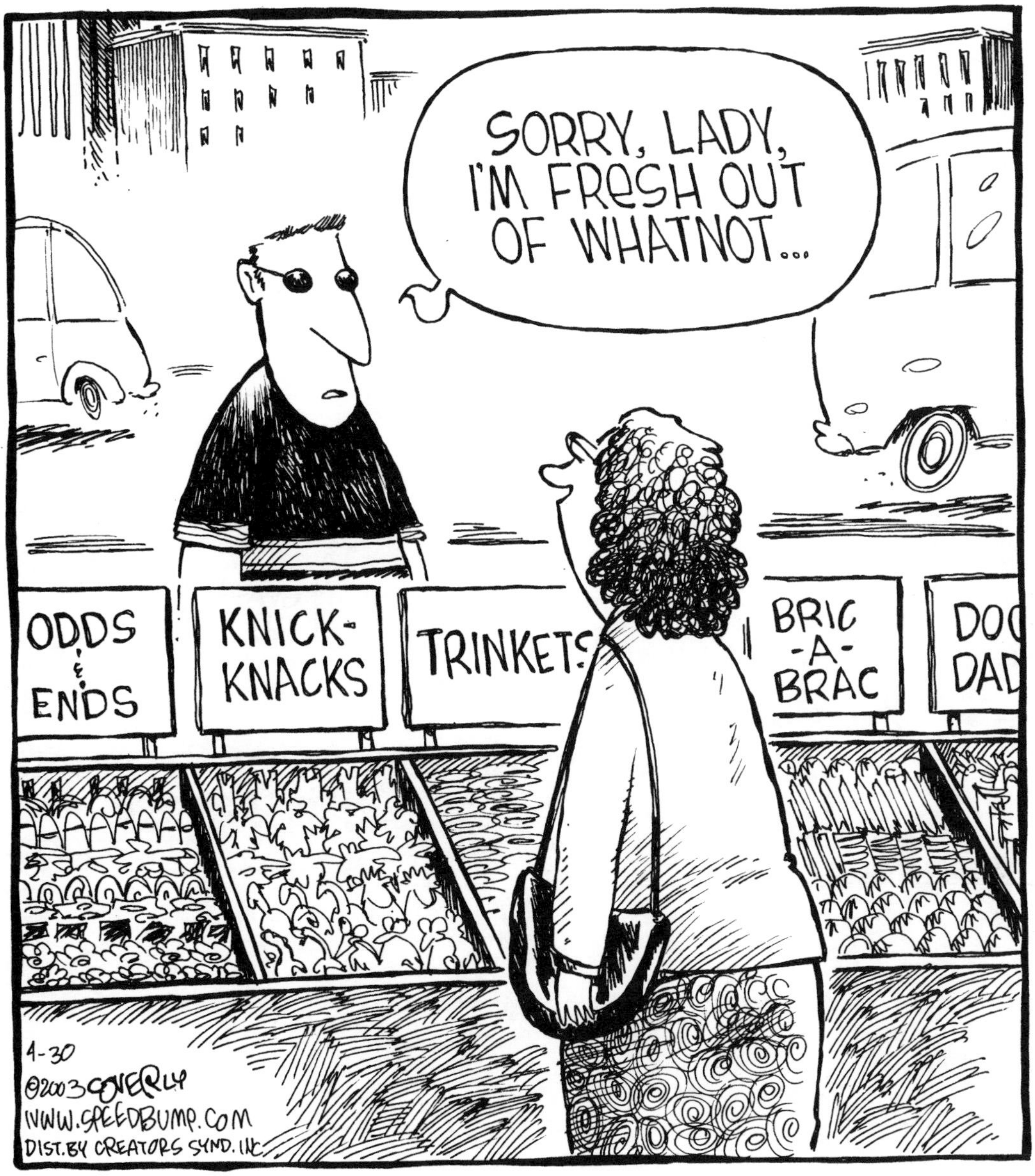
SORRY, LADY, I'M FRESH OUT OF WHATNOT...
ODDS & ENDS
KNICK-KNACKS
TRINKETS
BRIC -A- BRAC
DOO DAD
4-30
©2003 COVERLY
WWW.SPEEDBUMP.COM
DIST. BY CREATORS SYND. INC.

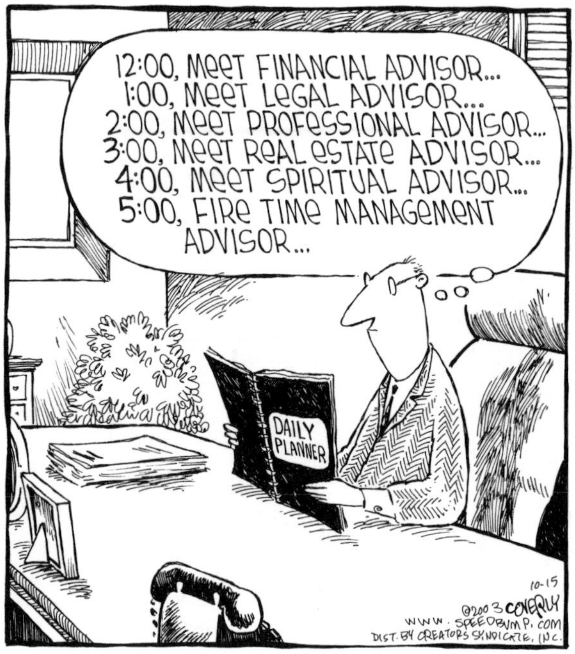
12:00, MEET FINANCIAL ADVISOR...
1:00, MEET LEGAL ADVISOR...
2:00, MEET PROFESSIONAL ADVISOR...
3:00, MEET REAL ESTATE ADVISOR...
4:00, MEET SPIRITUAL ADVISOR...
5:00, FIRE TIME MANAGEMENT ADVISOR...
DAILY PLANNER
10-15
©2003 COVERLY
WWW. SPEEDBUMP. COM
DIST. BY CREATORS SYNDICATE, INC.

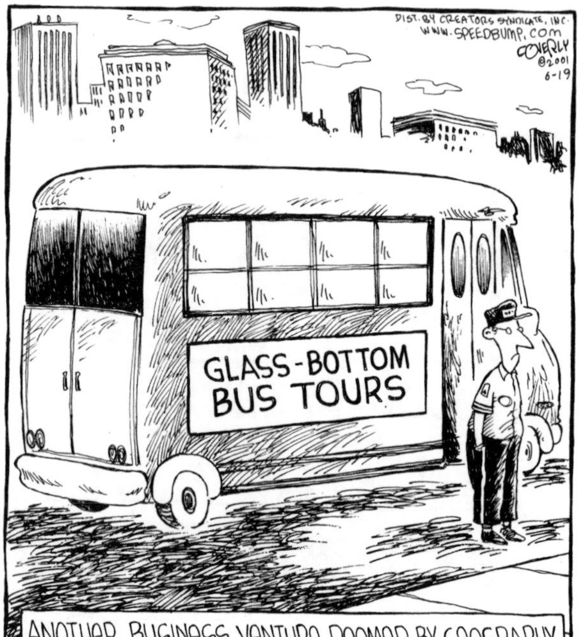
DIST. BY CREATORS SYNDICATE, INC.
WWW.SPEEDBUMP.COM
COVERLY
©2001
6-19
GLASS-BOTTOM BUS TOURS

ANOTHER BUSINESS VENTURE DOOMED BY GEOGRAPHY

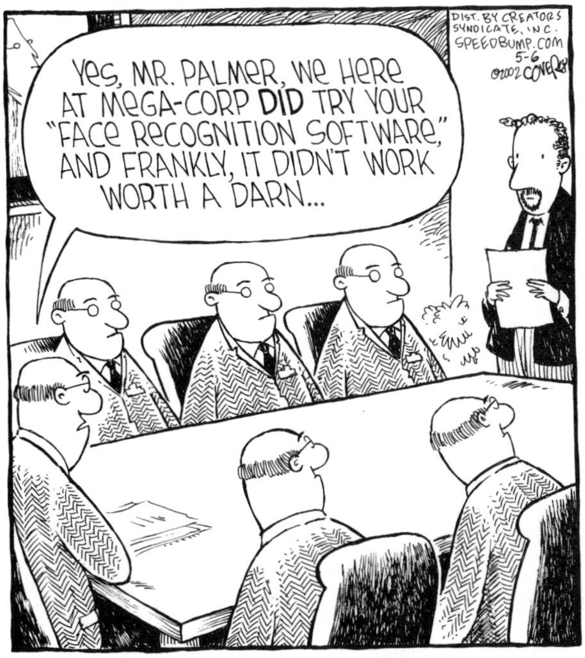
YES, MR. PALMER, WE HERE AT MEGA-CORP DID TRY YOUR "FACE RECOGNITION SOFTWARE," AND FRANKLY, IT DIDN'T WORK WORTH A DARN...
DIST. BY CREATORS SYNDICATE, INC. SPEEDBUMP.COM 5-6 ©2002 COVERLY

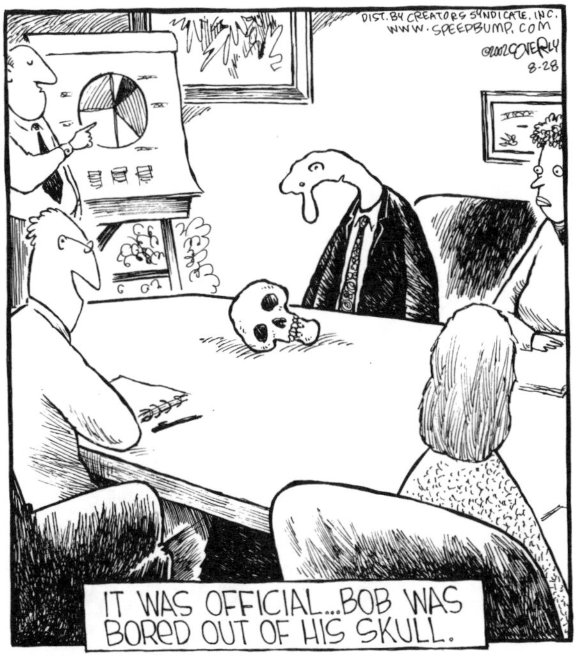
DIST. BY CREATORS SYNDICATE, INC. WWW.SPEEDBUMP.COM ©2002 COVERLY 8-28
IT WAS OFFICIAL...BOB WAS BORED OUT OF HIS SKULL.

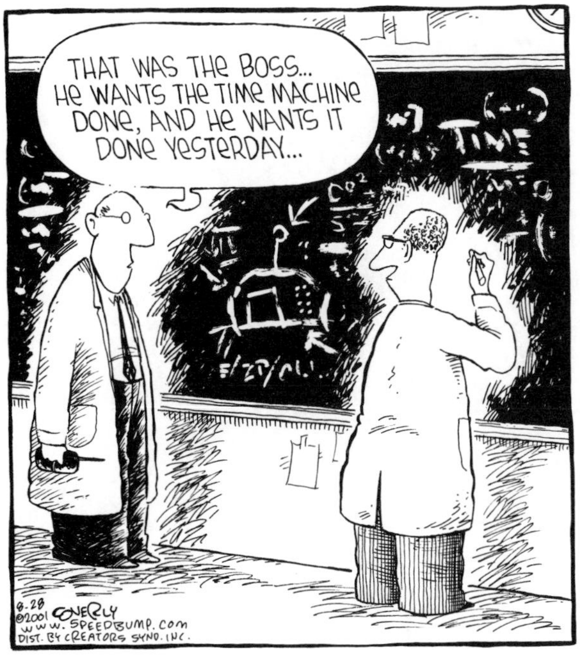
THAT WAS THE BOSS... HE WANTS THE TIME MACHINE DONE, AND HE WANTS IT DONE YESTERDAY...
TIME
8-28 ©2001 COVERLY WWW.SPEEDBUMP.COM DIST. BY CREATORS SYND. INC.

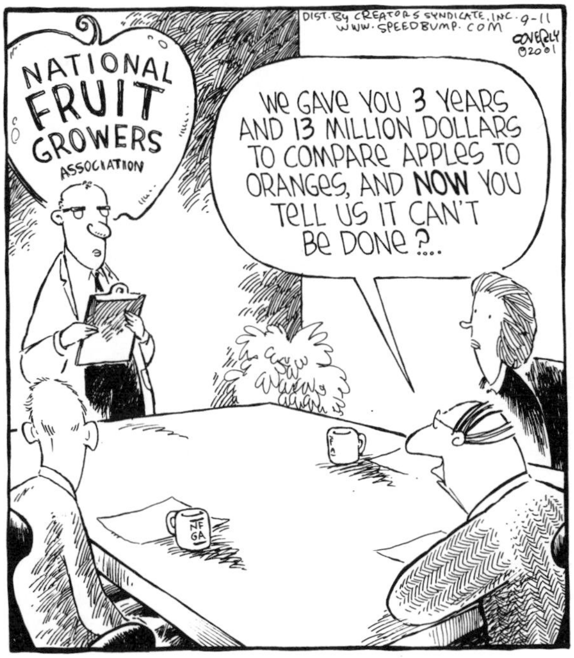
DIST. BY CREATORS SYNDICATE, INC. WWW.SPEEDBUMP.COM 9-11 COVERLY ©2001
NATIONAL FRUIT GROWERS ASSOCIATION
WE GAVE YOU 3 YEARS AND 13 MILLION DOLLARS TO COMPARE APPLES TO ORANGES, AND NOW YOU TELL US IT CAN'T BE DONE?...
NFGA

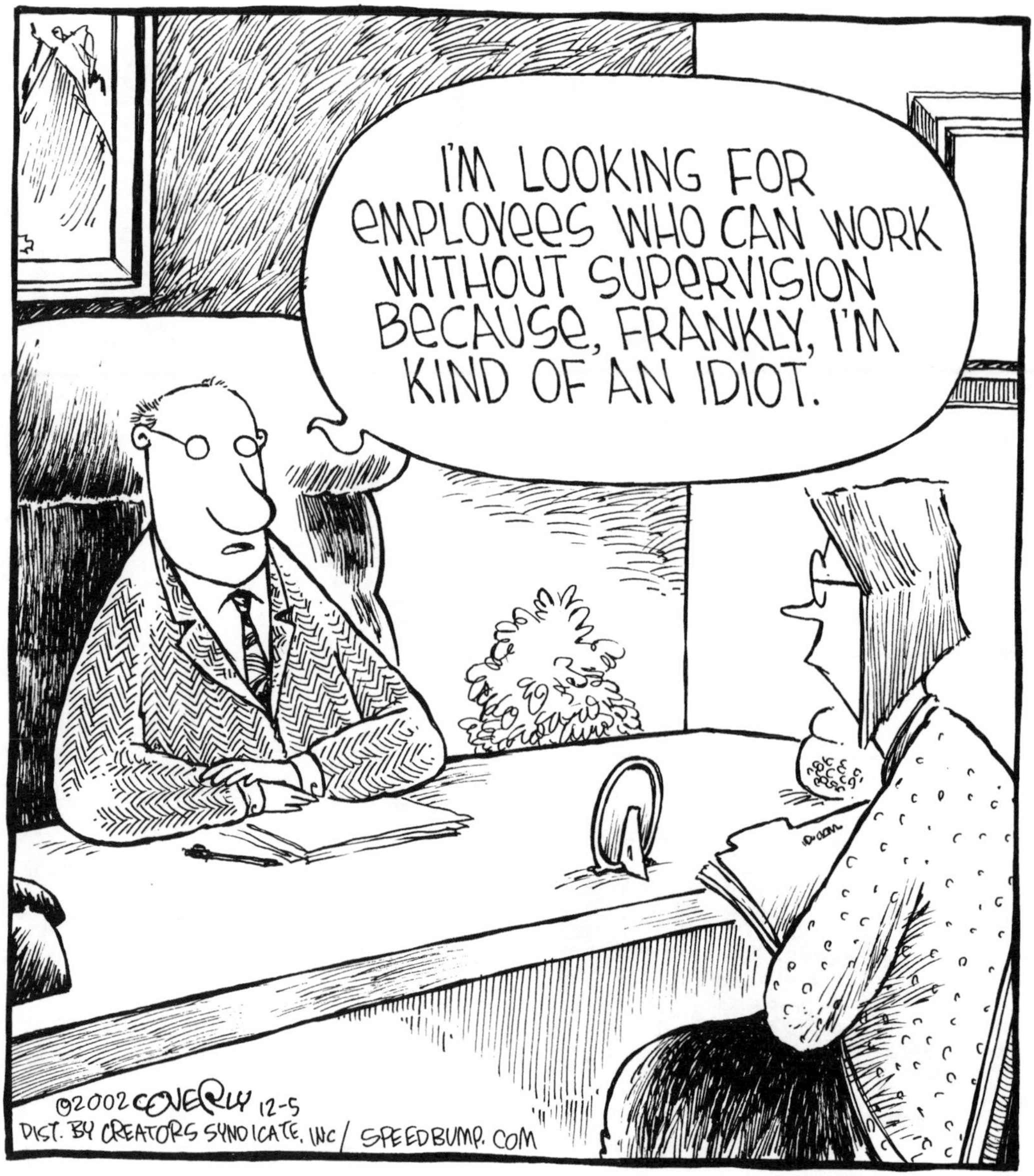
I'M LOOKING FOR EMPLOYEES WHO CAN WORK WITHOUT SUPERVISION BECAUSE, FRANKLY, I'M KIND OF AN IDIOT.
©2002 COVERLY 12-5
DIST. BY CREATORS SYNDICATE, INC / SPEEDBUMP.COM

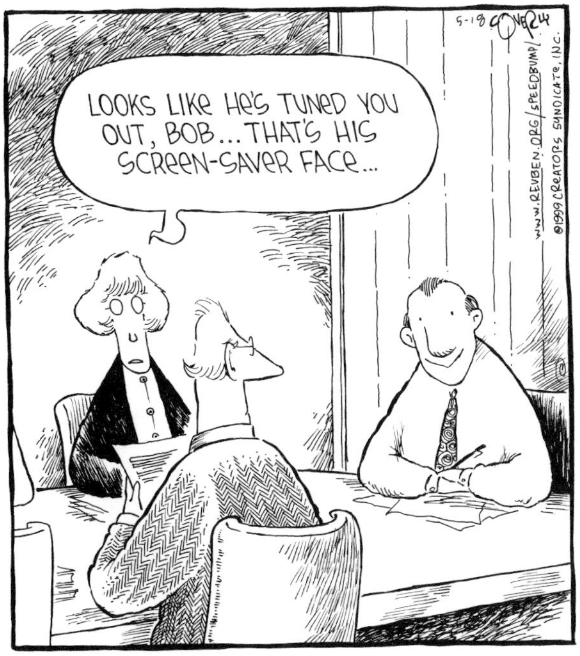
LOOKS LIKE HE'S TUNED YOU OUT, BOB... THAT'S HIS SCREEN-SAVER FACE...
5-18 COVERLY
WWW.REUBEN.ORG/SPEEDBUMP/
©1999 CREATORS SYNDICATE, INC.

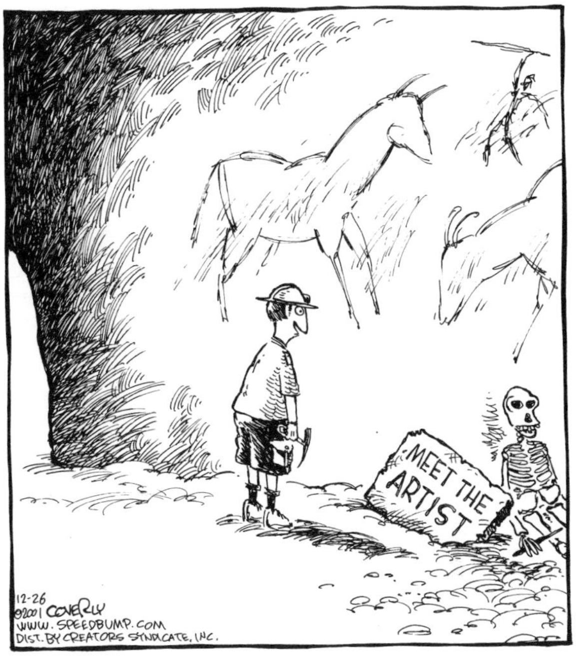
MEET THE ARTIST
12-26
©2001 COVERLY
WWW.SPEEDBUMP.COM
DIST. BY CREATORS SYNDICATE, INC.

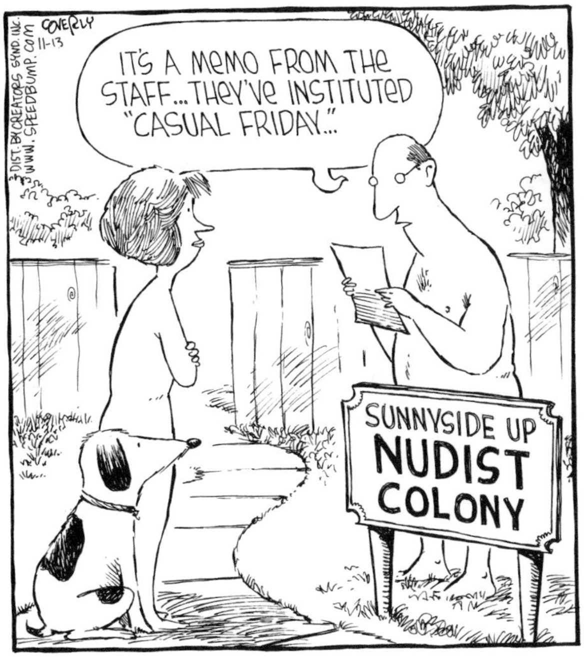
COVERLY
11-13
DIST. BY CREATORS SYND. INC.
WWW.SPEEDBUMP.COM
IT'S A MEMO FROM THE STAFF... THEY'VE INSTITUTED "CASUAL FRIDAY."
SUNNYSIDE UP
NUDIST
COLONY

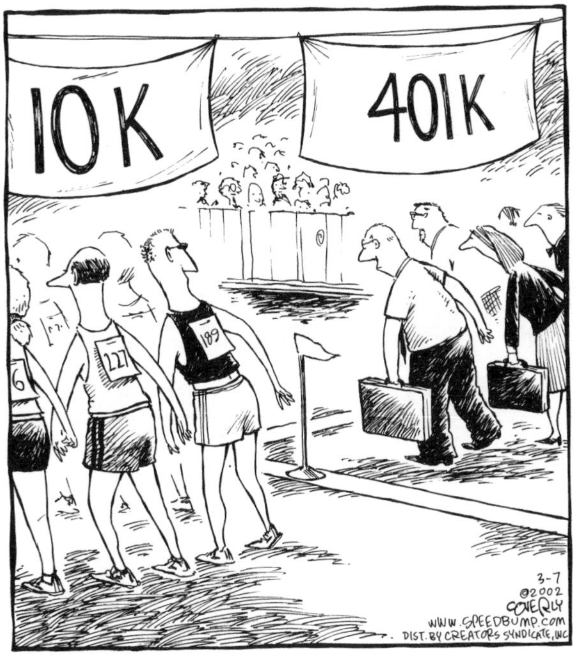
10K
401K
227
189
3-7
©2002
COVERLY
WWW.SPEEDBUMP.COM
DIST. BY CREATORS SYNDICATE, INC

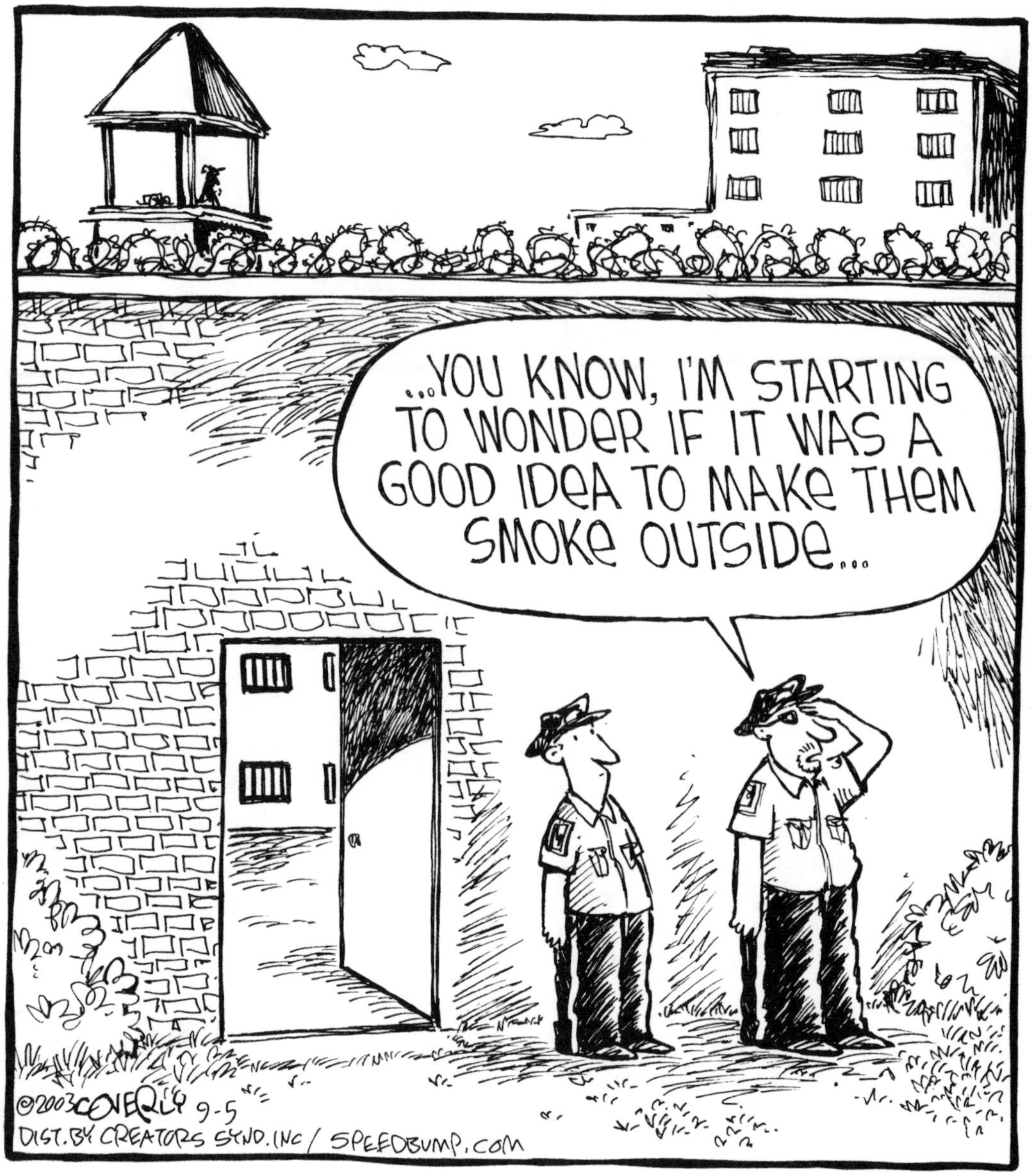
...YOU KNOW, I'M STARTING TO WONDER IF IT WAS A GOOD IDEA TO MAKE THEM SMOKE OUTSIDE...
©2003 COVERLY 9-5
DIST. BY CREATORS SYND. INC / SPEEDBUMP.COM

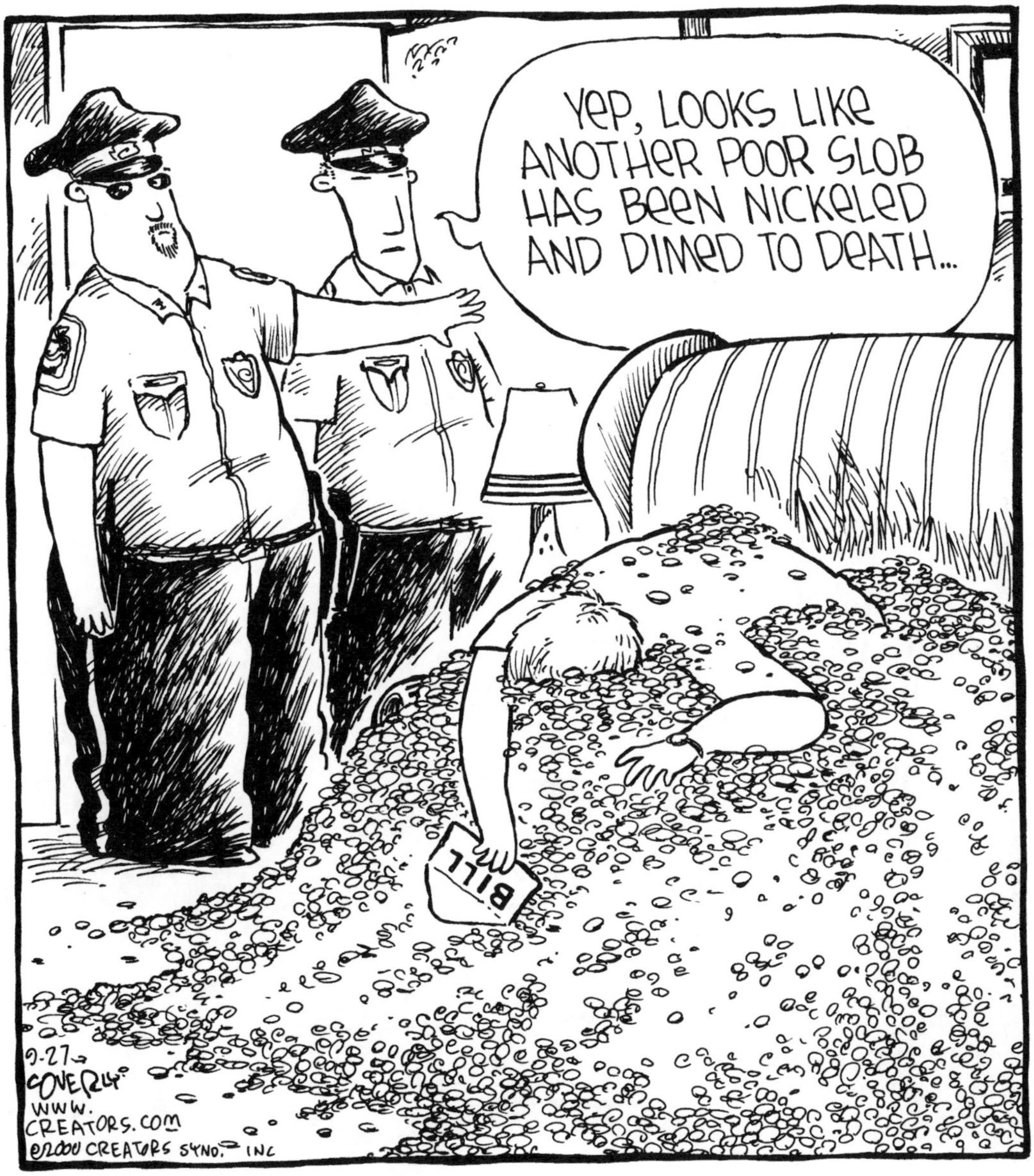
YEP, LOOKS LIKE ANOTHER POOR SLOB HAS BEEN NICKELED AND DIMED TO DEATH...
BILL
9-27
COVERLY
WWW.
CREATORS.COM
©2000 CREATORS SYND. INC

Animals

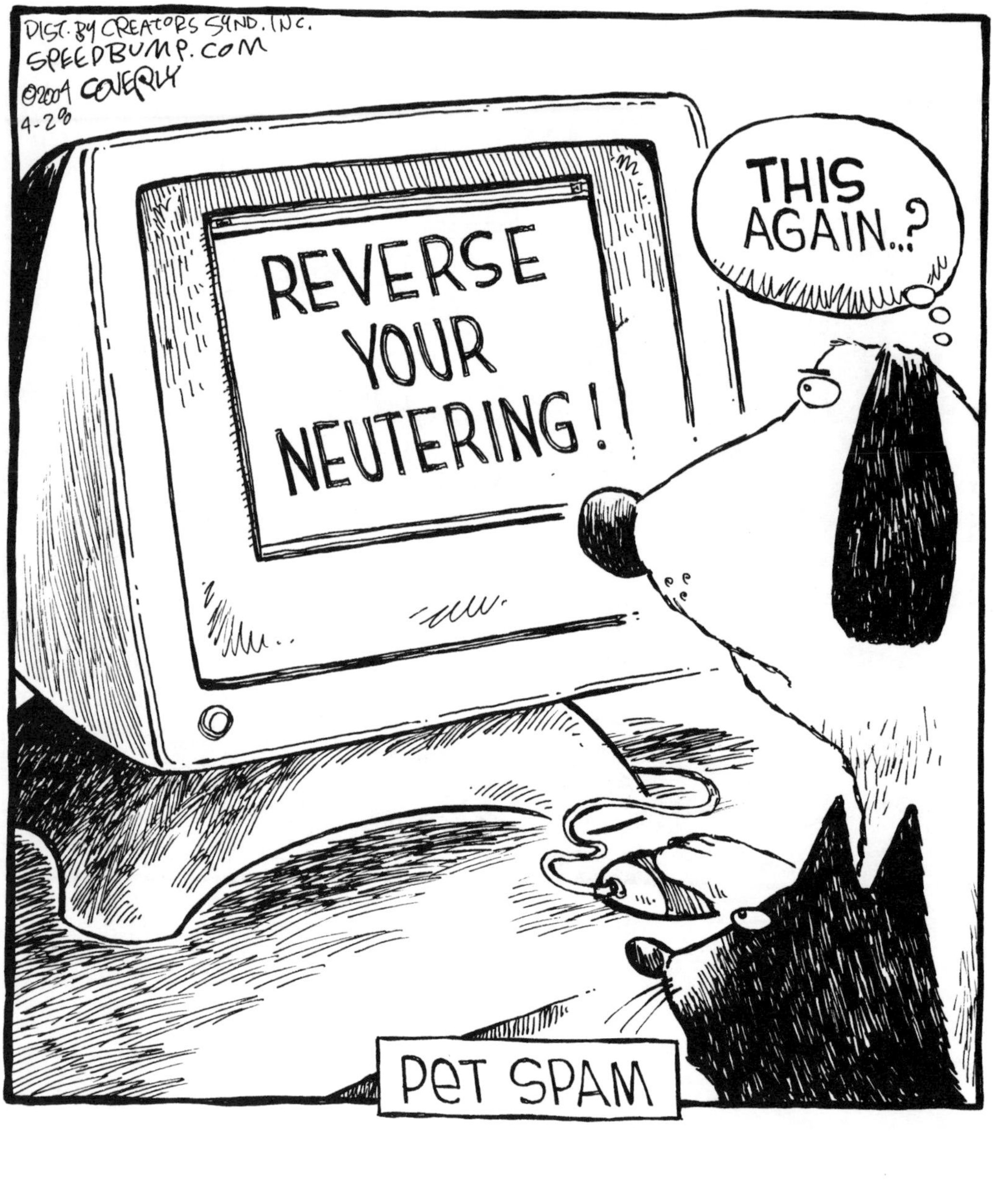
DIST. BY CREATORS SYND. INC.
SPEEDBUMP.COM
©2004 COVERLY
4-28
REVERSE YOUR NEUTERING!
THIS AGAIN..?
PET SPAM

Dave says that cartoonists are like bird watchers. The truth is that cartoonists are like birds. Birds sense things in ways humans only dream of. They certainly see better than bird watchers. And they're more amusing.

A sparrow, for instance, is a little person with a very different sense of time. She sees a crumb fall off the table as if in slow motion, and flits down and plucks it out of the air before it touches the floor, sometimes managing to work in a somersault on her way out.

Birds have a great sense of humor. Crows in St. Petersburg have been sliding down the stained glass windows of St. Petersburg cathedral on their rumps, just for fun, for so long that they've worn away the paint on the panes.

I knew a parrot named L'Oro who taught herself to imitate the sound of the front door bell, the back door buzzer, the telephone, and the wife's "Honey, can you get that?" Sometimes, when L'Oro saw the "lady of the house" was safely out of earshot in the garden, she'd "do" the door bell, the phone, the buzzer, and the "Honey . . ." in rapid succession just to get that man off the couch. She would sit ever so innocently, bottling up her feelings, until he'd fallen for the lot. Then, she'd cackle!

Or take Pearly Girl, a male vulture (it's hard to tell with birds and it's not polite to get that personal anyway) with a wingspan of over six feet. Pearly Girl loved to play "peek-a-boo," laughing every time his loved one's fingers revealed a face; and when he heard music, he would jump down onto the floor and do the Twist. Visitors were shocked to see him ever so delicately combing his guardian's eyelashes with his giant beak.

Pearly Girl made people smile and feel good, and conveyed the important message that all animals have feelings and interests in life too, just as we do, if we'd just pay attention to them.

Dave obviously has a bird in his family tree. You can tell because his senses are so keen, his humor so fresh, and his smile so fresh as we absorb the message.

— Ingrid E. Newkirk, President, People for the Ethical Treatment of Animals

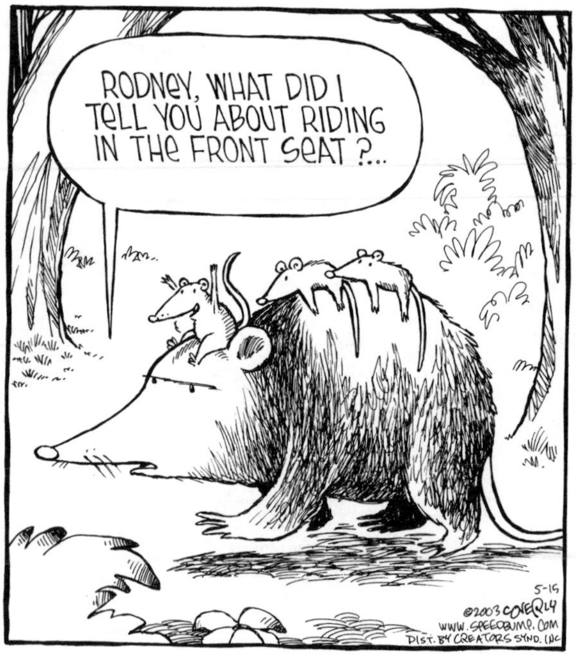
RODNEY, WHAT DID I TELL YOU ABOUT RIDING IN THE FRONT SEAT ?...
5-15
©2003 COVERLY
WWW.SPEEDBUMP.COM
DIST. BY CREATORS SYND. INC

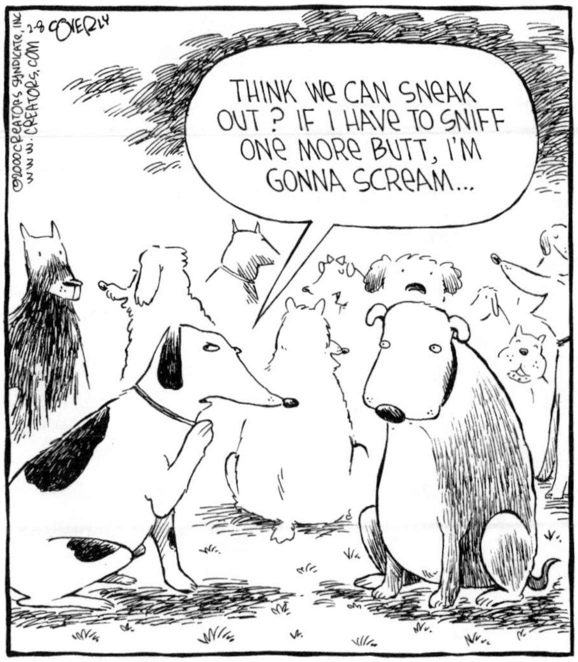
©2000 CREATORS SYNDICATE, INC
WWW.CREATORS.COM
2-8 COVERLY
THINK WE CAN SNEAK OUT ? IF I HAVE TO SNIFF ONE MORE BUTT, I'M GONNA SCREAM...

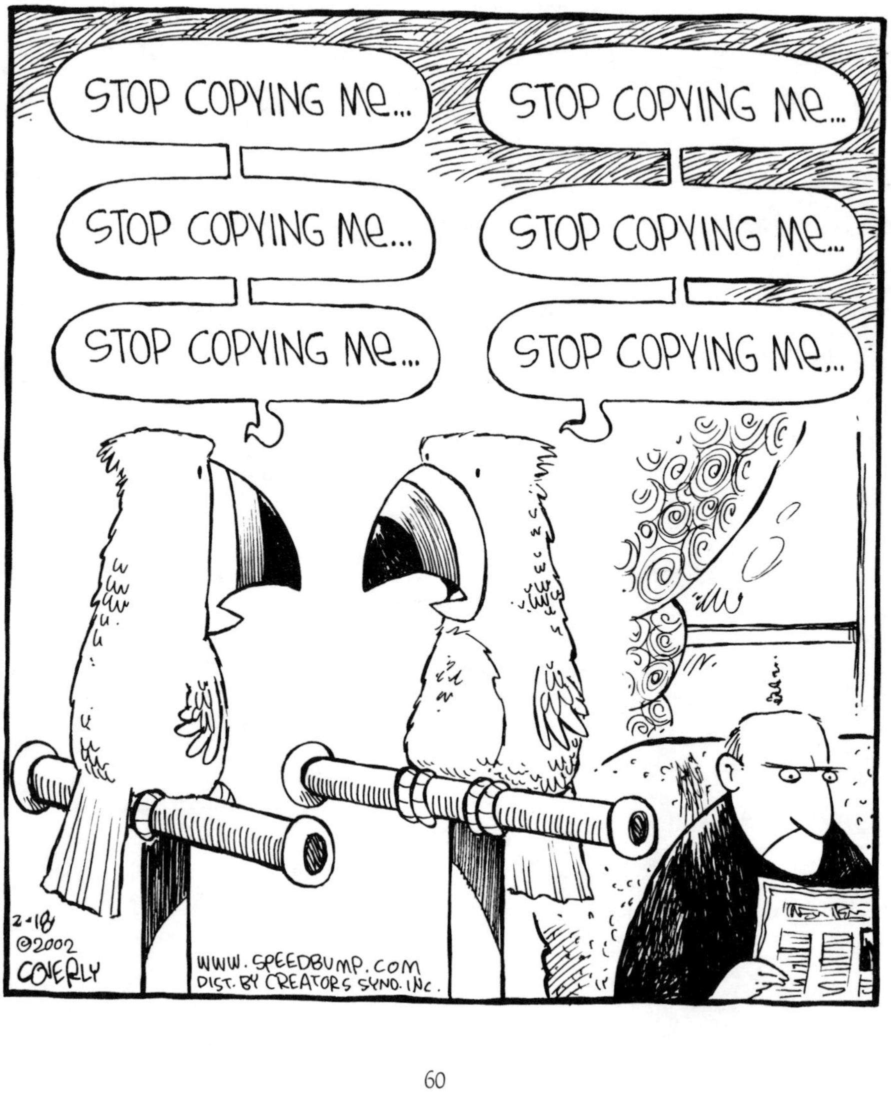
STOP COPYING ME...
STOP COPYING ME...
STOP COPYING ME...
STOP COPYING ME...
STOP COPYING ME...
STOP COPYING ME...
2-18
©2002
COVERLY
WWW.SPEEDBUMP.COM
DIST. BY CREATORS SYND. INC.

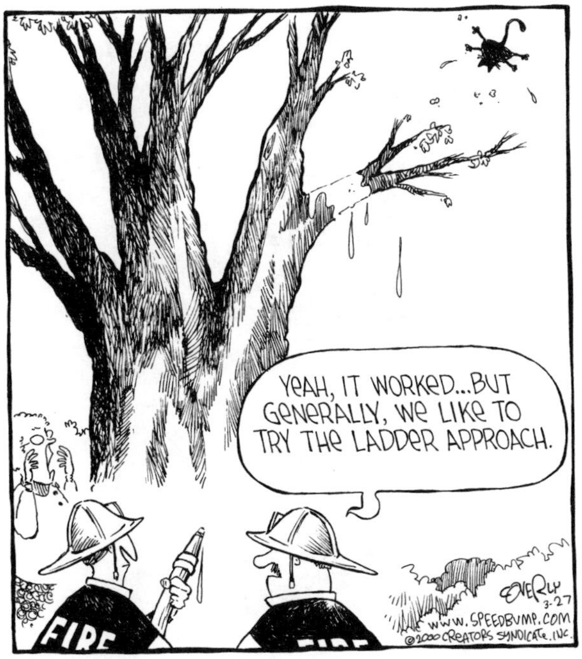
YEAH, IT WORKED...BUT GENERALLY, WE LIKE TO TRY THE LADDER APPROACH.
FIRE
3-27
WWW.SPEEDBUMP.COM
©2000 CREATORS SYNDICATE, INC.

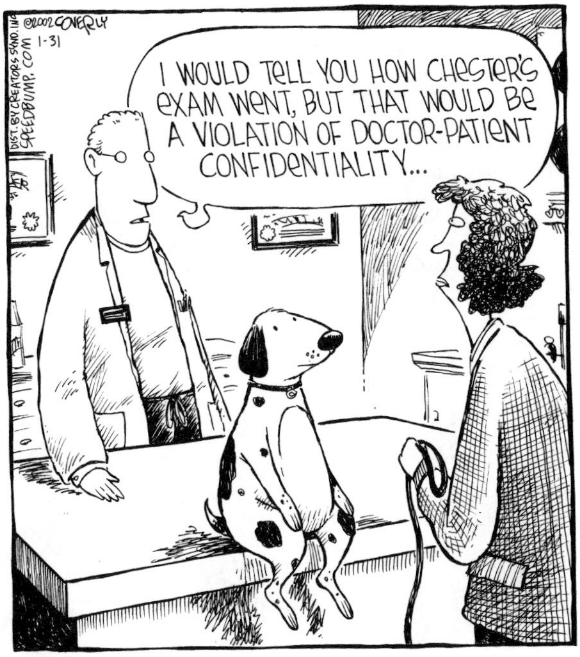
I WOULD TELL YOU HOW CHESTER'S EXAM WENT, BUT THAT WOULD BE A VIOLATION OF DOCTOR-PATIENT CONFIDENTIALITY...
©2002 COVERLY 1-31
DIST. BY CREATORS SYND. INC. SPEEDBUMP.COM

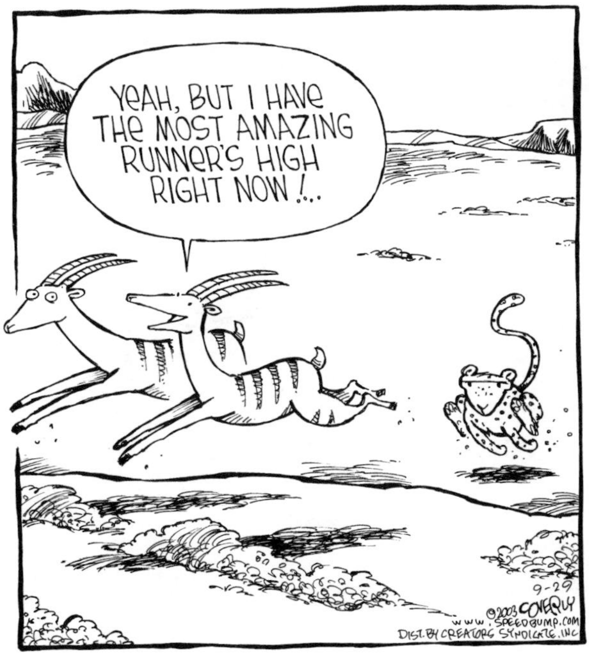
YEAH, BUT I HAVE THE MOST AMAZING RUNNER'S HIGH RIGHT NOW!...
9-29
©2003 COVERLY
WWW.SPEEDBUMP.COM
DIST. BY CREATORS SYNDICATE, INC.

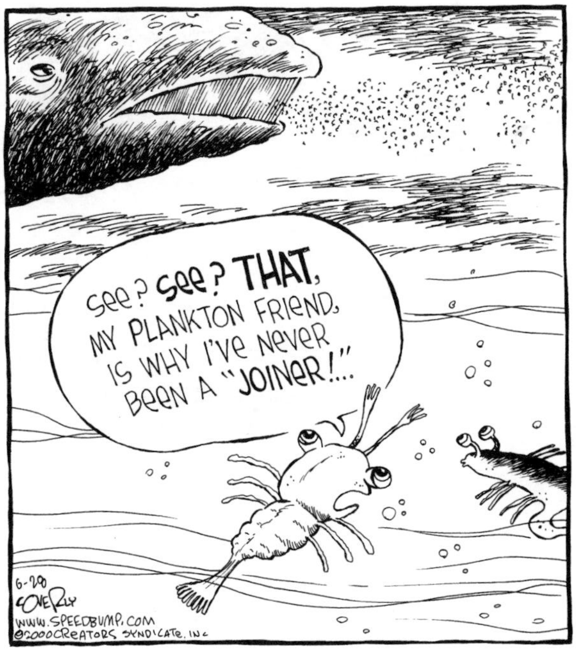
SEE? SEE? THAT, MY PLANKTON FRIEND, IS WHY I'VE NEVER BEEN A "JOINER!"...
6-20
COVERLY
WWW.SPEEDBUMP.COM
©2000 CREATORS SYNDICATE, INC.

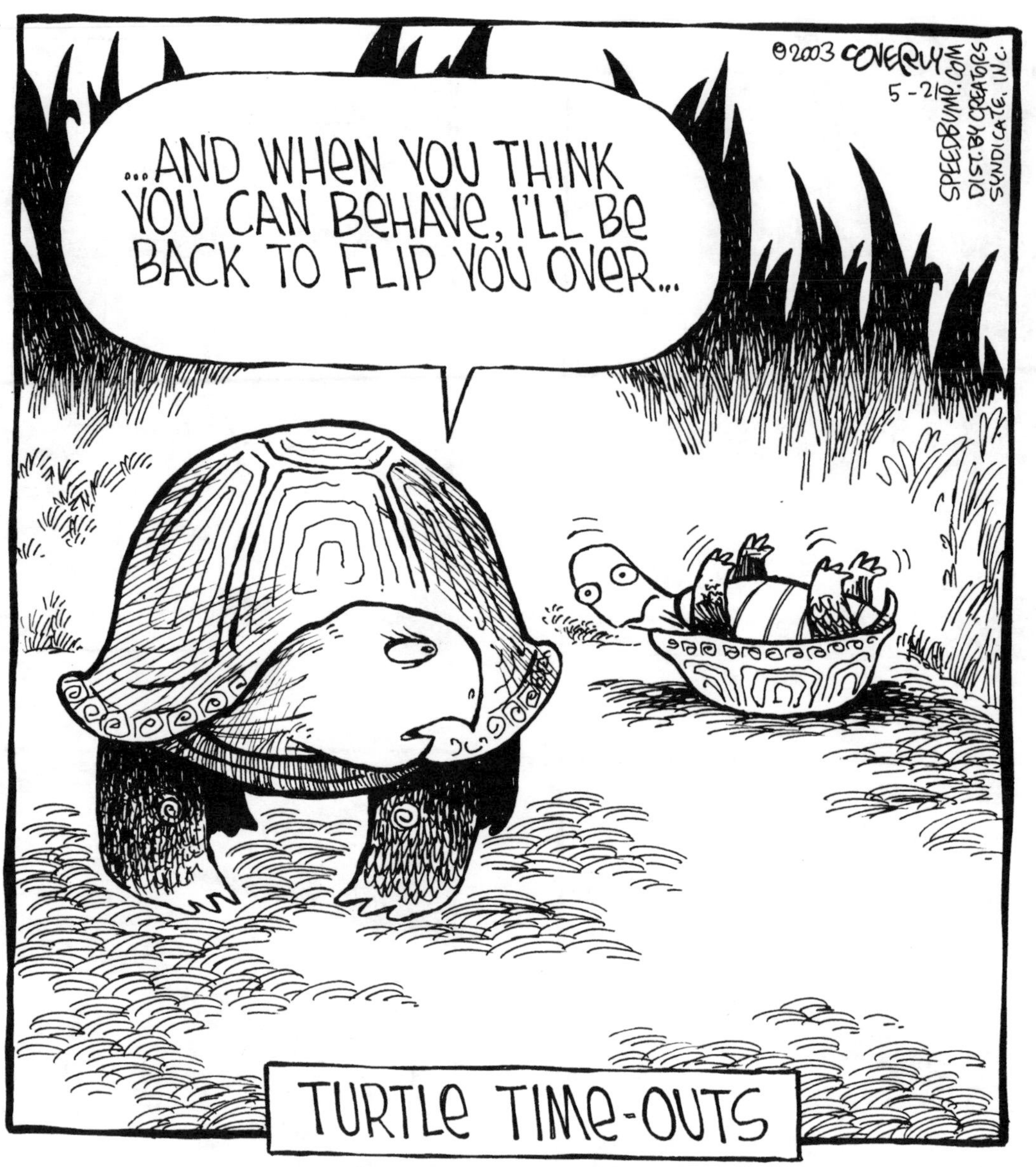
...AND WHEN YOU THINK YOU CAN BEHAVE, I'LL BE BACK TO FLIP YOU OVER...
TURTLE TIME-OUTS
©2003 COVERLY 5-21
SPEEDBUMP.COM
DIST. BY CREATORS SYNDICATE, INC.

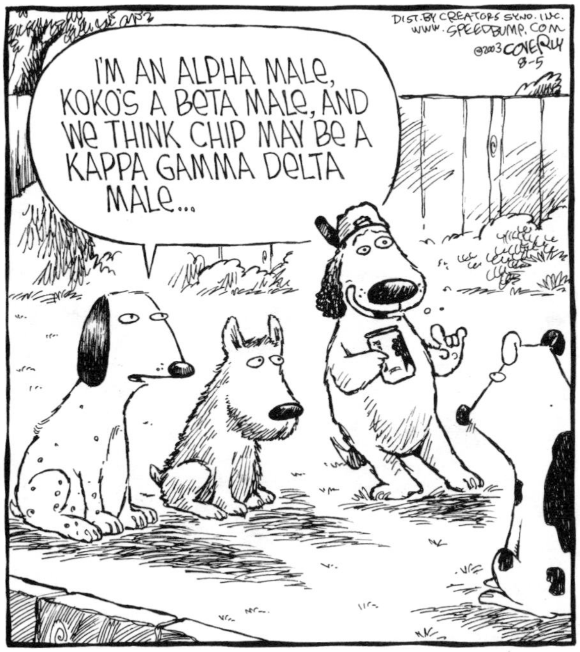
DIST. BY CREATORS SYND. INC.
WWW.SPEEDBUMP.COM
©2003 COVERLY 8-5
I'M AN ALPHA MALE, KOKO'S A BETA MALE, AND WE THINK CHIP MAY BE A KAPPA GAMMA DELTA MALE...

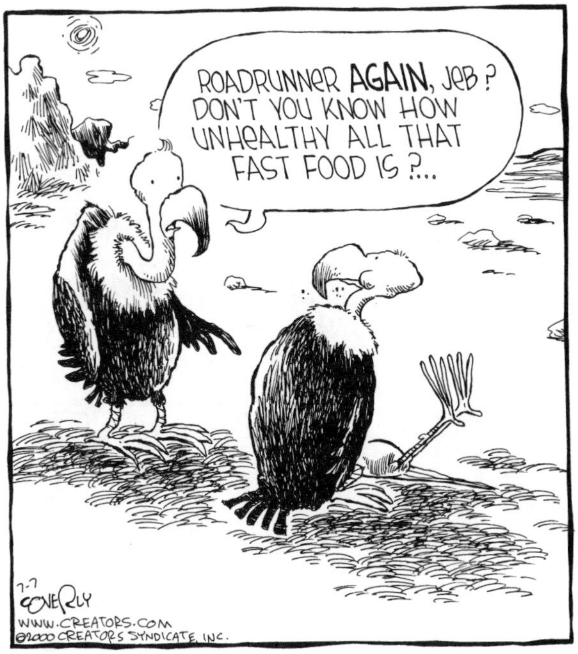
ROADRUNNER **AGAIN**, JEB? DON'T YOU KNOW HOW UNHEALTHY ALL THAT FAST FOOD IS?...
7-7
COVERLY
WWW.CREATORS.COM
©2000 CREATORS SYNDICATE, INC.

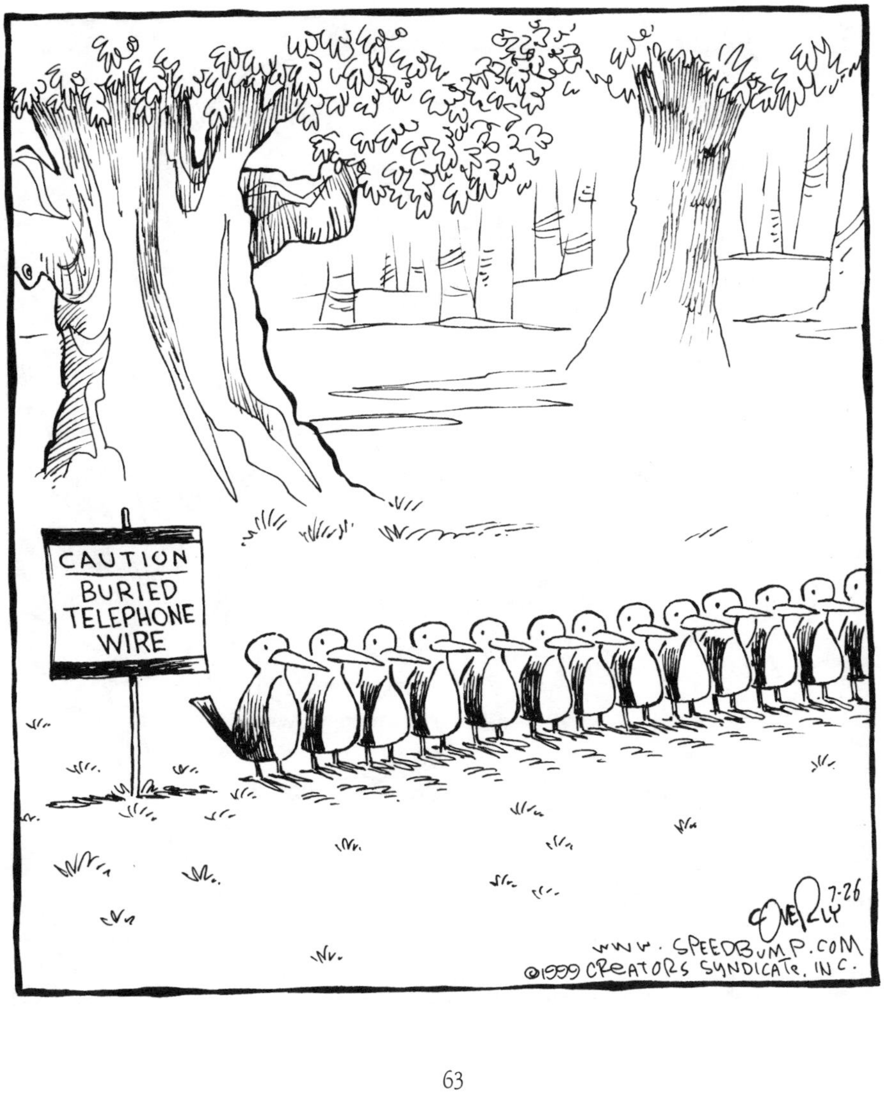
CAUTION
BURIED TELEPHONE WIRE
COVERLY 7-26
WWW.SPEEDBUMP.COM
©1999 CREATORS SYNDICATE, INC.

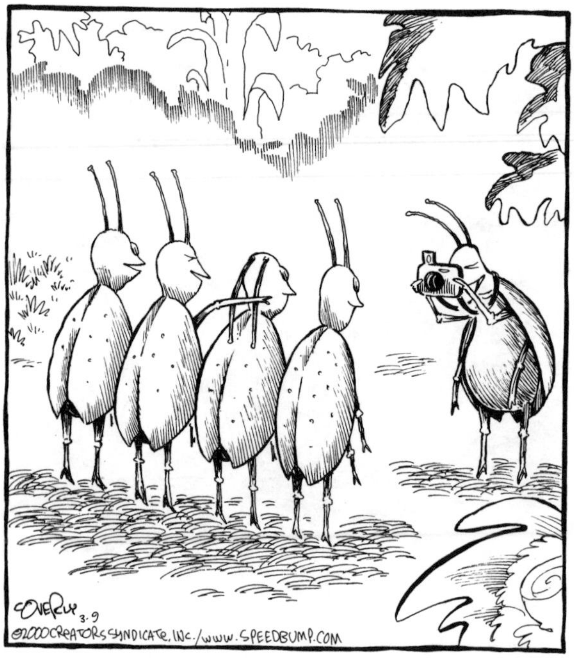
OVERLY 3-9
©2000 CREATORS SYNDICATE, INC./www.SPEEDBUMP.COM

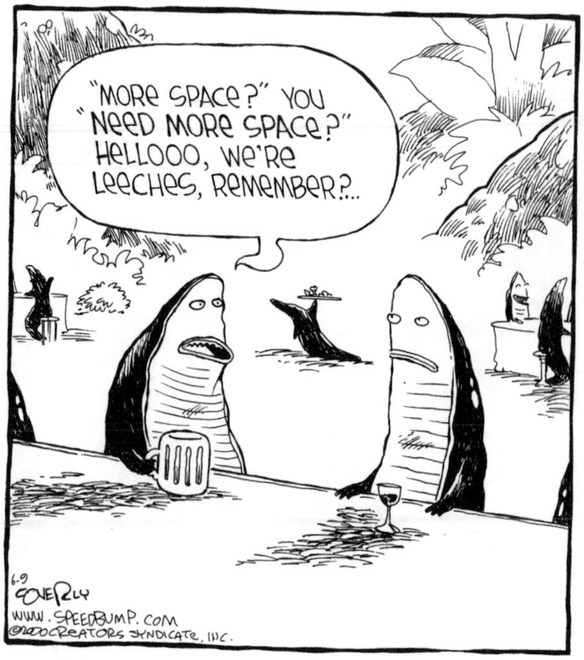
"MORE SPACE?" YOU "NEED MORE SPACE?" HELLOOO, WE'RE LEECHES, REMEMBER?...
6-9 OVERLY
www.SPEEDBUMP.COM
©2000 CREATORS SYNDICATE, INC.

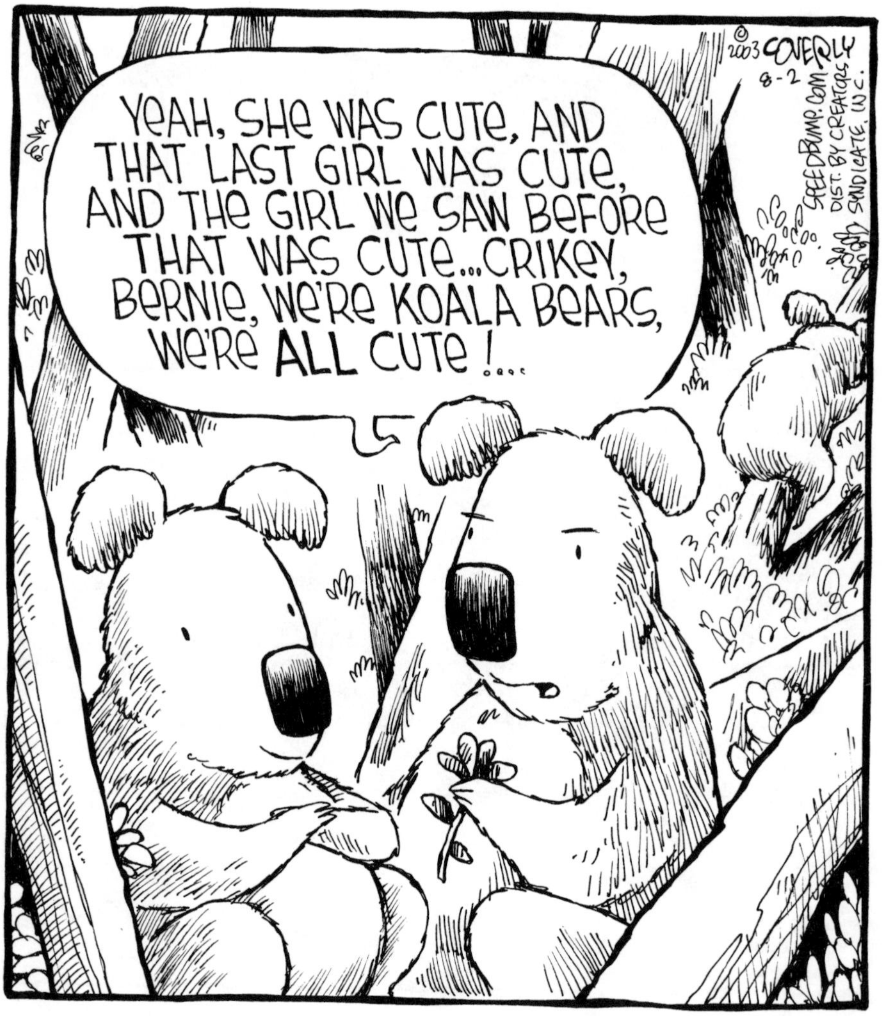
© 2003 OVERLY 8-2
SPEEDBUMP.COM
DIST. BY CREATORS SYNDICATE, INC.
YEAH, SHE WAS CUTE, AND THAT LAST GIRL WAS CUTE, AND THE GIRL WE SAW BEFORE THAT WAS CUTE...CRIKEY, BERNIE, WE'RE KOALA BEARS, WE'RE **ALL** CUTE!...

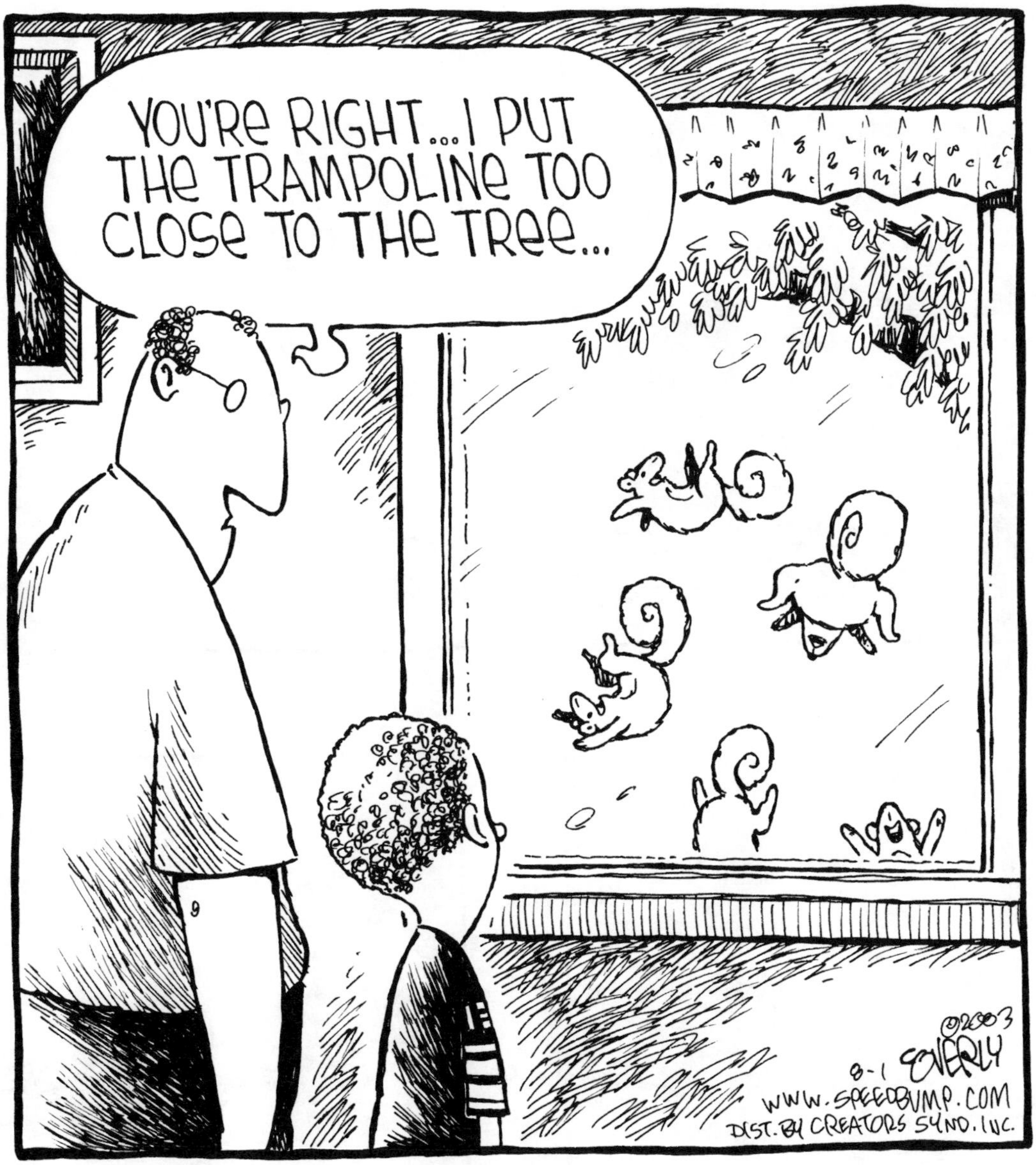
YOU'RE RIGHT...I PUT THE TRAMPOLINE TOO CLOSE TO THE TREE...
©2003
8-1 COVERLY
WWW.SPEEDBUMP.COM
DIST. BY CREATORS SYND. INC.

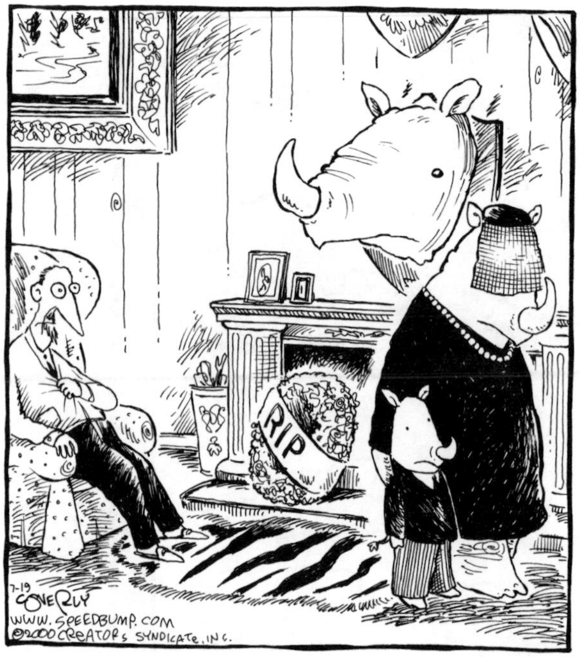
RIP
7-19
COVERLY
WWW.SPEEDBUMP.COM
©2000 CREATORS SYNDICATE, INC.

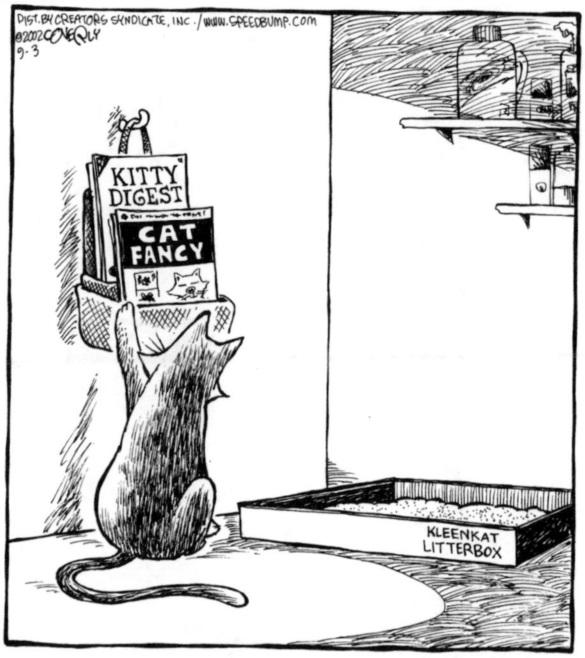
DIST. BY CREATORS SYNDICATE, INC. / WWW.SPEEDBUMP.COM
©2002 COVERLY
9-3
KITTY DIGEST
CAT FANCY
KLEENKAT LITTERBOX

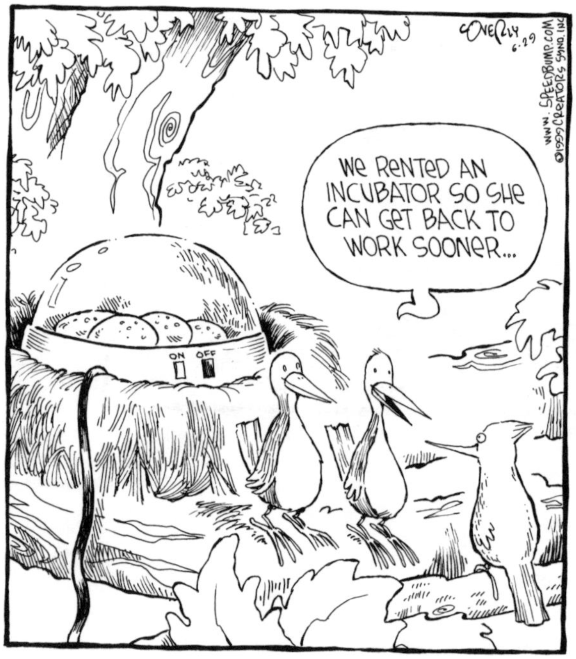
COVERLY 6-29
WWW.SPEEDBUMP.COM ©1999 CREATORS SYND. INC
WE RENTED AN INCUBATOR SO SHE CAN GET BACK TO WORK SOONER...
ON OFF

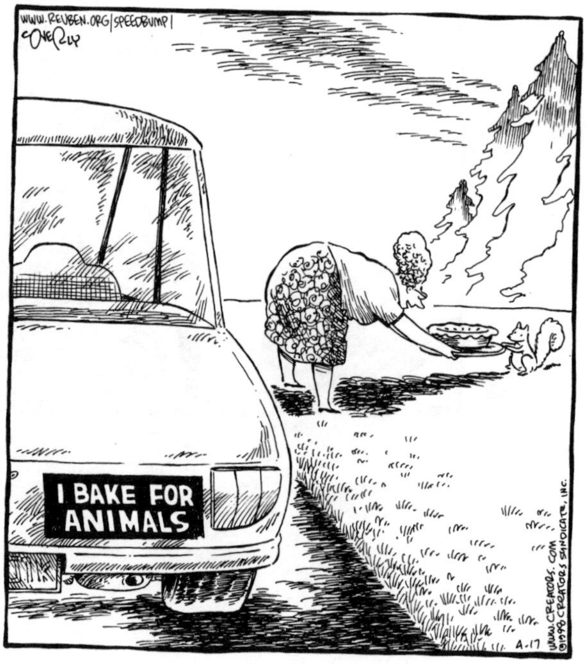
WWW.REUBEN.ORG/SPEEDBUMP/
COVERLY
I BAKE FOR ANIMALS
WWW.CREATORS.COM ©1998 CREATORS SYNDICATE, INC.
4-17

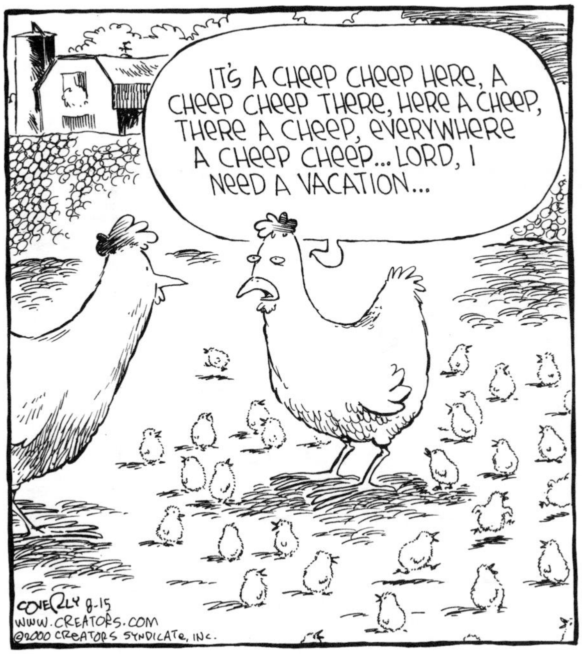
IT'S A CHEEP CHEEP HERE, A CHEEP CHEEP THERE, HERE A CHEEP, THERE A CHEEP, EVERYWHERE A CHEEP CHEEP... LORD, I NEED A VACATION...
COVERLY 8-15
WWW.CREATORS.COM
©2000 CREATORS SYNDICATE, INC.

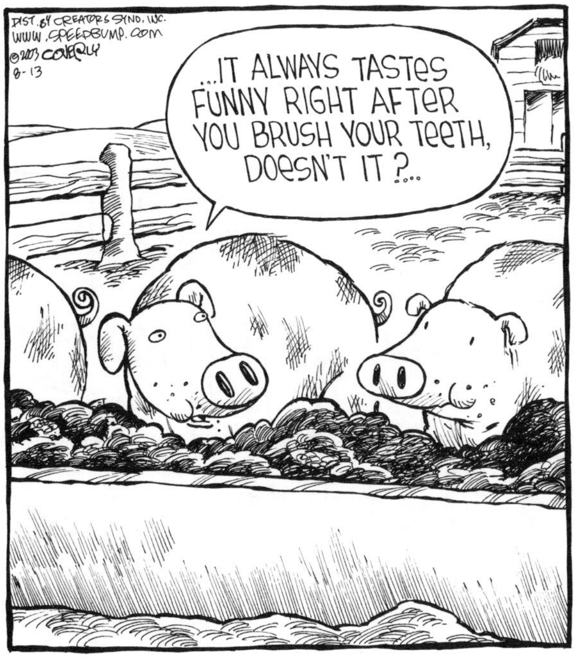
DIST. BY CREATORS SYND. INC.
WWW.SPEEDBUMP.COM
©2003 COVERLY
8-13
...IT ALWAYS TASTES FUNNY RIGHT AFTER YOU BRUSH YOUR TEETH, DOESN'T IT ?...

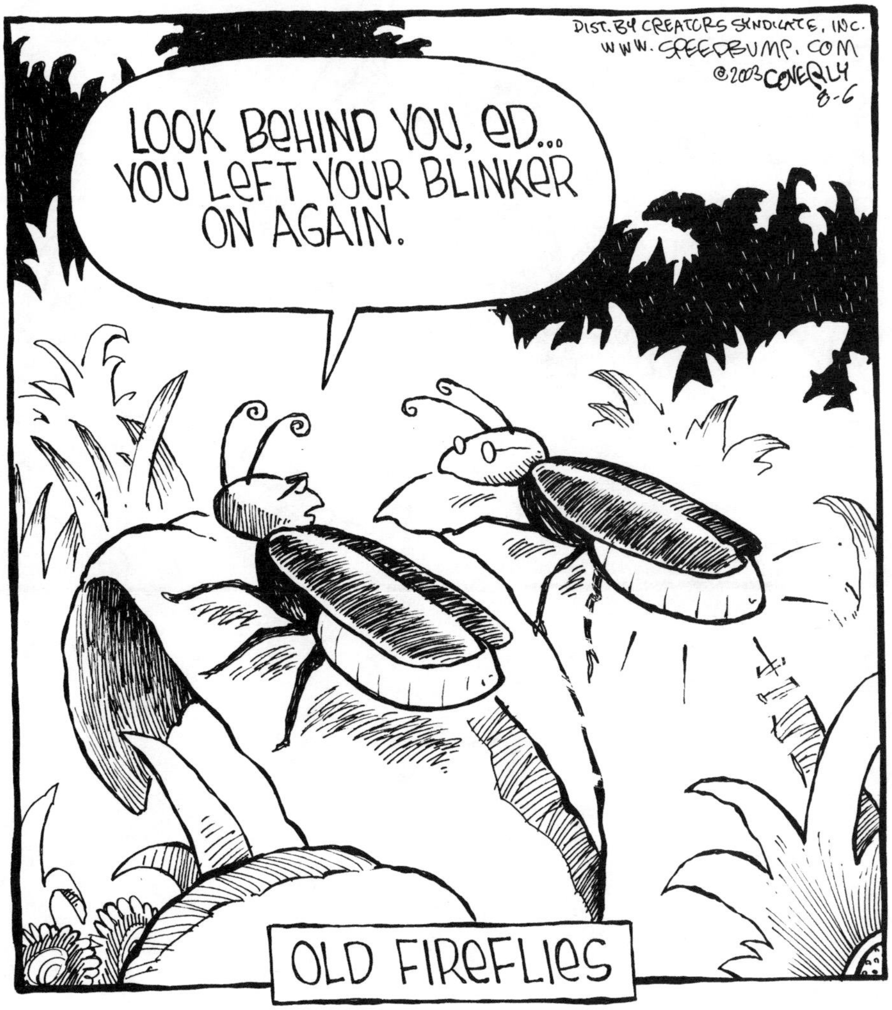
DIST. BY CREATORS SYNDICATE, INC.
WWW.SPEEDBUMP.COM
©2003 COVERLY 8-6
LOOK BEHIND YOU, ED... YOU LEFT YOUR BLINKER ON AGAIN.
OLD FIREFLIES

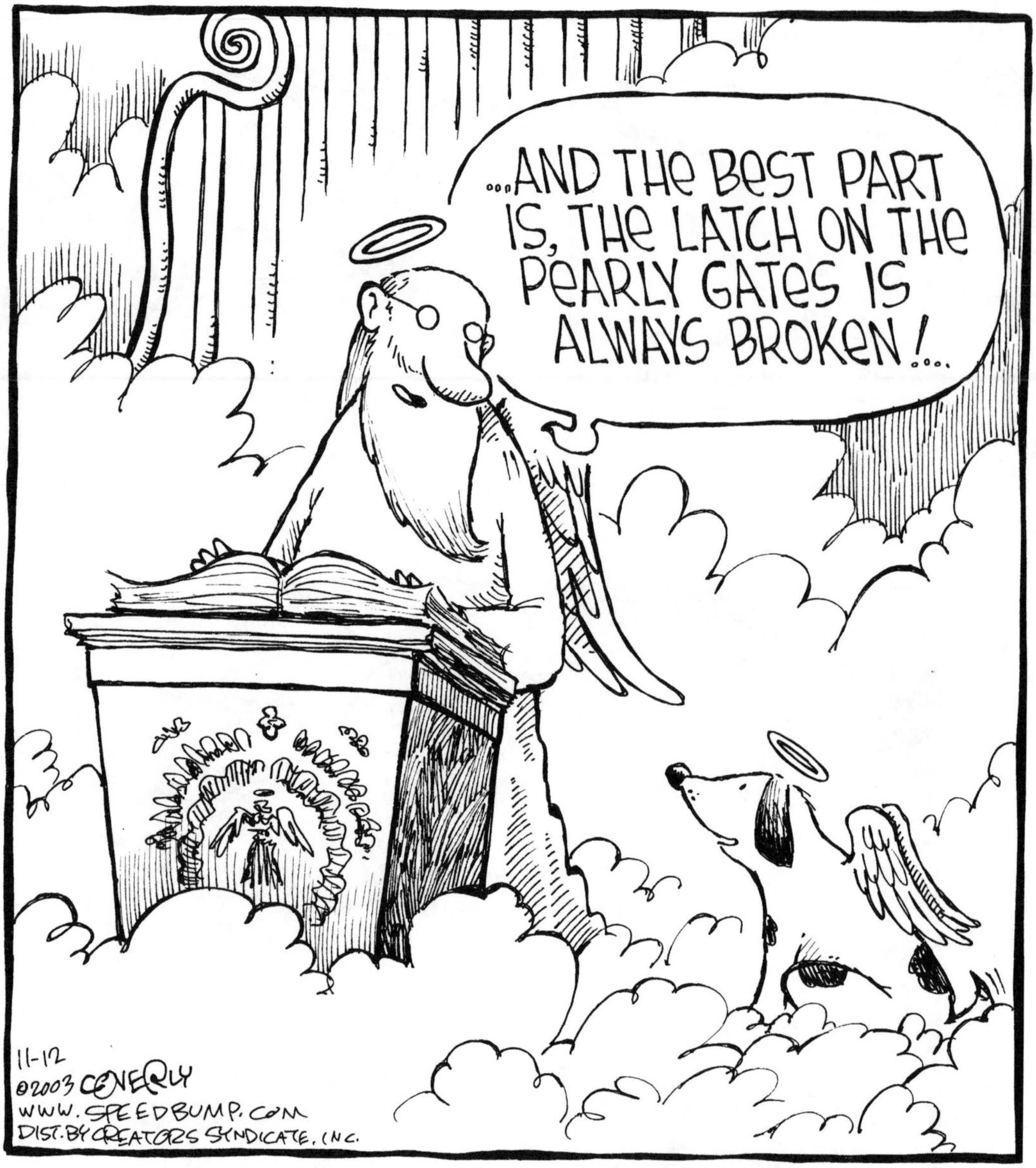
...AND THE BEST PART IS, THE LATCH ON THE PEARLY GATES IS ALWAYS BROKEN!...
11-12
©2003 COVERLY
WWW.SPEEDBUMP.COM
DIST. BY CREATORS SYNDICATE, INC.

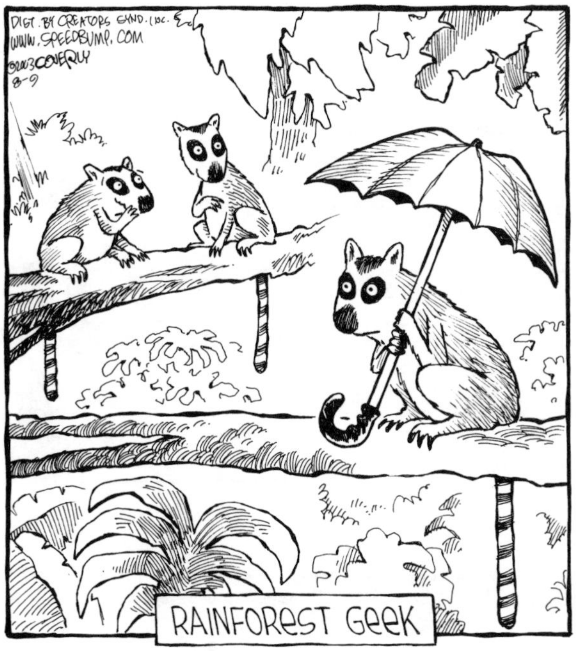
DIST. BY CREATORS SYND. INC.
WWW.SPEEDBUMP.COM
©2003 COVERLY
8-9
RAINFOREST GEEK

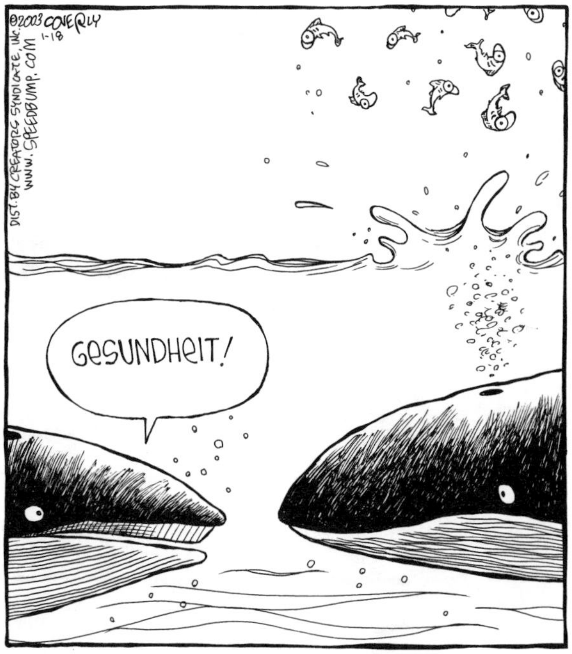
©2003 COVERLY
1-18
DIST. BY CREATORS SYNDICATE, INC.
WWW.SPEEDBUMP.COM
GESUNDHEIT!

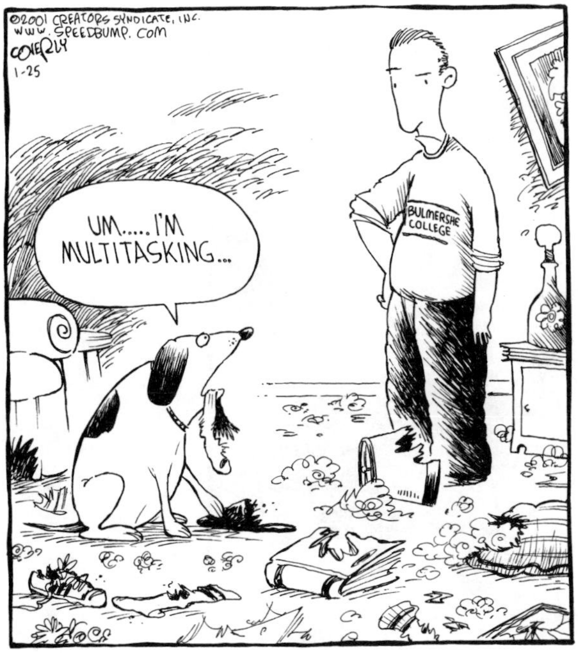
©2001 CREATORS SYNDICATE, INC.
WWW.SPEEDBUMP.COM
COVERLY
1-25
UM..... I'M MULTITASKING...
BULMERSHE COLLEGE

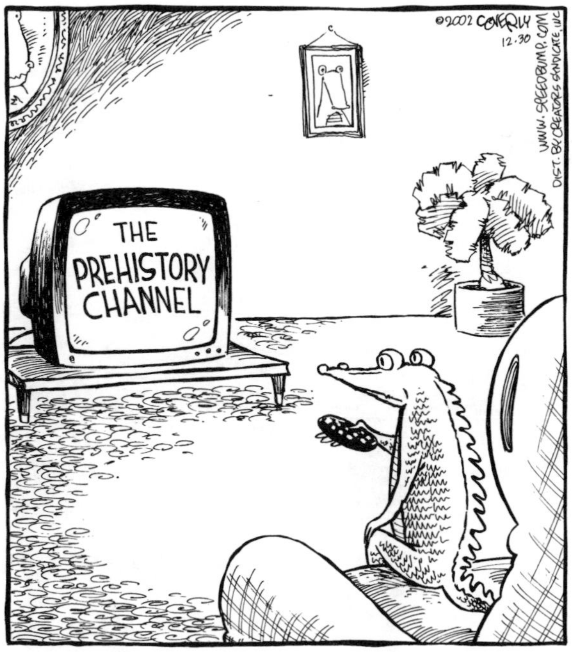
©2002 COVERLY
12-30
WWW.SPEEDBUMP.COM
DIST. BY CREATORS SYNDICATE INC.
THE PREHISTORY CHANNEL

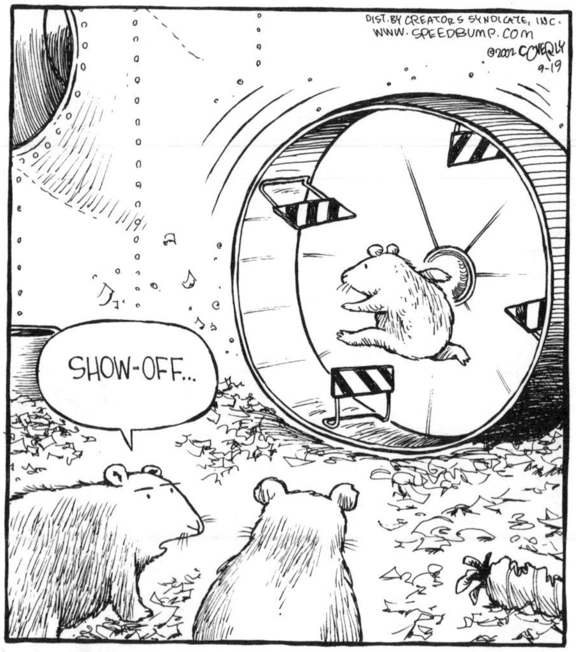
DIST. BY CREATORS SYNDICATE, INC.
WWW.SPEEDBUMP.COM
©2002 COVERLY
9-19
SHOW-OFF...

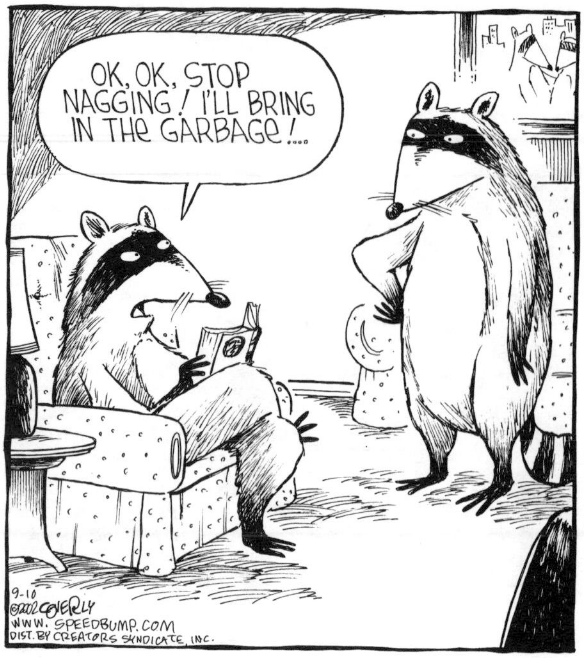
OK, OK, STOP NAGGING! I'LL BRING IN THE GARBAGE!...
9-10
©2002 COVERLY
WWW.SPEEDBUMP.COM
DIST. BY CREATORS SYNDICATE, INC.

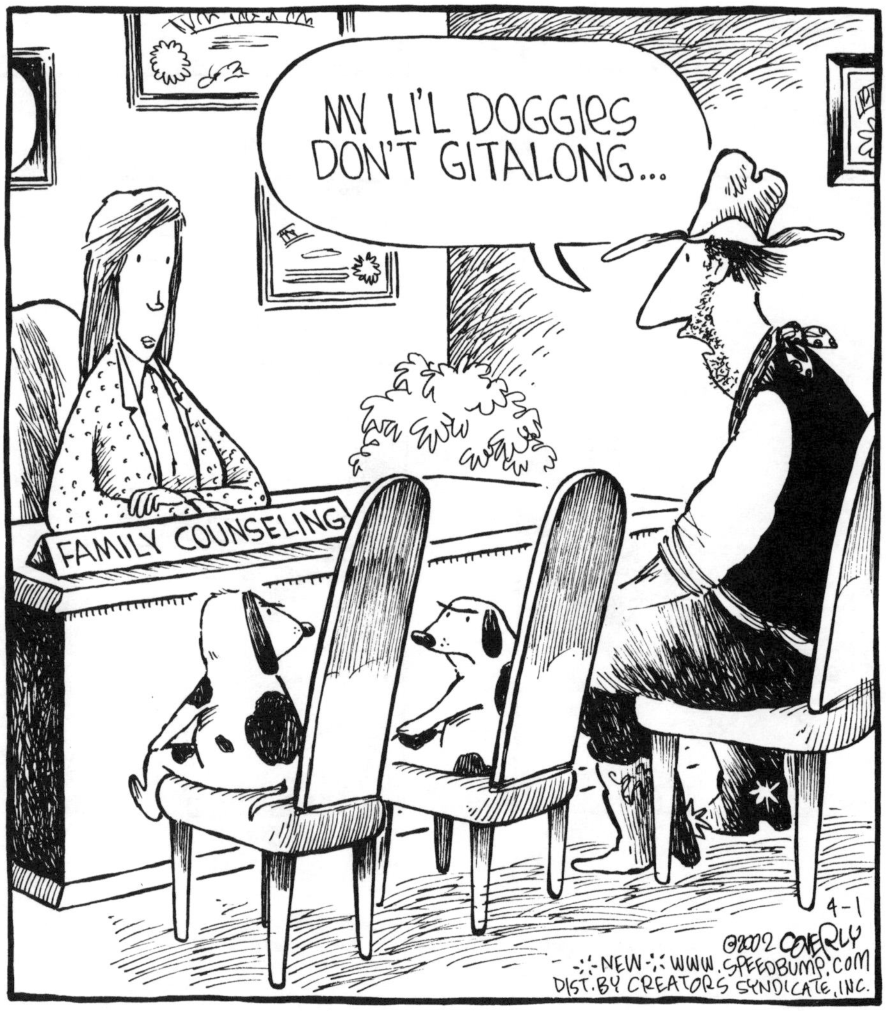
MY LI'L DOGGIES DON'T GITALONG...
FAMILY COUNSELING
4-1
©2002 COVERLY
NEW WWW.SPEEDBUMP.COM
DIST. BY CREATORS SYNDICATE, INC.

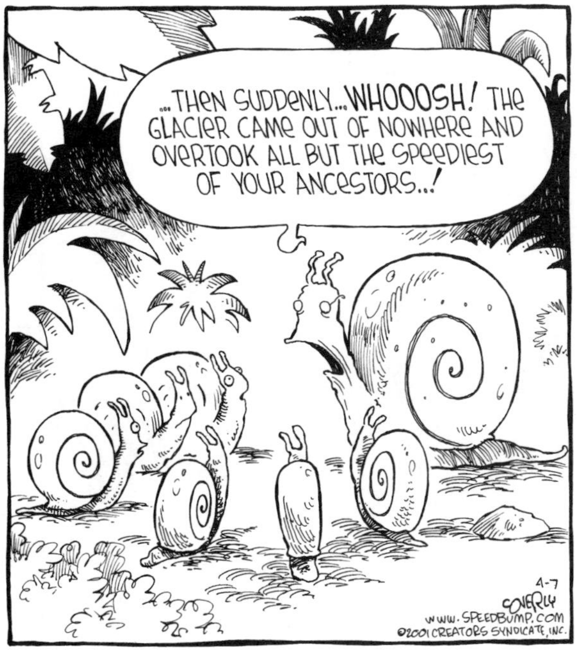
...THEN SUDDENLY...WHOOOSH! THE GLACIER CAME OUT OF NOWHERE AND OVERTOOK ALL BUT THE SPEEDIEST OF YOUR ANCESTORS...!
4-7
COVERLY
WWW.SPEEDBUMP.COM
©2001 CREATORS SYNDICATE, INC.

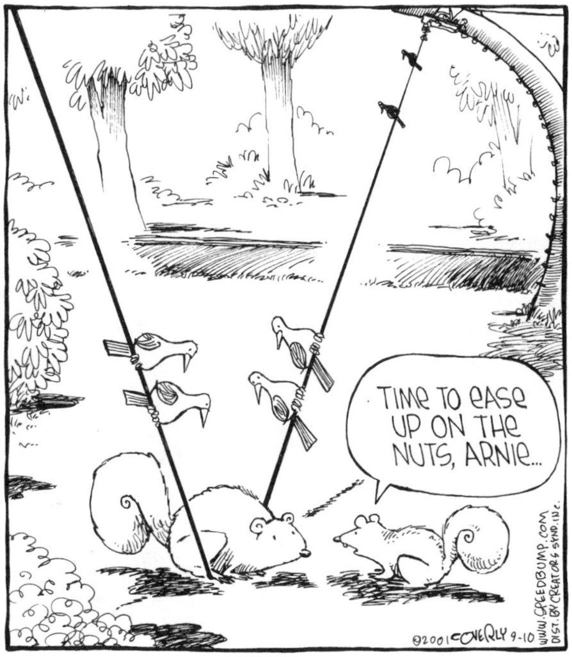
TIME TO EASE UP ON THE NUTS, ARNIE...
©2001 COVERLY 9-10
WWW.SPEEDBUMP.COM
DIST. BY CREATORS SYND. INC.

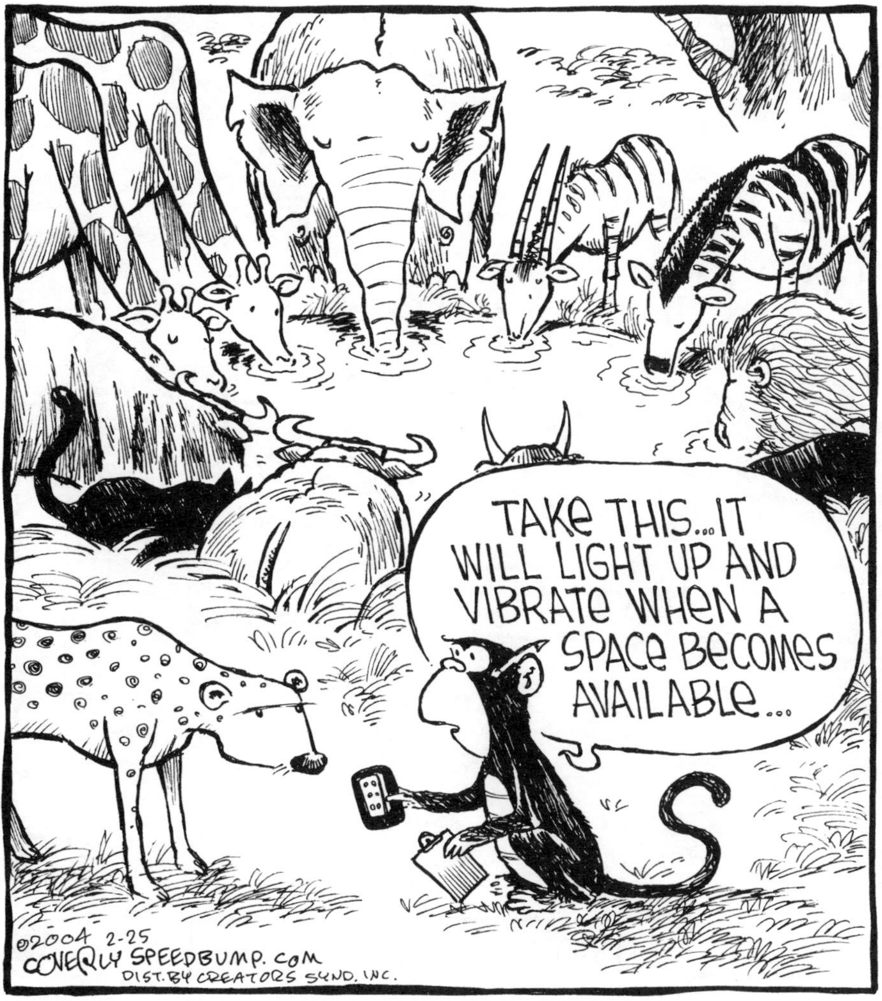
TAKE THIS... IT WILL LIGHT UP AND VIBRATE WHEN A SPACE BECOMES AVAILABLE...
©2004 2-25
COVERLY SPEEDBUMP.COM
DIST. BY CREATORS SYND. INC.

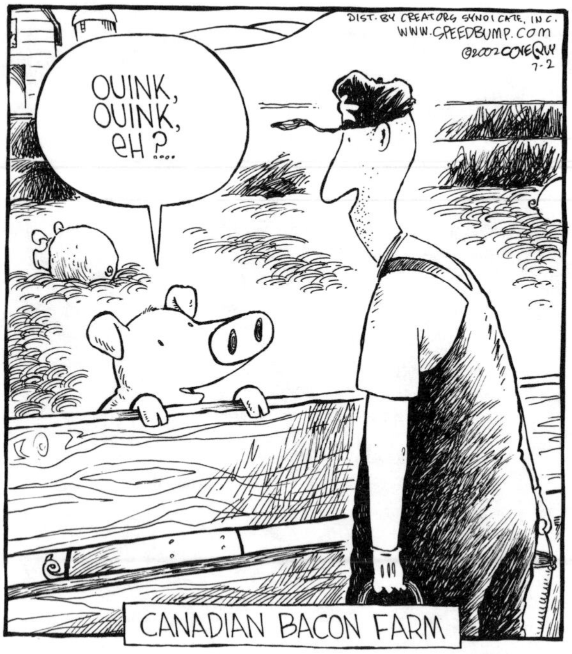
DIST. BY CREATORS SYNDICATE, INC.
WWW.SPEEDBUMP.COM
©2002 COVERLY
7-2
OUINK, OUINK, EH?...
CANADIAN BACON FARM

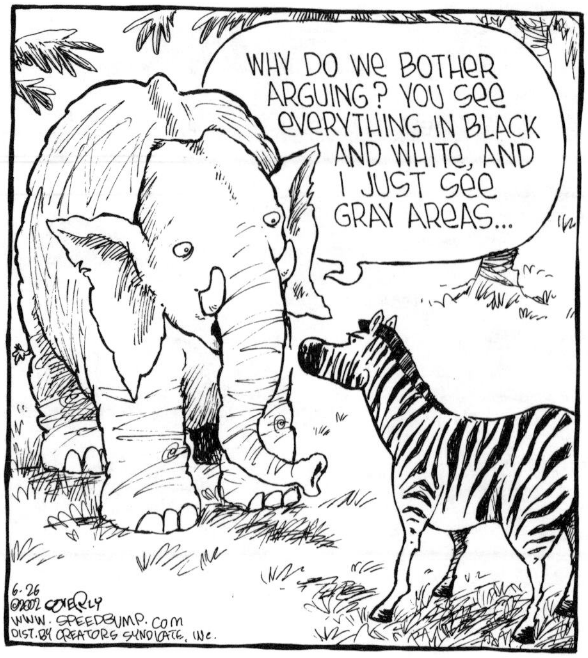
WHY DO WE BOTHER ARGUING? YOU SEE EVERYTHING IN BLACK AND WHITE, AND I JUST SEE GRAY AREAS...
6-26
©2002 COVERLY
WWW.SPEEDBUMP.COM
DIST. BY CREATORS SYNDICATE, INC.

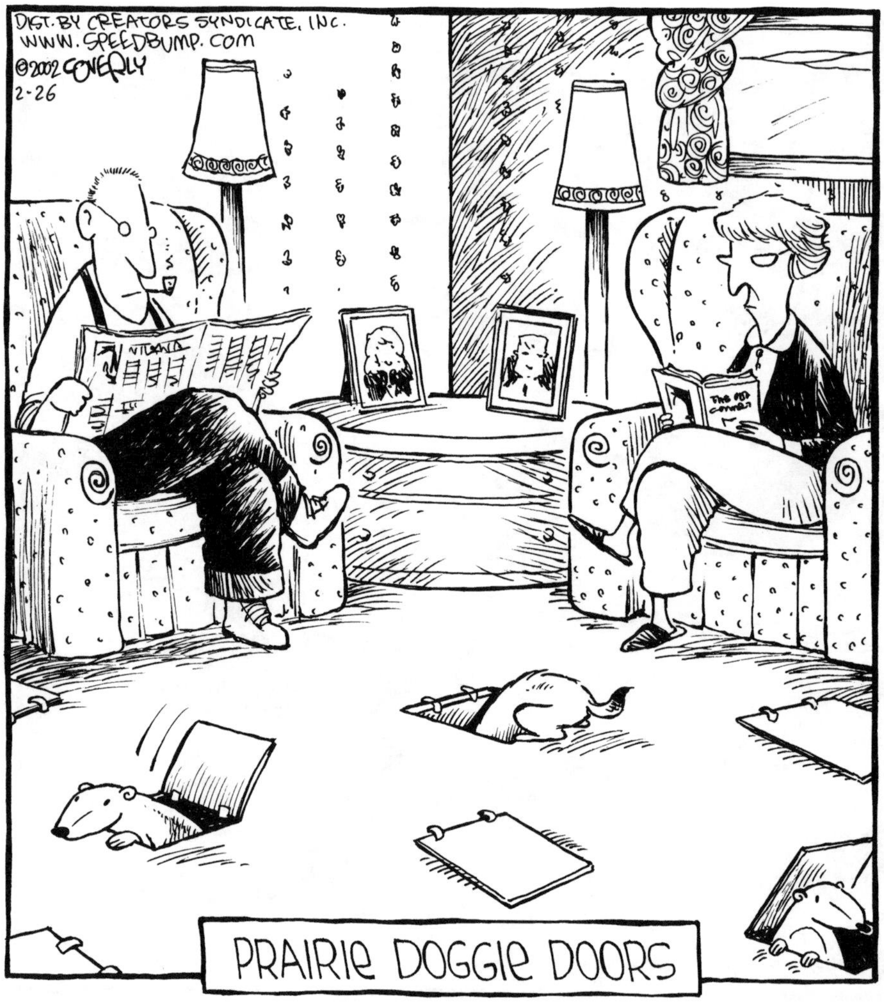
DIST. BY CREATORS SYNDICATE, INC.
WWW.SPEEDBUMP.COM
©2002 COVERLY
2-26
PRAIRIE DOGGIE DOORS

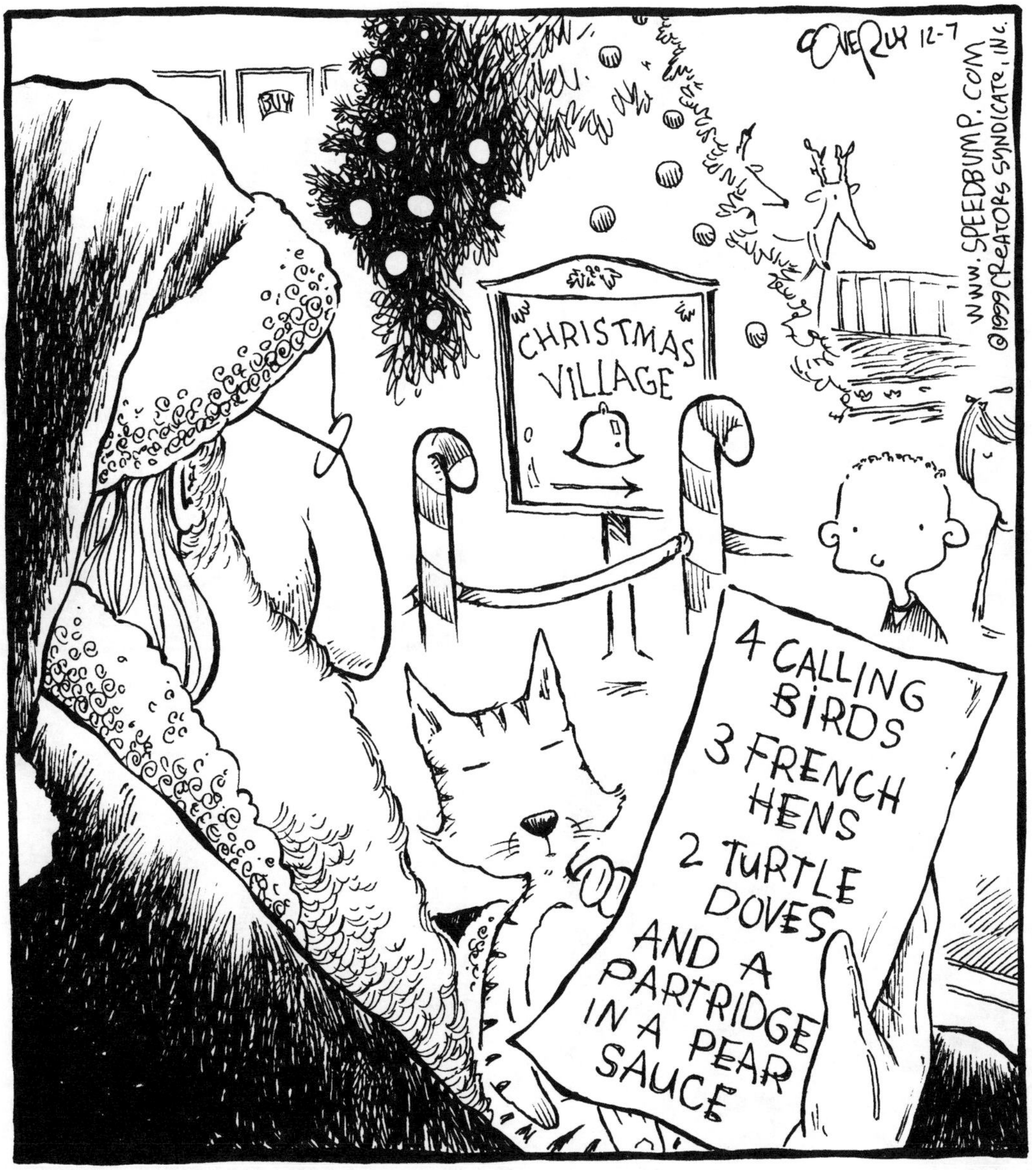

CHRISTMAS VILLAGE
4 CALLING BIRDS
3 FRENCH HENS
2 TURTLE DOVES
AND A PARTRIDGE IN A PEAR SAUCE
12-7
WWW.SPEEDBUMP.COM
©1999 CREATORS SYNDICATE, INC.

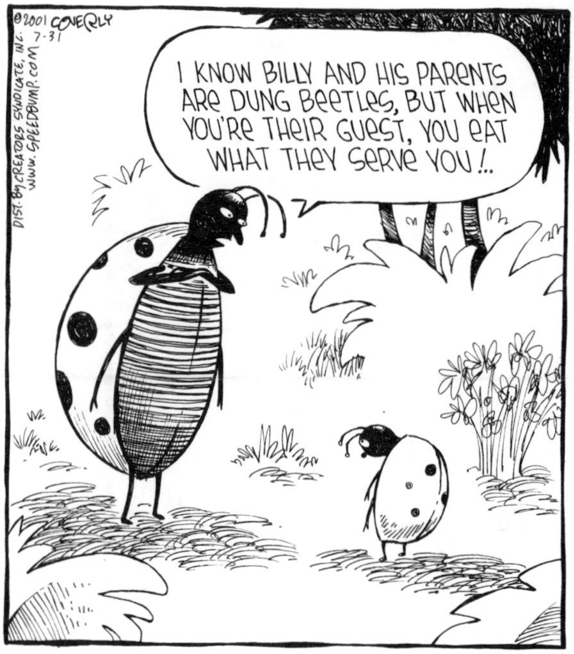
©2001 COVERLY 7-31
DIST. BY CREATORS SYNDICATE, INC. WWW.SPEEDBUMP.COM
I KNOW BILLY AND HIS PARENTS ARE DUNG BEETLES, BUT WHEN YOU'RE THEIR GUEST, YOU EAT WHAT THEY SERVE YOU!..

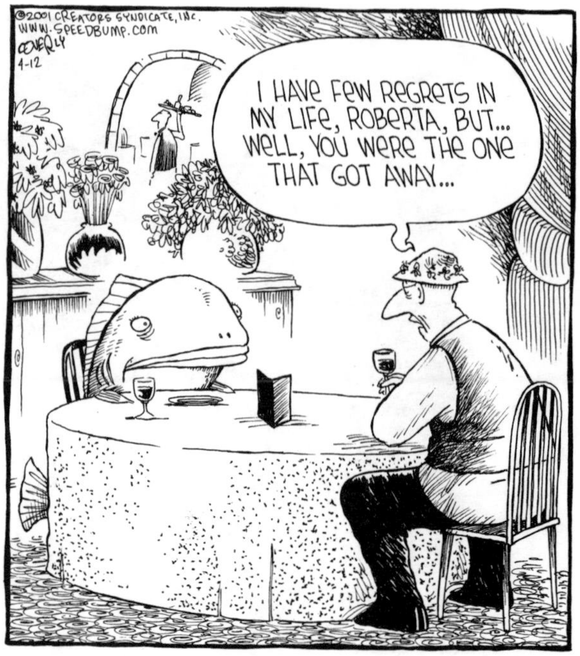
©2001 CREATORS SYNDICATE, INC. WWW.SPEEDBUMP.COM COVERLY 4-12
I HAVE FEW REGRETS IN MY LIFE, ROBERTA, BUT... WELL, YOU WERE THE ONE THAT GOT AWAY...

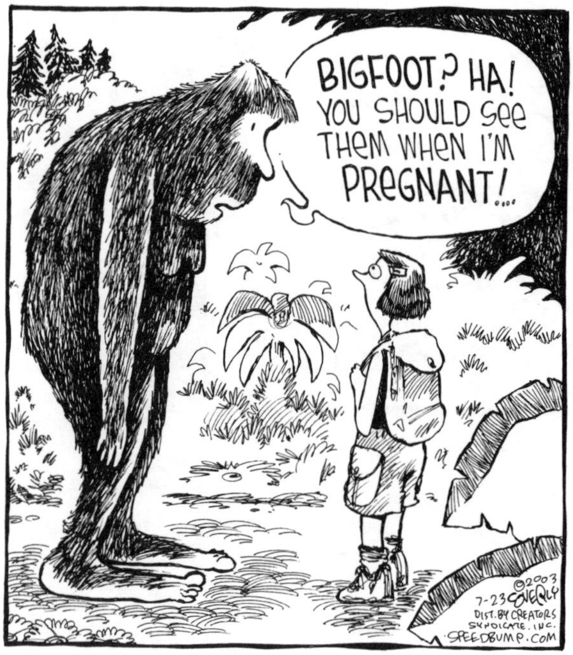
BIGFOOT? HA! YOU SHOULD SEE THEM WHEN I'M PREGNANT!
7-23 ©2003 COVERLY DIST. BY CREATORS SYNDICATE, INC. SPEEDBUMP.COM

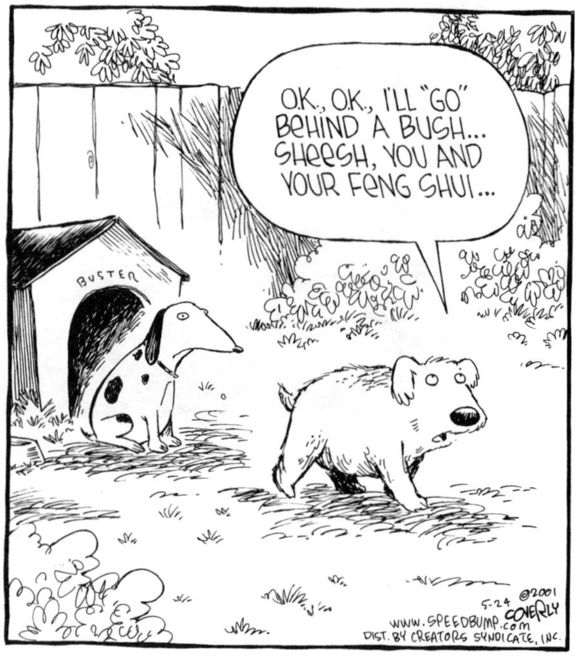
O.K., O.K., I'LL "GO" BEHIND A BUSH... SHEESH, YOU AND YOUR FENG SHUI...
BUSTER
5-24 ©2001 WWW.SPEEDBUMP.COM COVERLY DIST. BY CREATORS SYNDICATE, INC.

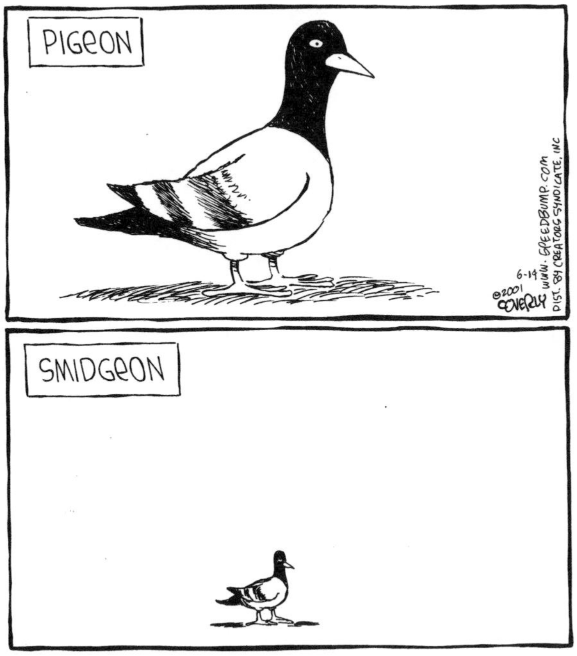
PIGEON
SMIDGEON

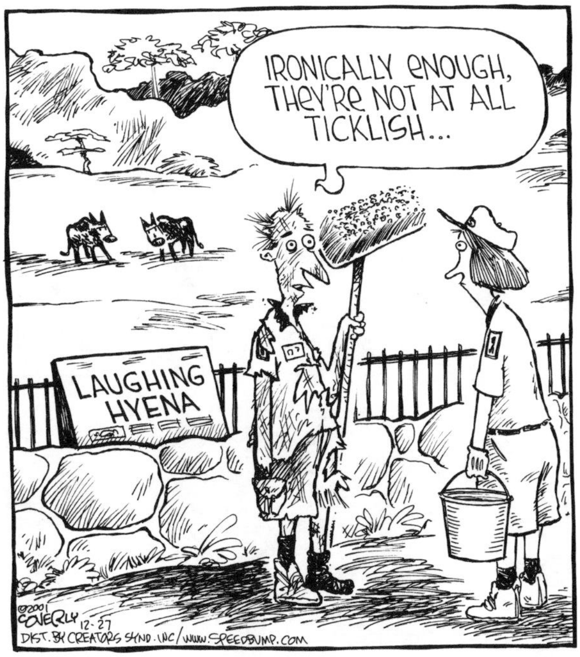
IRONICALLY ENOUGH, THEY'RE NOT AT ALL TICKLISH...
LAUGHING HYENA
DIST. BY CREATORS SYND. INC/WWW.SPEEDBUMP.COM

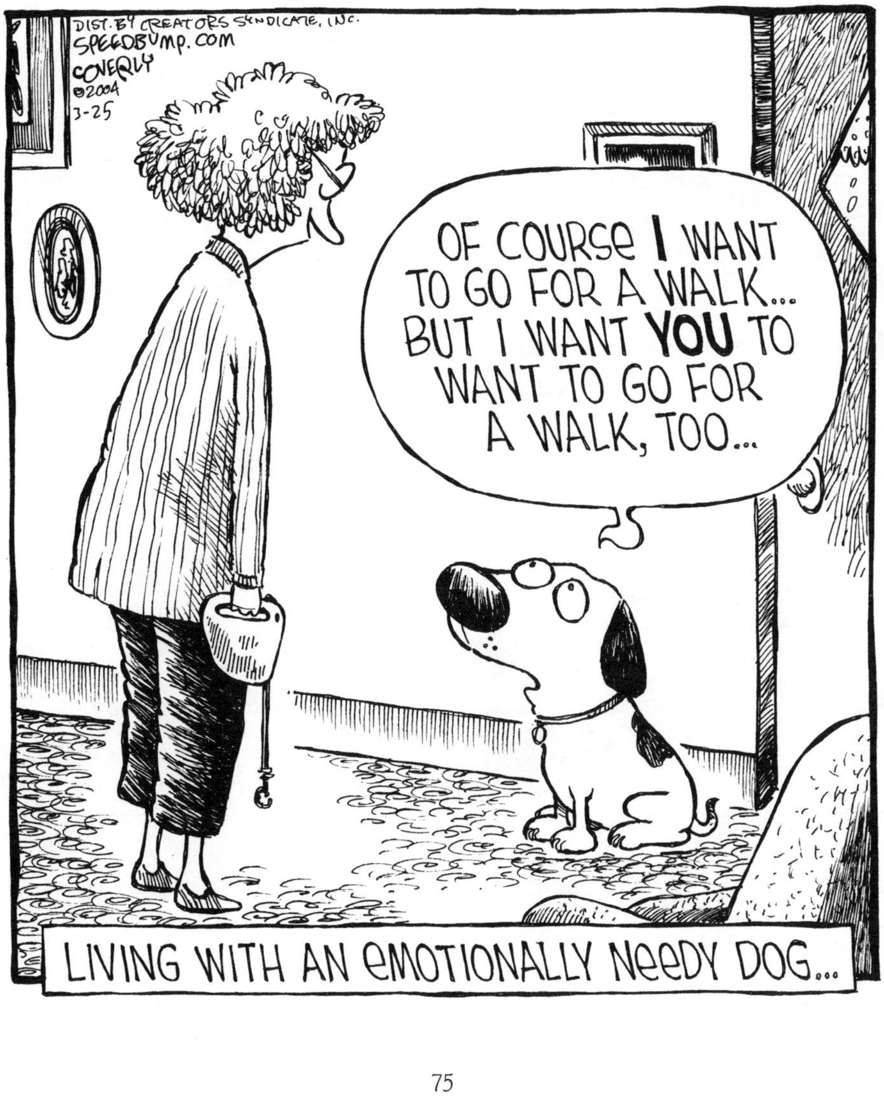
DIST. BY CREATORS SYNDICATE, INC.
SPEEDBUMP.COM
COVERLY
©2004
3-25
OF COURSE I WANT TO GO FOR A WALK... BUT I WANT YOU TO WANT TO GO FOR A WALK, TOO...
LIVING WITH AN EMOTIONALLY NEEDY DOG...

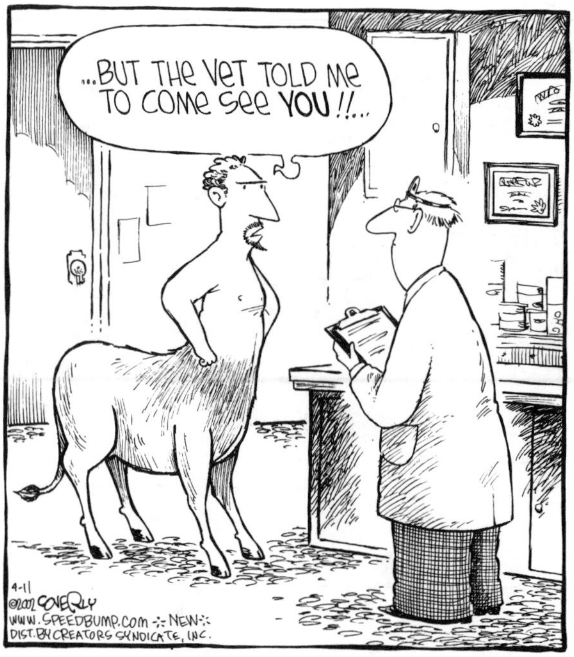
...BUT THE VET TOLD ME TO COME SEE YOU!!...
4-11
©2002 COVERLY
WWW.SPEEDBUMP.COM NEW
DIST. BY CREATORS SYNDICATE, INC.

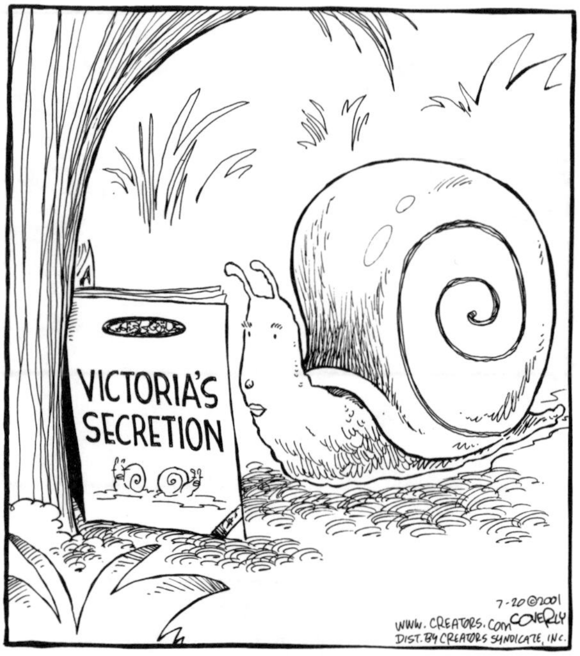
VICTORIA'S SECRETION
7-20 ©2001
WWW.CREATORS.COM COVERLY
DIST. BY CREATORS SYNDICATE, INC.

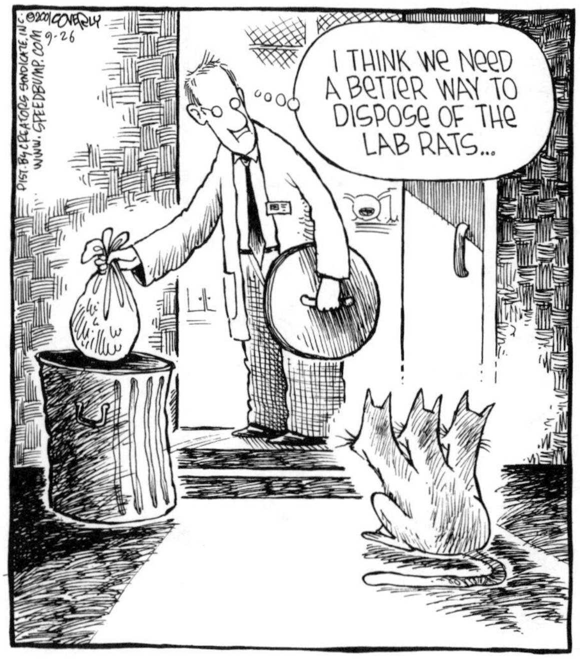
I THINK WE NEED A BETTER WAY TO DISPOSE OF THE LAB RATS...
©2001 COVERLY
9-26
DIST. BY CREATORS SYNDICATE, INC.
WWW.SPEEDBUMP.COM

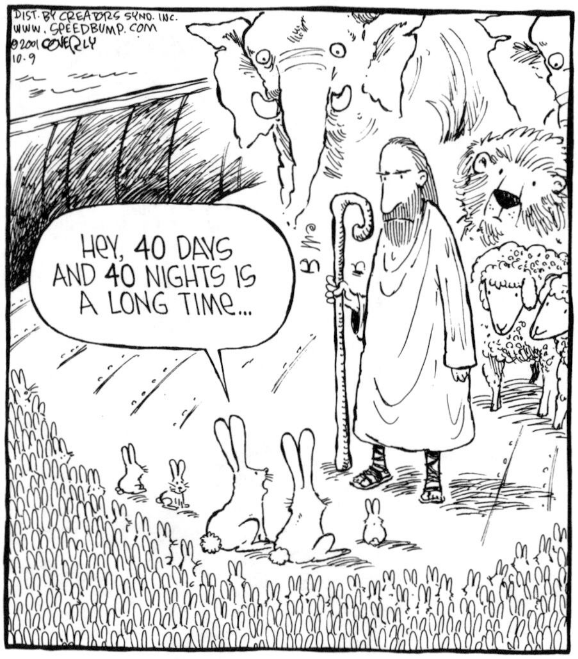
HEY, 40 DAYS AND 40 NIGHTS IS A LONG TIME...
DIST. BY CREATORS SYNO. INC.
WWW.SPEEDBUMP.COM
©2001 COVERLY
10-9

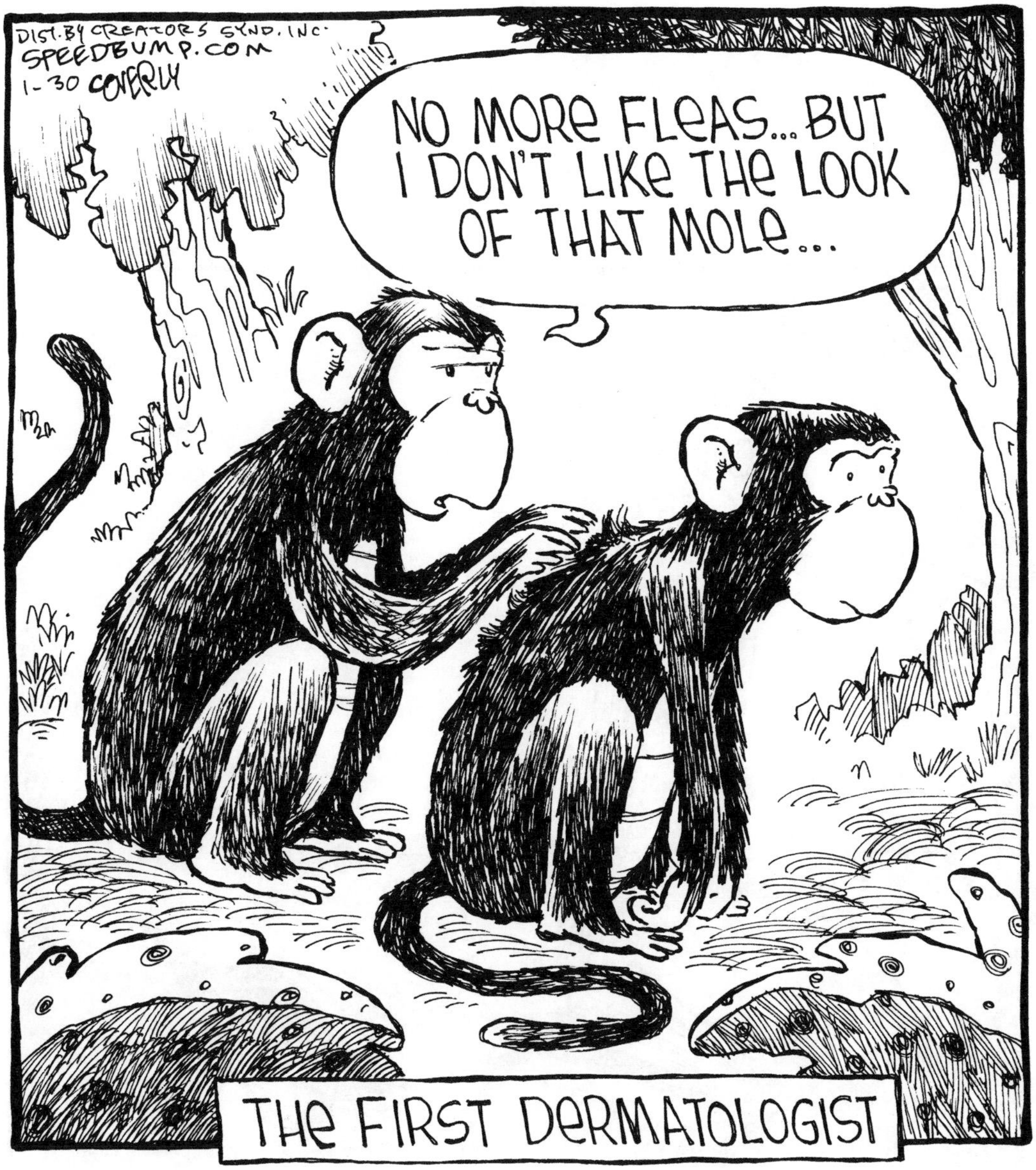
DIST. BY CREATORS SYND. INC.
SPEEDBUMP.COM
1-30 COVERLY
NO MORE FLEAS... BUT I DON'T LIKE THE LOOK OF THAT MOLE...
THE FIRST DERMATOLOGIST

Reading

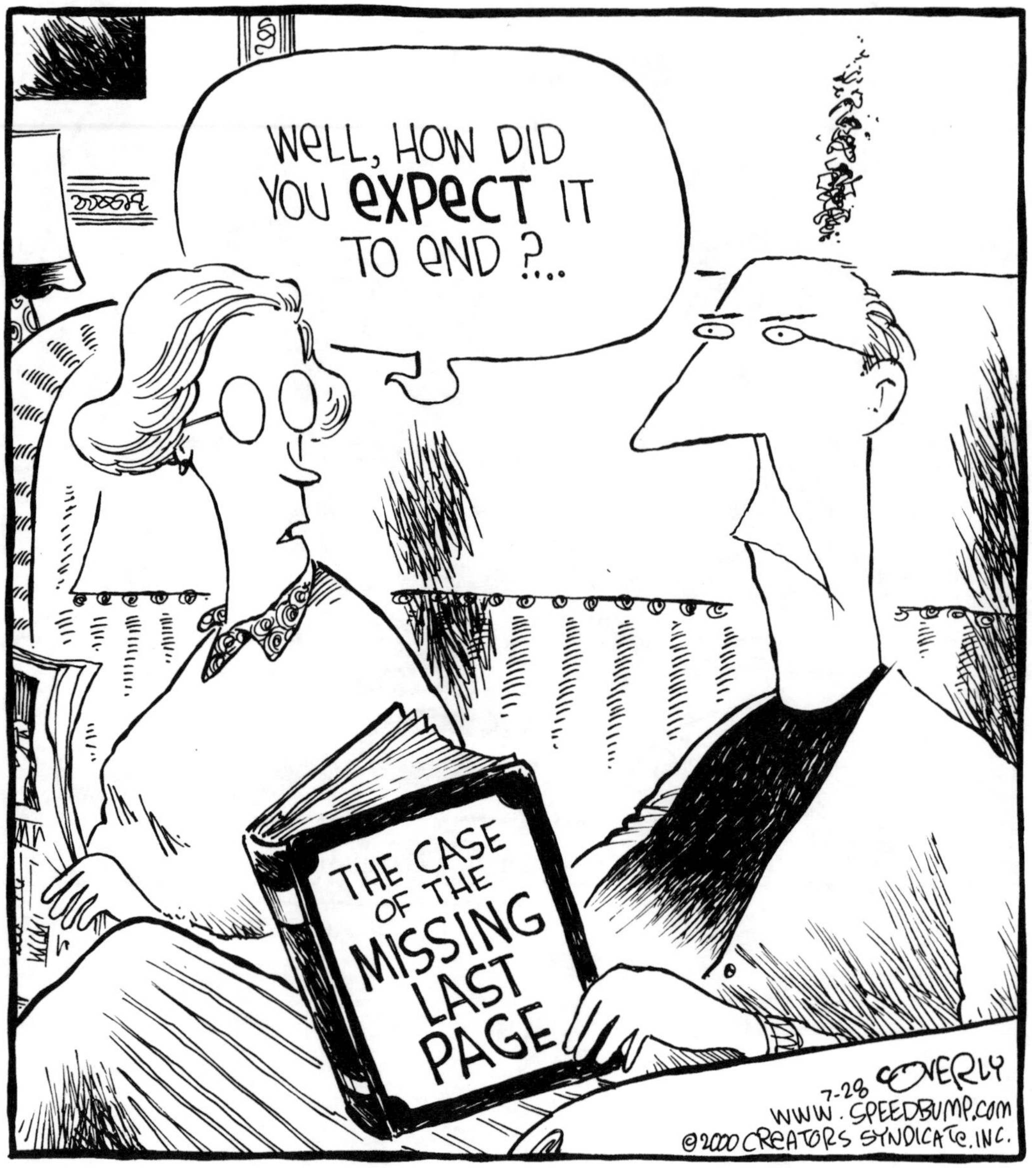

WELL, HOW DID YOU EXPECT IT TO END ?...
THE CASE OF THE MISSING LAST PAGE
7-28 COVERLY
WWW.SPEEDBUMP.COM
©2000 CREATORS SYNDICATE, INC.

There's a stereotype about cartoonists and other artists that we're flaky head-cases who shut ourselves in an attic and create our works in a fit of madness. This is true, but seems unhealthy to tell someone who wants to be a cartoonist . . . so whenever I talk with a young person who wants to try cartooning, I always stress two things: one, get out and experience life so that you'll have a larger reservoir of experiences to tap into for ideas . . . and two, read. A lot. You can't personally experience everything, but you can travel vicariously and absorb new perspectives by reading. This is important if you don't want the idea pool to dry up.

For those of you who keep lists, like I do, the following books have been mental landmarks on the Speed Bump Cartoon Map, and are all heartily recommended by the crack staff up here in the Belfry:

> *The Life of Pi* by Yann Martel
> *Ignorance* by Milan Kundera
> *Marcovaldo* by Italo Calvino
> *I'm With Stupid* by Gene Weingarten and Gina Barreca
> *Maus I* and *Maus II* by Art Spiegelman
> *The Essential George Booth* by Lee Lorenz
> *The Essential Jack Ziegler* by Lee Lorenz
> *The Essential Charles Barsotti* by Lee Lorenz
> *The World of Quino*
> *A Prayer for Owen Meany* by John Irving
> *Ernie Pyle's War* by James Tobin
> *Me Talk Pretty One Day* by David Sedaris
> *Mutts: The Comic Art of Patrick McDonnell* by Patrick McDonnell
> *Darkness Visible* by William Styron
> *Trinity* by Leon Uris
> *The Complete Fiction of Bruno Schulz*
> *The Essential Ellison* by Harlan Ellison
> *Snow White* by Donald Barthelme

and anything by Dave Barry.

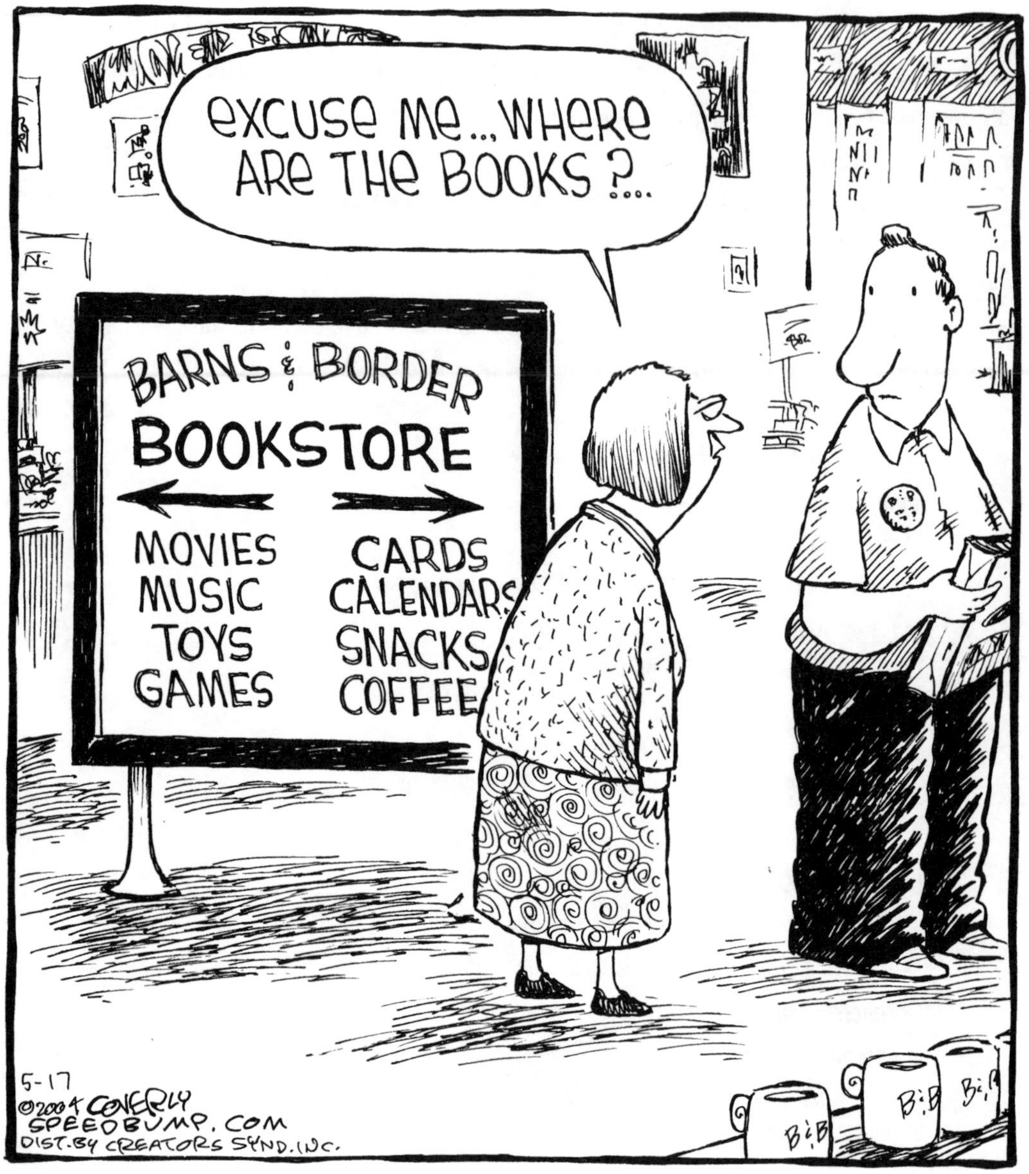
EXCUSE ME..., WHERE ARE THE BOOKS ?...
BARNS & BORDER
BOOKSTORE
MOVIES
MUSIC
TOYS
GAMES
CARDS
CALENDARS
SNACKS
COFFEE
5-17
©2004 COVERLY
SPEEDBUMP.COM
DIST. BY CREATORS SYND. INC.

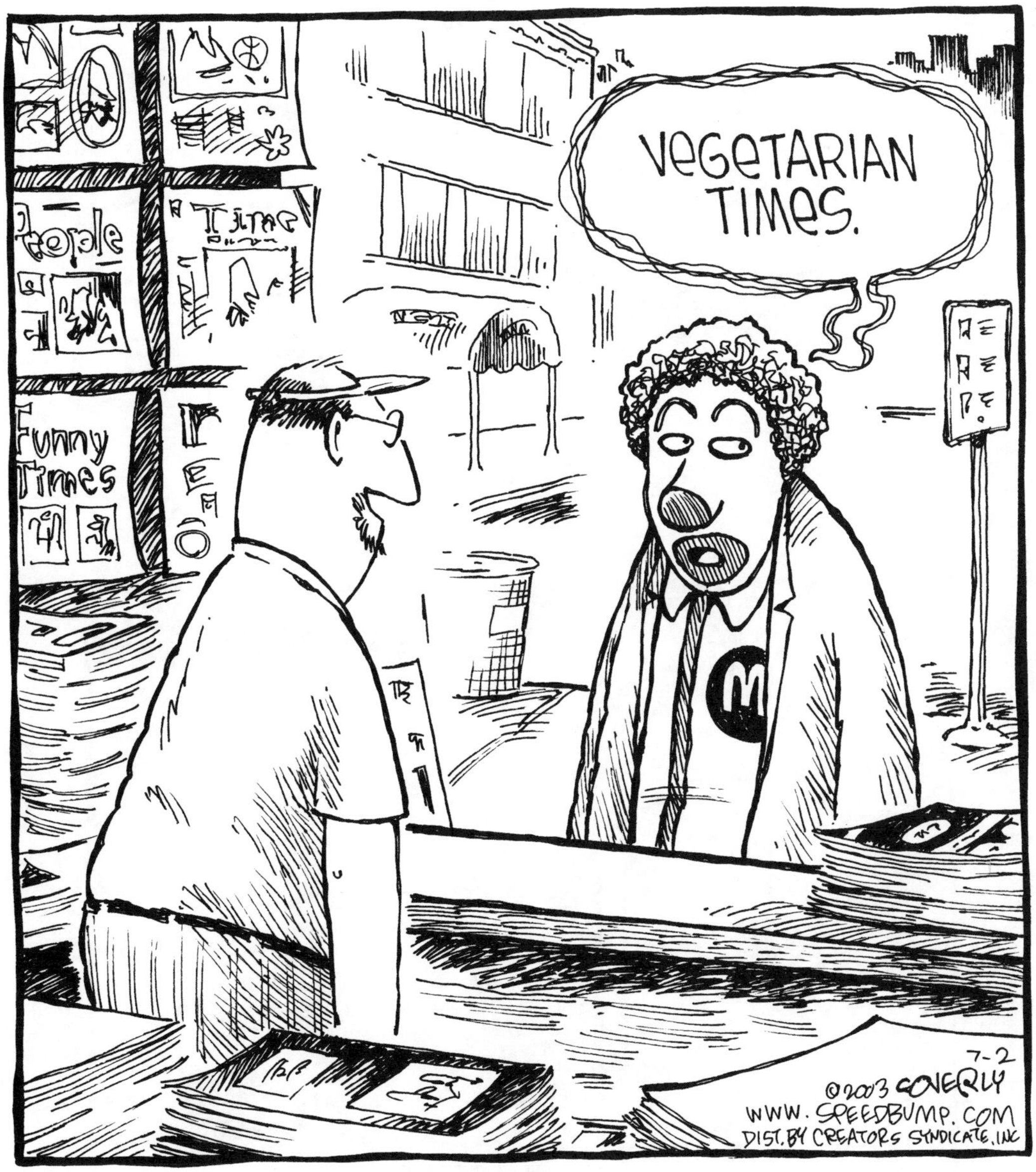
VEGETARIAN TIMES.
People
Time
Funny Times
7-2
©2003 COVERLY
WWW.SPEEDBUMP.COM
DIST. BY CREATORS SYNDICATE, INC

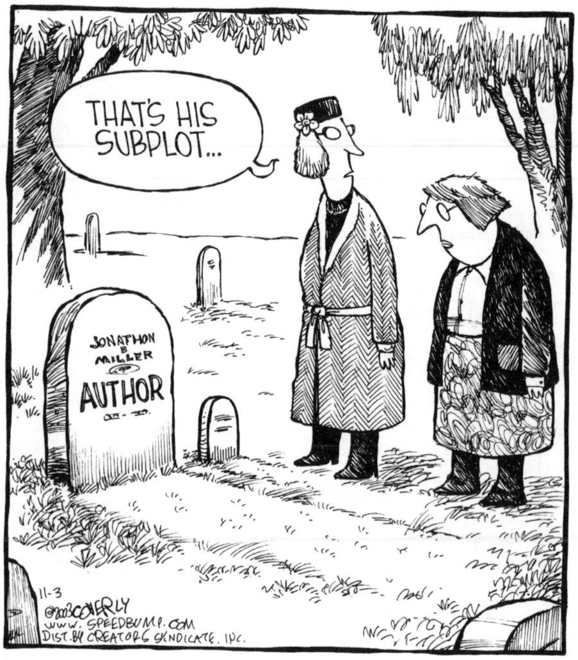
THAT'S HIS SUBPLOT...
JONATHON E MILLER
AUTHOR
11-3
©2003 COVERLY
WWW.SPEEDBUMP.COM
DIST. BY CREATORS SYNDICATE, INC.

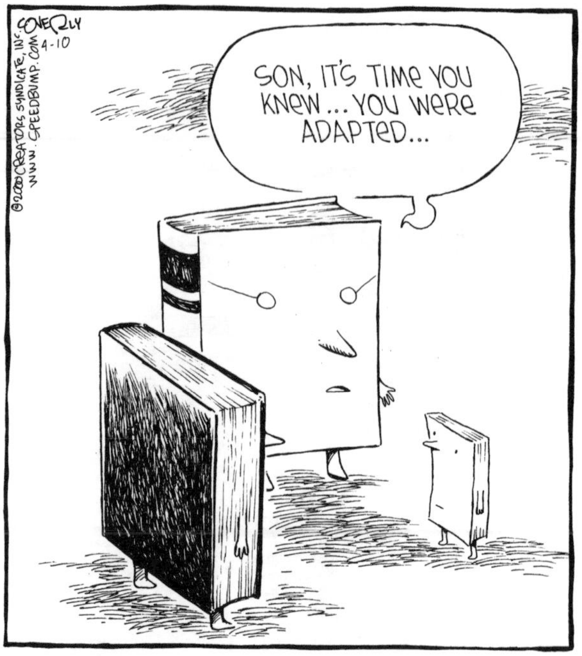
SON, IT'S TIME YOU KNEW... YOU WERE ADAPTED...
©2000 CREATORS SYNDICATE, INC.
WWW.SPEEDBUMP.COM
COVERLY
4-10

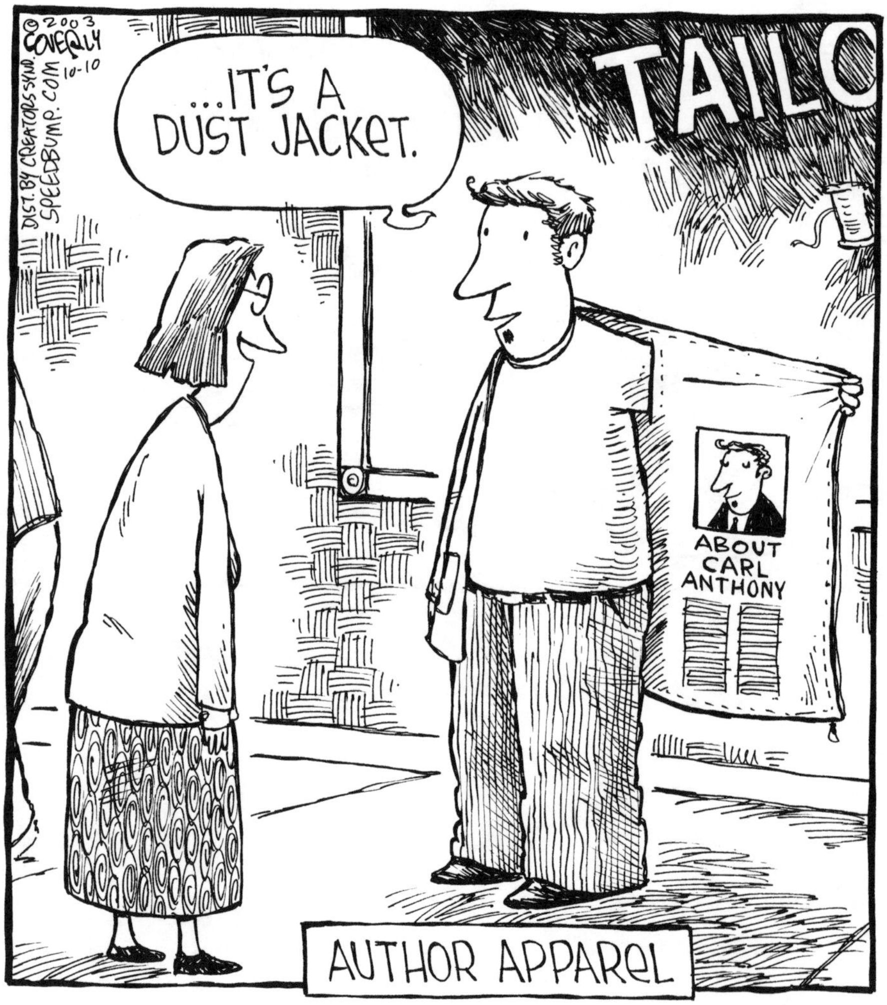
©2003 COVERLY
10-10
DIST. BY CREATORS SYND.
SPEEDBUMP.COM
...IT'S A DUST JACKET.
TAILO
ABOUT CARL ANTHONY
AUTHOR APPAREL

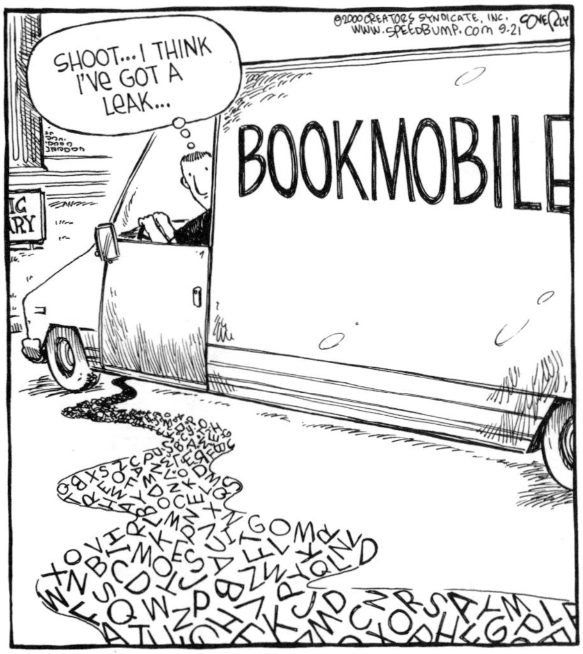
©2000 CREATORS SYNDICATE, INC.
WWW.SPEEDBUMP.COM 9-21
COVERLY
SHOOT...I THINK I'VE GOT A LEAK...
BOOKMOBILE

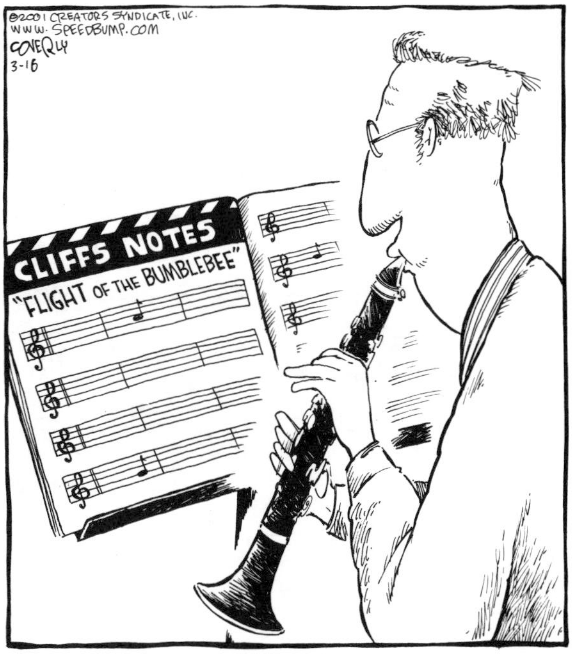
©2001 CREATORS SYNDICATE, INC.
WWW.SPEEDBUMP.COM
COVERLY
3-16
CLIFFS NOTES
"FLIGHT OF THE BUMBLEBEE"

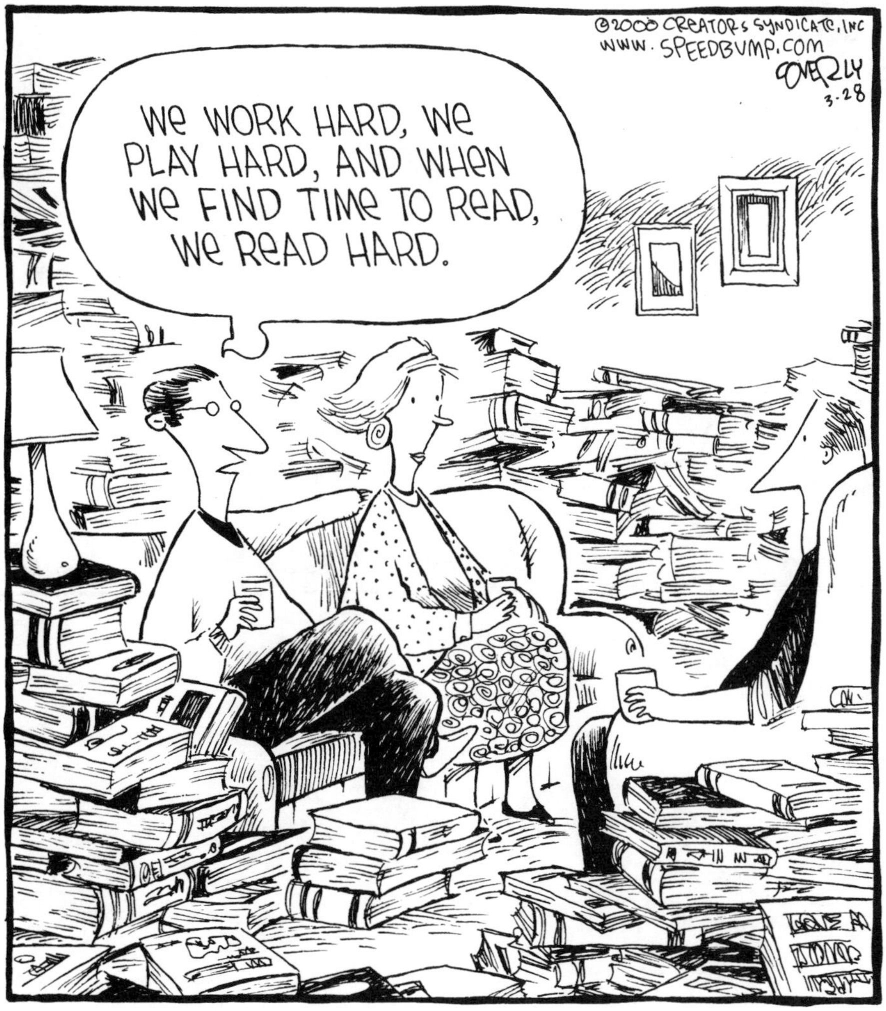
©2000 CREATORS SYNDICATE, INC
WWW.SPEEDBUMP.COM
COVERLY
3-28
WE WORK HARD, WE PLAY HARD, AND WHEN WE FIND TIME TO READ, WE READ HARD.

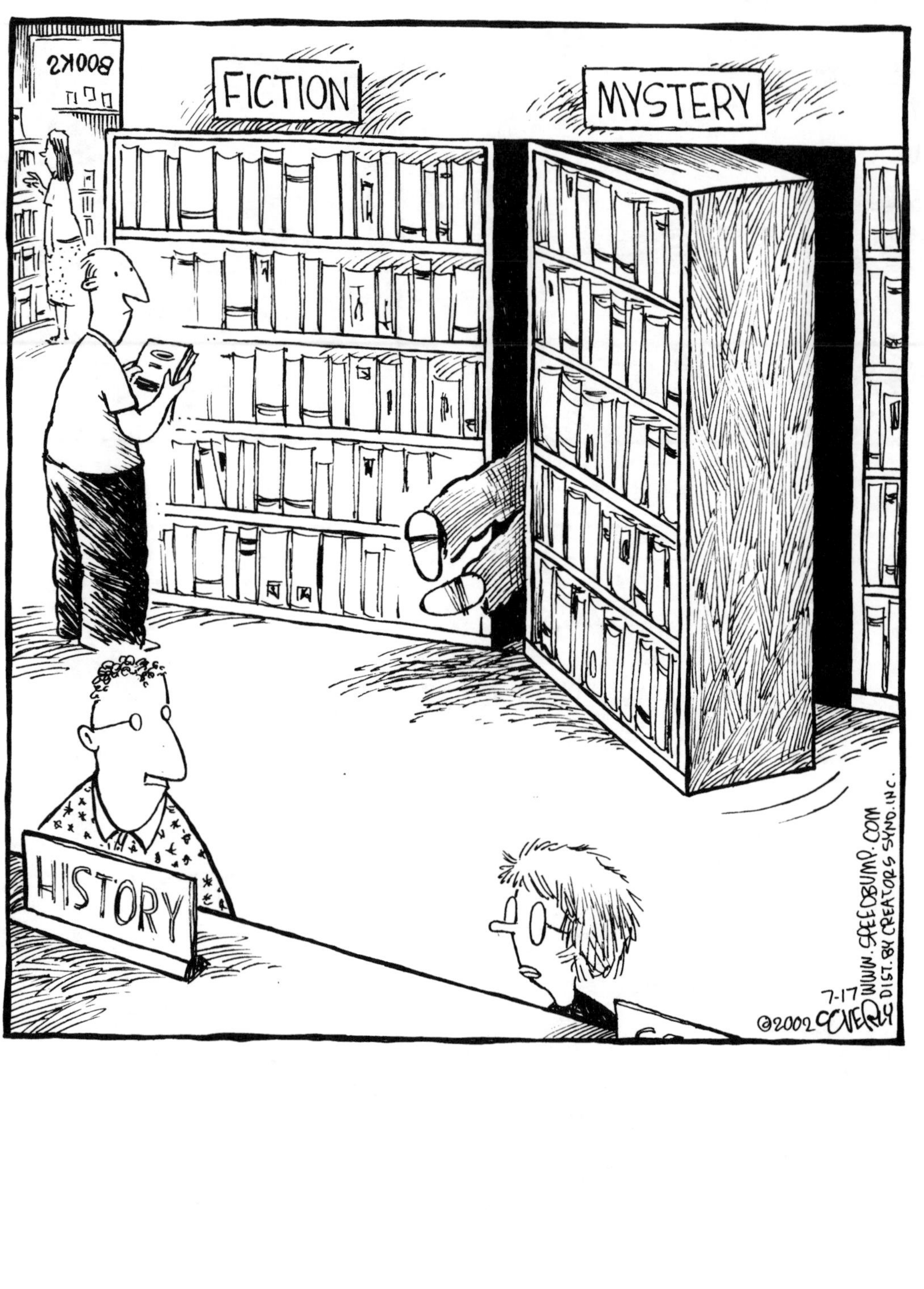
BOOKS
FICTION
MYSTERY
HISTORY
7-17
WWW.SPEEDBUMP.COM
DIST. BY CREATORS SYND. INC.
©2002 COVERLY

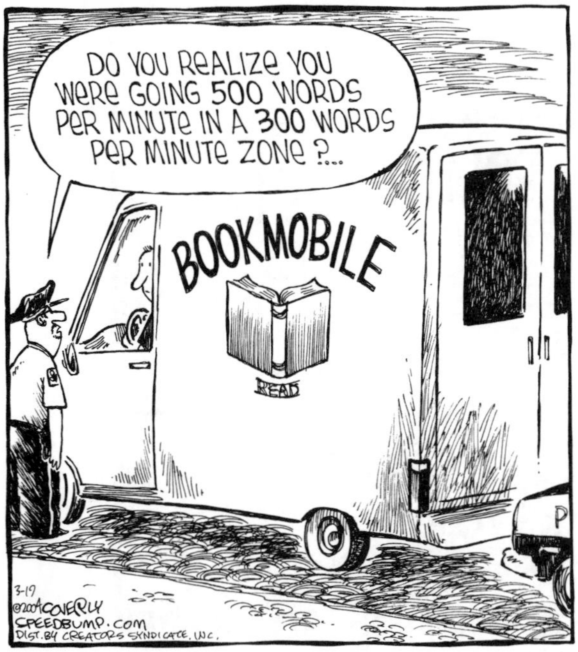
DO YOU REALIZE YOU WERE GOING 500 WORDS PER MINUTE IN A 300 WORDS PER MINUTE ZONE ?...
BOOKMOBILE
READ
3-19 ©2004 COVERLY SPEEDBUMP.COM DIST. BY CREATORS SYNDICATE, INC.

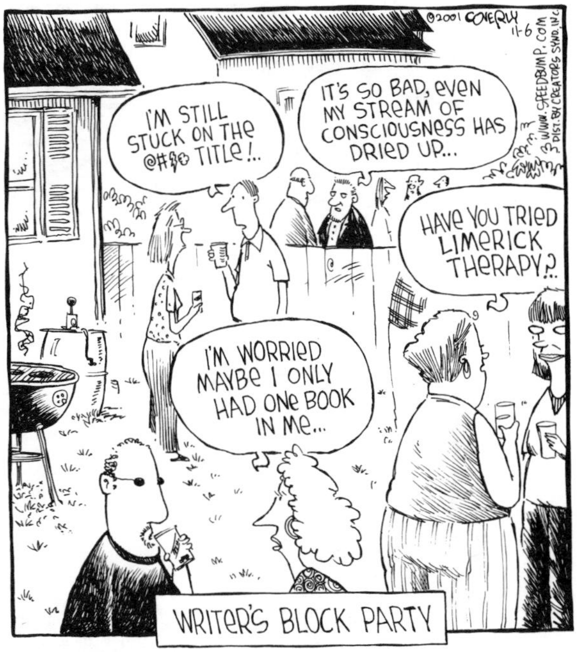
©2001 COVERLY 11-6
WWW.SPEEDBUMP.COM DIST. BY CREATORS SYND. INC.
I'M STILL STUCK ON THE @#$© TITLE!..
IT'S SO BAD, EVEN MY STREAM OF CONSCIOUSNESS HAS DRIED UP...
HAVE YOU TRIED LIMERICK THERAPY?...
I'M WORRIED MAYBE I ONLY HAD ONE BOOK IN ME...
WRITER'S BLOCK PARTY

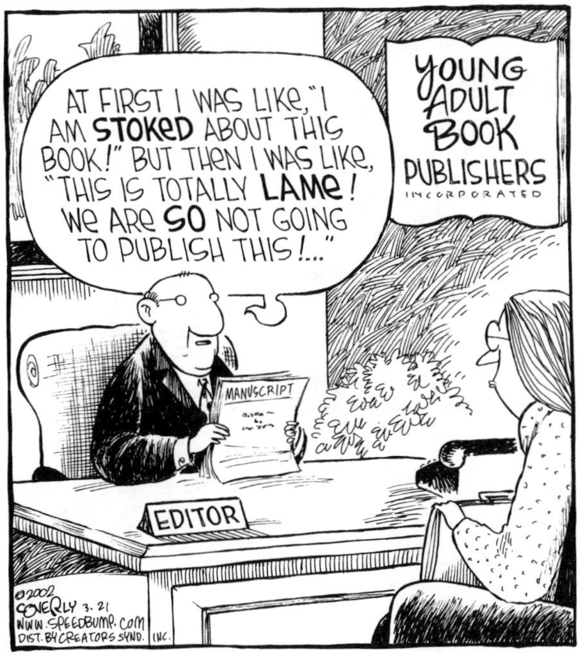
AT FIRST I WAS LIKE, "I AM STOKED ABOUT THIS BOOK!" BUT THEN I WAS LIKE, "THIS IS TOTALLY LAME! WE ARE SO NOT GOING TO PUBLISH THIS!..."
YOUNG ADULT BOOK PUBLISHERS INCORPORATED
MANUSCRIPT
EDITOR
©2002 COVERLY 3-21 WWW.SPEEDBUMP.COM DIST. BY CREATORS SYND. INC.

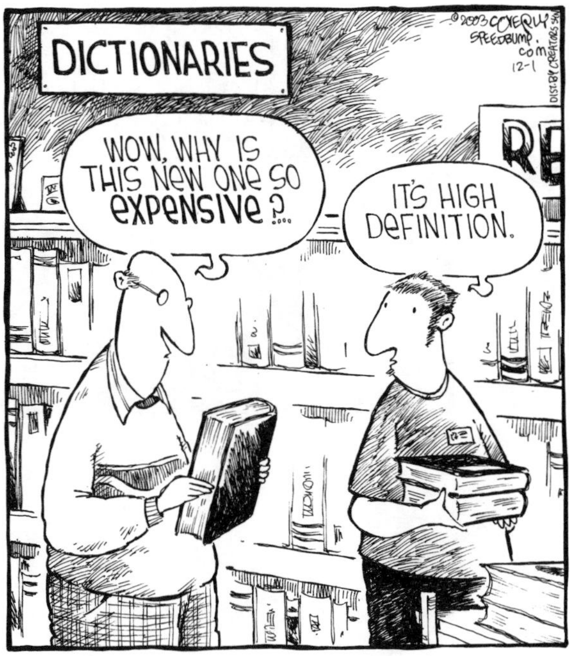
DICTIONARIES
©2003 COVERLY SPEEDBUMP.COM 12-1 DIST. BY CREATORS SYND.
WOW, WHY IS THIS NEW ONE SO EXPENSIVE?...
IT'S HIGH DEFINITION.

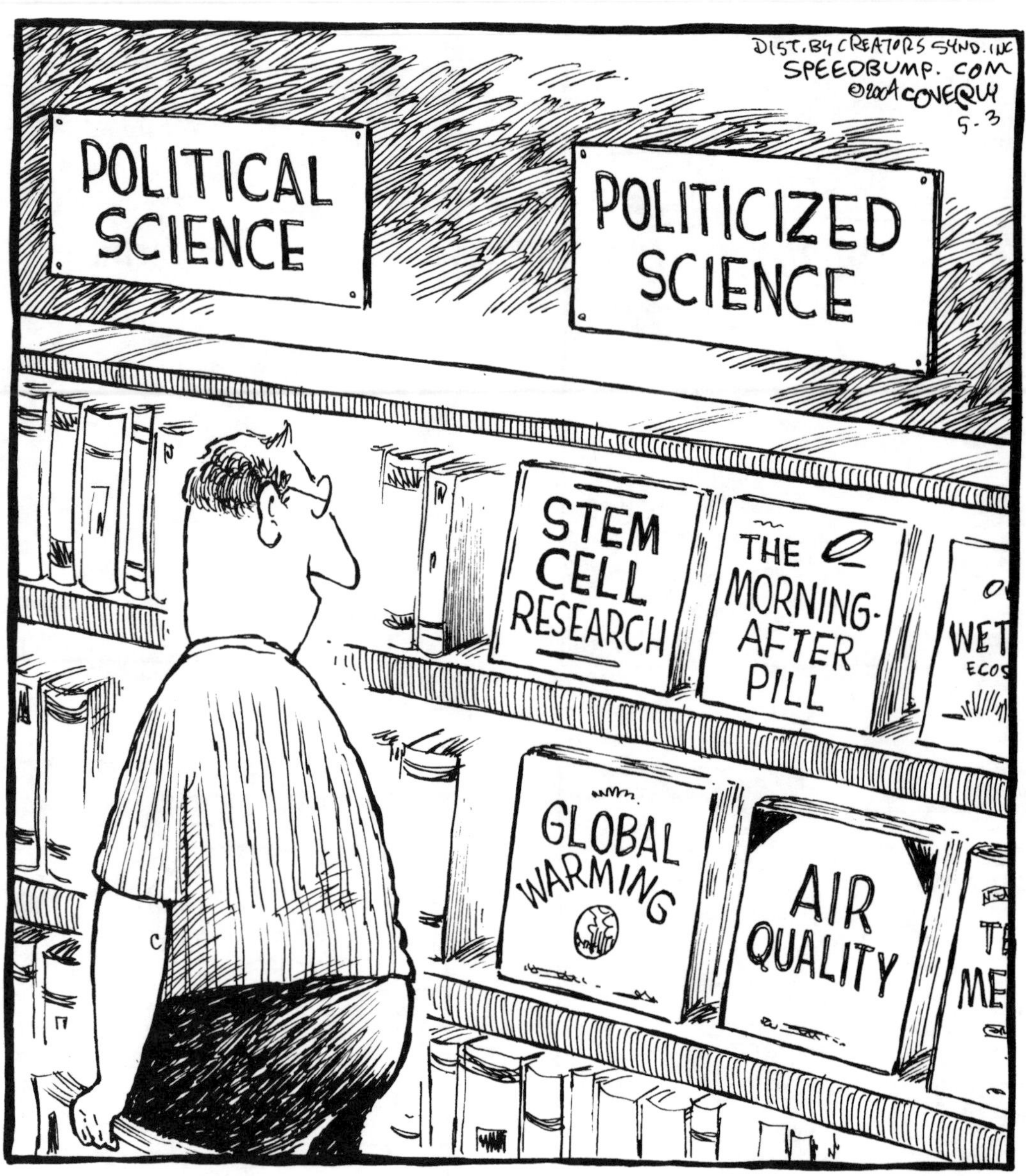
DIST. BY CREATORS SYND. INC
SPEEDBUMP. COM
©2004 COVERLY
5-3
POLITICAL SCIENCE
POLITICIZED SCIENCE
STEM CELL RESEARCH
THE MORNING-AFTER PILL
GLOBAL WARMING
AIR QUALITY

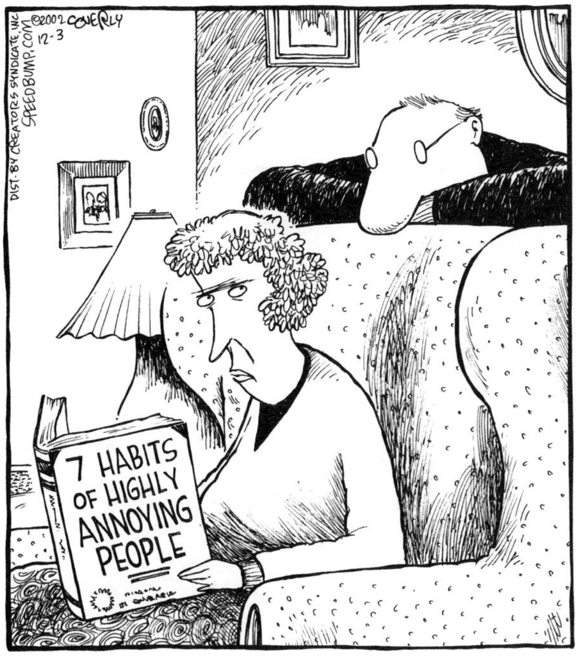
DIST. BY CREATORS SYNDICATE, INC. SPEEDBUMP.COM ©2002 COVERLY 12-3
7 HABITS OF HIGHLY ANNOYING PEOPLE

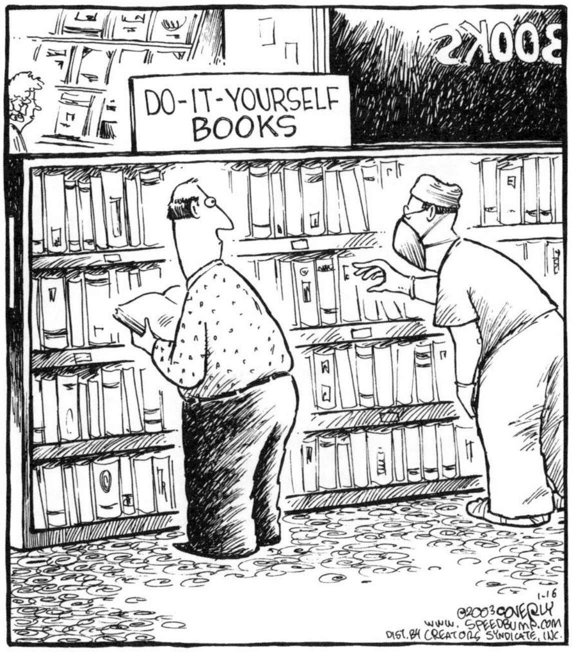
BOOKS
DO-IT-YOURSELF BOOKS
1-16 ©2003 COVERLY WWW. SPEEDBUMP.COM DIST. BY CREATORS SYNDICATE, INC.

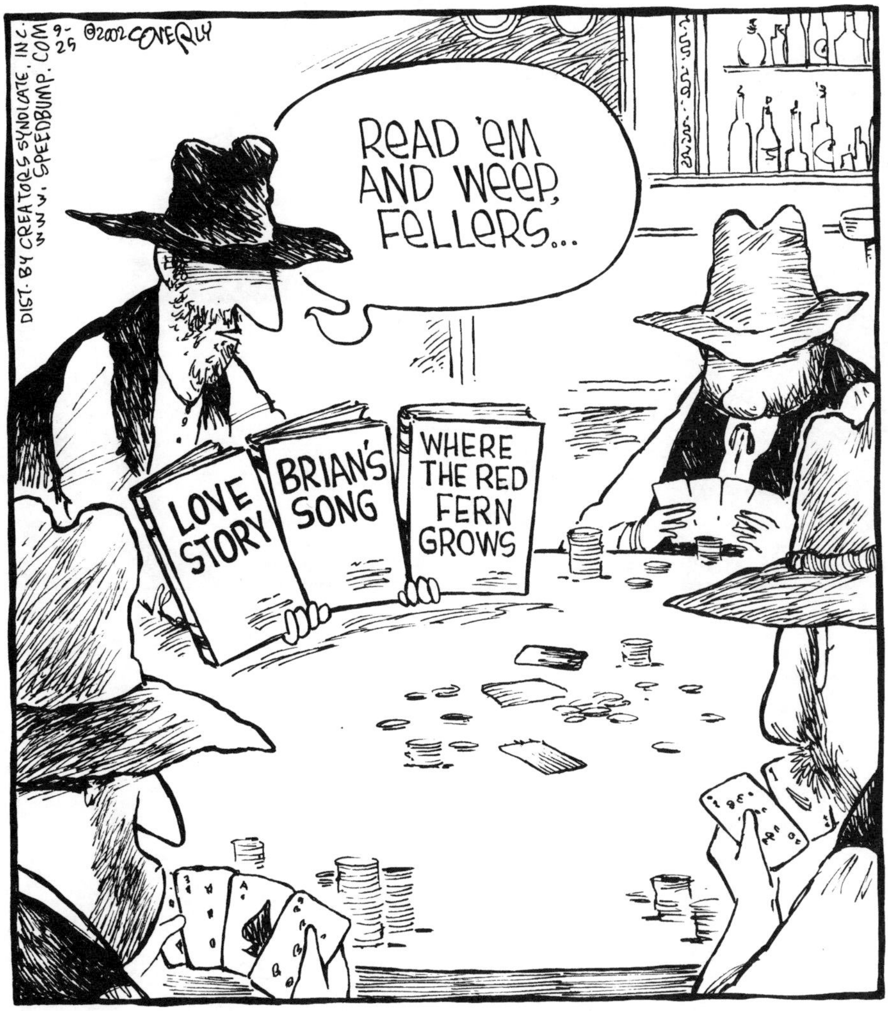
DIST. BY CREATORS SYNDICATE, INC. WWW. SPEEDBUMP.COM 9-25 ©2002 COVERLY
Read 'em and weep, fellers...
LOVE STORY
BRIAN'S SONG
WHERE THE RED FERN GROWS

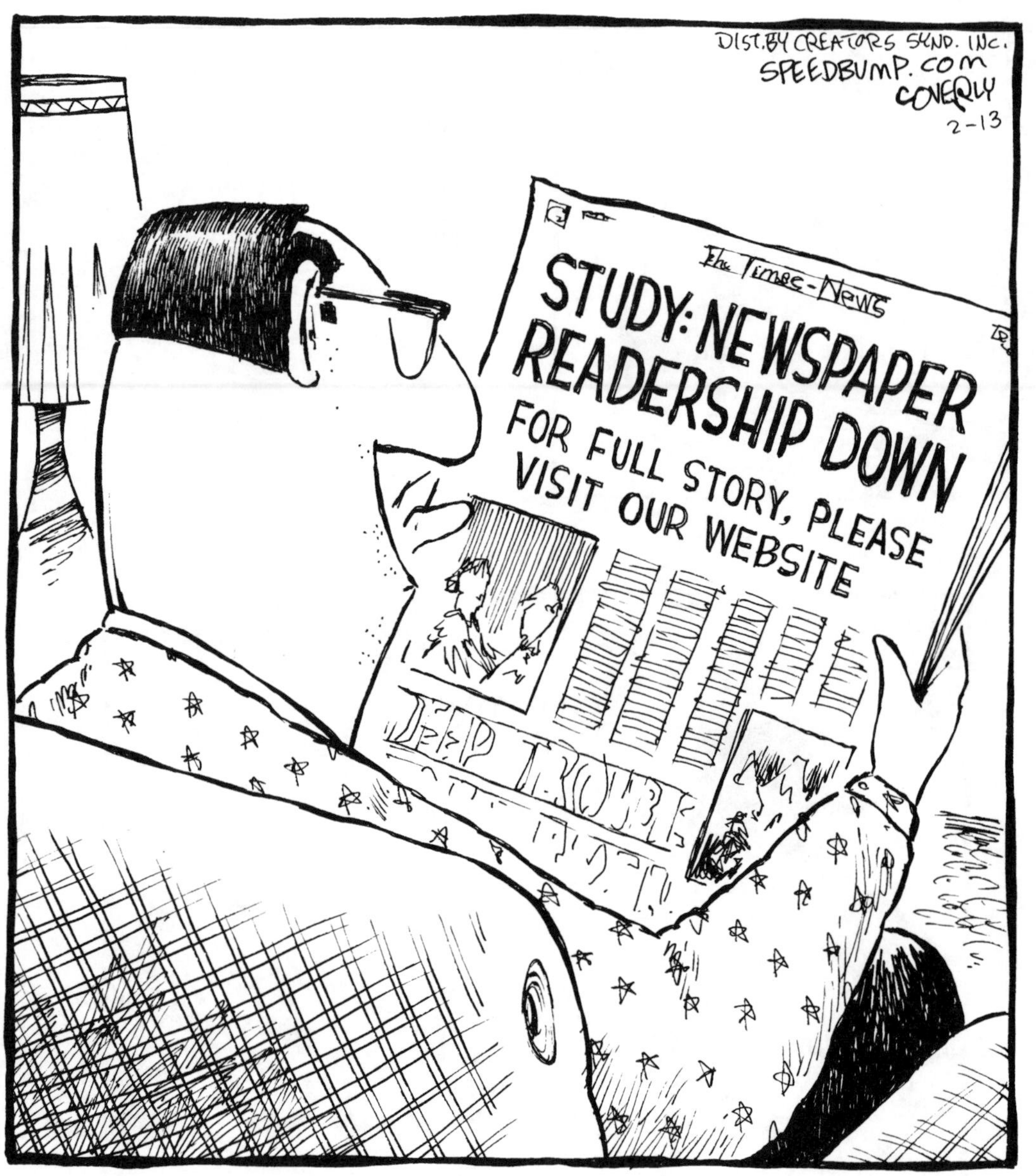
DIST. BY CREATORS SYND. INC.
SPEEDBUMP.COM
COVERLY
2-13
The Times-News
STUDY: NEWSPAPER READERSHIP DOWN
FOR FULL STORY, PLEASE VISIT OUR WEBSITE
DEEP TROUBLE

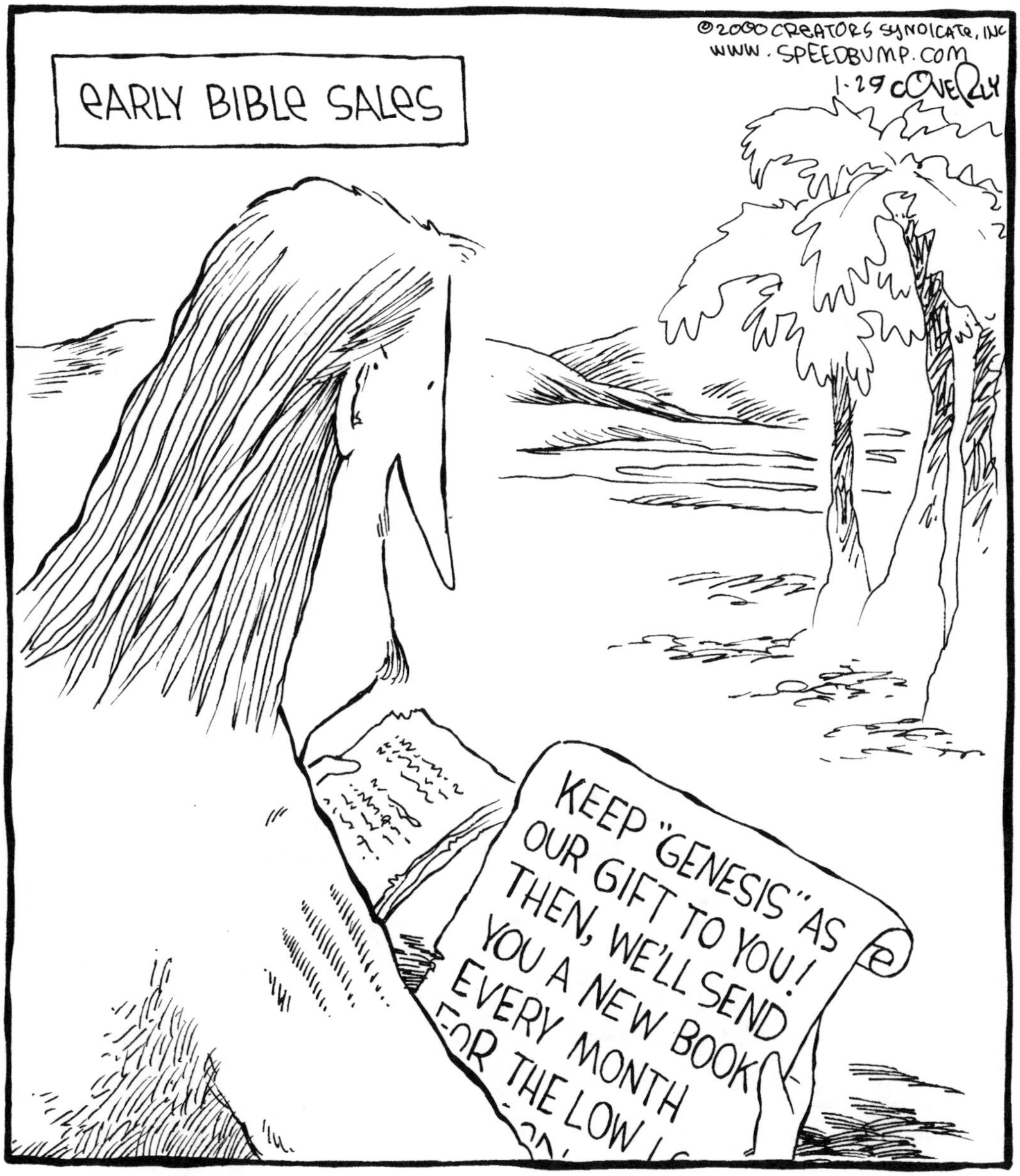
©2000 CREATORS SYNDICATE, INC
WWW.SPEEDBUMP.COM
1·29 COVERLY
EARLY BIBLE SALES
KEEP "GENESIS" AS
OUR GIFT TO YOU!
THEN, WE'LL SEND
YOU A NEW BOOK
EVERY MONTH
FOR THE LOW

Beverages

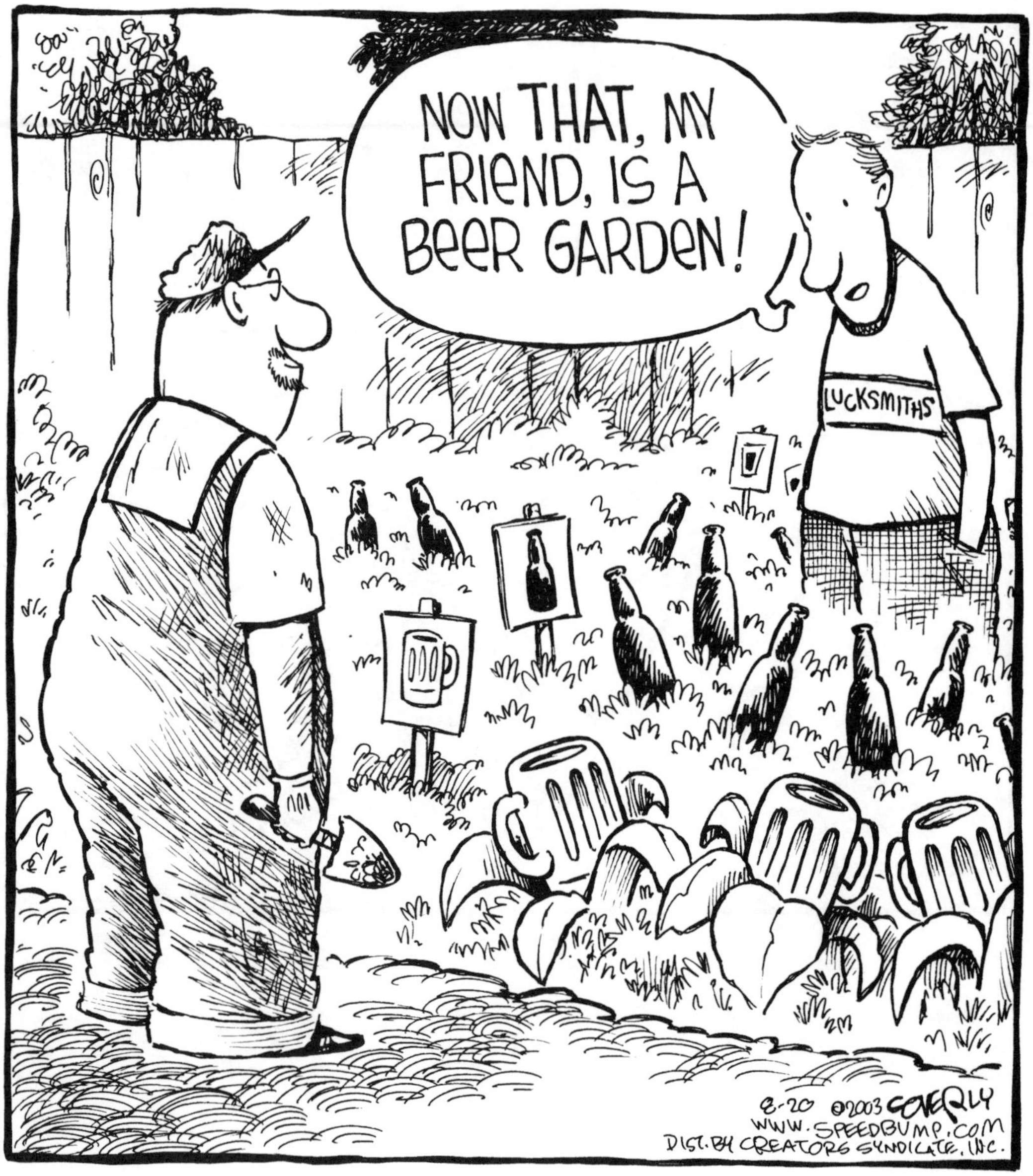
NOW THAT, MY FRIEND, IS A BEER GARDEN!
LUCKSMITHS
8-20 ©2003 COVERLY
WWW.SPEEDBUMP.COM
DIST. BY CREATORS SYNDICATE, INC.

If you've had a hard week at work, or if you're just feeling generally listless, we here at Speed Bump Incorporated heartily recommend the following cure. There's a big ol' clawfoot bathtub up here in the Belfry Studio that gets plenty of use:

Coffee Bath

That's right, coffee's not just for drinking anymore.

Just add three (3) to six (6) cups of strong coffee to your hot bath water and soak in it for at least fifteen (15) minutes. Do not soak more than an hour, however, as you'll look prunish and will be up all night. And pamper yourself with good coffee, for crying out loud — don't insult your skin with generic or store brands. Instant coffee will not revitalize you any faster, either, and those flavor crystals tend to find their way into awkward places.

Do not add frothed milk, nor should you add milk and then froth it. Not that there's anything wrong with that.

Hangover Cure

Now, if you had a hard week at work, and instead of soaking in a cuppa joe you opted to drown your worries in the harder stuff (not that we here in the Belfry would know anything about that), here's a little something that will cool your brain and settle your stomach the morning after:

Grab a blender. Add one frozen banana, some orange juice, a handful of raw almonds, and whatever other fruit is around — strawberries or blueberries are particularly good.

The secret ingredient is Nature's Plus energy supplement vegetarian Fruitein. This is a high protein, low calorie, Banana Orange Creme energy shake. I'm no paid spokesperson (yet), but this stuff is delicious.

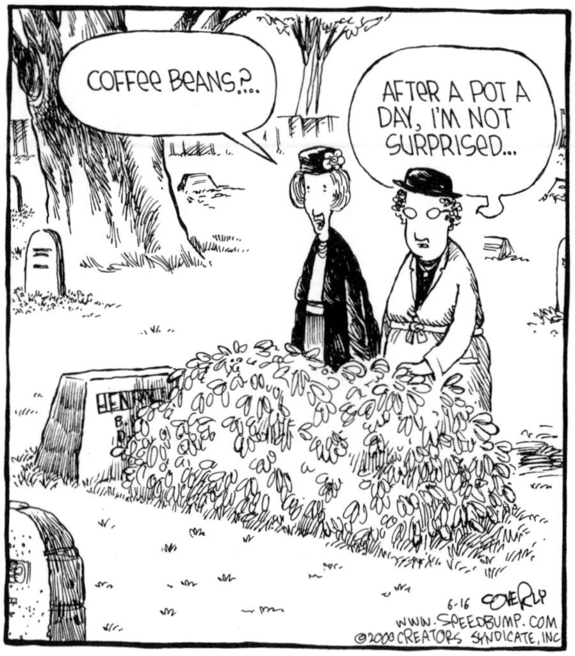
COFFEE BEANS?...
AFTER A POT A DAY, I'M NOT SURPRISED...
6-16 COVERLY
WWW.SPEEDBUMP.COM
©2000 CREATORS SYNDICATE, INC

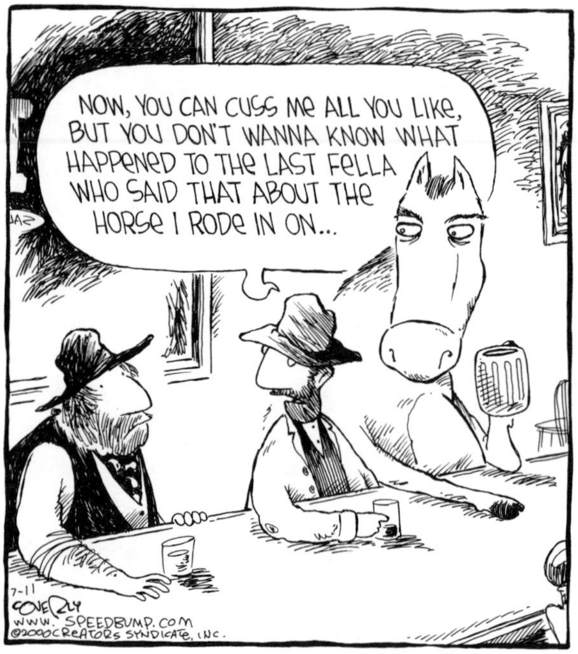
NOW, YOU CAN CUSS ME ALL YOU LIKE, BUT YOU DON'T WANNA KNOW WHAT HAPPENED TO THE LAST FELLA WHO SAID THAT ABOUT THE HORSE I RODE IN ON...
7-11 COVERLY
WWW.SPEEDBUMP.COM
©2000 CREATORS SYNDICATE, INC.

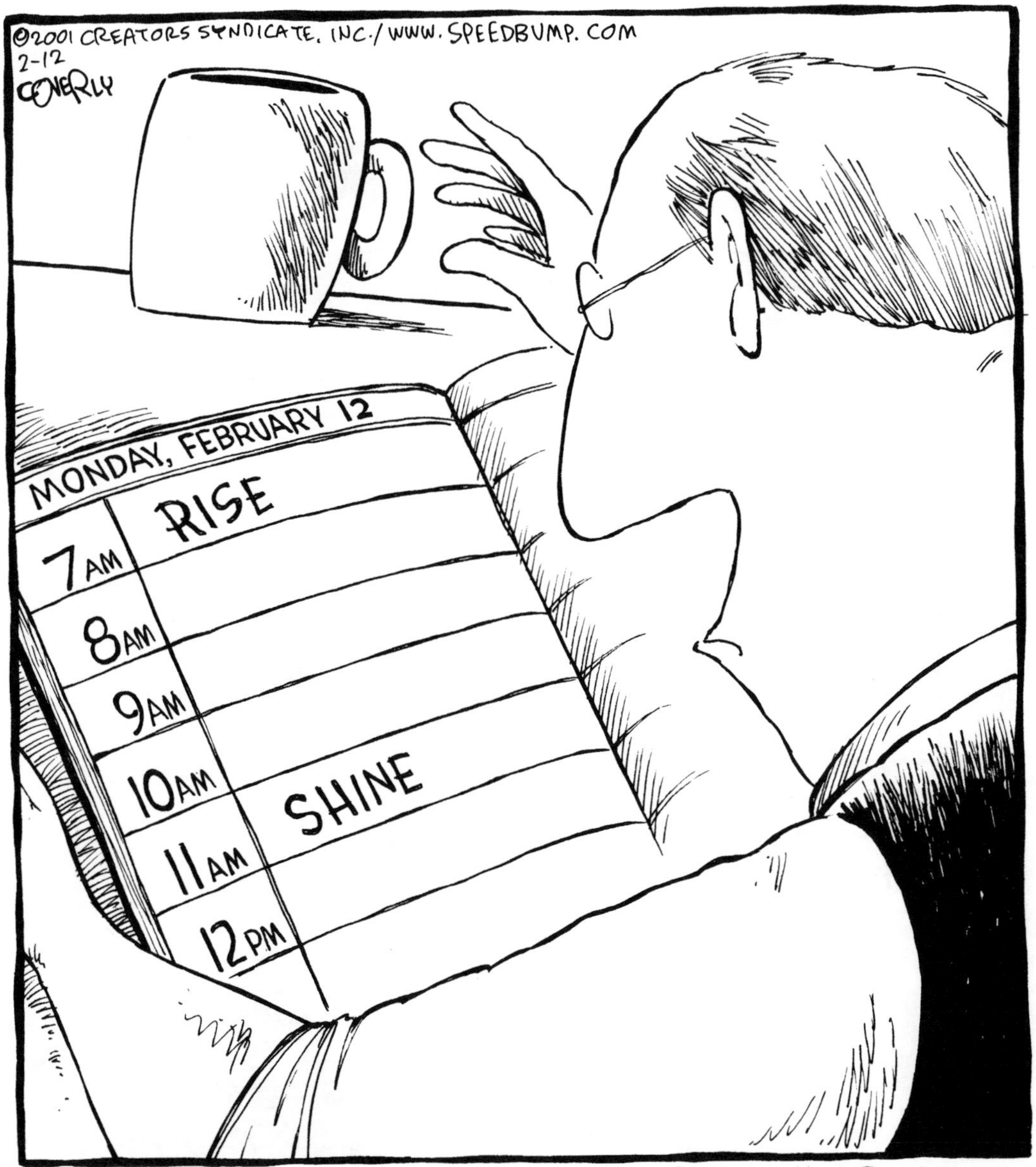
©2001 CREATORS SYNDICATE, INC./ WWW.SPEEDBUMP.COM
2-12
COVERLY
MONDAY, FEBRUARY 12
7AM RISE
8AM
9AM
10AM
11AM SHINE
12PM

DAY PLANNER OF A COFFEE DRINKER

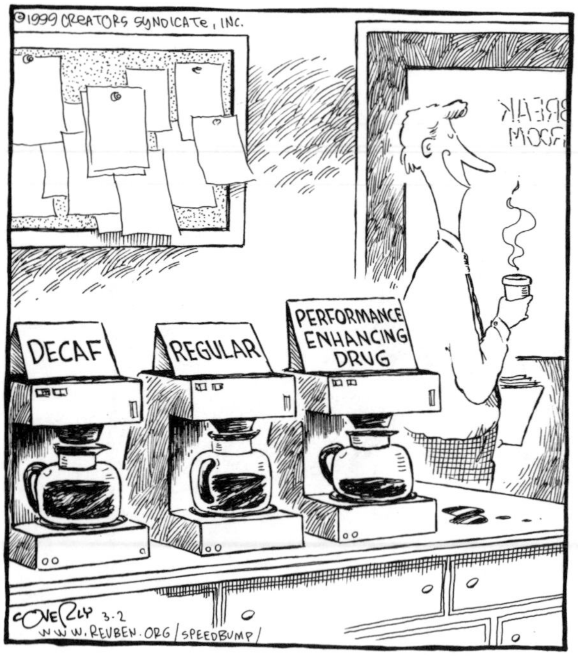
©1999 CREATORS SYNDICATE, INC.
DECAF
REGULAR
PERFORMANCE ENHANCING DRUG
COVERLY 3-2
WWW.REUBEN.ORG/SPEEDBUMP/

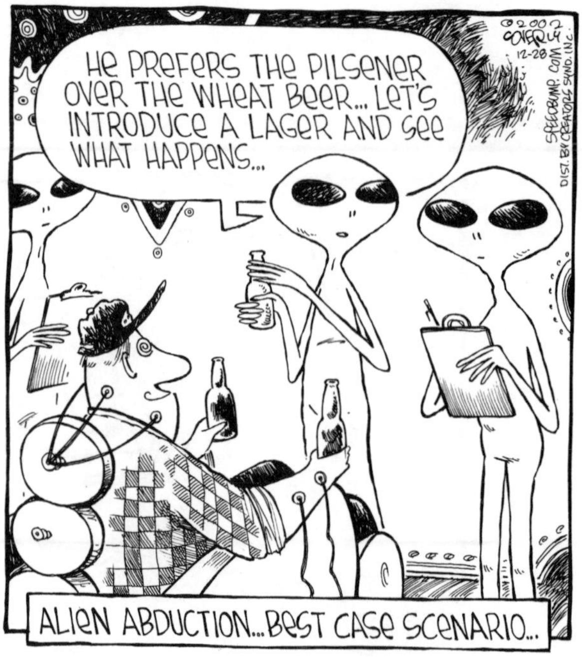
HE PREFERS THE PILSENER OVER THE WHEAT BEER... LET'S INTRODUCE A LAGER AND SEE WHAT HAPPENS...
©2002 COVERLY 12-28
SPEEDBUMP.COM
DIST. BY CREATORS SYND. INC.
ALIEN ABDUCTION... BEST CASE SCENARIO...

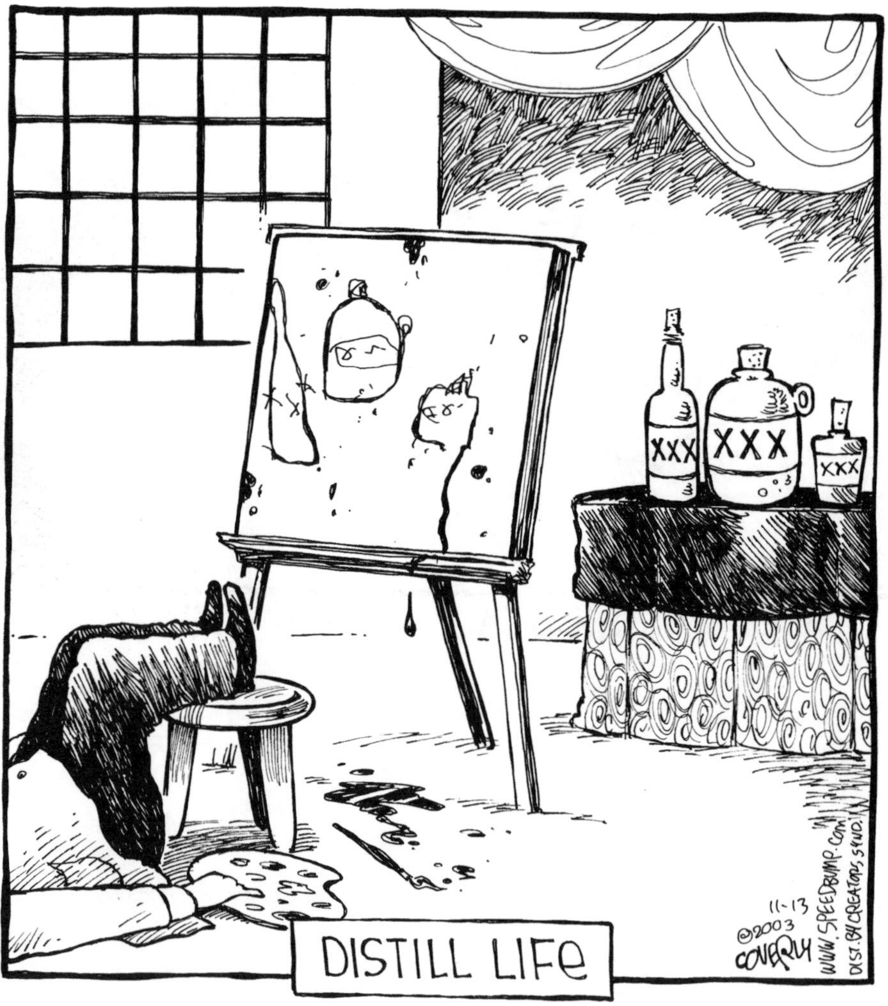
XXX
XXX
XXX
11-13
©2003
COVERLY
WWW.SPEEDBUMP.COM
DIST. BY CREATORS SYND.
DISTILL LIFE

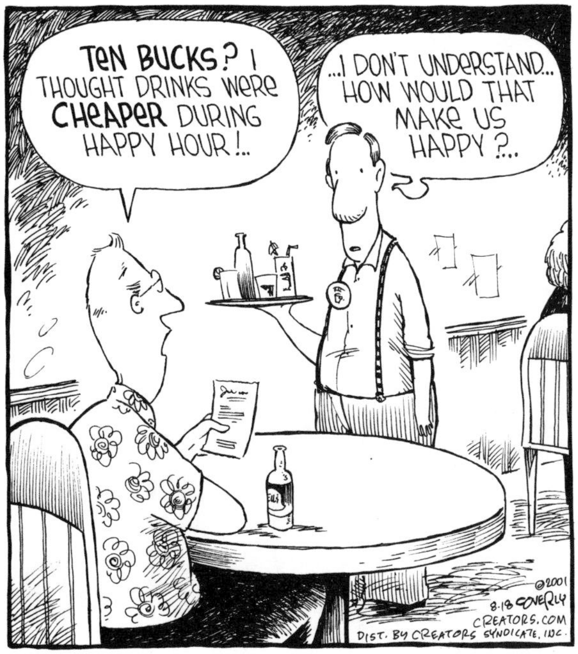

TEN BUCKS? I THOUGHT DRINKS WERE CHEAPER DURING HAPPY HOUR!..
...I DON'T UNDERSTAND... HOW WOULD THAT MAKE US HAPPY?..
©2001 8-18 COVERLY
CREATORS.COM
DIST. BY CREATORS SYNDICATE, INC.

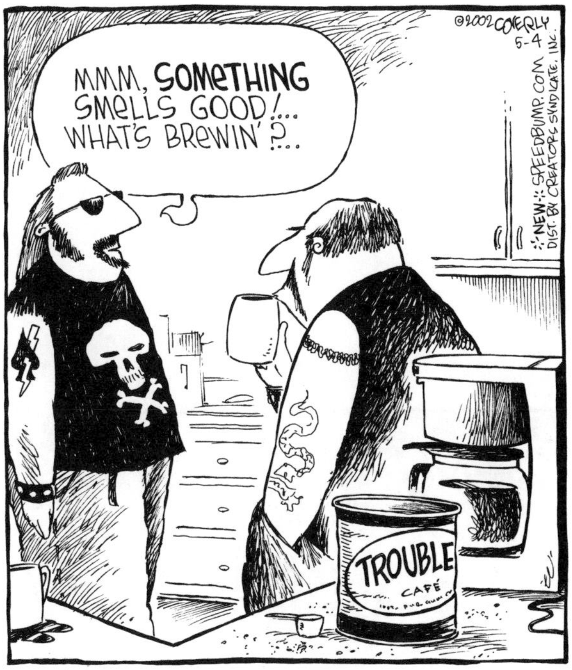

MMM, SOMETHING SMELLS GOOD!... WHAT'S BREWIN'?...
©2002 COVERLY 5-4
NEW: SPEEDBUMP.COM
DIST. BY CREATORS SYNDICATE, INC.
TROUBLE
CAFÉ

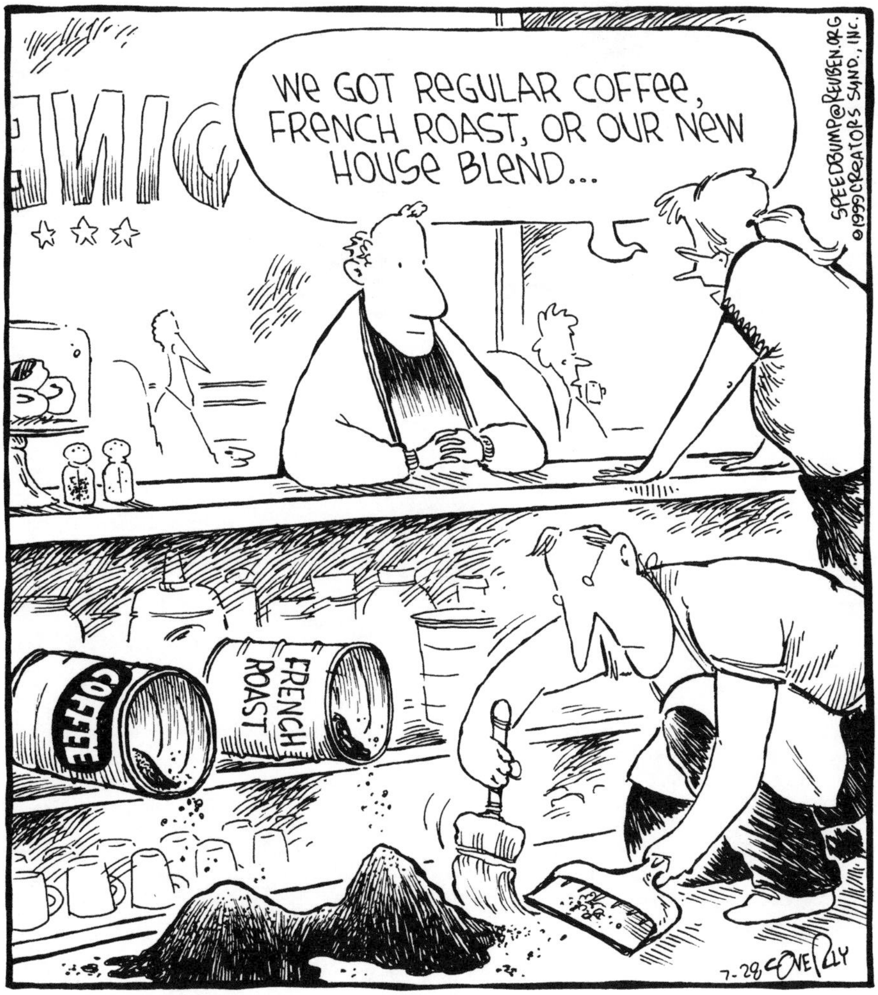

WE GOT REGULAR COFFEE, FRENCH ROAST, OR OUR NEW HOUSE BLEND...
SPEEDBUMP@REUBEN.ORG
©1999 CREATORS SYND., INC.
COFFEE
FRENCH ROAST
7-28 COVERLY

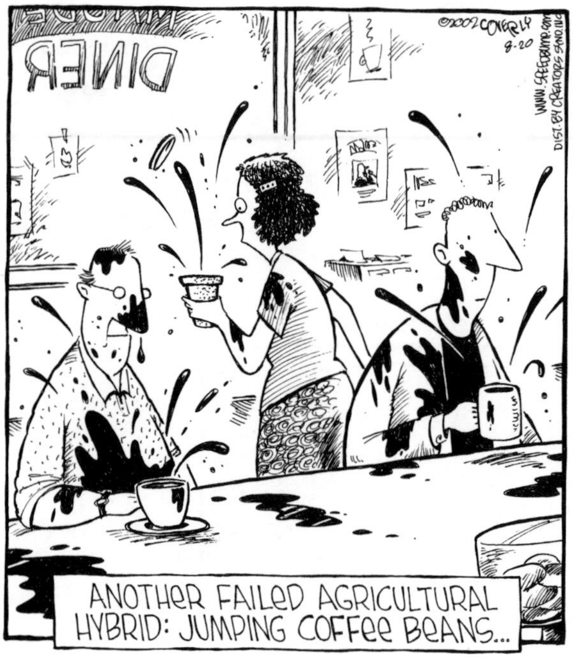
DINER
ANOTHER FAILED AGRICULTURAL HYBRID: JUMPING COFFEE BEANS...

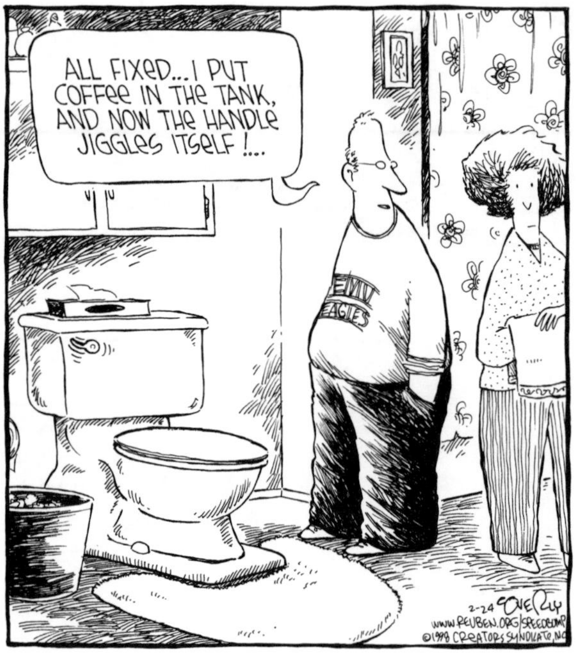
ALL FIXED... I PUT COFFEE IN THE TANK, AND NOW THE HANDLE JIGGLES ITSELF !...
EAGLES

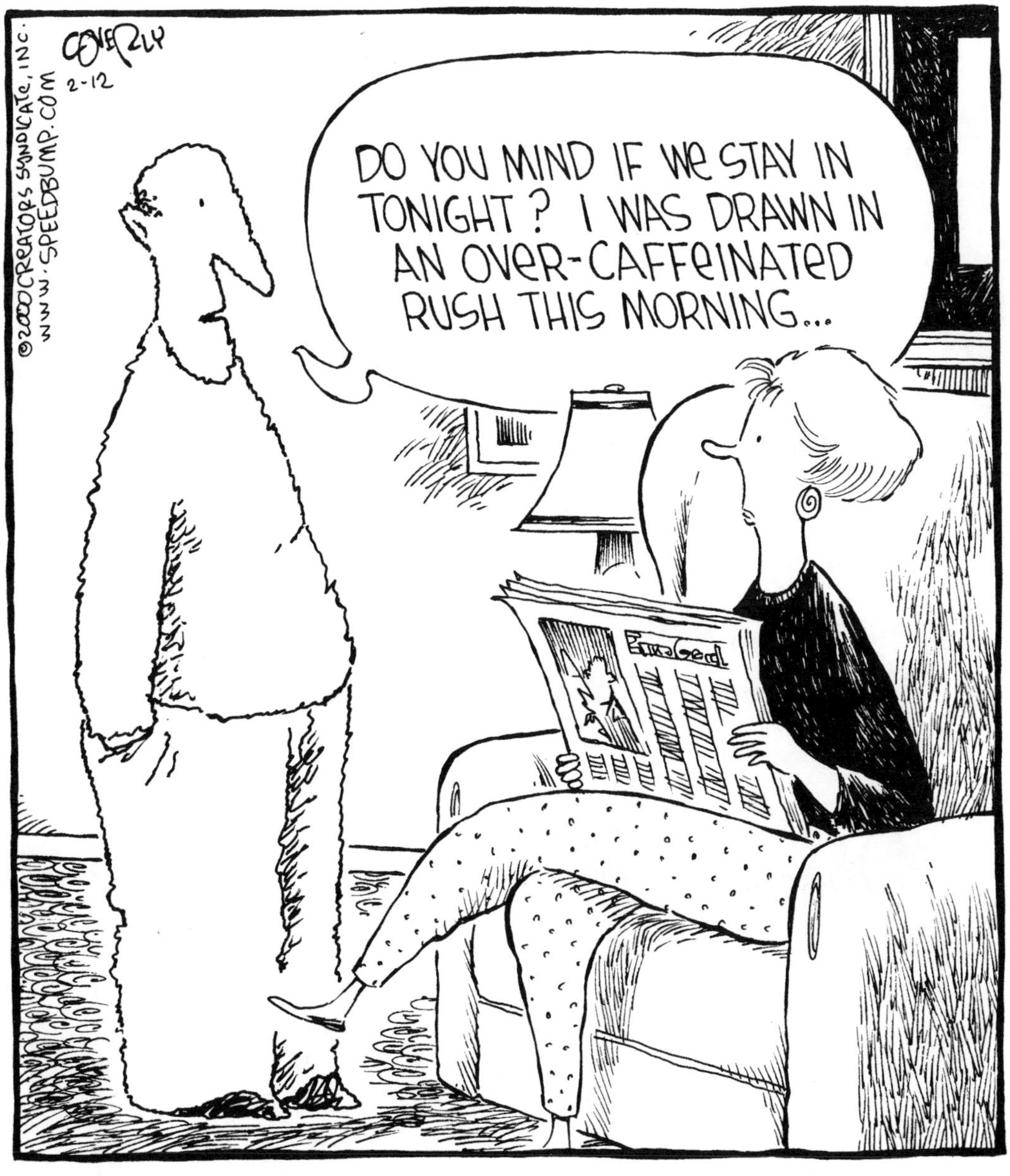
COVERLY
2-12
©2000 CREATORS SYNDICATE, INC.
WWW.SPEEDBUMP.COM
DO YOU MIND IF WE STAY IN TONIGHT? I WAS DRAWN IN AN OVER-CAFFEINATED RUSH THIS MORNING...

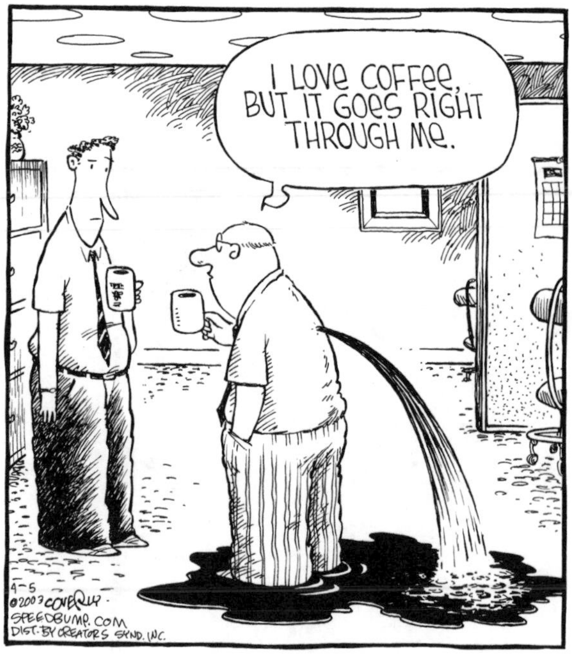
I LOVE COFFEE, BUT IT GOES RIGHT THROUGH ME.
4-5
©2003 COVERLY
SPEEDBUMP.COM
DIST. BY CREATORS SYND. INC.

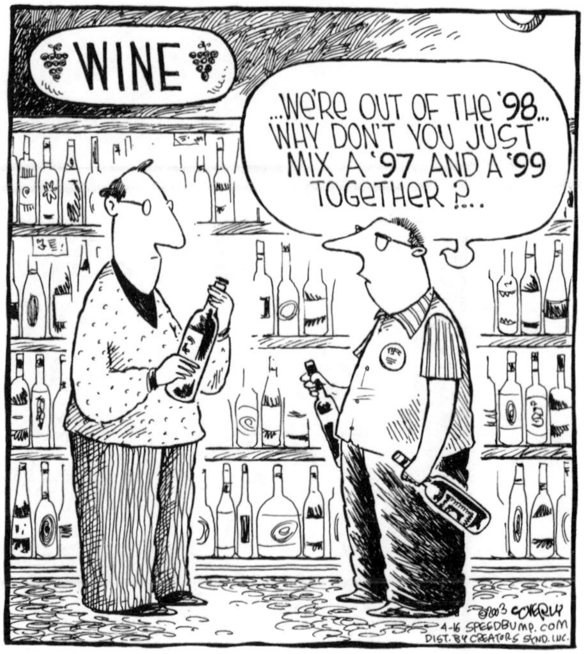
WINE
...WE'RE OUT OF THE '98... WHY DON'T YOU JUST MIX A '97 AND A '99 TOGETHER ?...
©2003 COVERLY
4-16 SPEEDBUMP.COM
DIST. BY CREATORS SYND. INC.

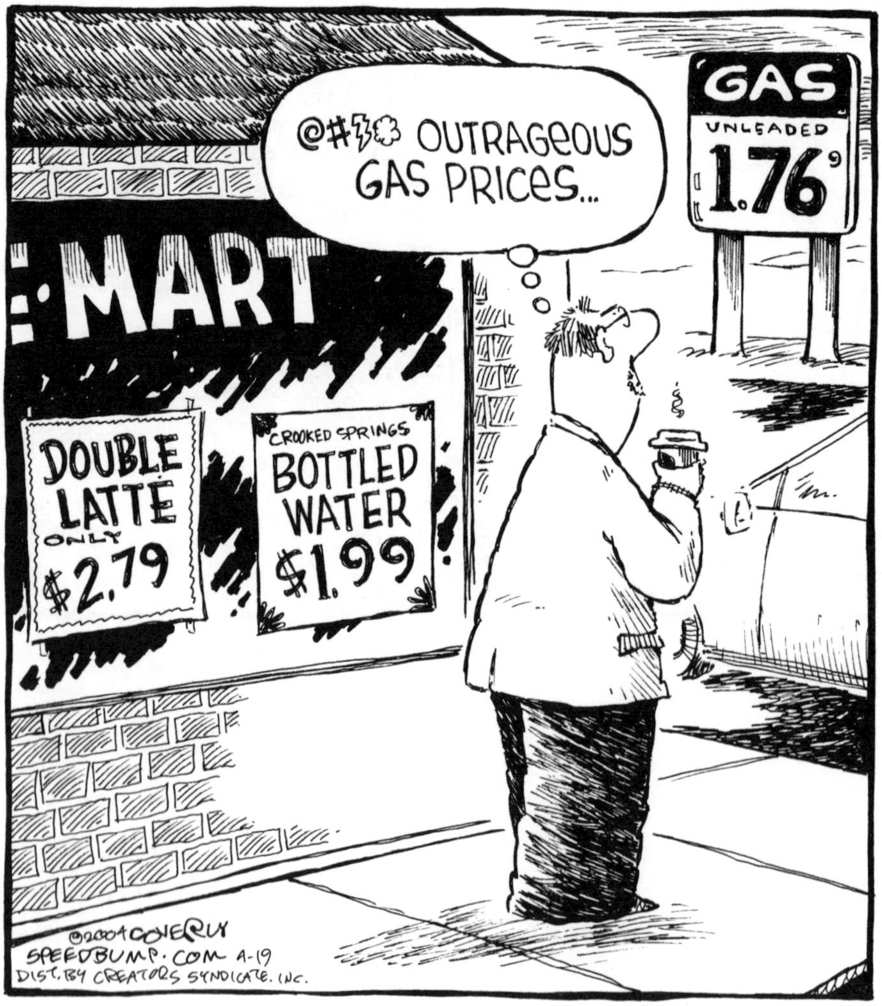
@#%@ OUTRAGEOUS GAS PRICES...
GAS
UNLEADED
1.76⁹
MART
DOUBLE LATTE ONLY $2.79
CROOKED SPRINGS BOTTLED WATER $1.99
©2004 COVERLY
SPEEDBUMP.COM 4-19
DIST. BY CREATORS SYNDICATE. INC.

©1999 CREATORS SYND., INC.
WWW.CREATORS.COM
COVERLY 6-5
WOW... I CAN'T WAIT TO HEAR **THEIR** PUNCHLINE!...
BAR

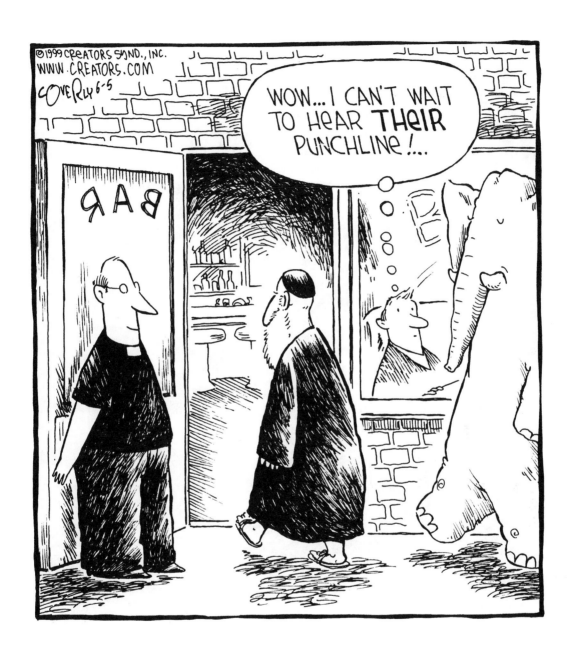

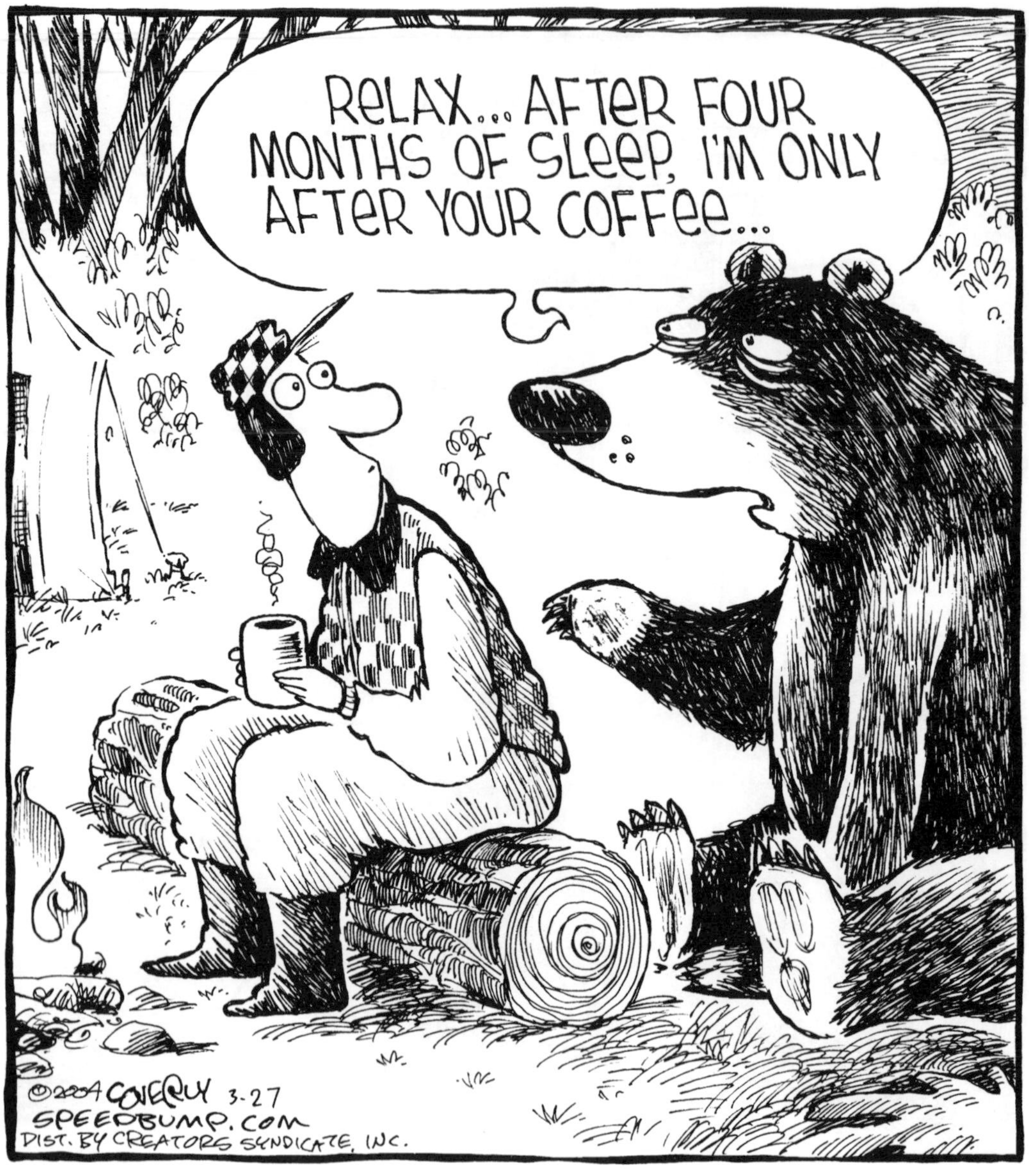
RELAX... AFTER FOUR MONTHS OF SLEEP, I'M ONLY AFTER YOUR COFFEE...
©2004 COVERLY 3-27
SPEEDBUMP.COM
DIST. BY CREATORS SYNDICATE, INC.

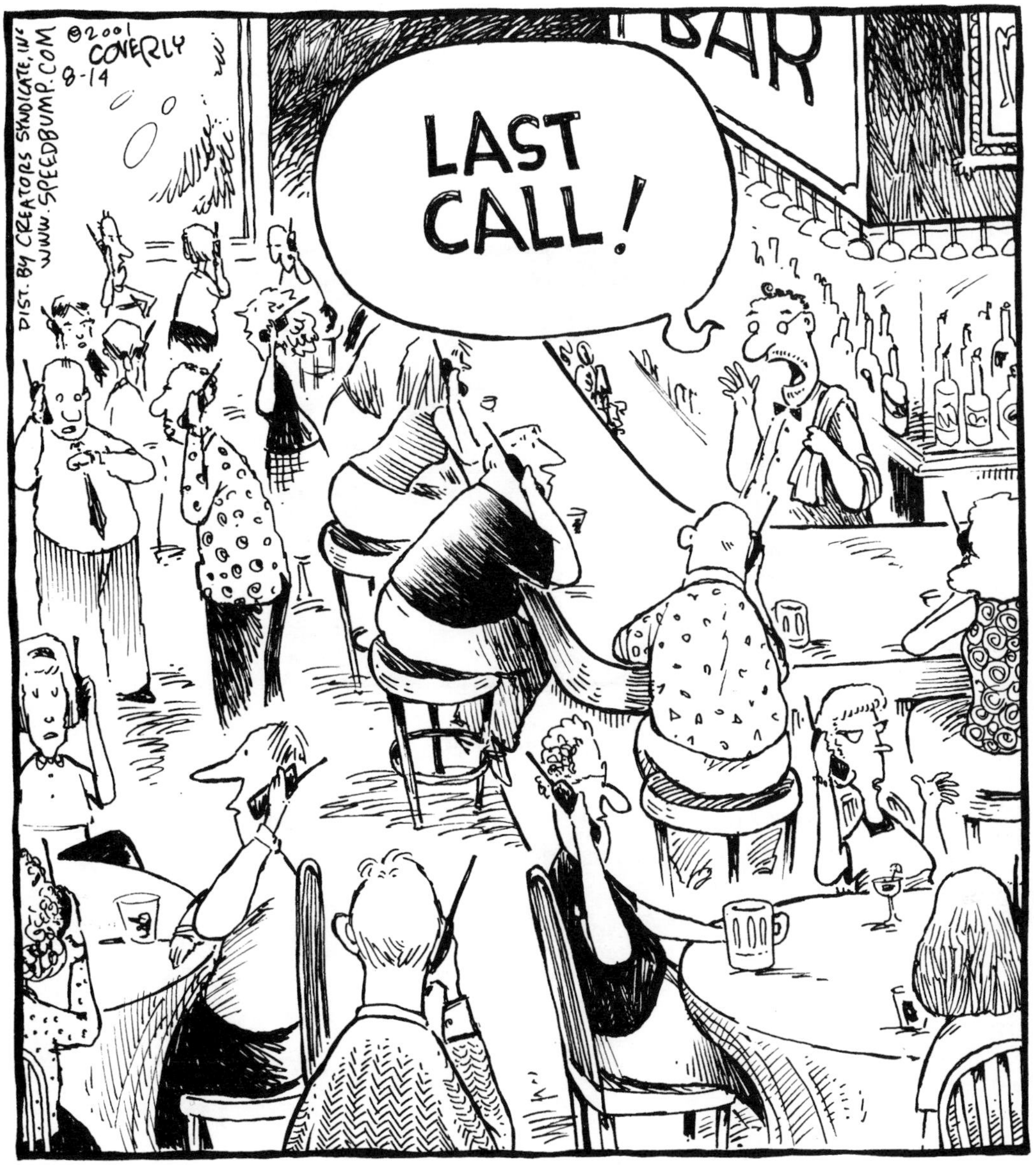

LAST CALL!
BAR
©2001 COVERLY 8-14
DIST. BY CREATORS SYNDICATE, INC
WWW.SPEEDBUMP.COM

Nuts & Dolts

Dave Coverly

"November 27, 1970: The author and his sister, Cathy,
descend slowly, almost imperceptibly, into madness."

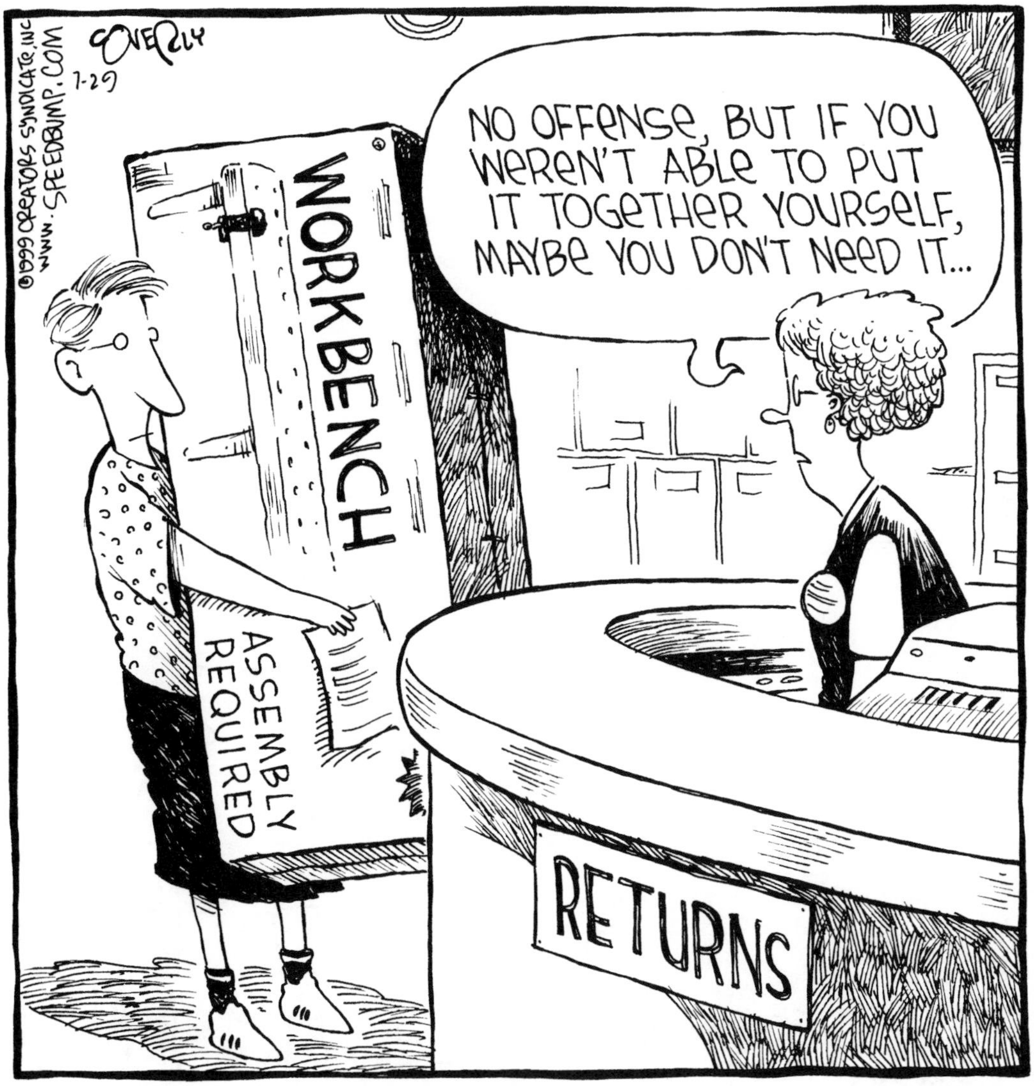
©1999 CREATORS SYNDICATE, INC
WWW.SPEEDBUMP.COM
COVERLY
7-29
NO OFFENSE, BUT IF YOU WEREN'T ABLE TO PUT IT TOGETHER YOURSELF, MAYBE YOU DON'T NEED IT...
WORKBENCH
ASSEMBLY REQUIRED
RETURNS

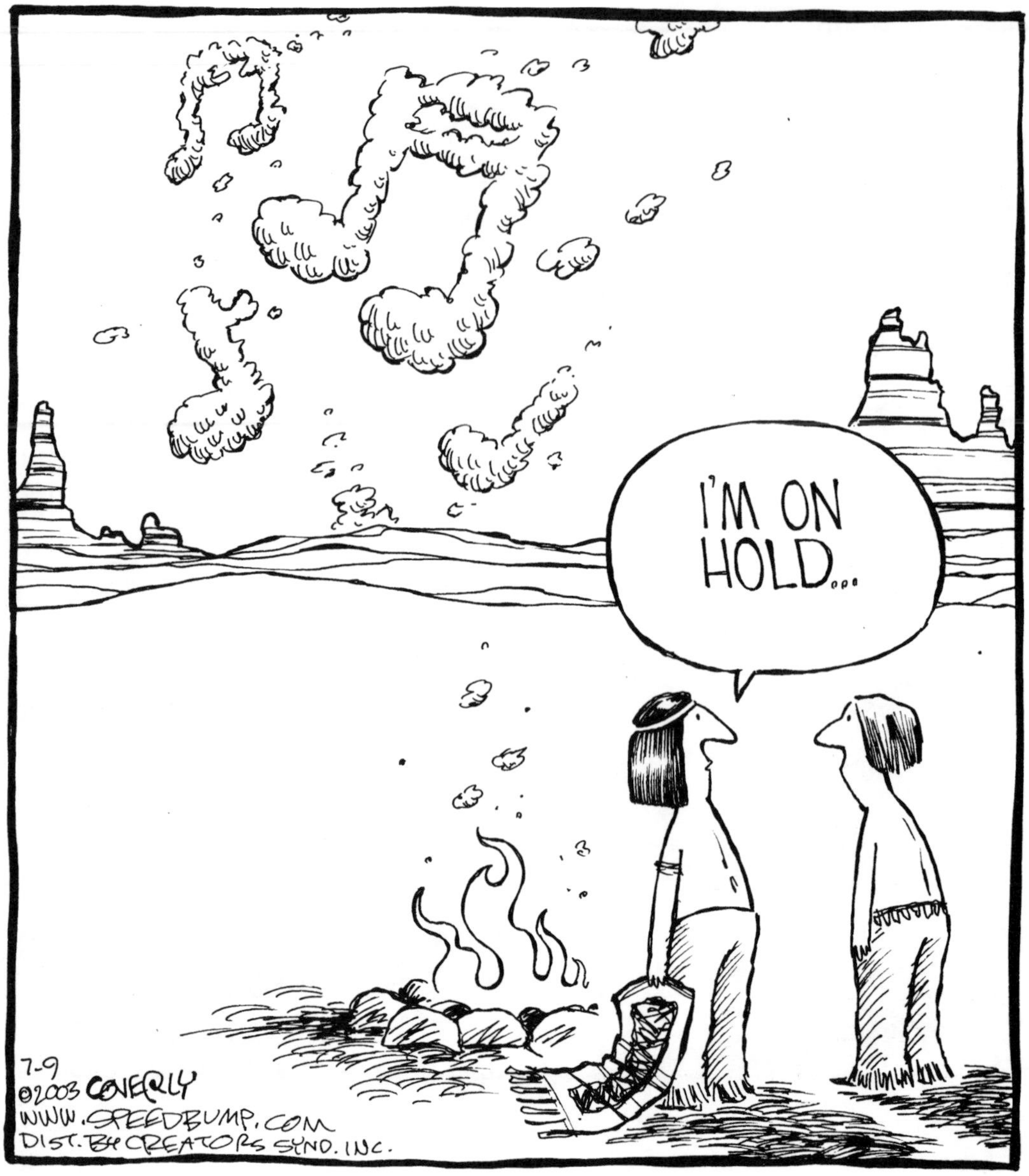
I'M ON HOLD...
7-9
©2003 COVERLY
WWW.SPEEDBUMP.COM
DIST. BY CREATORS SYND. INC.

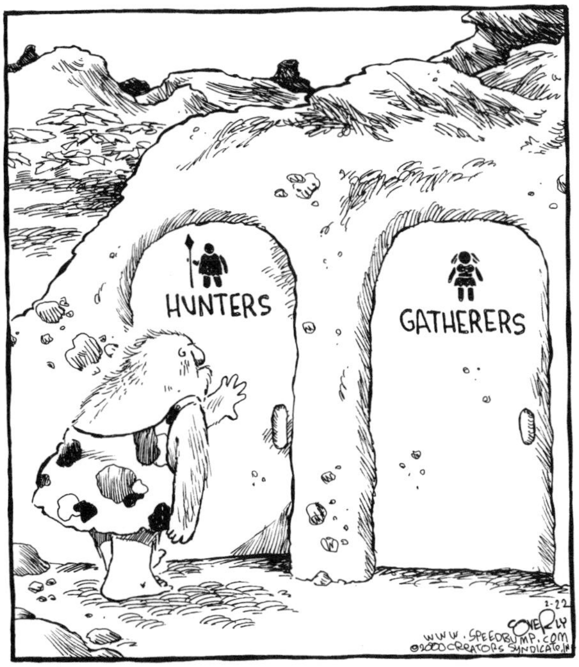
HUNTERS
GATHERERS
2-22
COVERLY
WWW.SPEEDBUMP.COM
©2000 CREATORS SYNDICATE INC

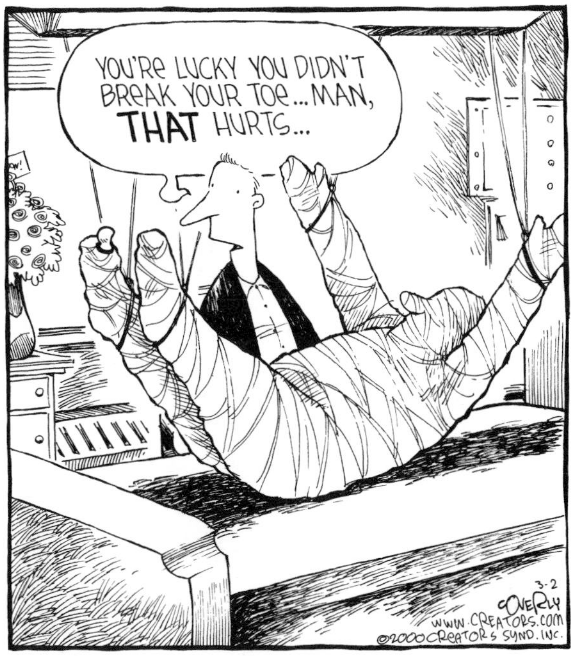
YOU'RE LUCKY YOU DIDN'T BREAK YOUR TOE...MAN, **THAT** HURTS...
3-2
COVERLY
WWW.CREATORS.COM
©2000 CREATORS SYND. INC.

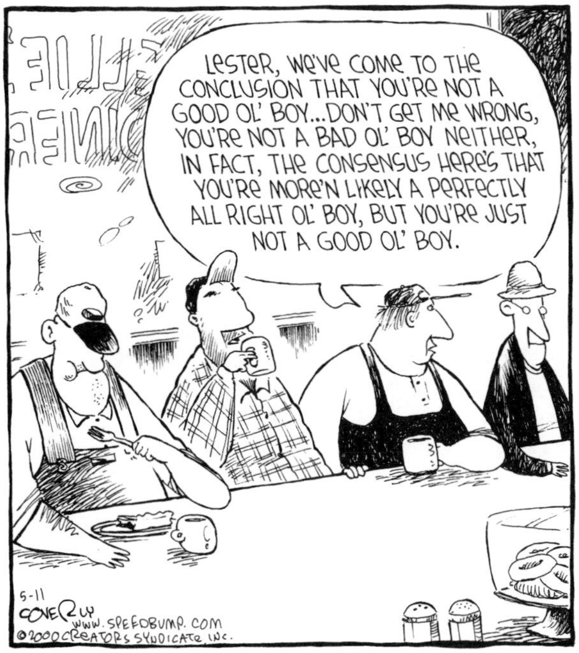
LESTER, WE'VE COME TO THE CONCLUSION THAT YOU'RE NOT A GOOD OL' BOY...DON'T GET ME WRONG, YOU'RE NOT A BAD OL' BOY NEITHER, IN FACT, THE CONSENSUS HERE'S THAT YOU'RE MORE'N LIKELY A PERFECTLY ALL RIGHT OL' BOY, BUT YOU'RE JUST NOT A GOOD OL' BOY.
5-11
COVERLY
WWW.SPEEDBUMP.COM
©2000 CREATORS SYNDICATE INC.

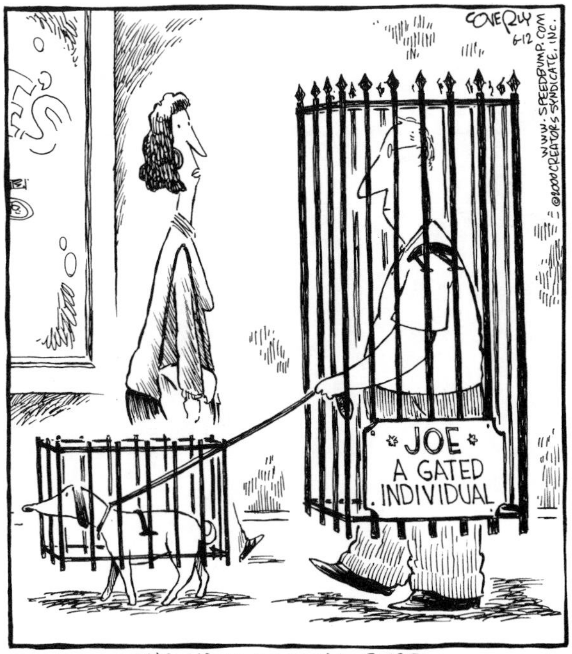
COVERLY
6-12
WWW.SPEEDBUMP.COM
©2000 CREATORS SYNDICATE, INC.
JOE
A GATED INDIVIDUAL

THE NEXT LOGICAL STEP...

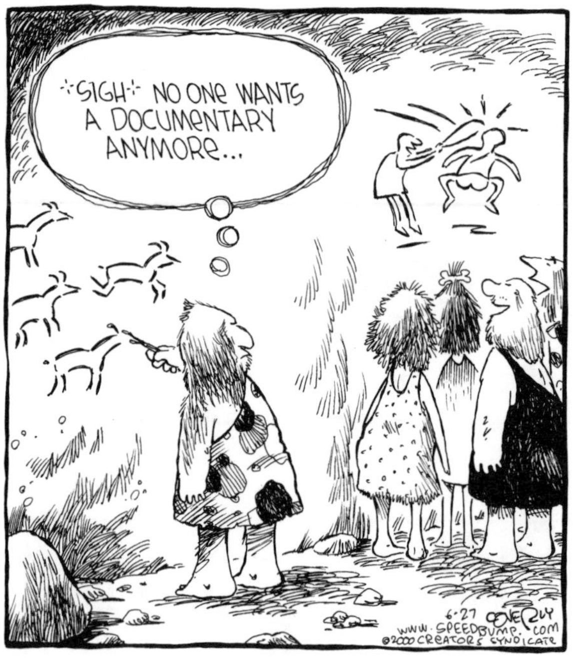
·SIGH· NO ONE WANTS A DOCUMENTARY ANYMORE...
6-27 COVERLY
WWW.SPEEDBUMP.COM
©2000 CREATORS SYNDICATE

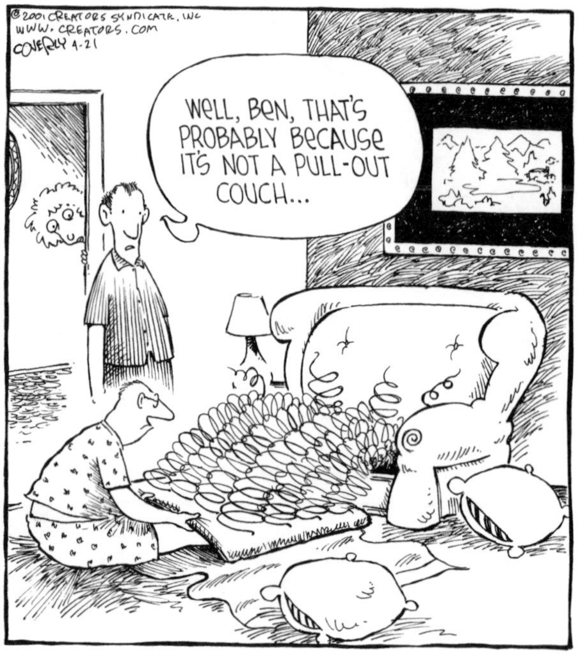
©2001 CREATORS SYNDICATE, INC
WWW.CREATORS.COM
COVERLY 4-21
WELL, BEN, THAT'S PROBABLY BECAUSE IT'S NOT A PULL-OUT COUCH...

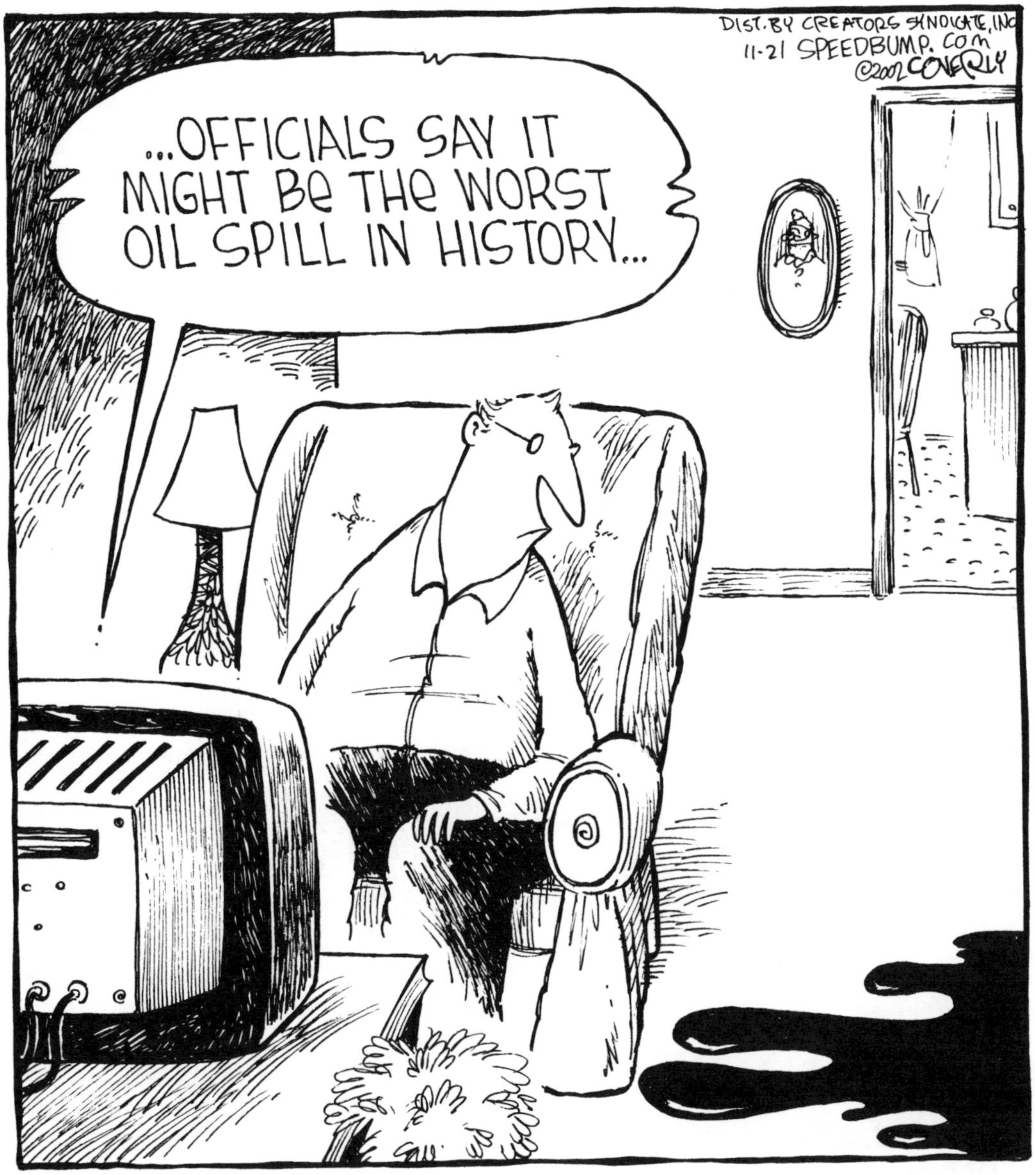
DIST. BY CREATORS SYNDICATE, INC
11-21 SPEEDBUMP.COM
©2002 COVERLY
...OFFICIALS SAY IT MIGHT BE THE WORST OIL SPILL IN HISTORY...

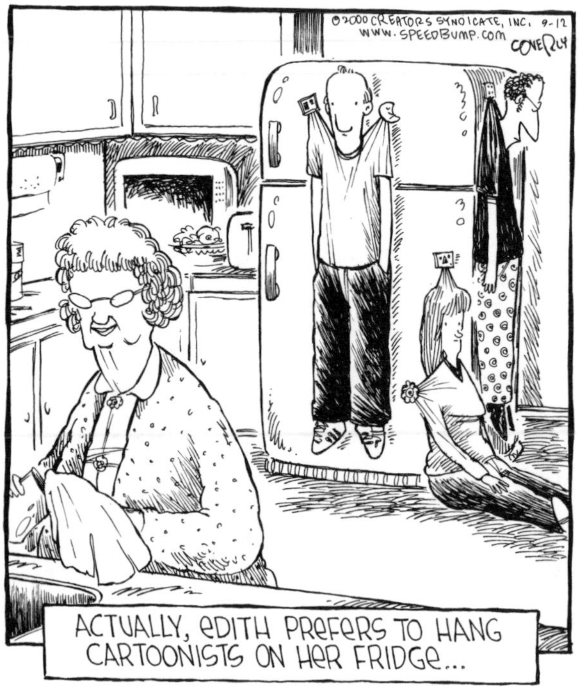
©2000 CREATORS SYNDICATE, INC. 9-12
WWW.SPEEDBUMP.COM
COVERLY
ACTUALLY, EDITH PREFERS TO HANG CARTOONISTS ON HER FRIDGE...

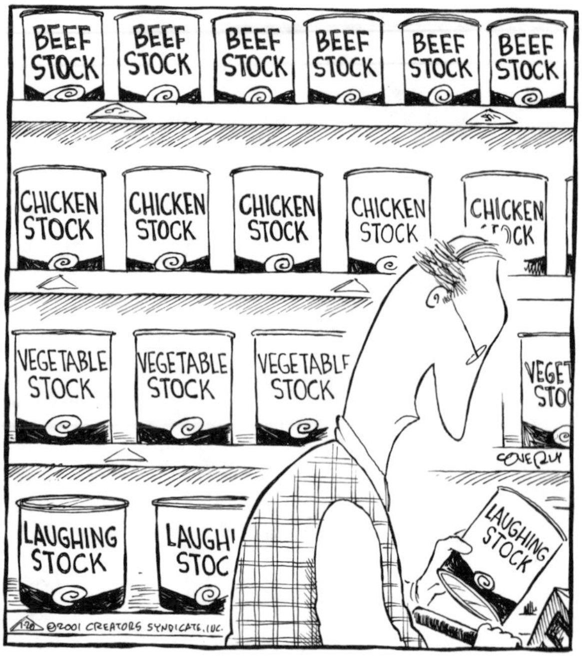
BEEF STOCK
CHICKEN STOCK
VEGETABLE STOCK
LAUGHING STOCK
COVERLY
©2001 CREATORS SYNDICATE, INC.

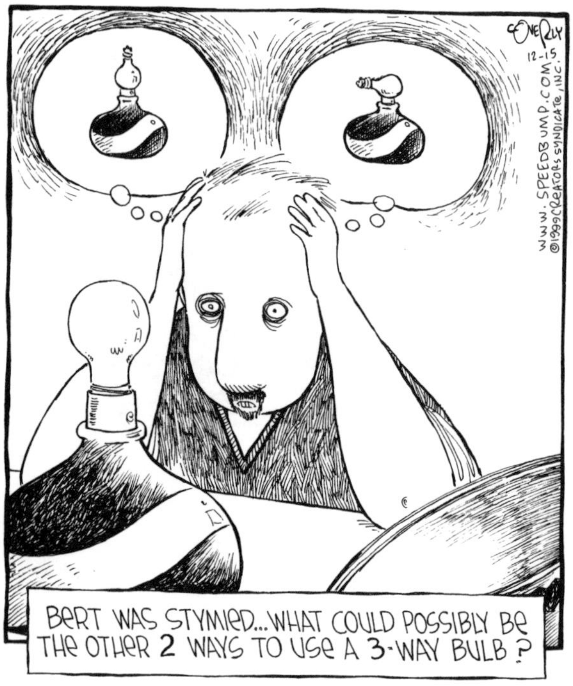
COVERLY
12-15
WWW.SPEEDBUMP.COM
©1999 CREATORS SYNDICATE, INC.
BERT WAS STYMIED...WHAT COULD POSSIBLY BE THE OTHER 2 WAYS TO USE A 3-WAY BULB ?

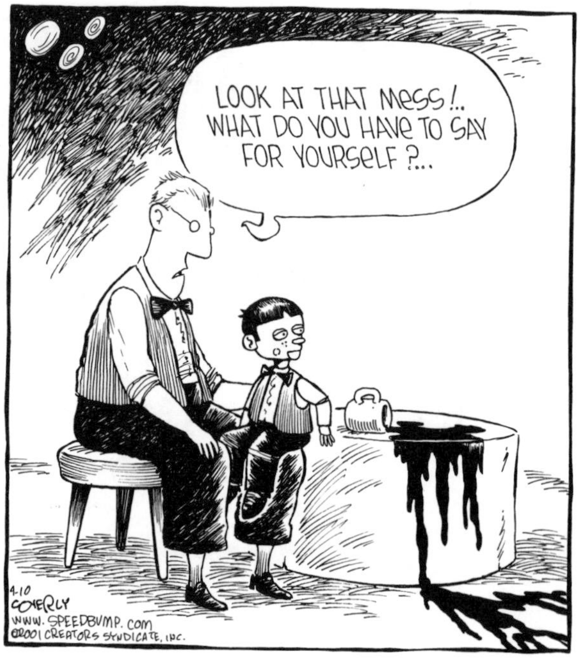
LOOK AT THAT MESS!.. WHAT DO YOU HAVE TO SAY FOR YOURSELF ?...
4-10
COVERLY
WWW.SPEEDBUMP.COM
©2001 CREATORS SYNDICATE, INC.

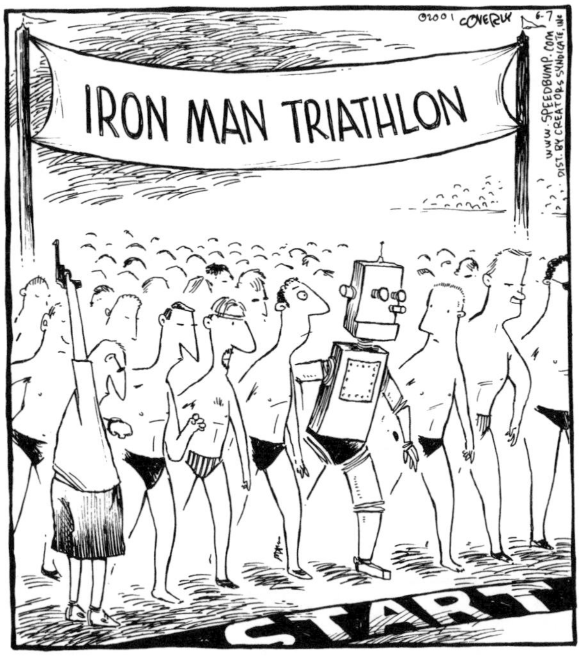
IRON MAN TRIATHLON
START
©2001 COVERLY 6-7
WWW.SPEEDBUMP.COM
DIST. BY CREATORS SYNDICATE, INC

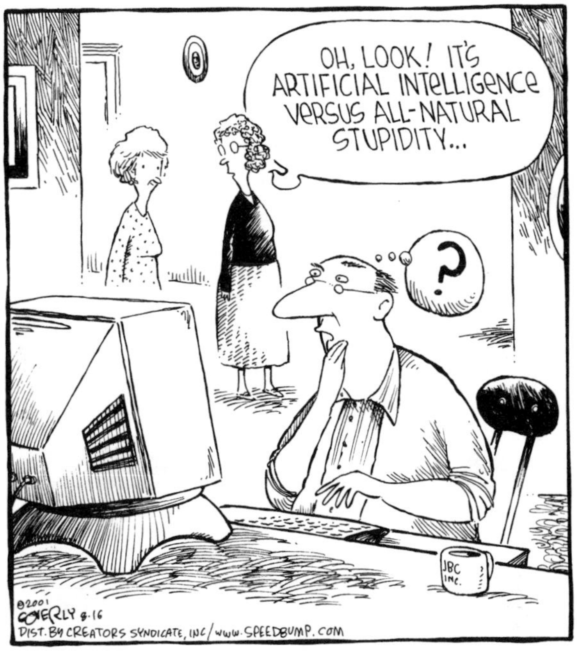
OH, LOOK! IT'S ARTIFICIAL INTELLIGENCE VERSUS ALL-NATURAL STUPIDITY...
?
JBC INC.
©2001 COVERLY 8-16
DIST. BY CREATORS SYNDICATE, INC/WWW.SPEEDBUMP.COM

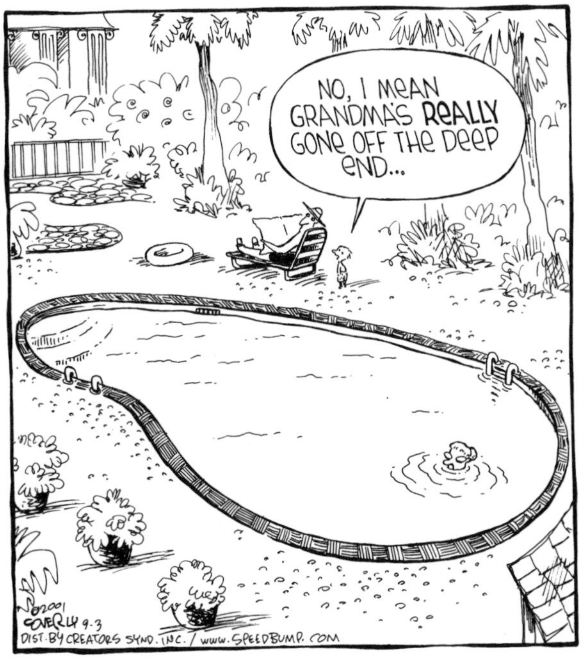
NO, I MEAN GRANDMA'S REALLY GONE OFF THE DEEP END...
©2001 COVERLY 9-3
DIST. BY CREATORS SYND. INC. / WWW.SPEEDBUMP.COM

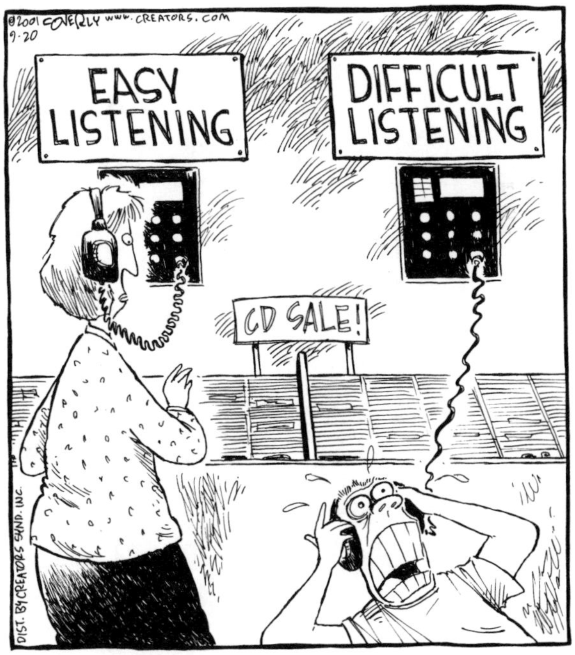
©2001 COVERLY WWW.CREATORS.COM 9-20
EASY LISTENING
DIFFICULT LISTENING
CD SALE!
DIST. BY CREATORS SYND. INC.

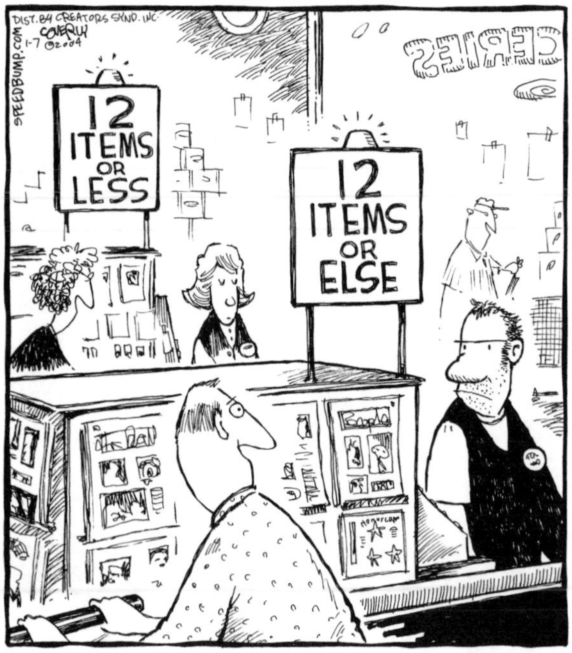
DIST. BY CREATORS SYND. INC.
COVERLY 1-7 ©2004
SPEEDBUMP.COM
12 ITEMS OR LESS
12 ITEMS OR ELSE

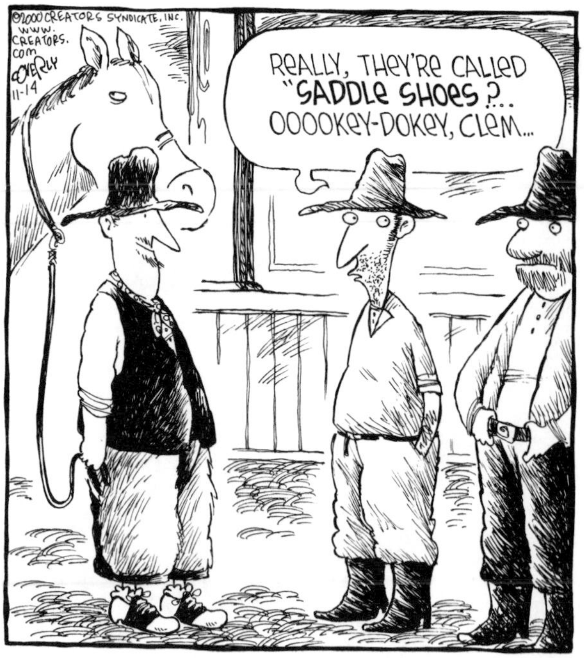
©2000 CREATORS SYNDICATE, INC. WWW.CREATORS.COM
COVERLY 11-14
REALLY, THEY'RE CALLED "SADDLE SHOES"?... OOOOKEY-DOKEY, CLEM...

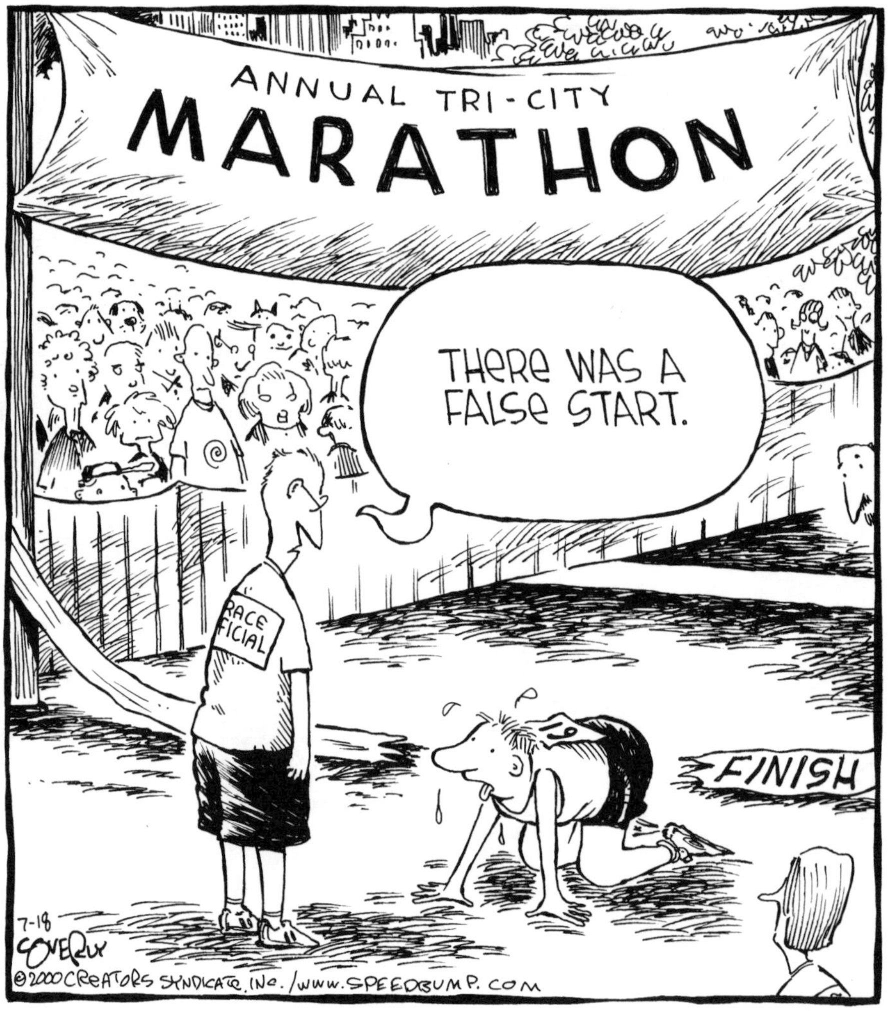
ANNUAL TRI-CITY
MARATHON
THERE WAS A FALSE START.
RACE OFFICIAL
FINISH
7-18
COVERLY
©2000 CREATORS SYNDICATE, INC. / WWW.SPEEDBUMP.COM

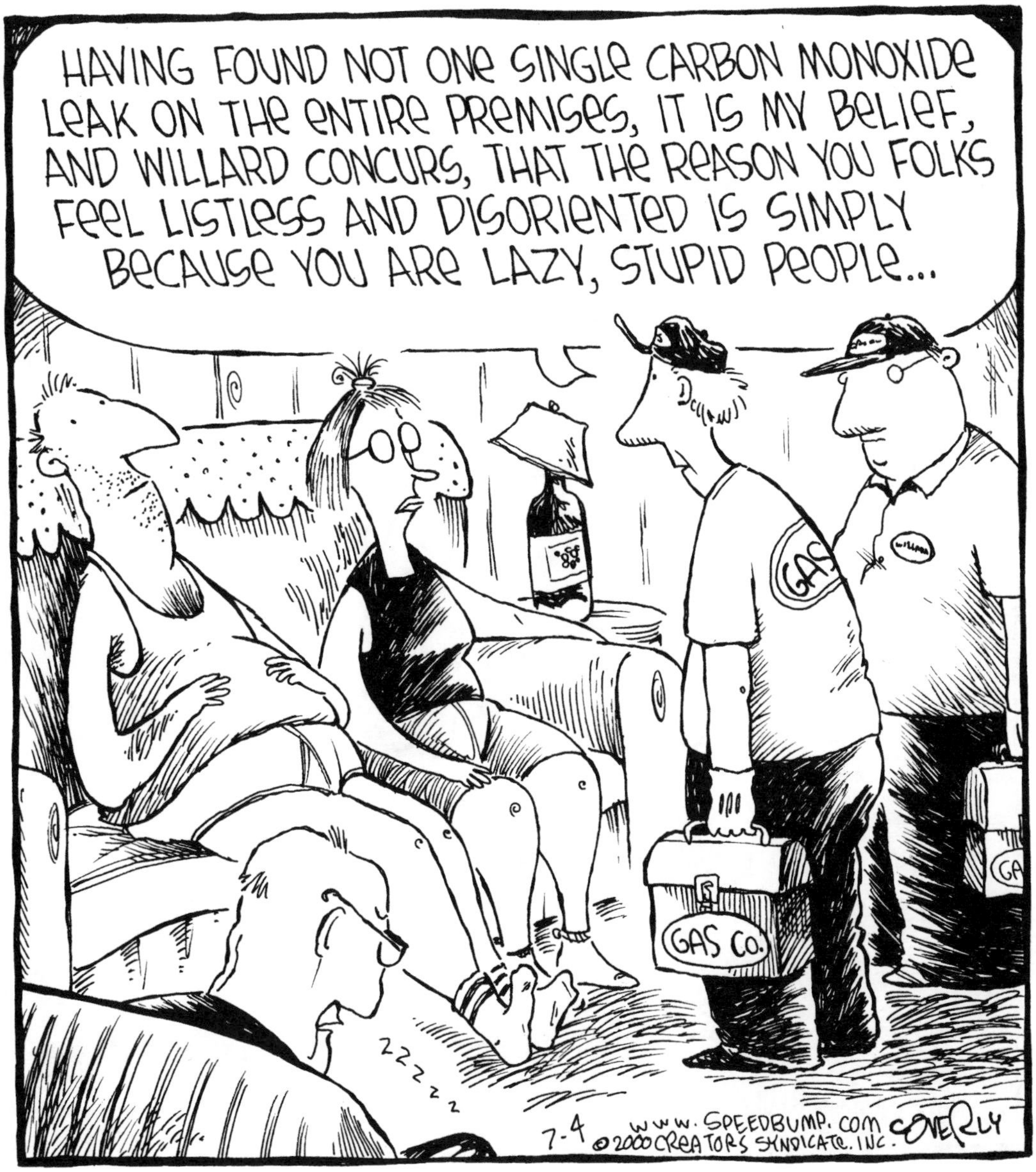
HAVING FOUND NOT ONE SINGLE CARBON MONOXIDE LEAK ON THE ENTIRE PREMISES, IT IS MY BELIEF, AND WILLARD CONCURS, THAT THE REASON YOU FOLKS FEEL LISTLESS AND DISORIENTED IS SIMPLY BECAUSE YOU ARE LAZY, STUPID PEOPLE...
GAS
GAS CO.
ZZZZZ
7-4
www.SPEEDBUMP.com
©2000 CREATORS SYNDICATE, INC.
COVERLY

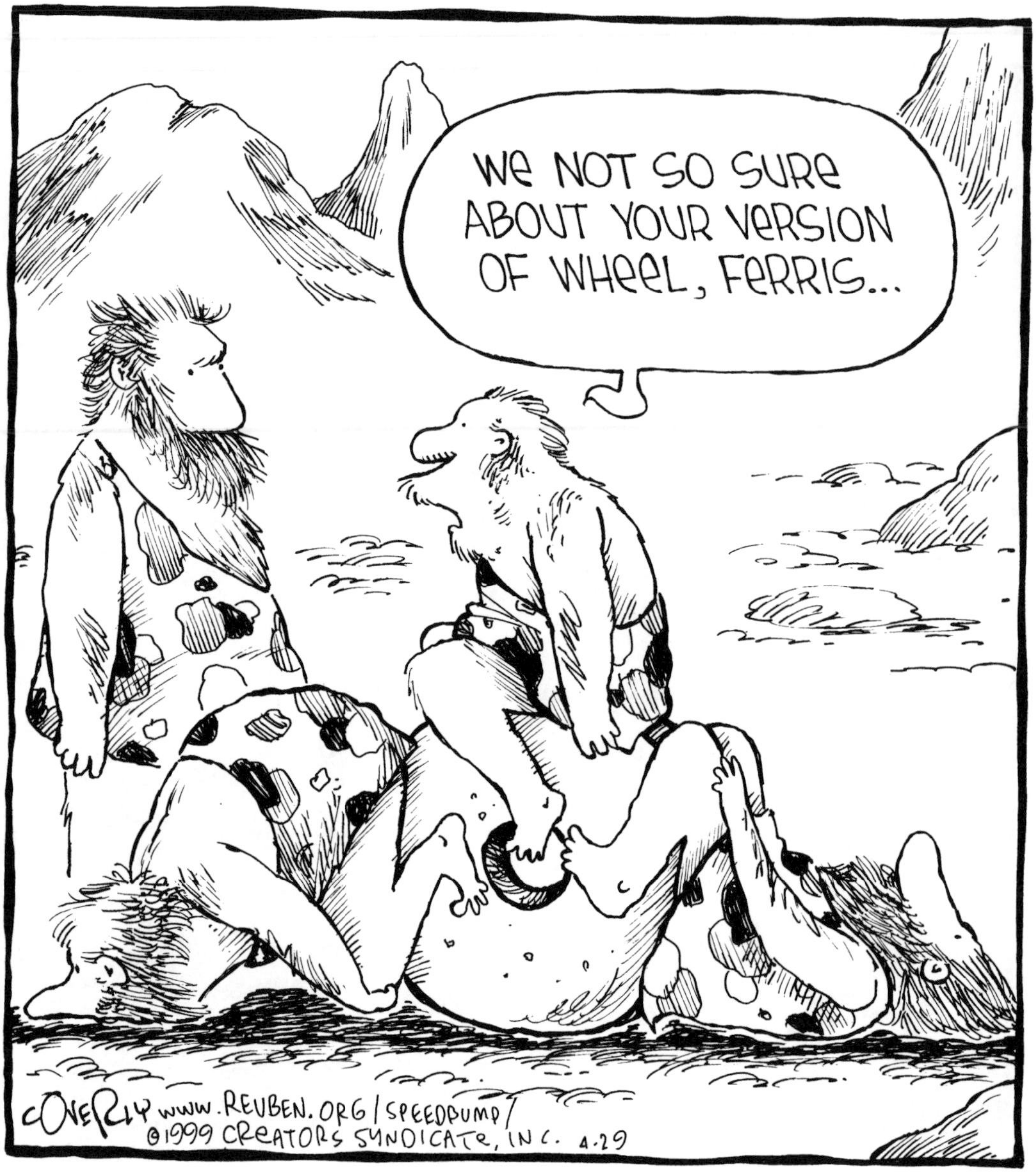
WE NOT SO SURE ABOUT YOUR VERSION OF WHEEL, FERRIS...
COVERLY www.REUBEN.ORG/SPEEDBUMP/
©1999 CREATORS SYNDICATE, INC. 4-29

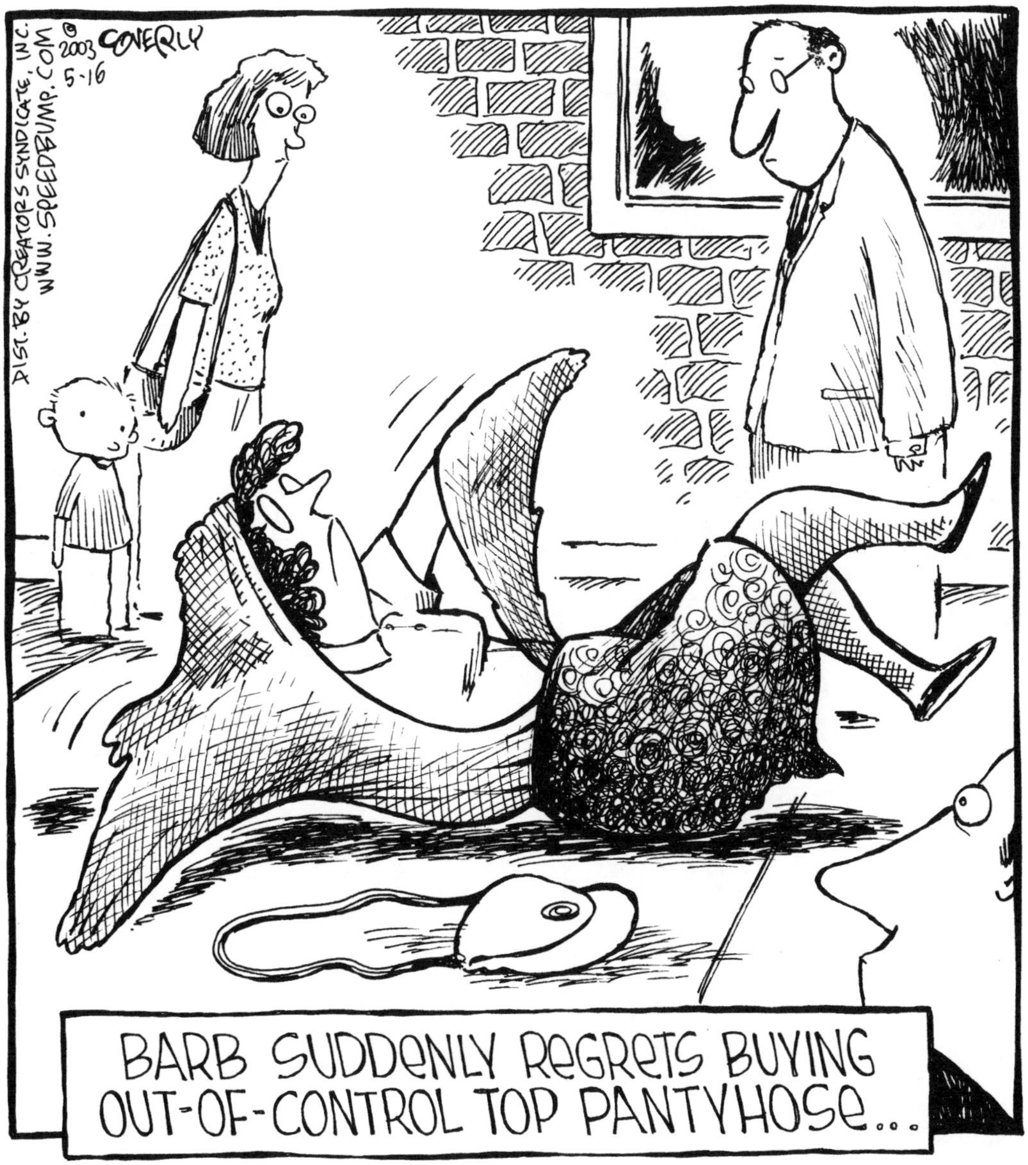
© 2003 COVERLY 5-16
DIST. BY CREATORS SYNDICATE, INC.
WWW.SPEEDBUMP.COM
BARB SUDDENLY REGRETS BUYING OUT-OF-CONTROL TOP PANTYHOSE...

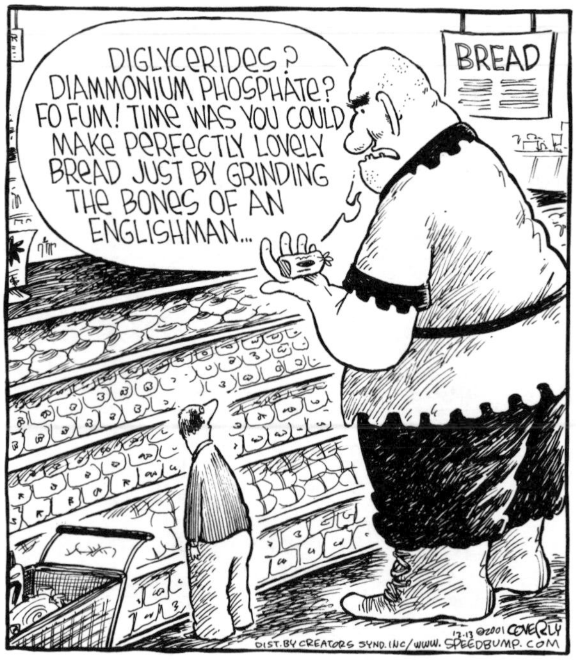
DIGLYCERIDES?
DIAMMONIUM PHOSPHATE?
FO FUM! TIME WAS YOU COULD
MAKE PERFECTLY LOVELY
BREAD JUST BY GRINDING
THE BONES OF AN
ENGLISHMAN...
BREAD
12-13 ©2001 COVERLY
DIST. BY CREATORS SYND. INC/WWW.SPEEDBUMP.COM

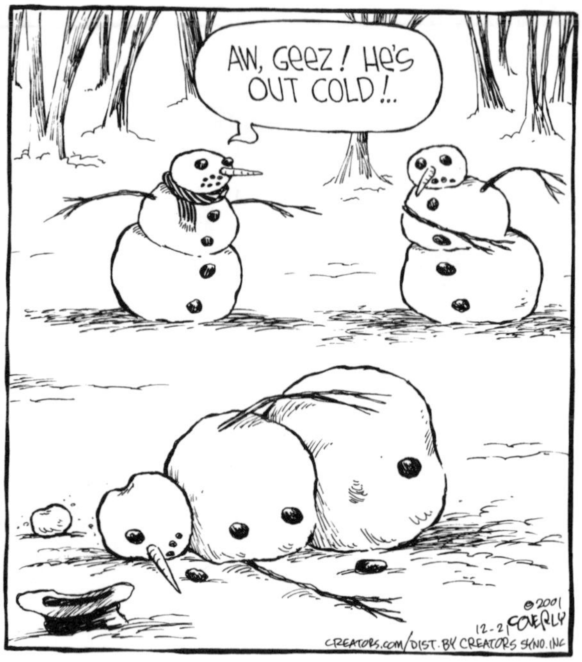
AW, GEEZ! HE'S
OUT COLD!..
©2001
12-2 COVERLY
CREATORS.COM/DIST. BY CREATORS SYND. INC

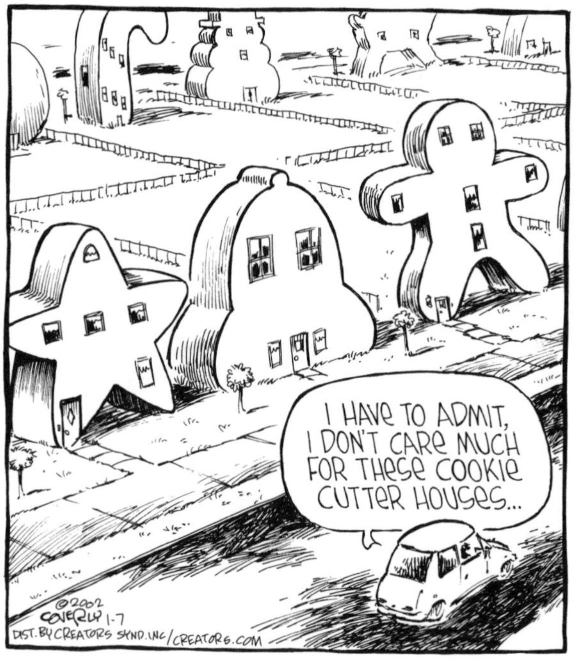
I HAVE TO ADMIT,
I DON'T CARE MUCH
FOR THESE COOKIE
CUTTER HOUSES...
©2002
COVERLY 1-7
DIST. BY CREATORS SYND. INC/CREATORS.COM

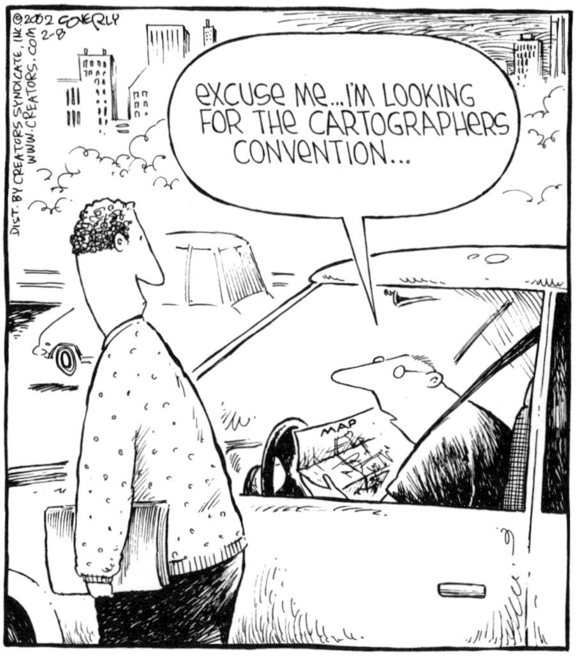
EXCUSE ME...I'M LOOKING
FOR THE CARTOGRAPHERS
CONVENTION...
MAP
©2002 COVERLY
2-8
DIST. BY CREATORS SYNDICATE, INC
WWW.CREATORS.COM

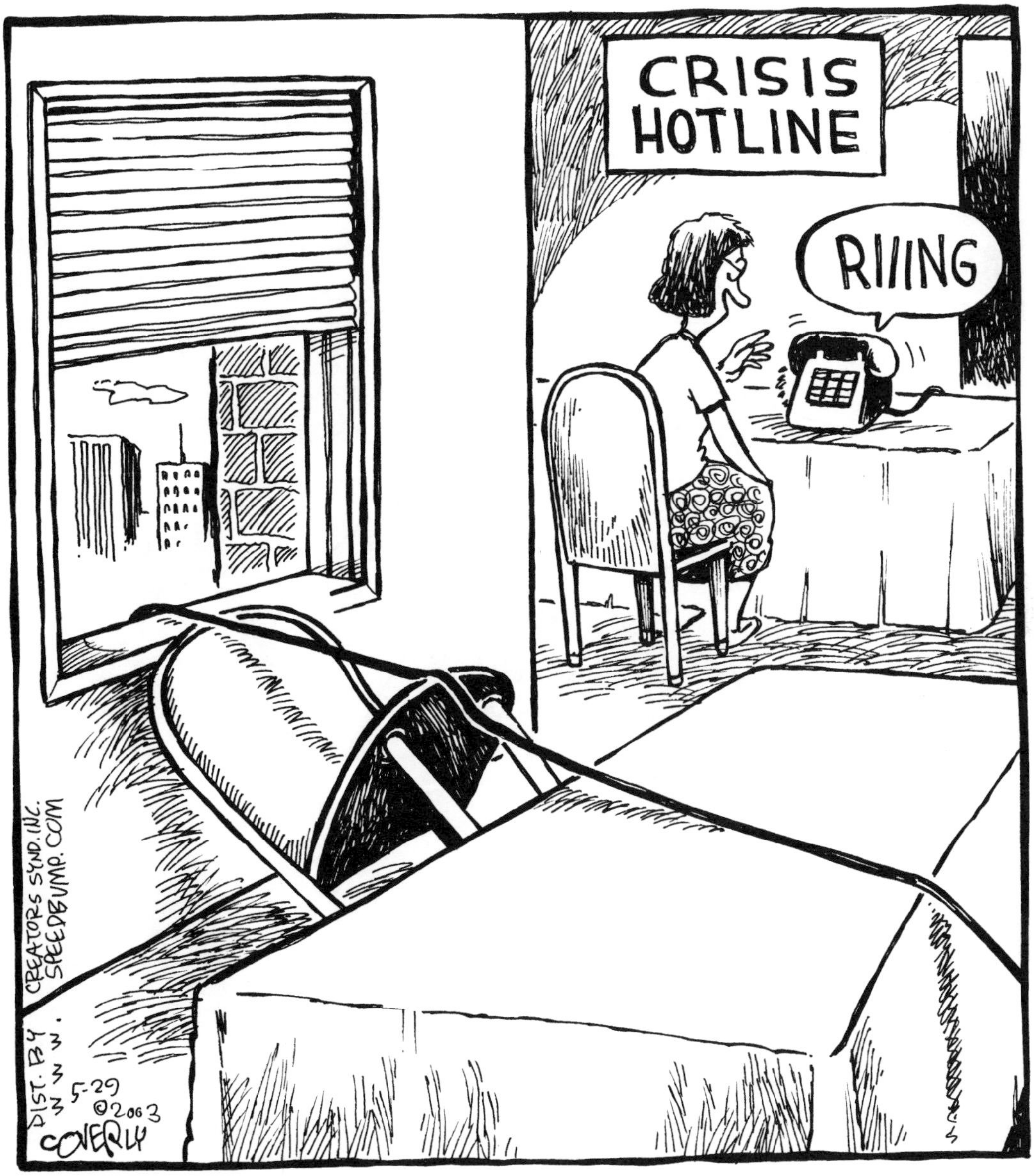
CRISIS
HOTLINE
RIIING
DIST. BY CREATORS SYND. INC.
WWW. SPEEDBUMP.COM
5-29 ©2003
COVERLY

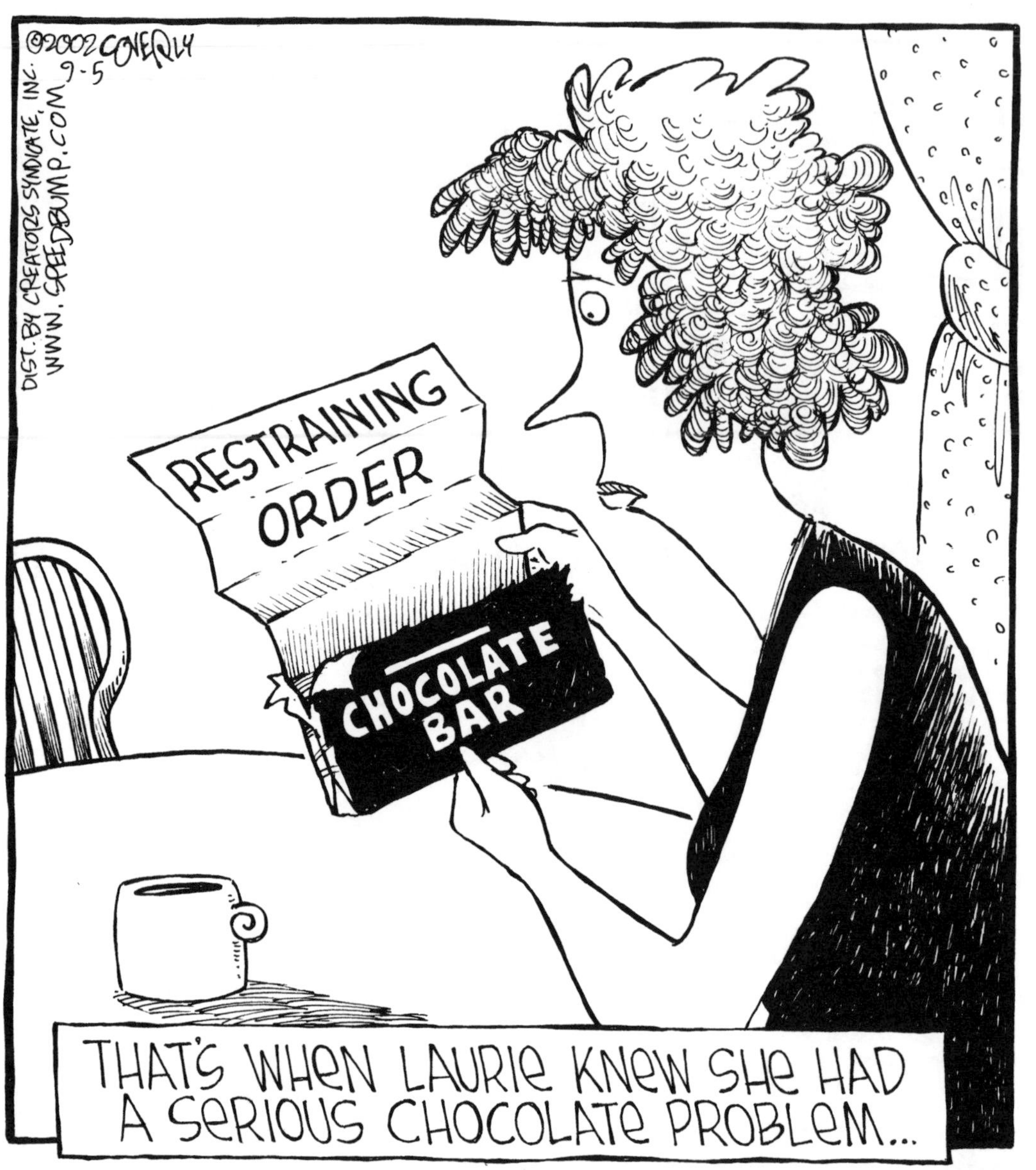
©2002 COVERLY
9-5
DIST. BY CREATORS SYNDICATE, INC.
WWW.SPEEDBUMP.COM
RESTRAINING ORDER
CHOCOLATE BAR
THAT'S WHEN LAURIE KNEW SHE HAD A SERIOUS CHOCOLATE PROBLEM...

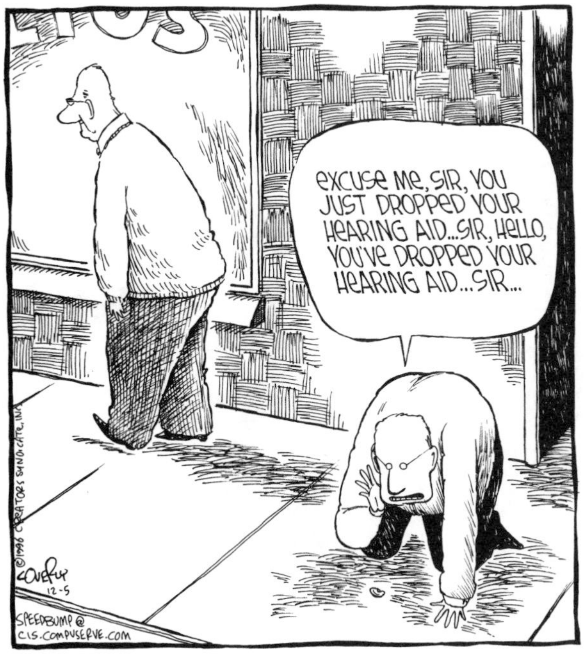
EXCUSE ME, SIR, YOU JUST DROPPED YOUR HEARING AID...SIR, HELLO, YOU'VE DROPPED YOUR HEARING AID...SIR...
SPEEDBUMP@ CIS.COMPUSERVE.COM

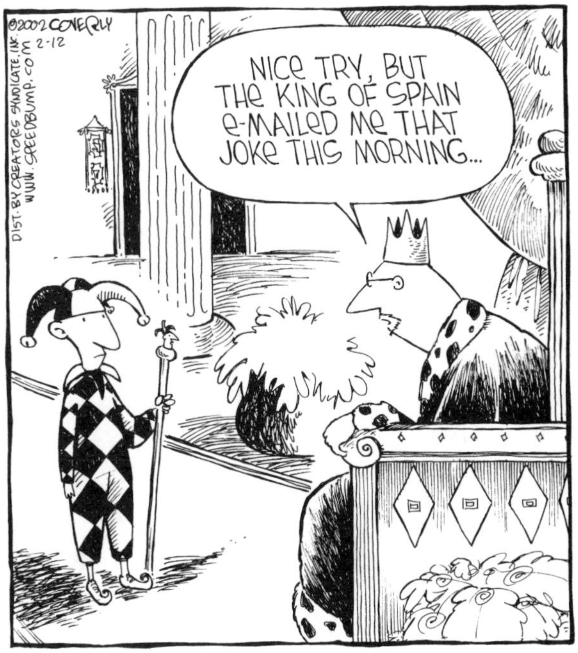
©2002 COVERLY 2-12
DIST. BY CREATORS SYNDICATE, INC. WWW.SPEEDBUMP.COM
NICE TRY, BUT THE KING OF SPAIN E-MAILED ME THAT JOKE THIS MORNING...

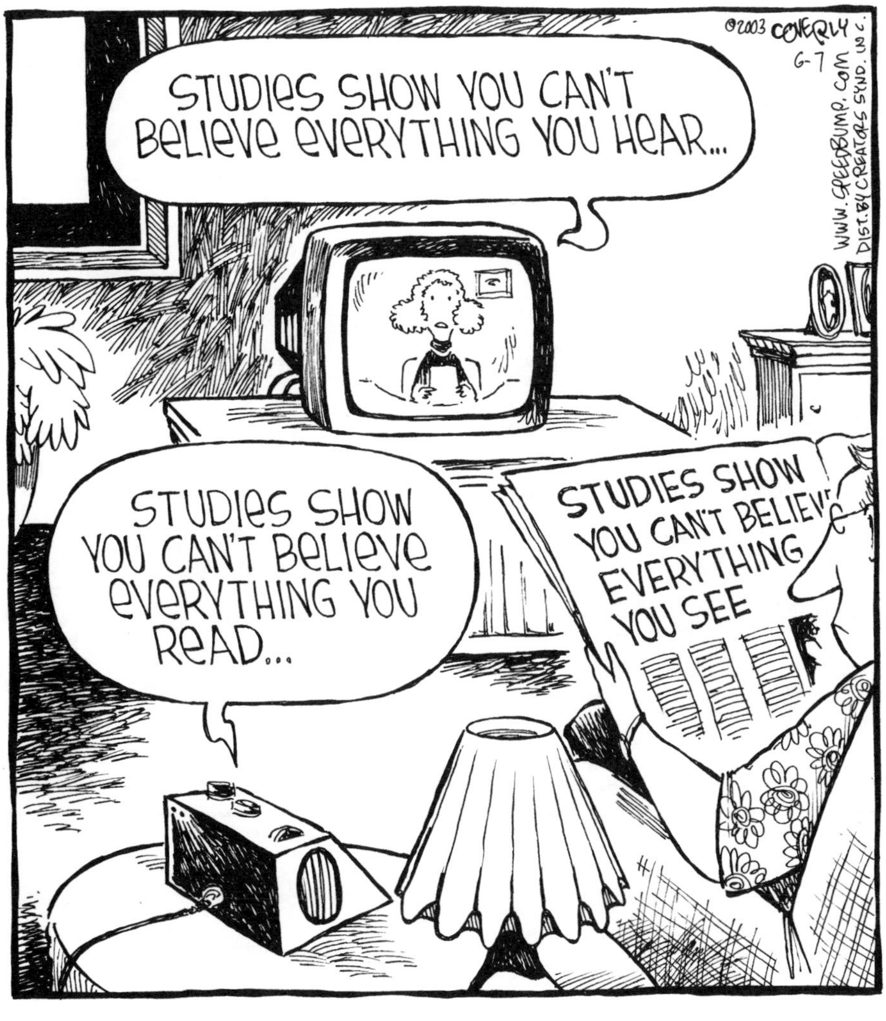
©2003 COVERLY 6-7
WWW.SPEEDBUMP.COM DIST. BY CREATORS SYND. INC.
STUDIES SHOW YOU CAN'T BELIEVE EVERYTHING YOU HEAR...
STUDIES SHOW YOU CAN'T BELIEVE EVERYTHING YOU READ...
STUDIES SHOW YOU CAN'T BELIEVE EVERYTHING YOU SEE

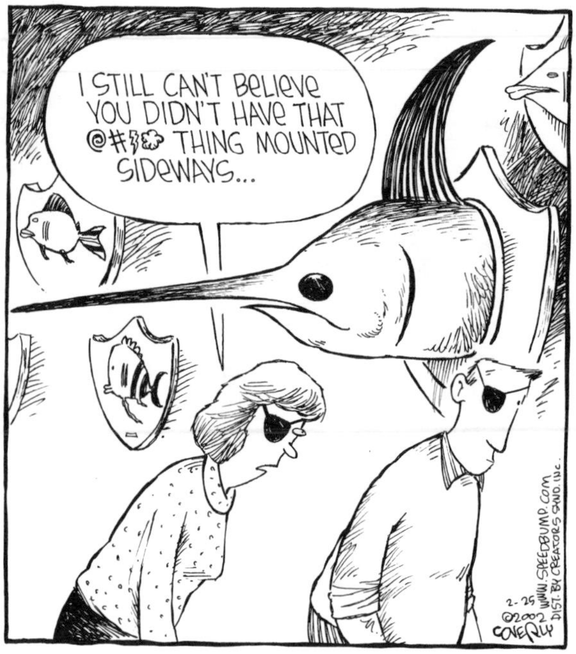
I STILL CAN'T BELIEVE YOU DIDN'T HAVE THAT @#$& THING MOUNTED SIDEWAYS...
2-25 ©2002 COVERLY
WWW.SPEEDBUMP.COM DIST. BY CREATORS SYND. INC.

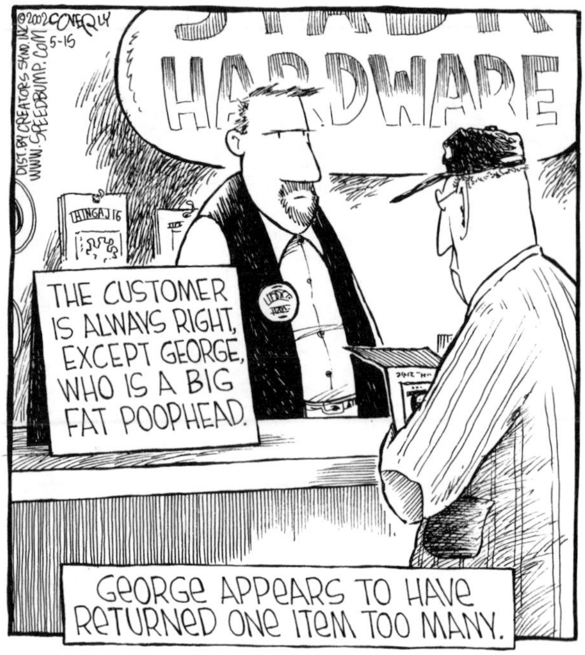
HARDWARE
THE CUSTOMER IS ALWAYS RIGHT, EXCEPT GEORGE, WHO IS A BIG FAT POOPHEAD.
GEORGE APPEARS TO HAVE RETURNED ONE ITEM TOO MANY.
©2002 COVERLY 5-15
DIST. BY CREATORS SYND. INC. WWW.SPEEDBUMP.COM

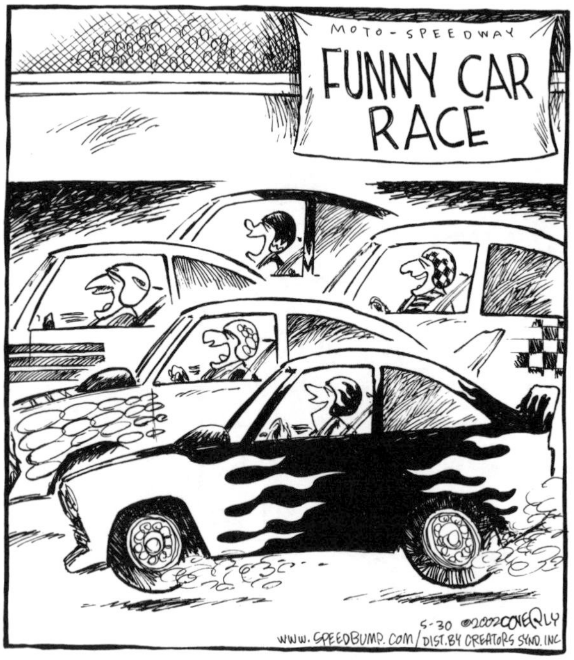
MOTO-SPEEDWAY
FUNNY CAR RACE
5-30 ©2002 COVERLY
WWW.SPEEDBUMP.COM/DIST. BY CREATORS SYND. INC.

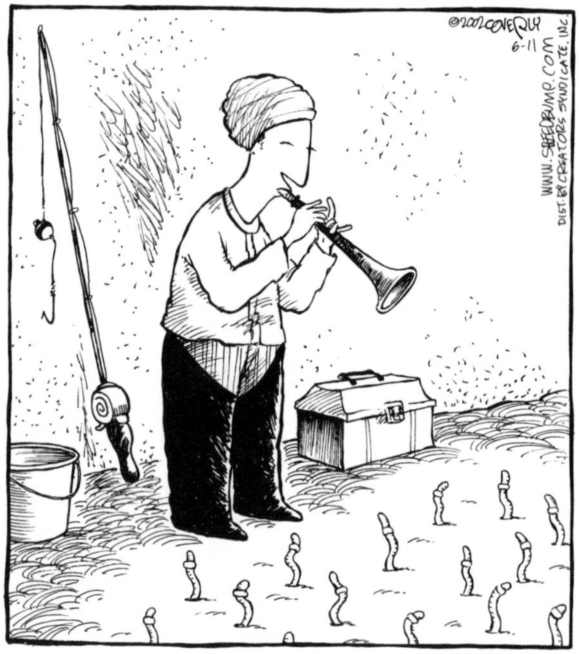
©2002 COVERLY 6-11
WWW.SPEEDBUMP.COM DIST. BY CREATORS SYNDICATE, INC.

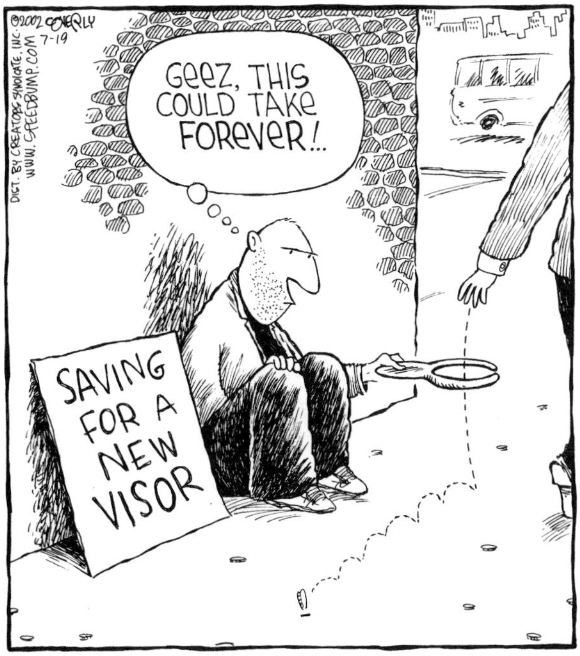
©2002 COVERLY 7-19
DIST. BY CREATORS SYNDICATE, INC.
WWW.SPEEDBUMP.COM
GEEZ, THIS COULD TAKE FOREVER!..
SAVING FOR A NEW VISOR

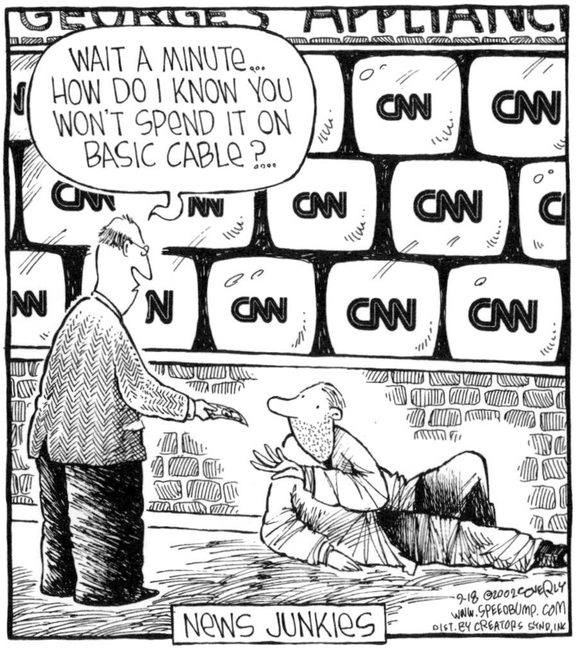
WAIT A MINUTE... HOW DO I KNOW YOU WON'T SPEND IT ON BASIC CABLE?...
9-18 ©2002 COVERLY
WWW.SPEEDBUMP.COM
DIST. BY CREATORS SYND, INC
NEWS JUNKIES

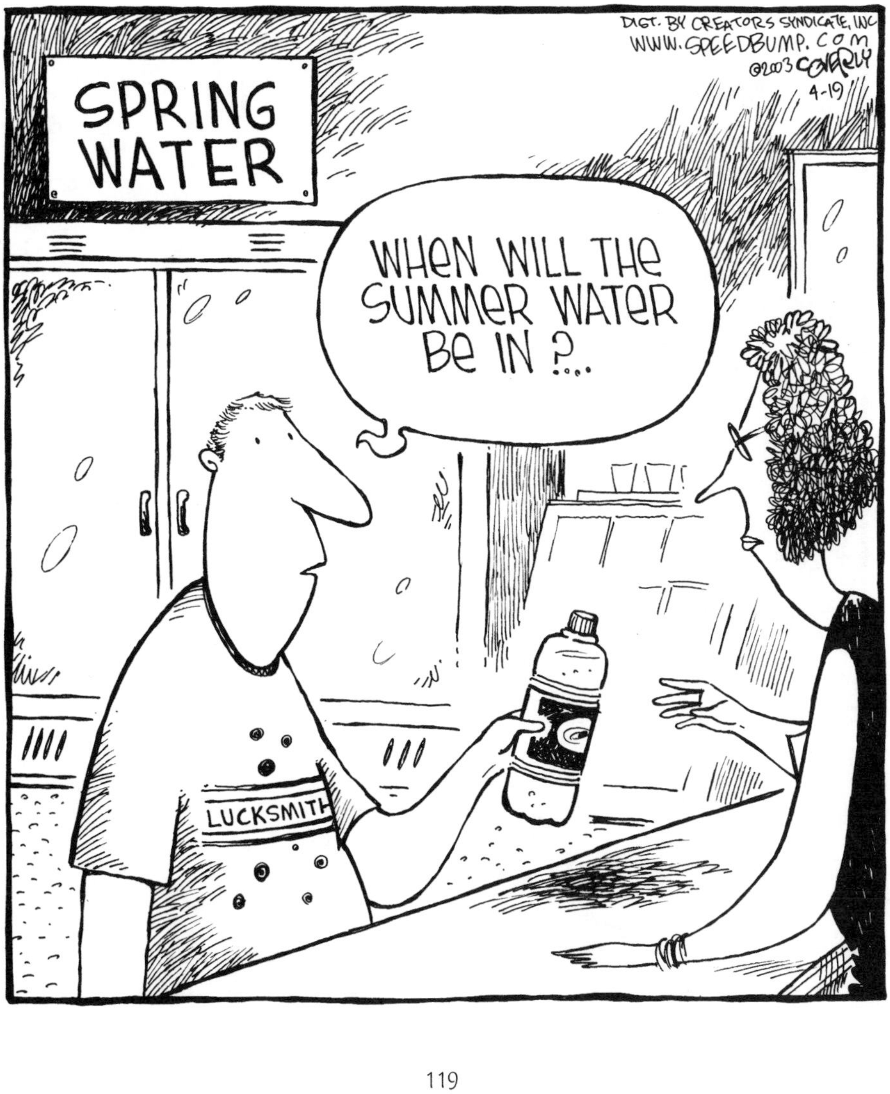
DIST. BY CREATORS SYNDICATE, INC
WWW.SPEEDBUMP.COM
©2003 COVERLY 4-19
SPRING WATER
WHEN WILL THE SUMMER WATER BE IN?...
LUCKSMITH

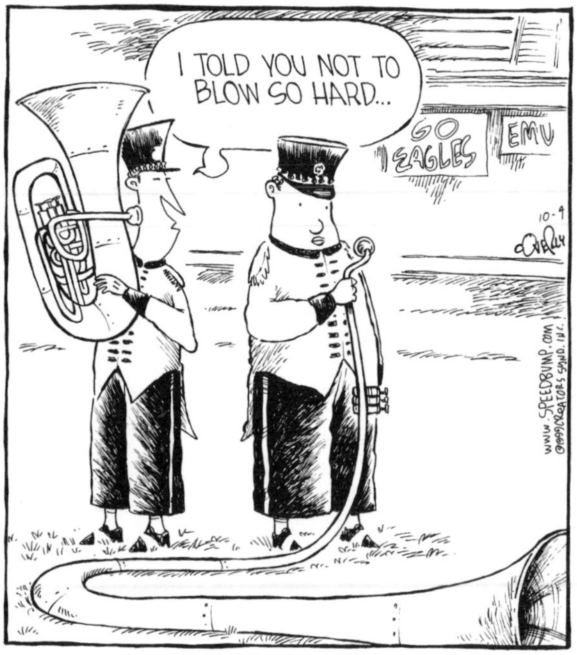
I TOLD YOU NOT TO BLOW SO HARD...
GO EAGLES
EMU
10-4
OVERLY
WWW.SPEEDBUMP.COM
©1999 CREATORS SYND. INC.

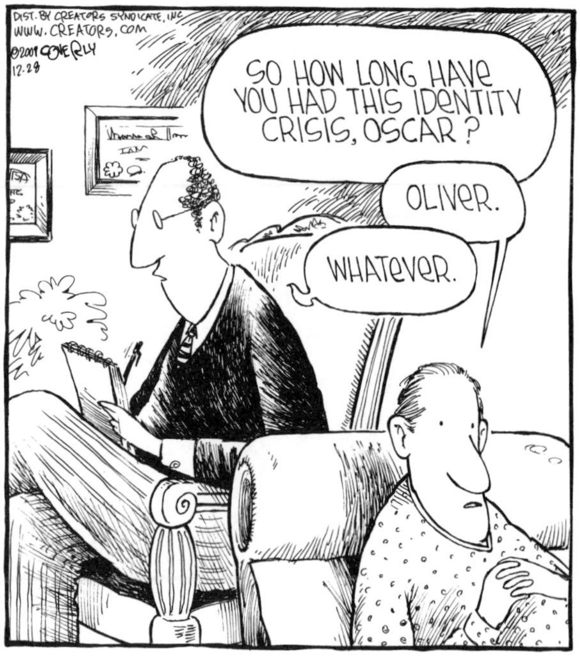
DIST. BY CREATORS SYNDICATE, INC
WWW.CREATORS.COM
©2009 OVERLY
12-28
SO HOW LONG HAVE YOU HAD THIS IDENTITY CRISIS, OSCAR?
OLIVER.
WHATEVER.

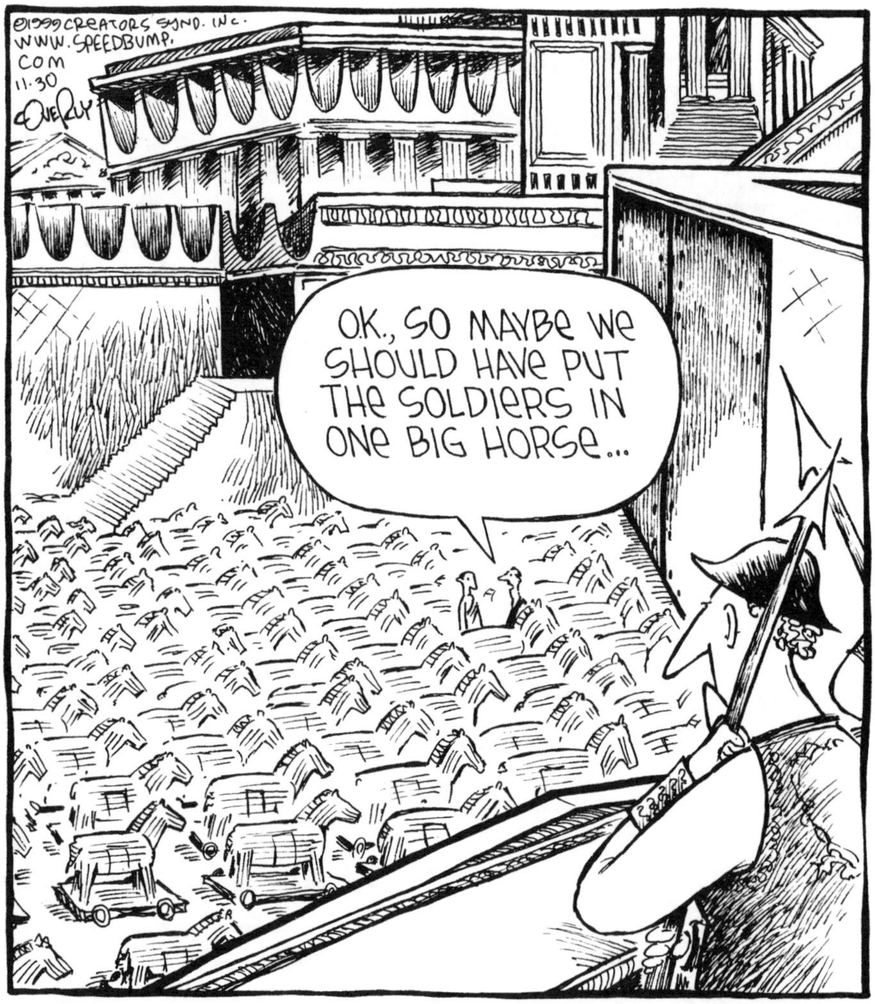
©1999 CREATORS SYND. INC.
WWW.SPEEDBUMP.COM
11.30
OVERLY
O.K., SO MAYBE WE SHOULD HAVE PUT THE SOLDIERS IN ONE BIG HORSE...

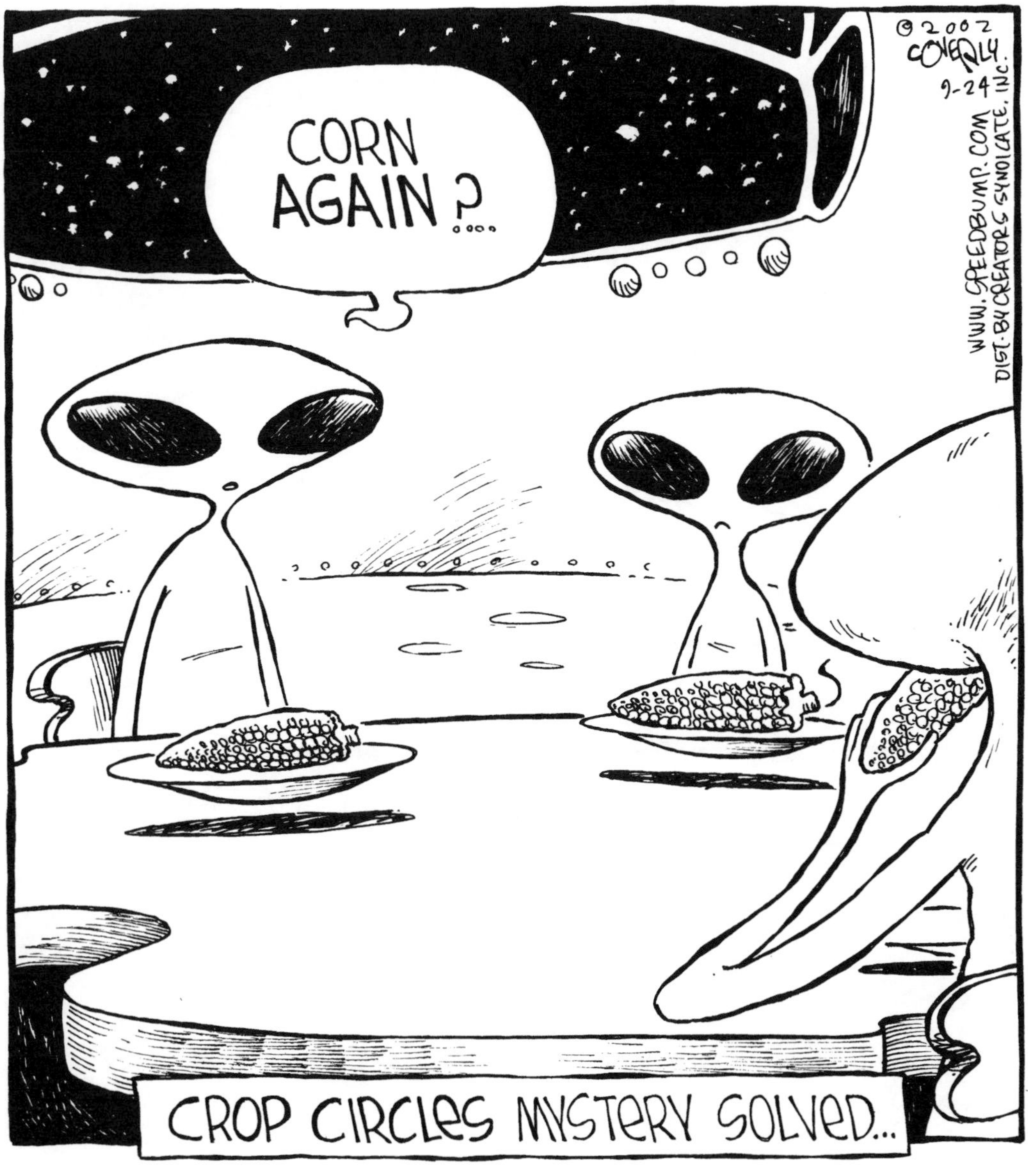
CORN AGAIN?...
©2002 COVERLY 9-24
WWW.SPEEDBUMP.COM DIST. BY CREATORS SYNDICATE, INC.
CROP CIRCLES MYSTERY SOLVED...

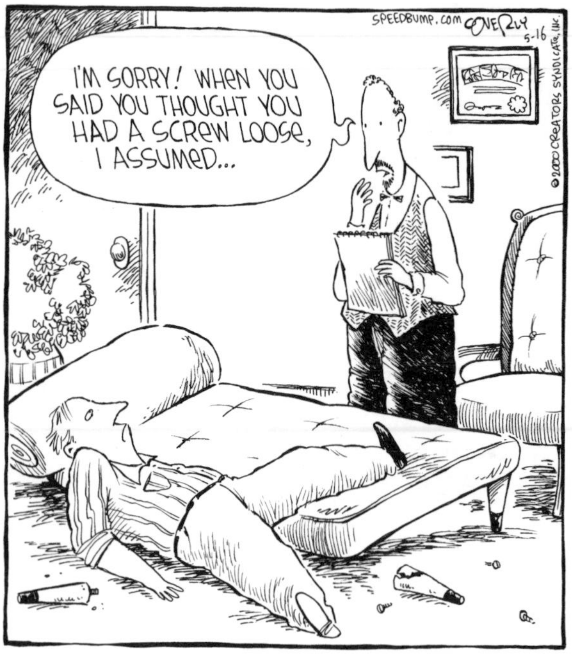
SPEEDBUMP.COM COVERLY 5-16
I'M SORRY! WHEN YOU SAID YOU THOUGHT YOU HAD A SCREW LOOSE, I ASSUMED...
©2000 CREATORS SYNDICATE, INC.

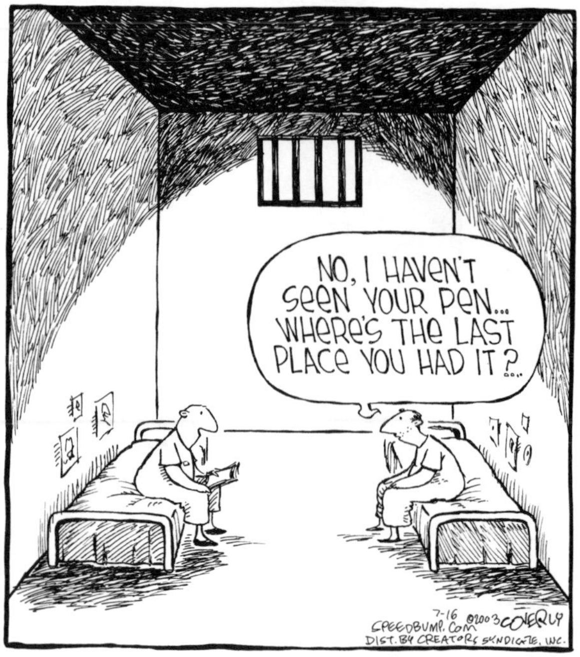
NO, I HAVEN'T SEEN YOUR PEN... WHERE'S THE LAST PLACE YOU HAD IT?...
7-16 SPEEDBUMP.COM ©2003 COVERLY
DIST. BY CREATORS SYNDICATE, INC.

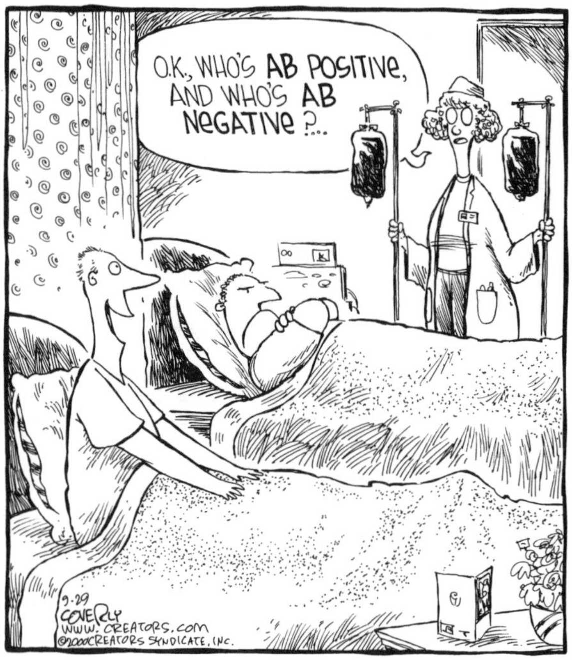
O.K., WHO'S AB POSITIVE, AND WHO'S AB NEGATIVE?...
9-29 COVERLY WWW.CREATORS.COM ©2000 CREATORS SYNDICATE, INC.

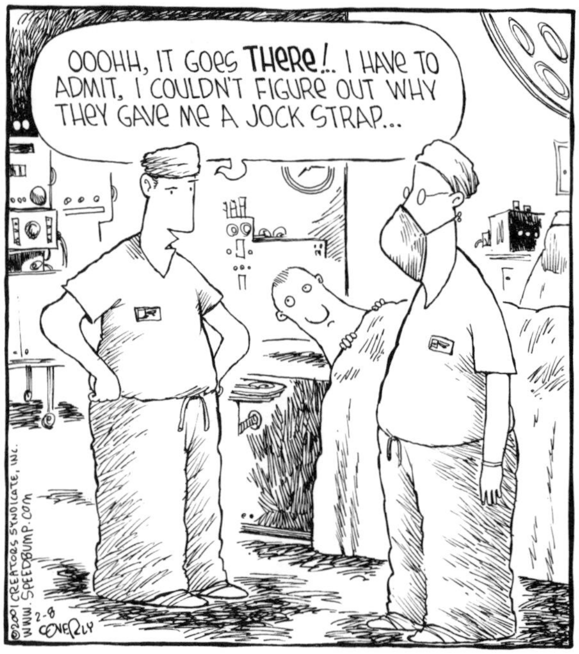
OOOHH, IT GOES THERE!.. I HAVE TO ADMIT, I COULDN'T FIGURE OUT WHY THEY GAVE ME A JOCK STRAP...
©2001 CREATORS SYNDICATE, INC. WWW.SPEEDBUMP.COM 2-8 COVERLY

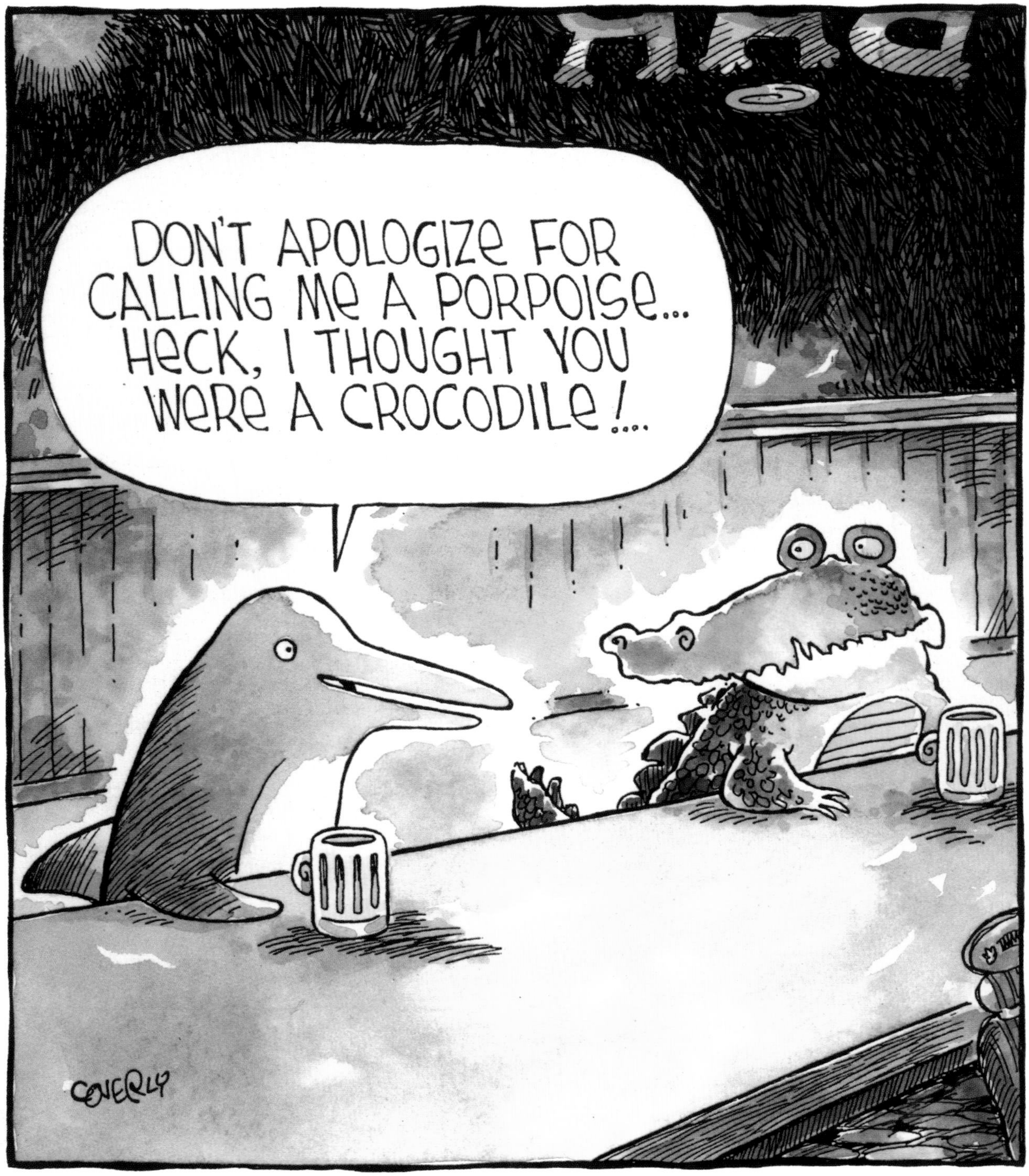
DON'T APOLOGIZE FOR CALLING ME A PORPOISE... HECK, I THOUGHT YOU WERE A CROCODILE!...
COVERLY

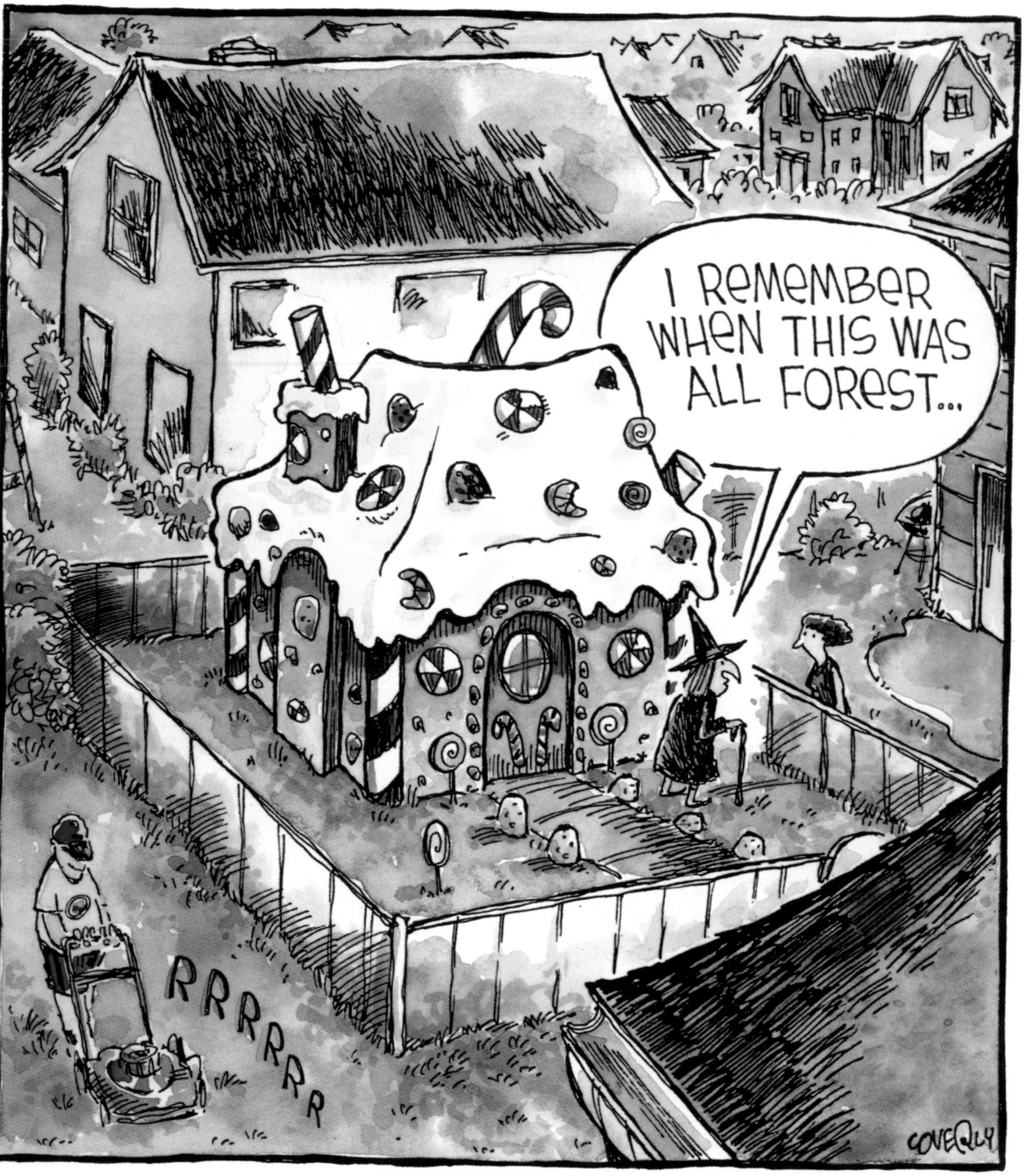
I REMEMBER WHEN THIS WAS ALL FOREST...
RRRRRRRR
COVERLY

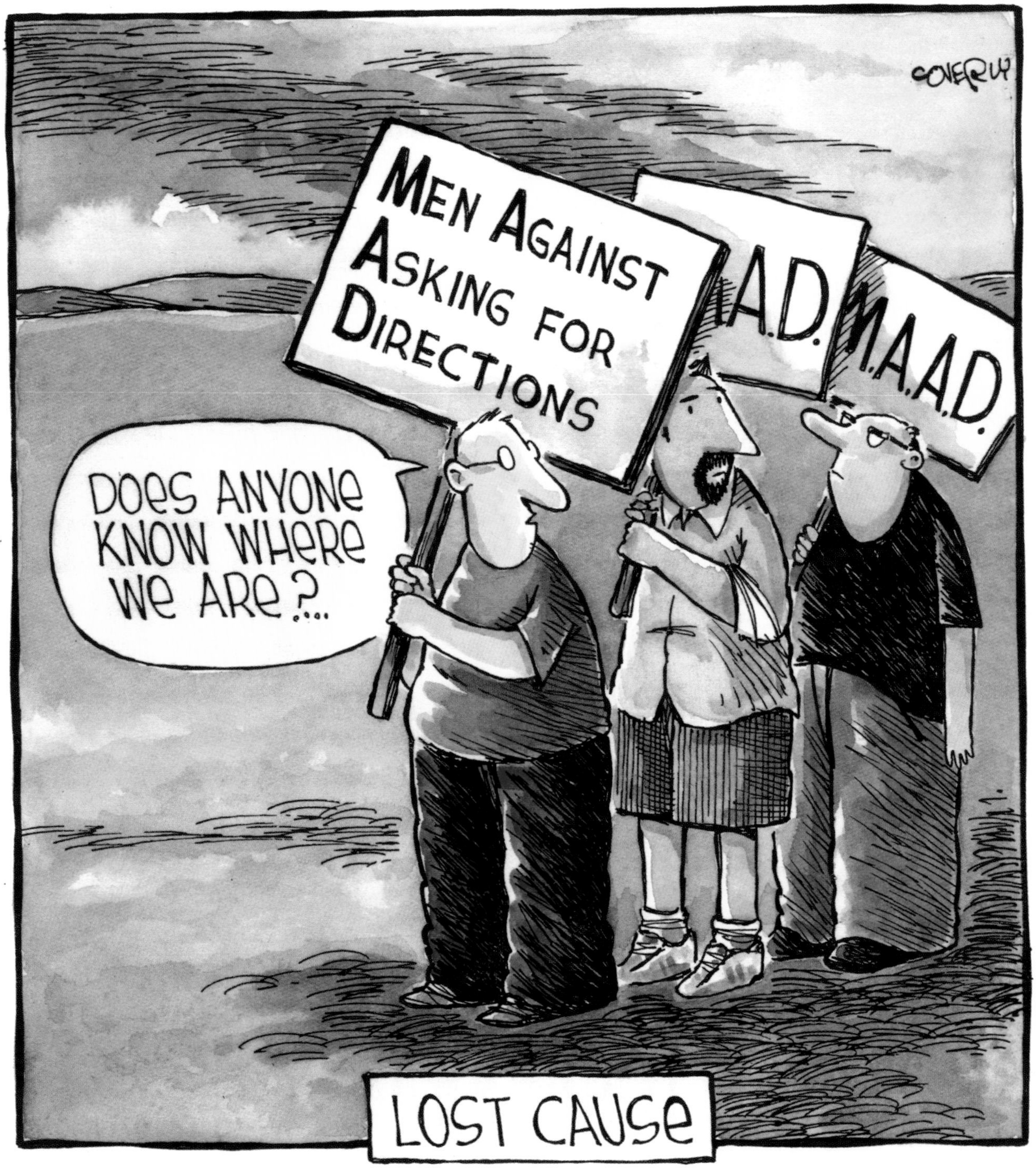
MEN AGAINST ASKING FOR DIRECTIONS
M.A.A.D.
DOES ANYONE KNOW WHERE WE ARE?...

LOST CAUSE

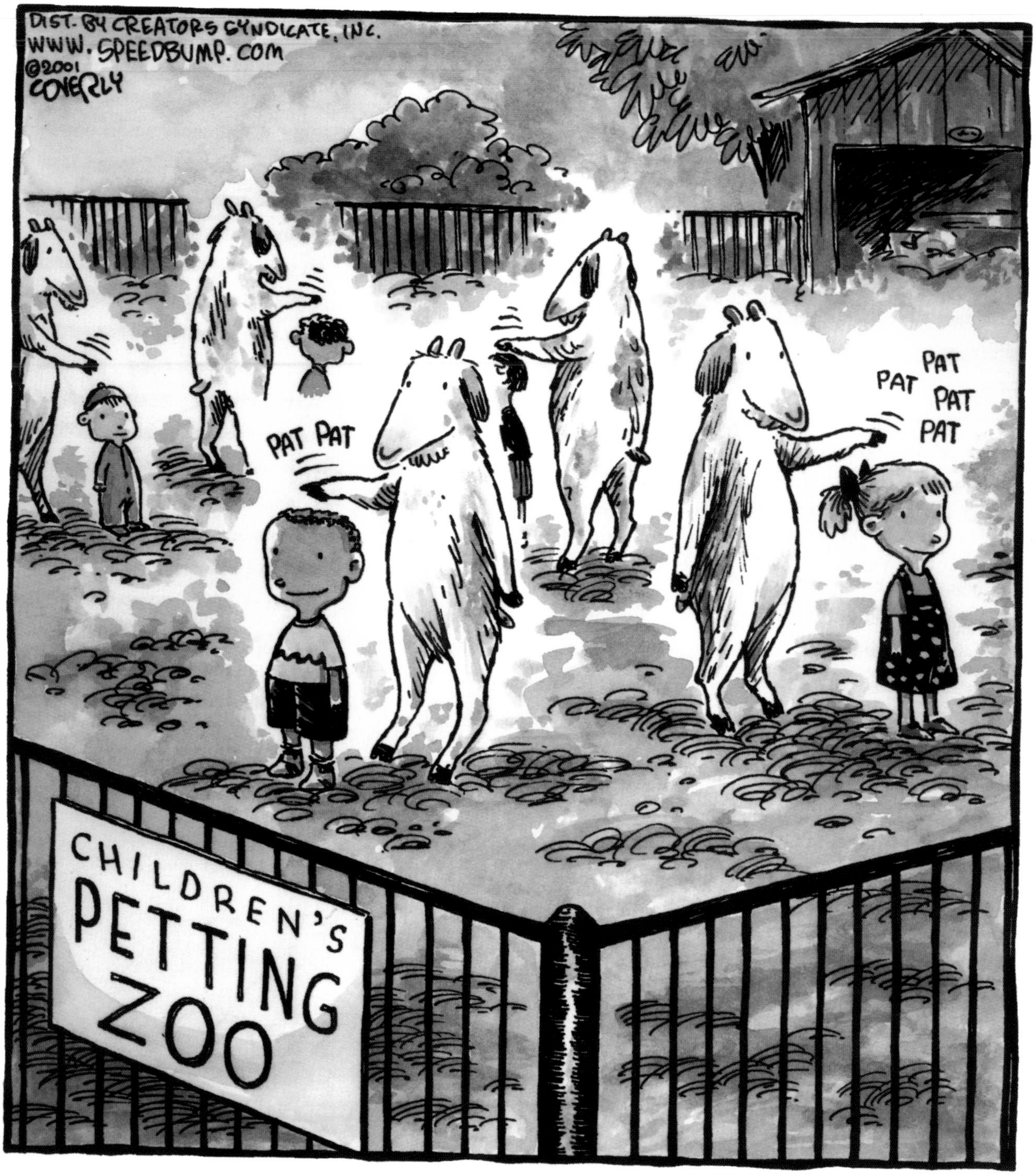
DIST. BY CREATORS SYNDICATE, INC.
WWW. SPEEDBUMP. COM
©2001
COVERLY
PAT PAT
PAT
PAT
PAT
PAT
CHILDREN'S
PETTING
ZOO

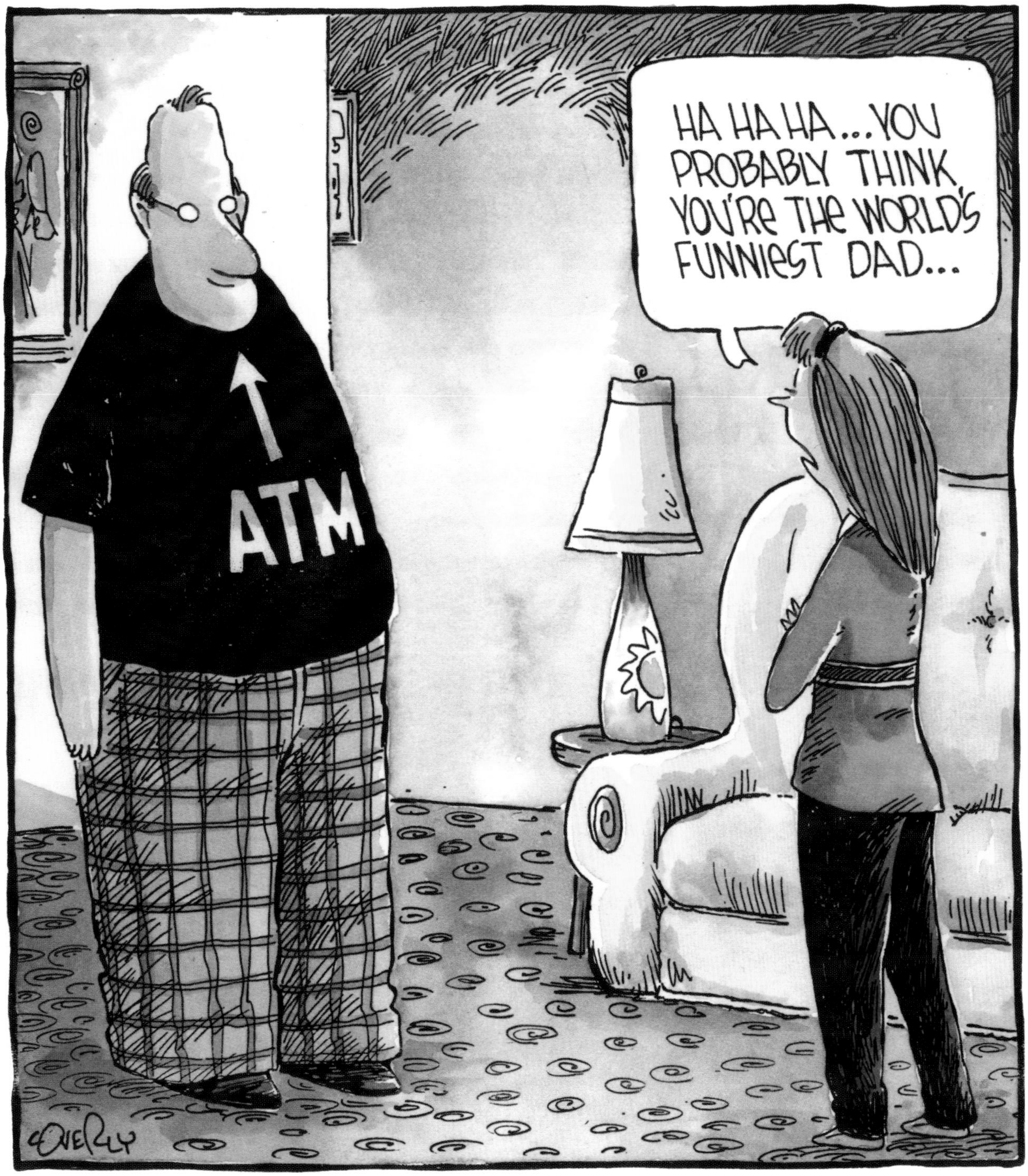
HA HA HA... YOU PROBABLY THINK YOU'RE THE WORLD'S FUNNIEST DAD...
ATM
COVERLY

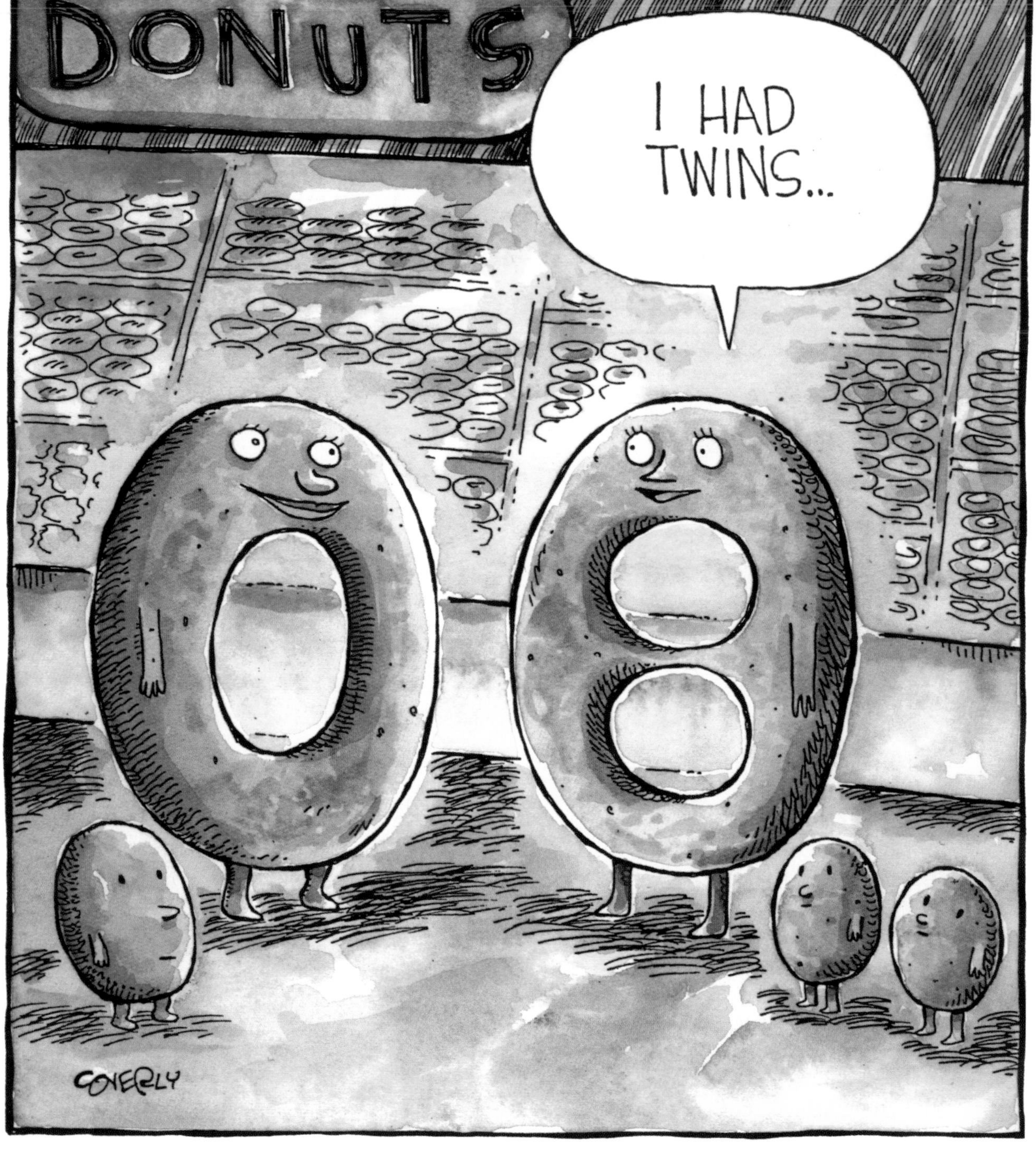
DONUTS
I HAD TWINS...
COVERLY

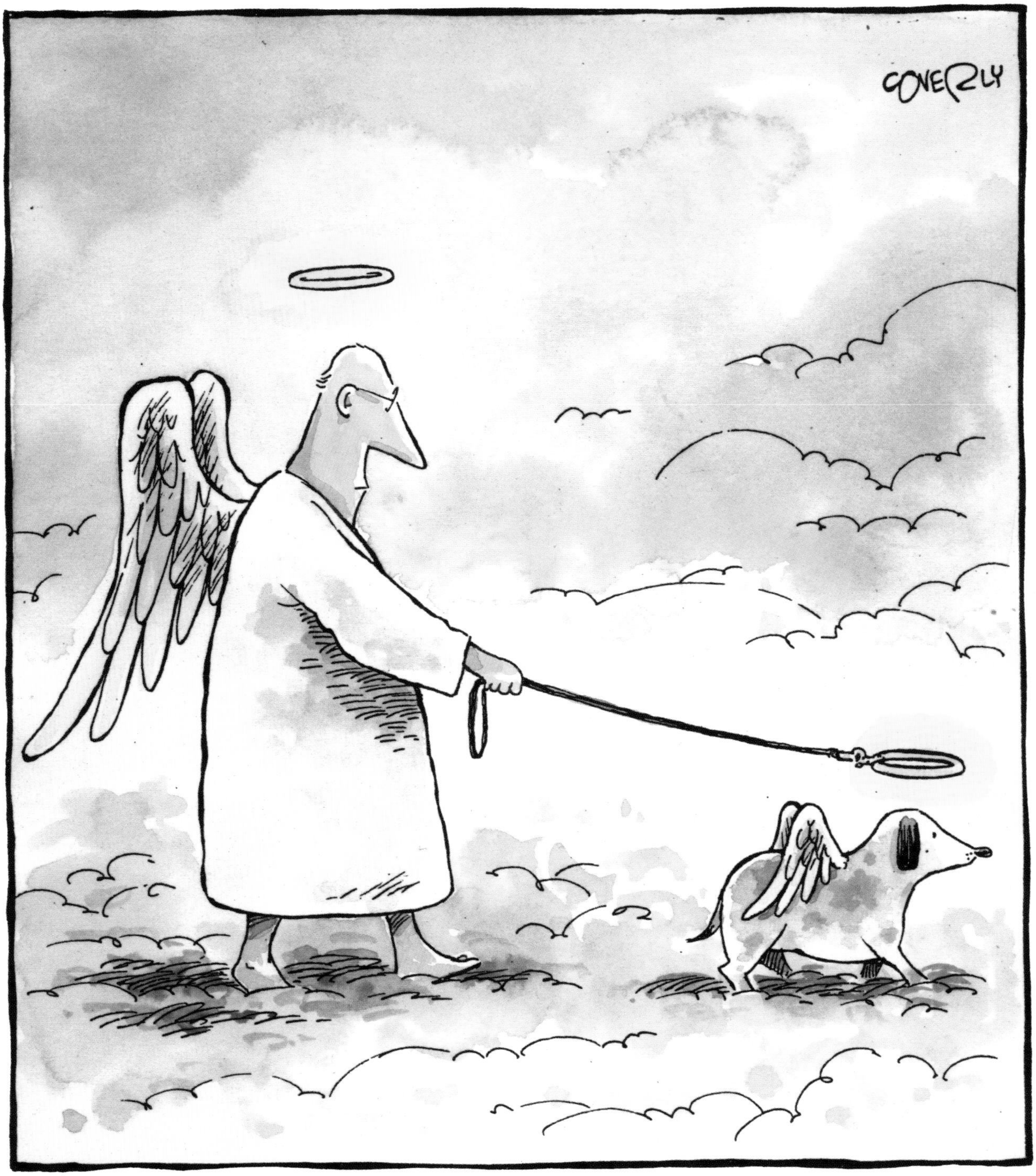
COVERLY

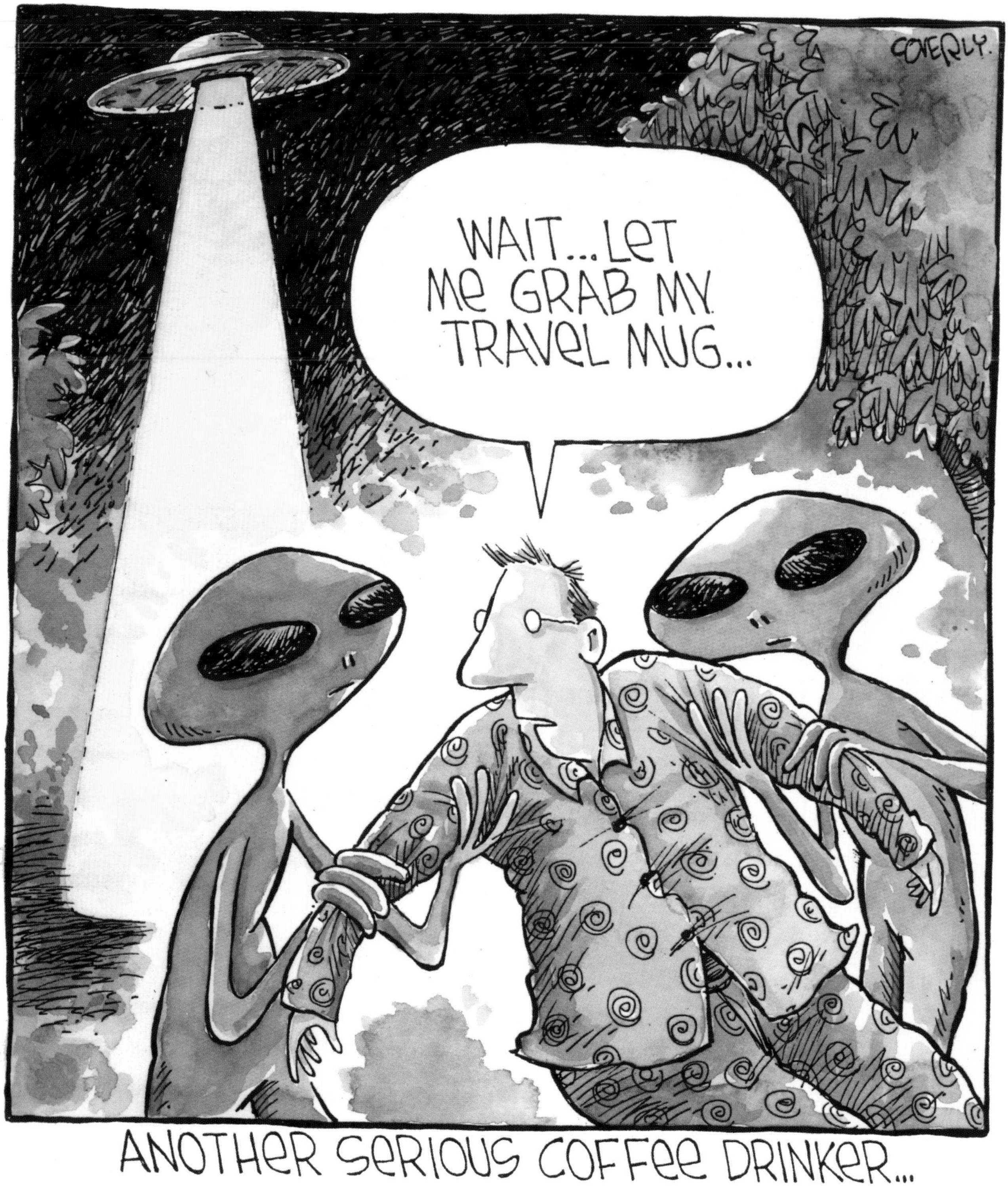
COVERLY.
WAIT... LET ME GRAB MY TRAVEL MUG...

ANOTHER SERIOUS COFFEE DRINKER...

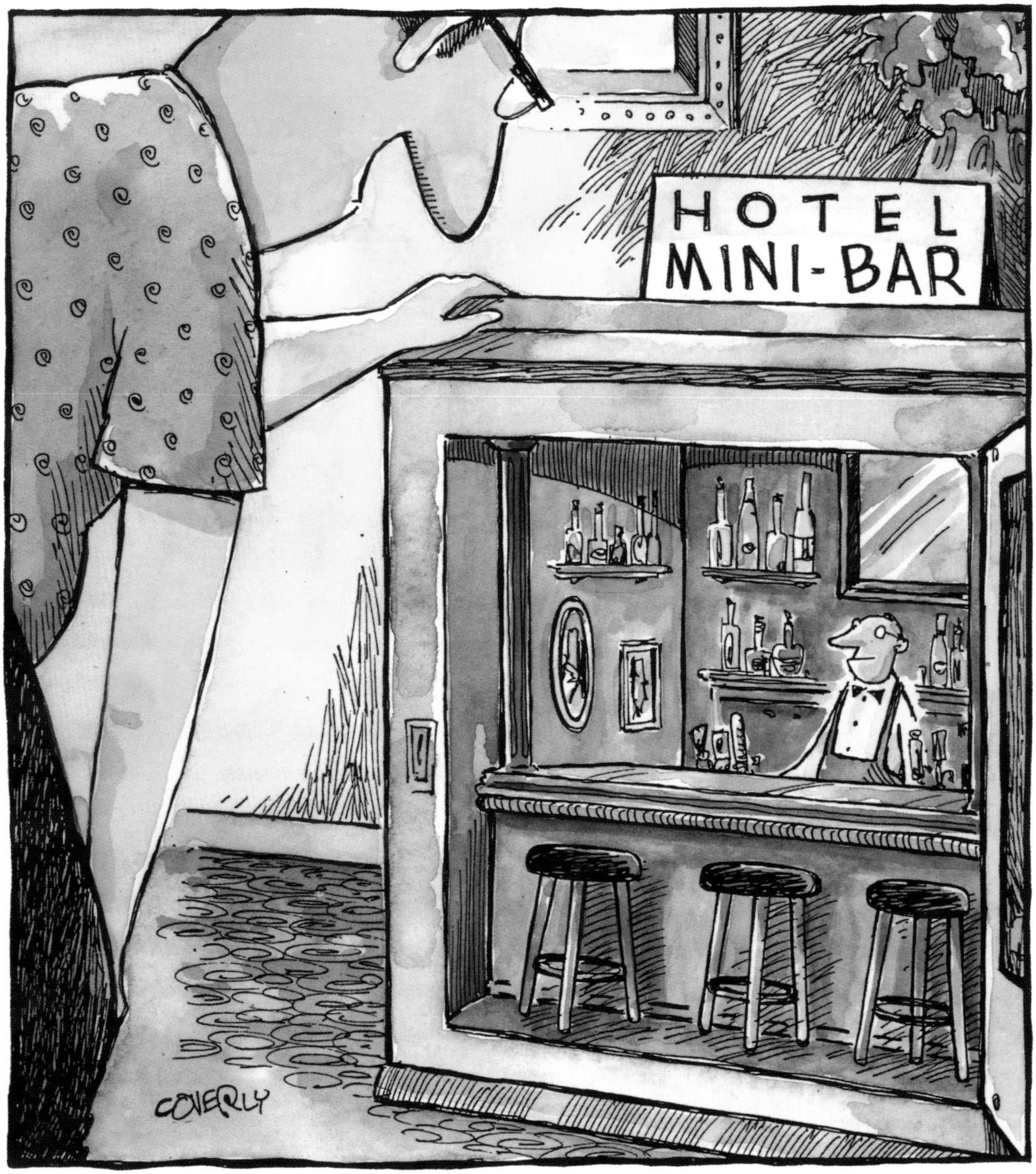
HOTEL
MINI-BAR
COVERLY

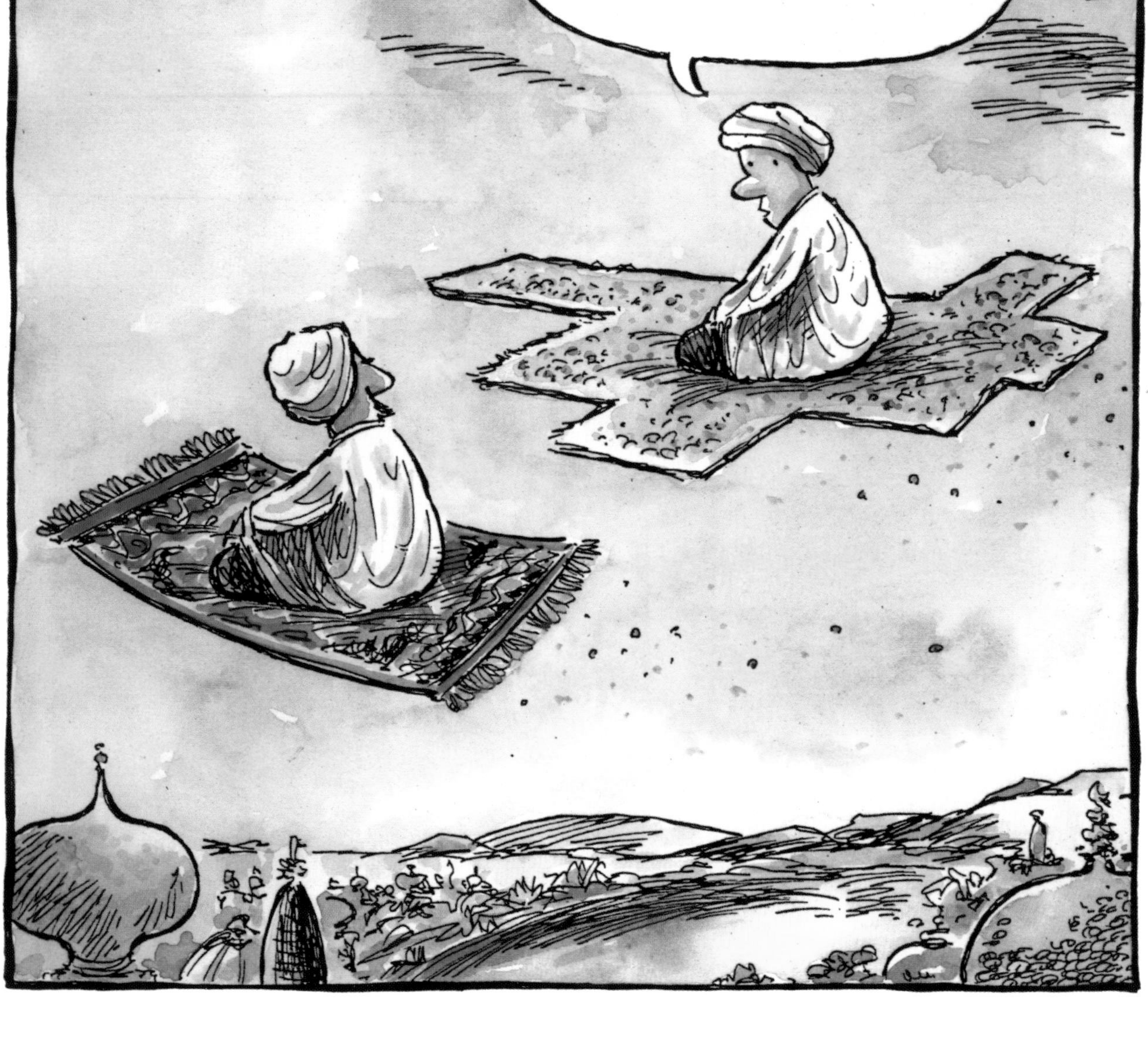
CONERLY
...I GOT A GOOD DEAL ON A REMNANT...

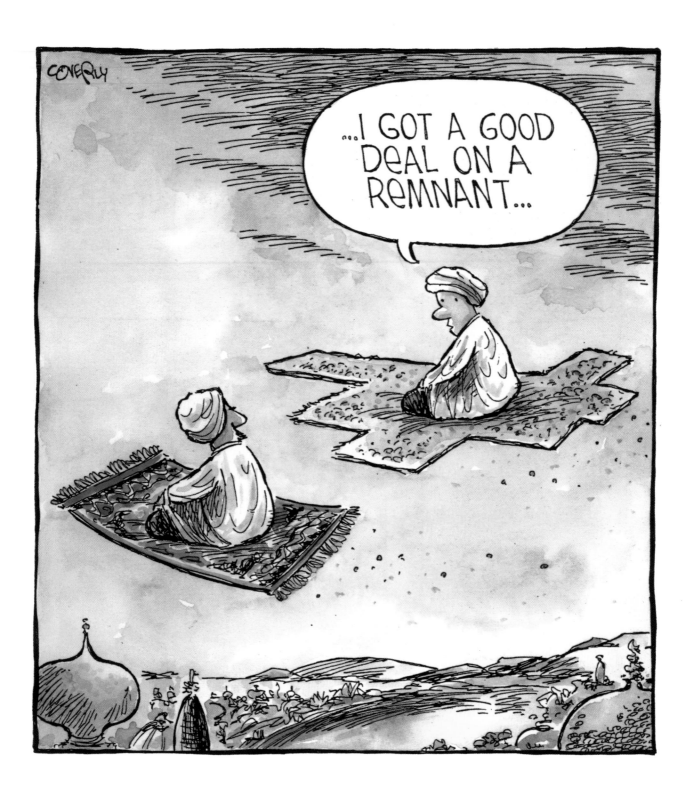

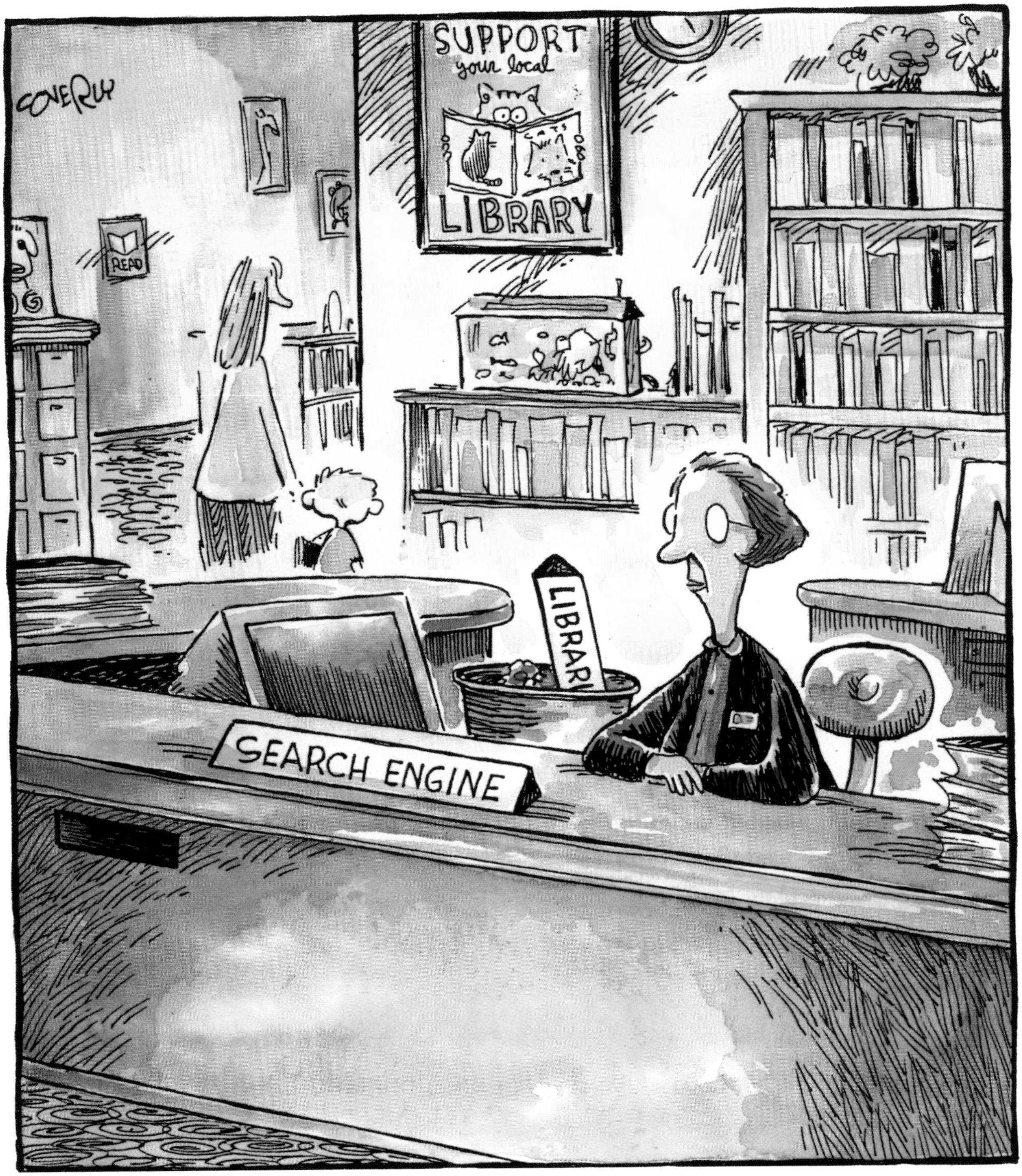
SUPPORT
your local
LIBRARY
READ
LIBRARY
SEARCH ENGINE

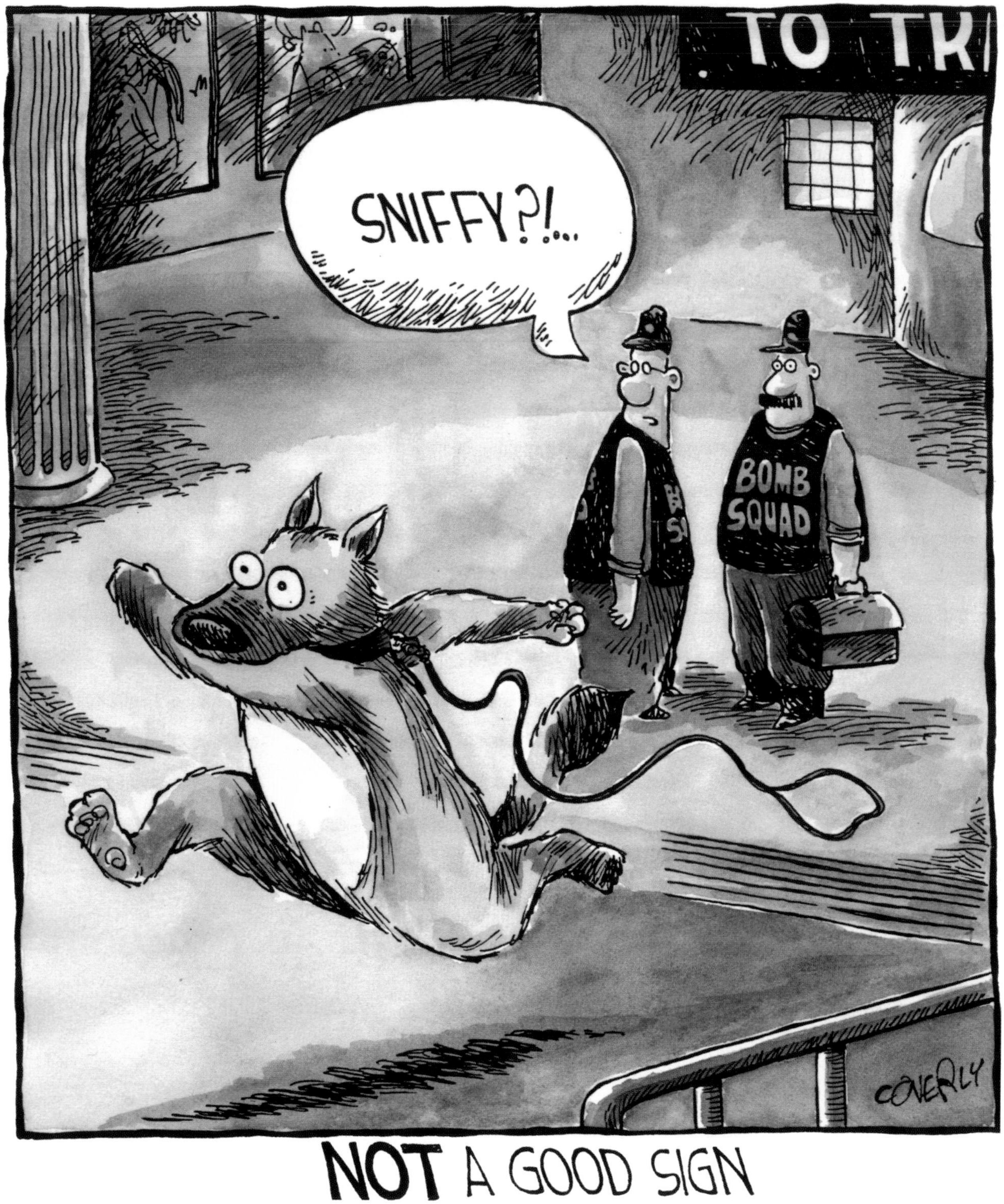
TO TR
SNIFFY?!...
BOMB SQUAD
CONERLY

NOT A GOOD SIGN

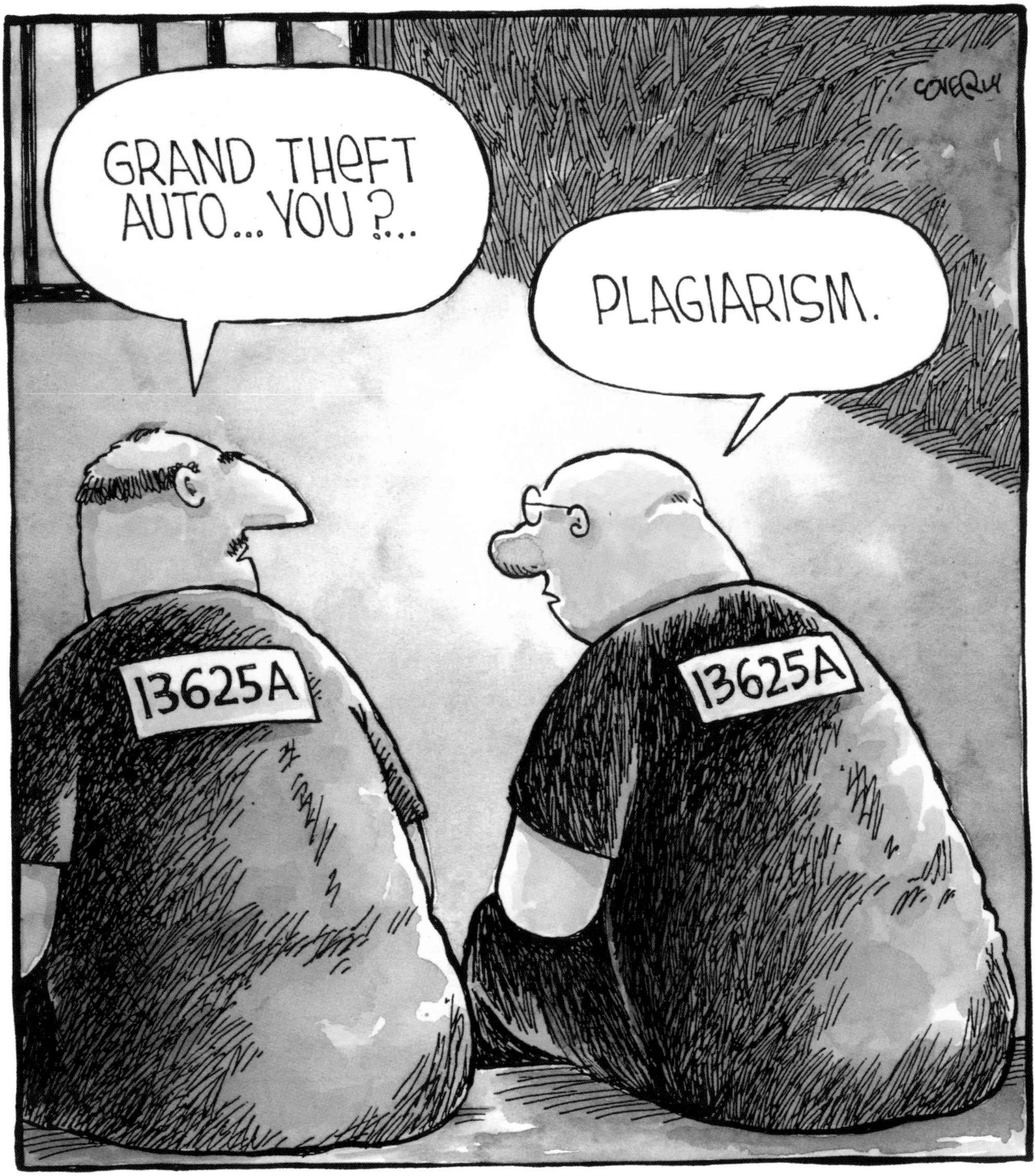
GRAND THEFT AUTO... YOU ?...
PLAGIARISM.
13625A
13625A

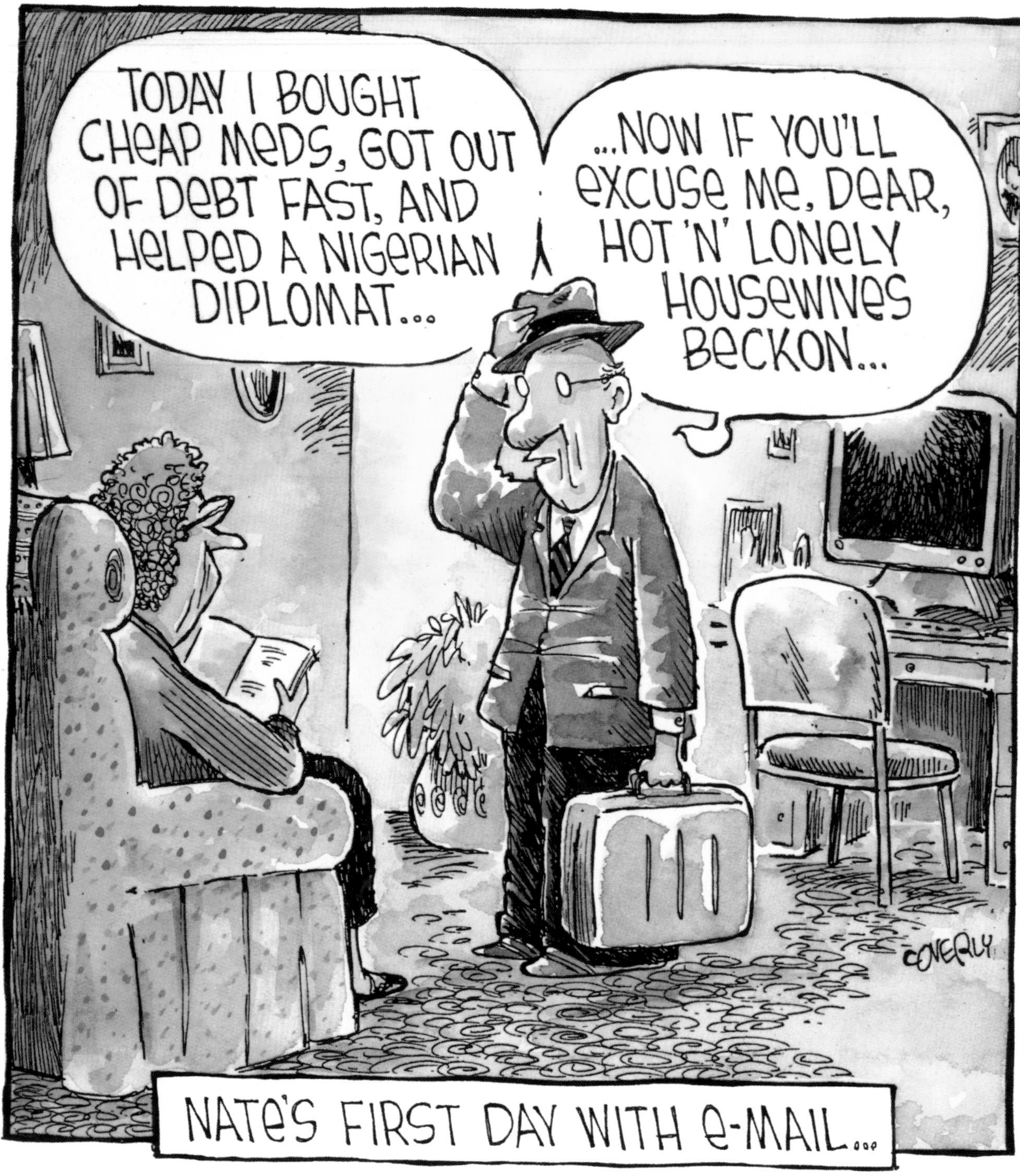
TODAY I BOUGHT CHEAP MEDS, GOT OUT OF DEBT FAST, AND HELPED A NIGERIAN DIPLOMAT...
...NOW IF YOU'LL EXCUSE ME, DEAR, HOT 'N' LONELY HOUSEWIVES BECKON...
CONERLY

NATE'S FIRST DAY WITH E-MAIL...

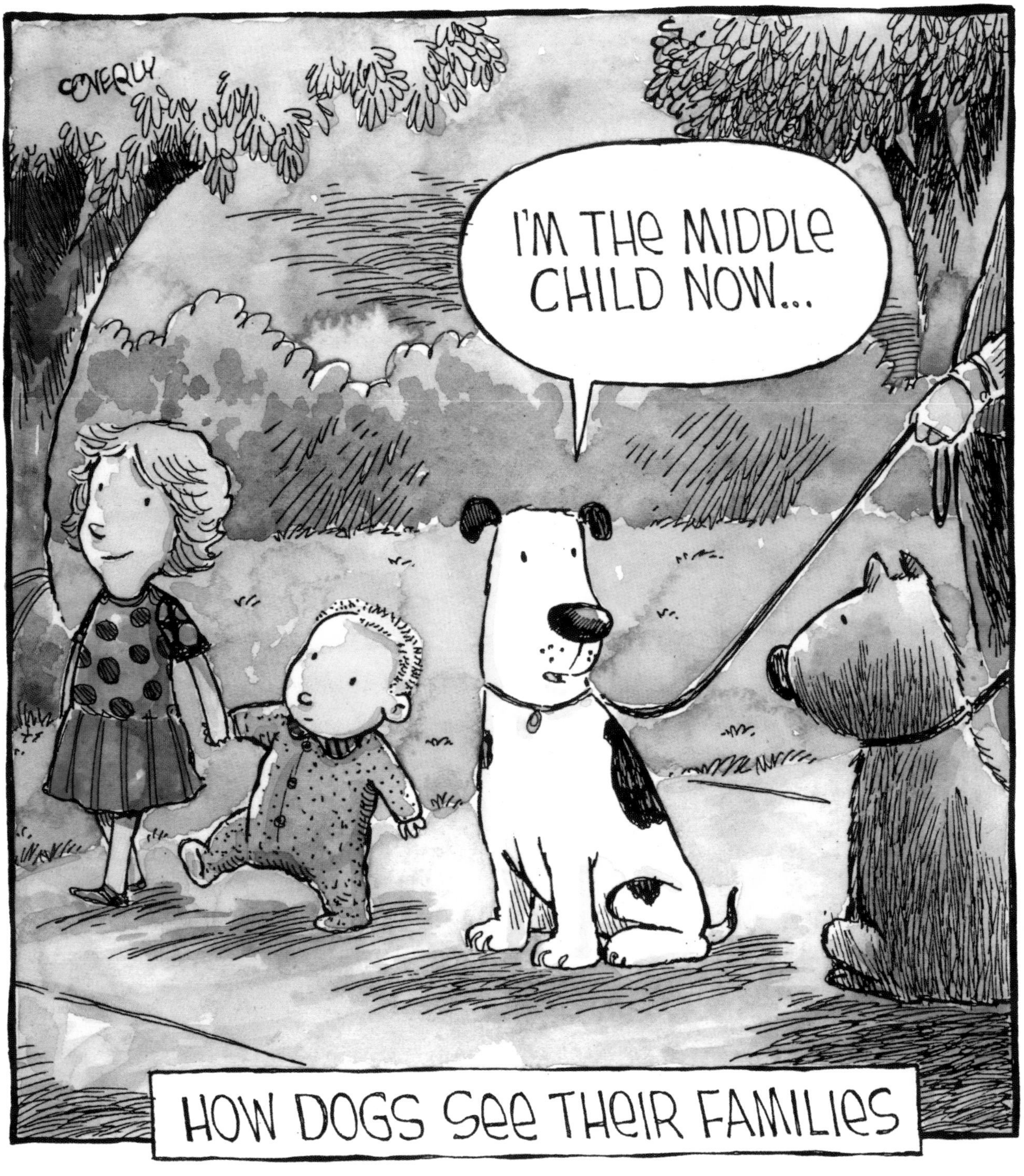
I'M THE MIDDLE CHILD NOW...

HOW DOGS SEE THEIR FAMILIES

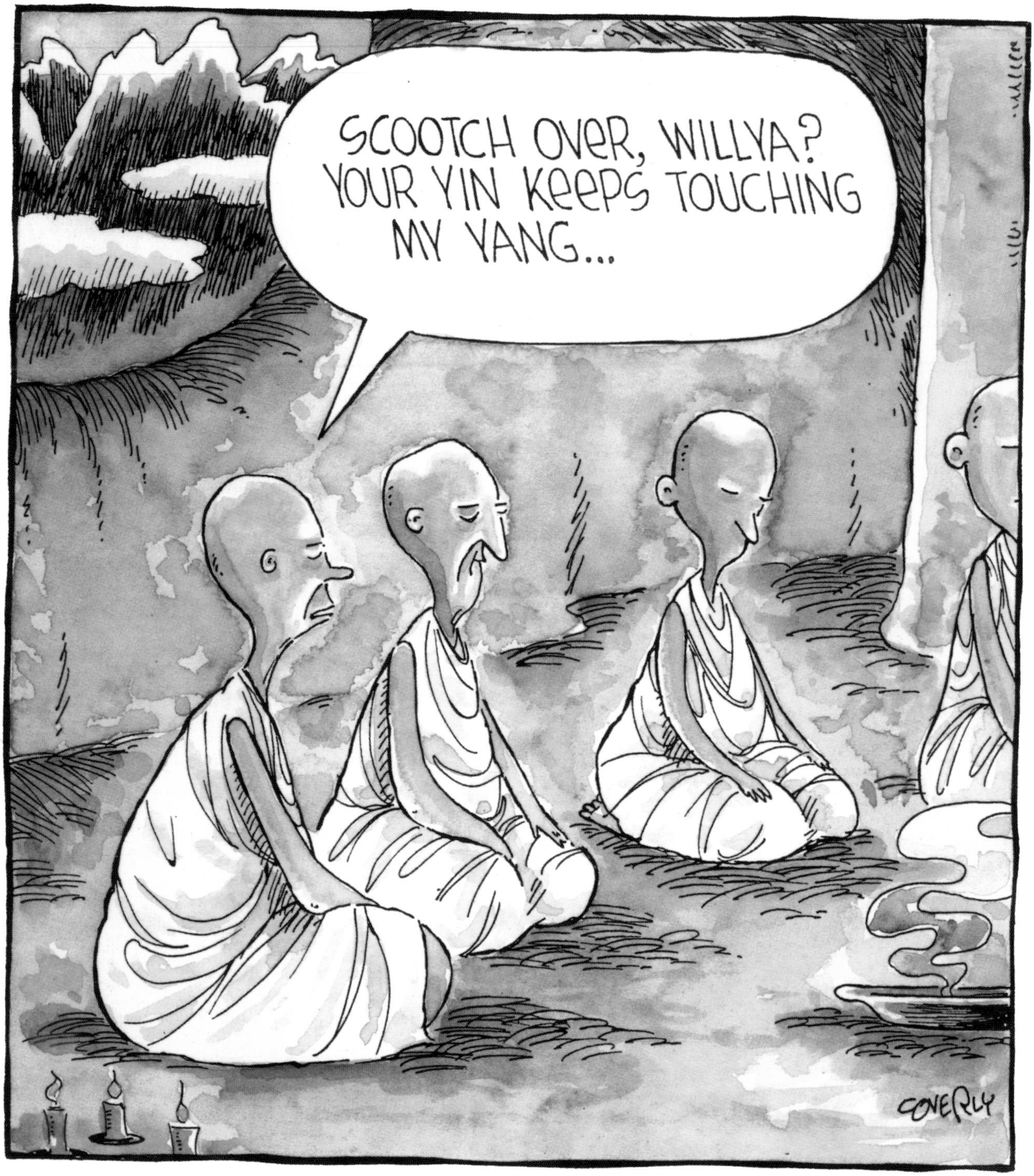
SCOOTCH OVER, WILLYA? YOUR YIN KEEPS TOUCHING MY YANG...
COVERLY

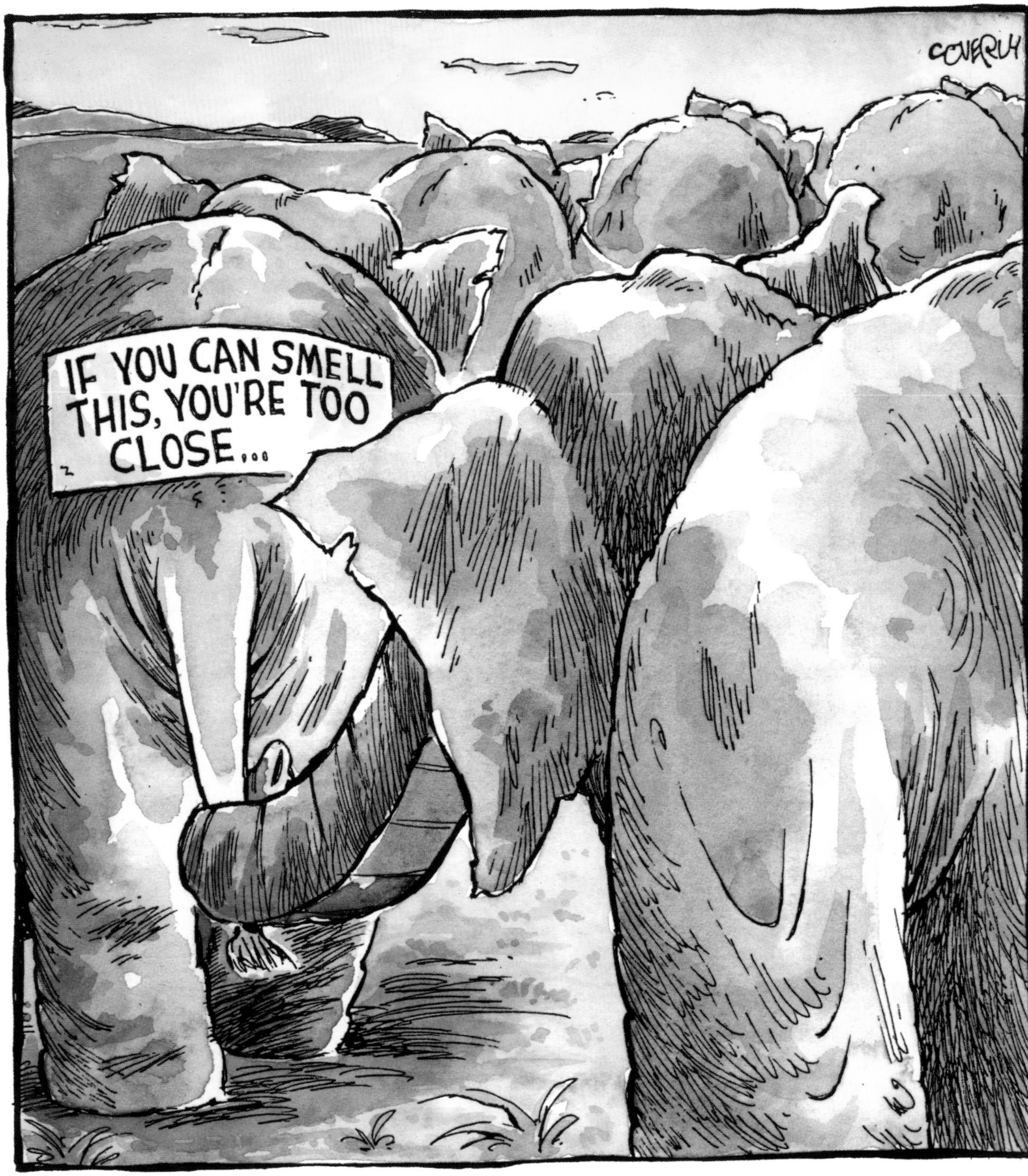
IF YOU CAN SMELL
THIS, YOU'RE TOO
CLOSE...

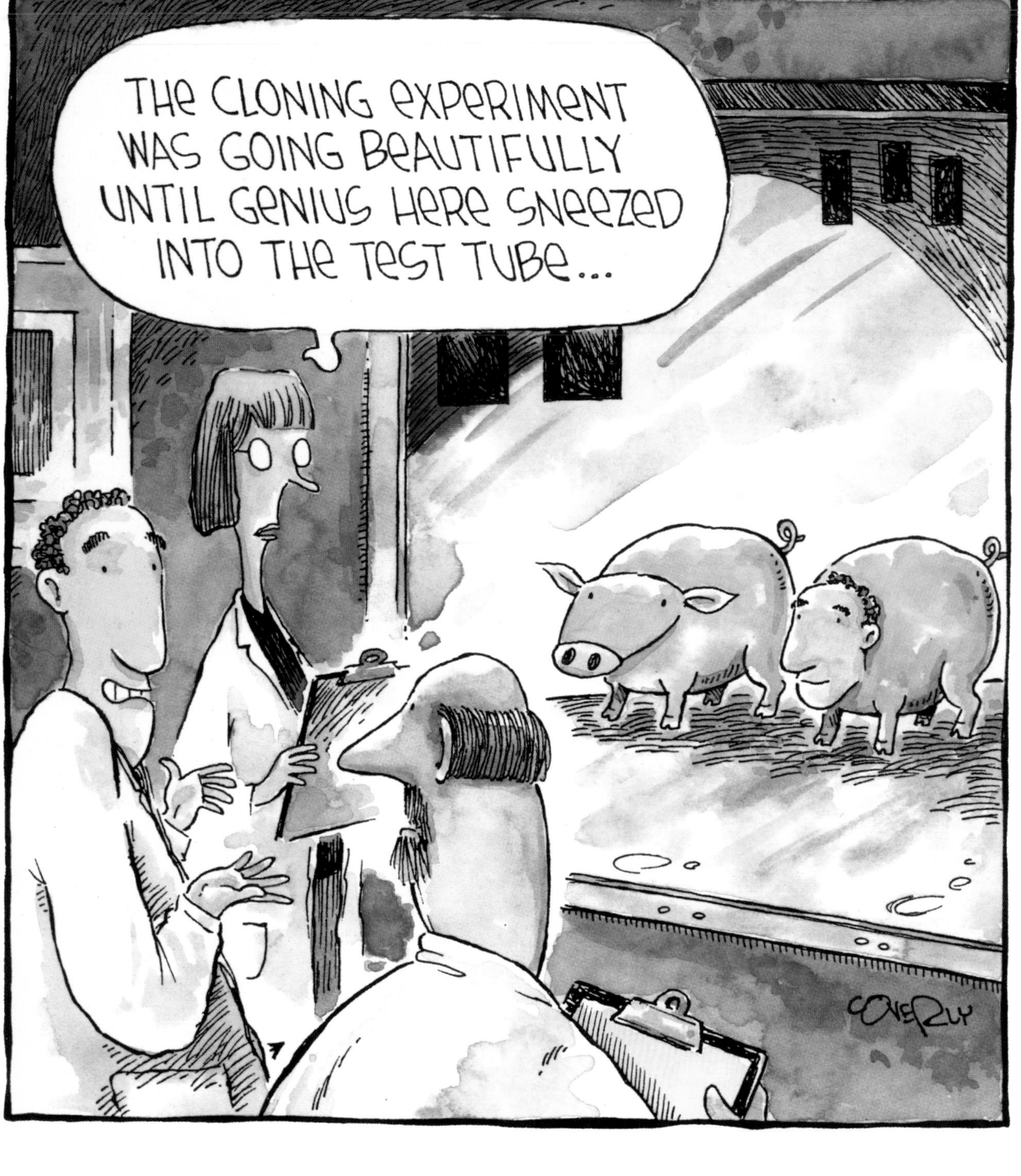
THE CLONING EXPERIMENT WAS GOING BEAUTIFULLY UNTIL GENIUS HERE SNEEZED INTO THE TEST TUBE...
COVERLY

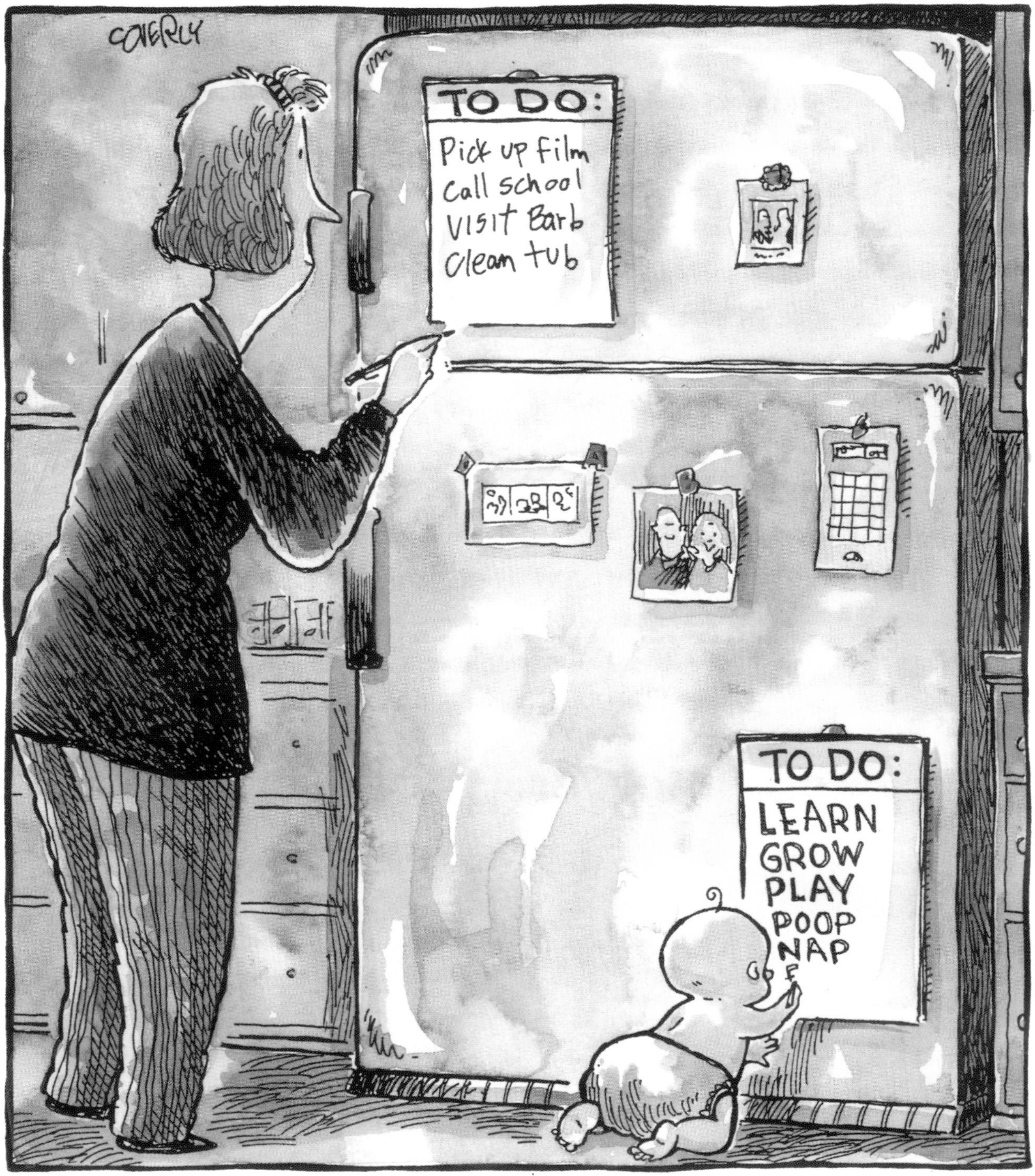
COVERLY
TO DO:
Pick up film
Call school
VISIT Barb
Clean tub
TO DO:
LEARN
GROW
PLAY
POOP
NAP

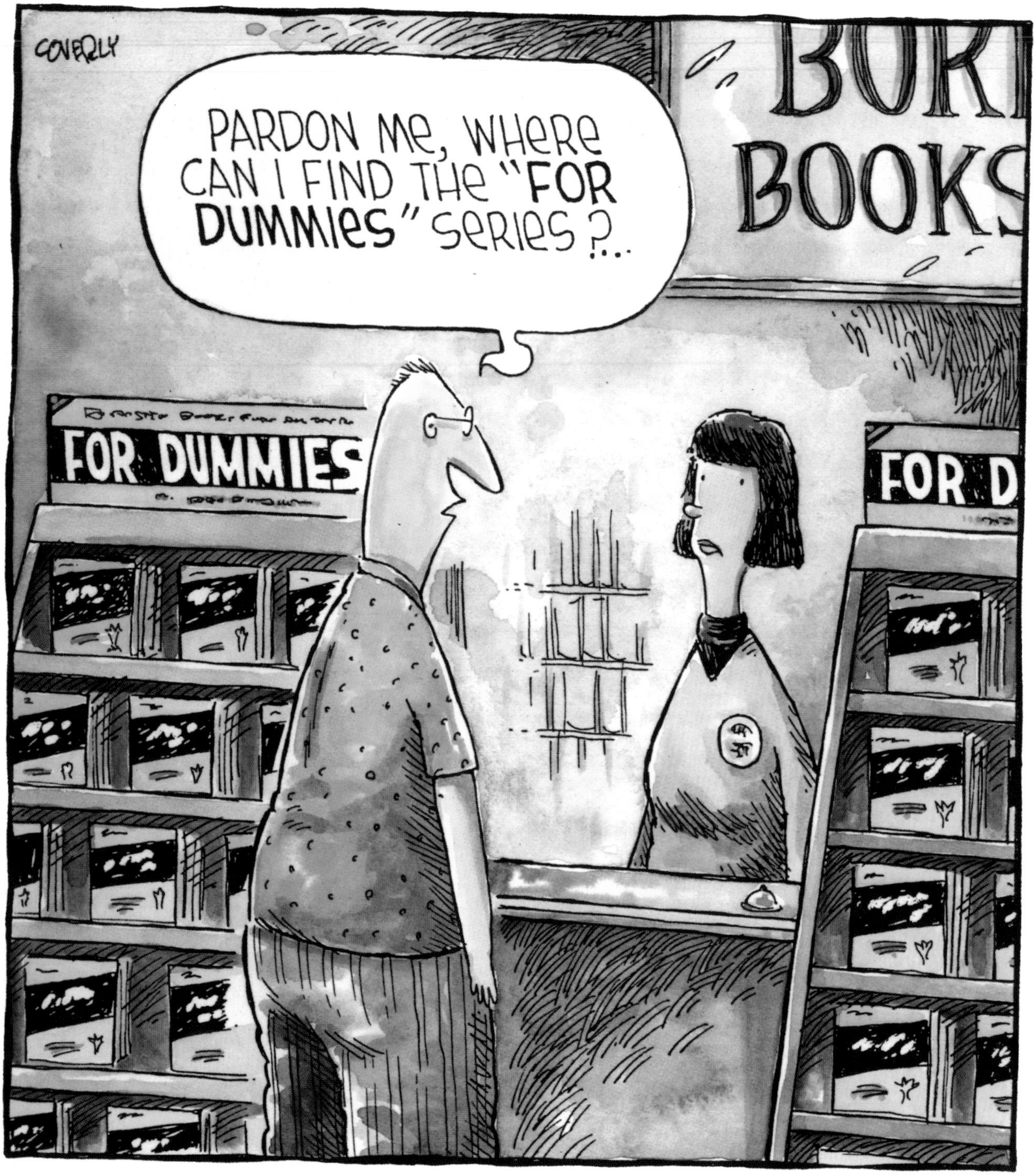
COVERLY
PARDON ME, WHERE CAN I FIND THE "FOR DUMMIES" SERIES ?...
BOR
BOOKS
FOR DUMMIES
FOR D

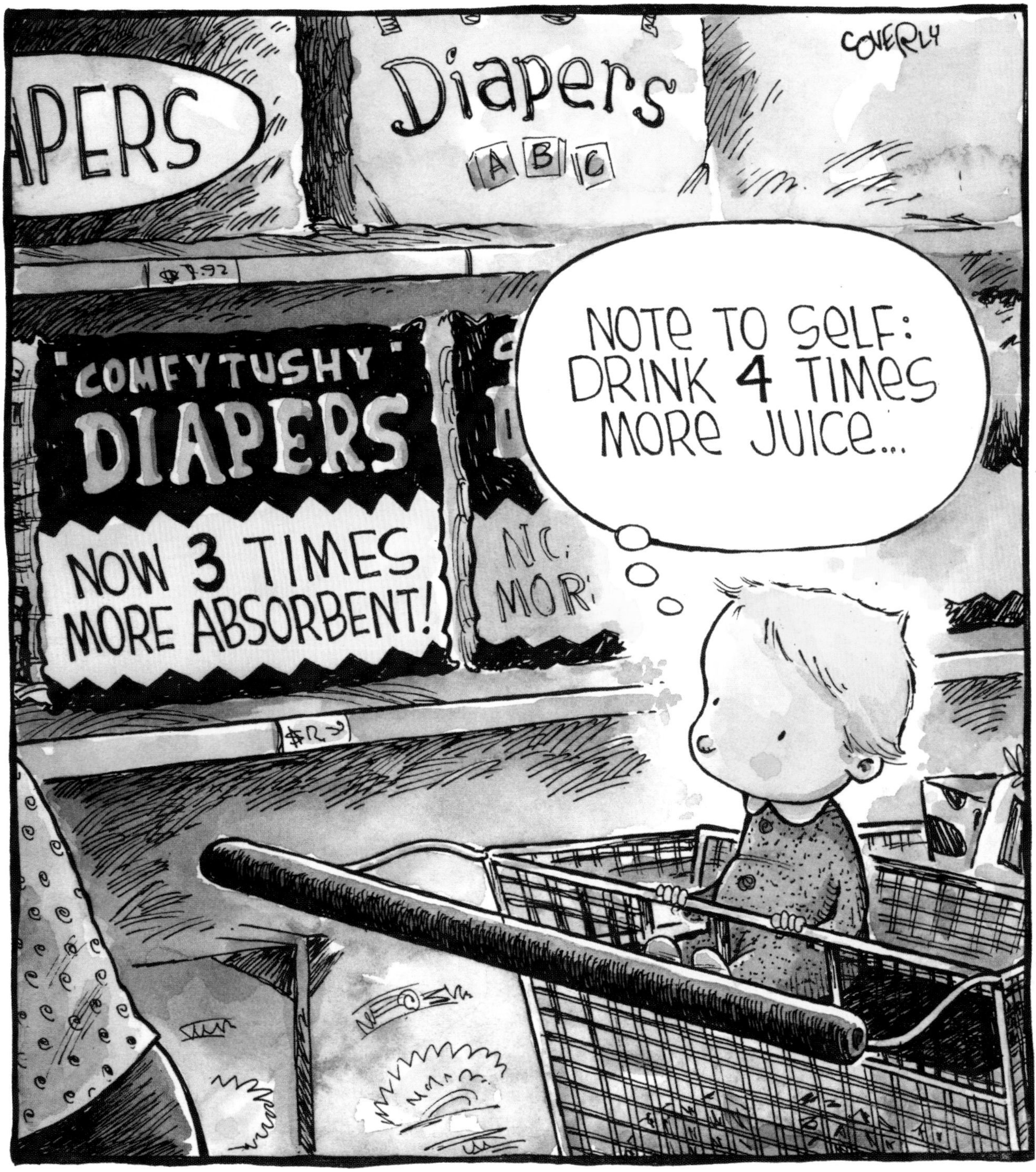
COVERLY
APERS
Diapers
A B C
"COMFY TUSHY"
DIAPERS
NOW 3 TIMES MORE ABSORBENT!
NOTE TO SELF: DRINK 4 TIMES MORE JUICE...

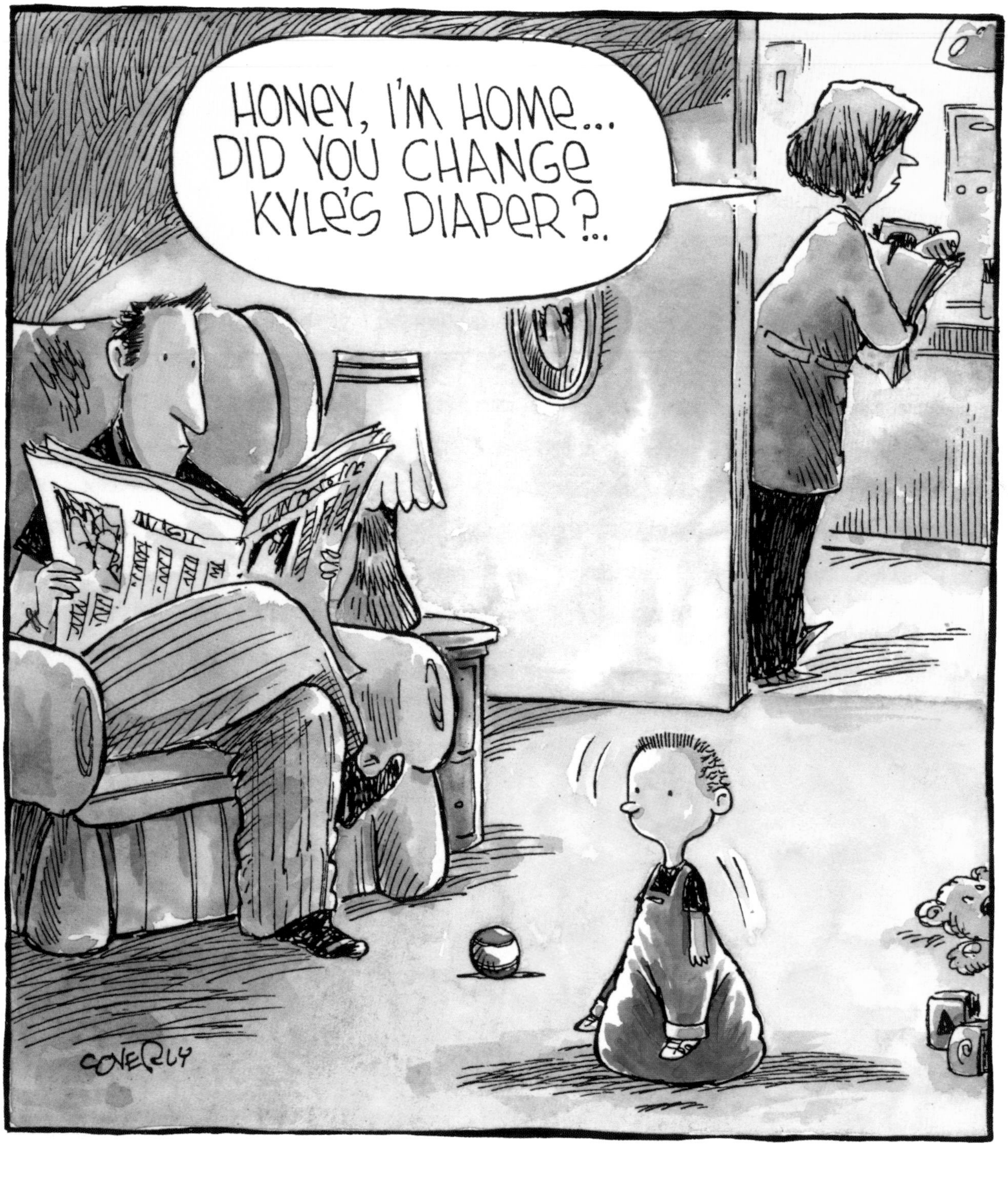
HONEY, I'M HOME...
DID YOU CHANGE
KYLE'S DIAPER?..
COVERLY

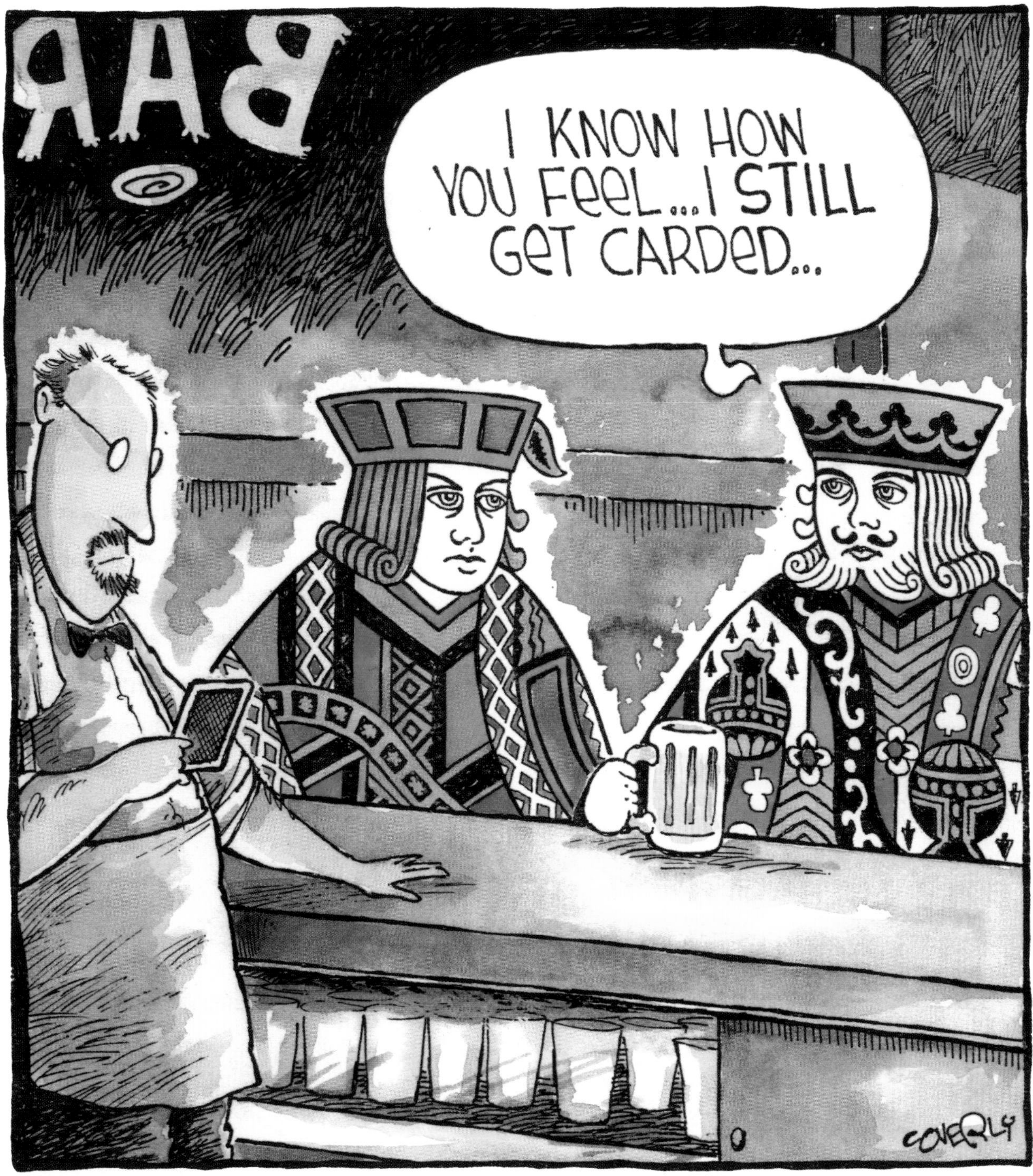
BAR
I KNOW HOW YOU FEEL...I STILL GET CARDED...
COVERLY

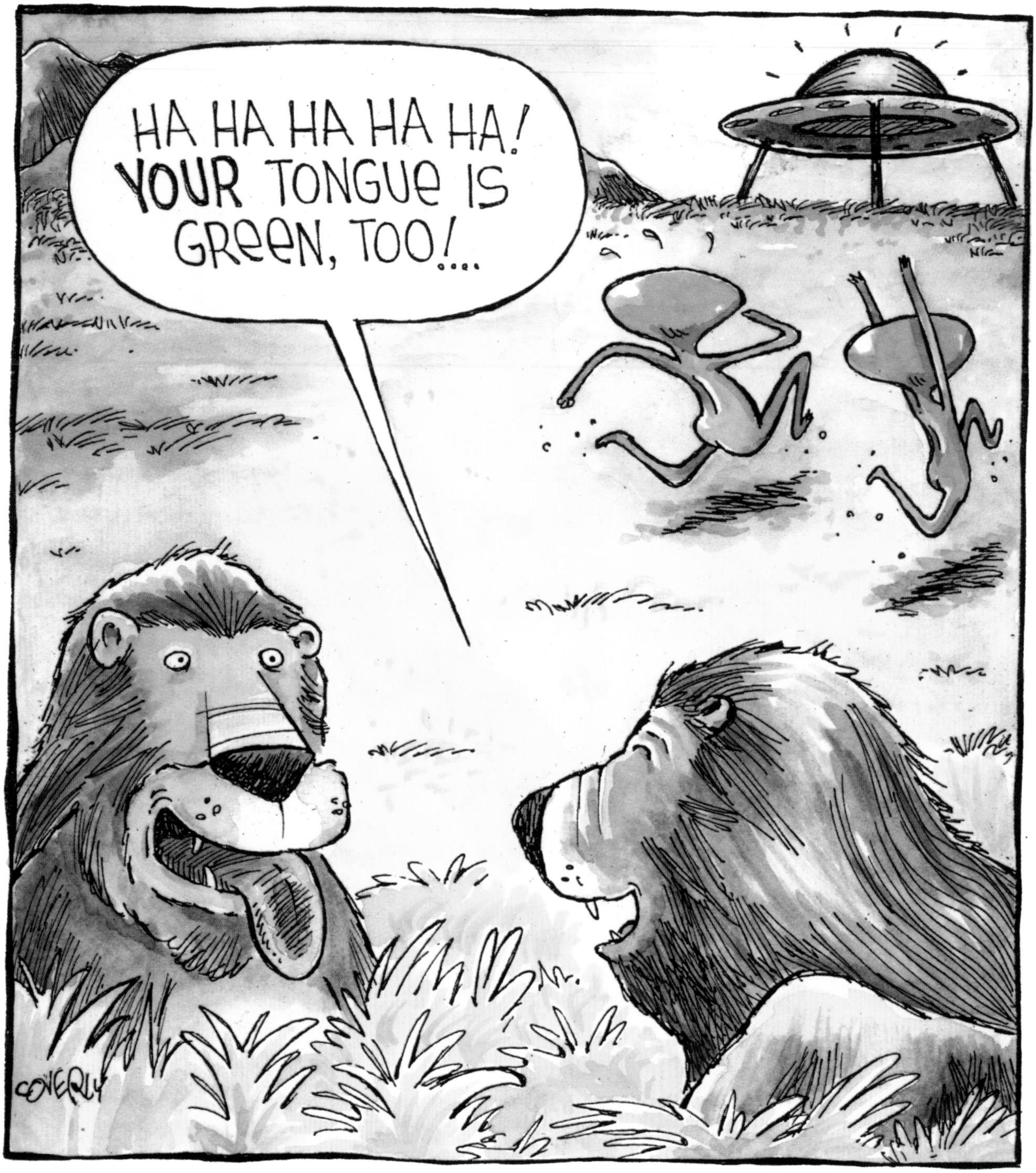
HA HA HA HA HA! YOUR TONGUE IS GREEN, TOO!...
COVERLY

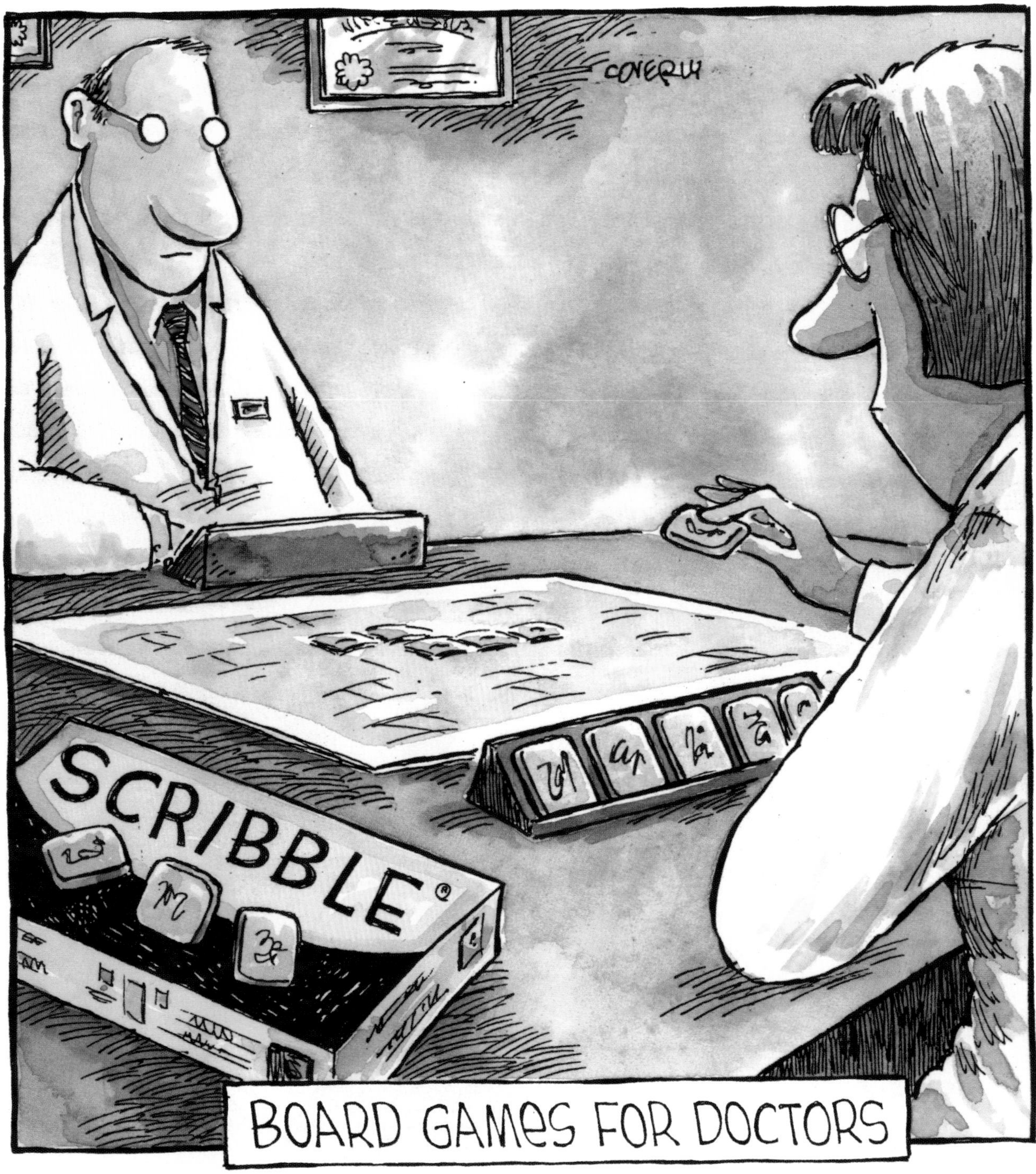
COVERLY
SCRIBBLE®

BOARD GAMES FOR DOCTORS

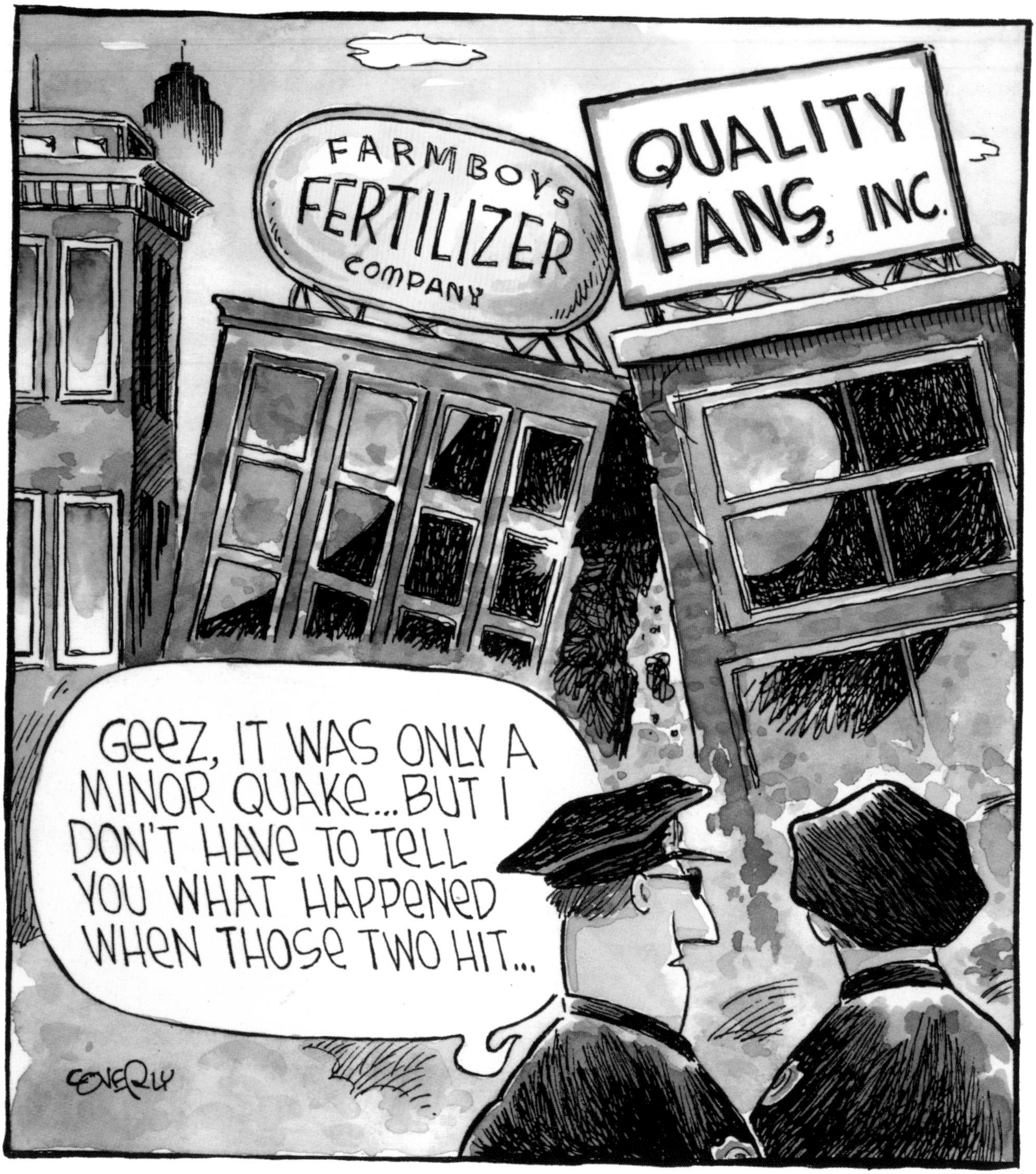
FARMBOYS
FERTILIZER
COMPANY
QUALITY
FANS, INC.
GEEZ, IT WAS ONLY A MINOR QUAKE...BUT I DON'T HAVE TO TELL YOU WHAT HAPPENED WHEN THOSE TWO HIT...
EVERLY

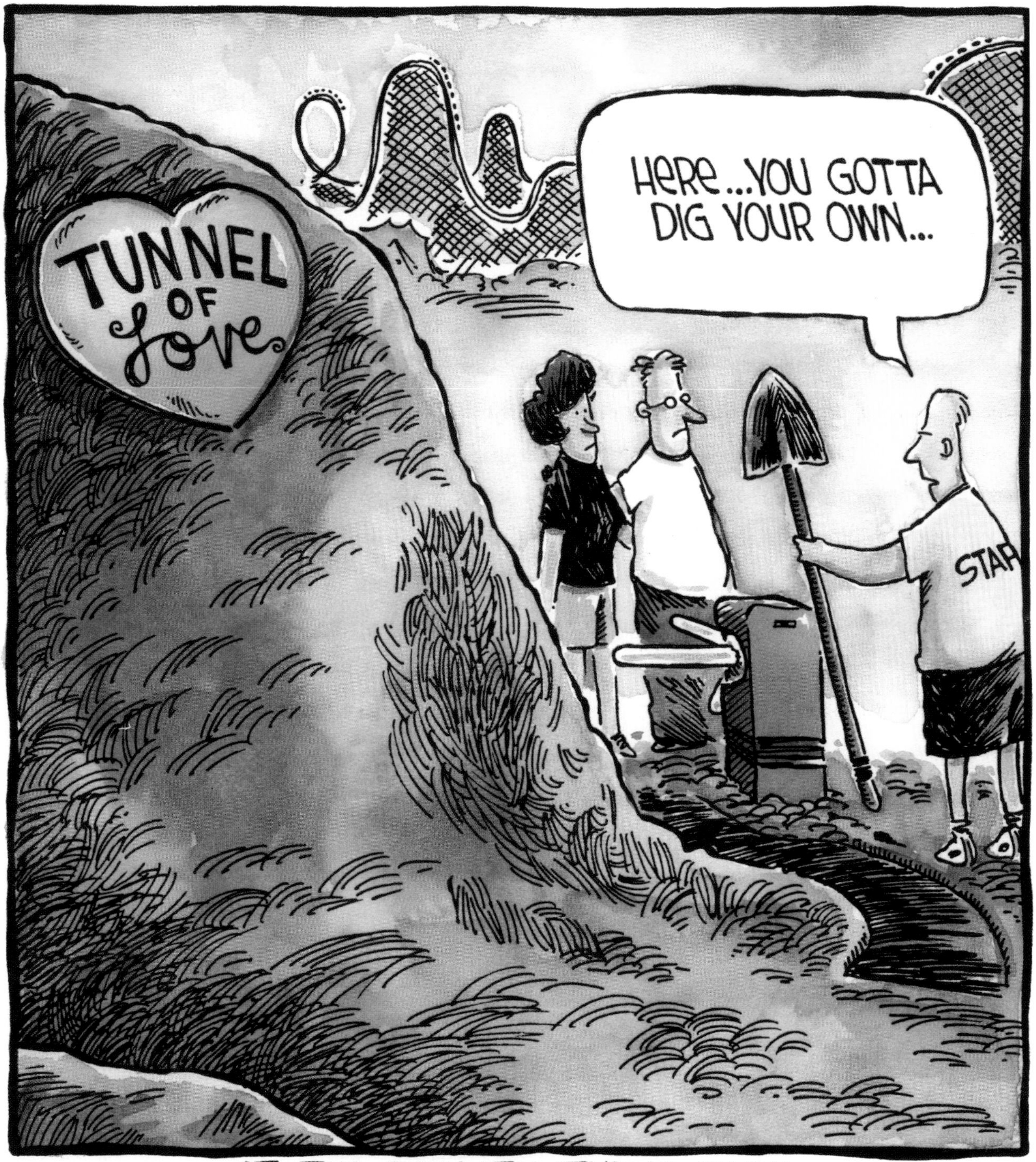
TUNNEL OF Love
HERE...YOU GOTTA DIG YOUR OWN...
STAF
AT THE REALITY THEME PARK

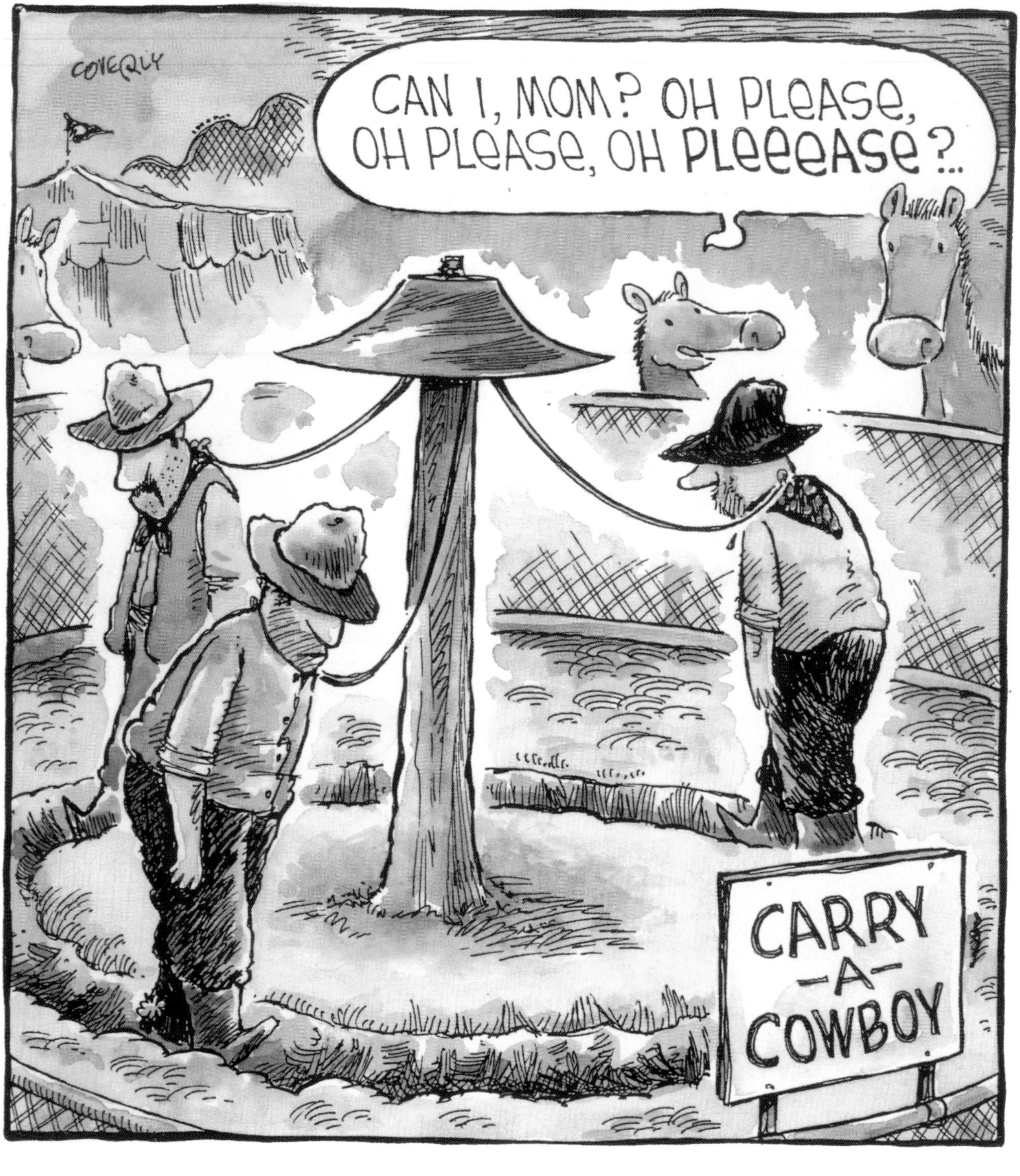
COVERLY
CAN I, MOM? OH PLEASE, OH PLEASE, OH PLEEEASE?..
CARRY -A- COWBOY

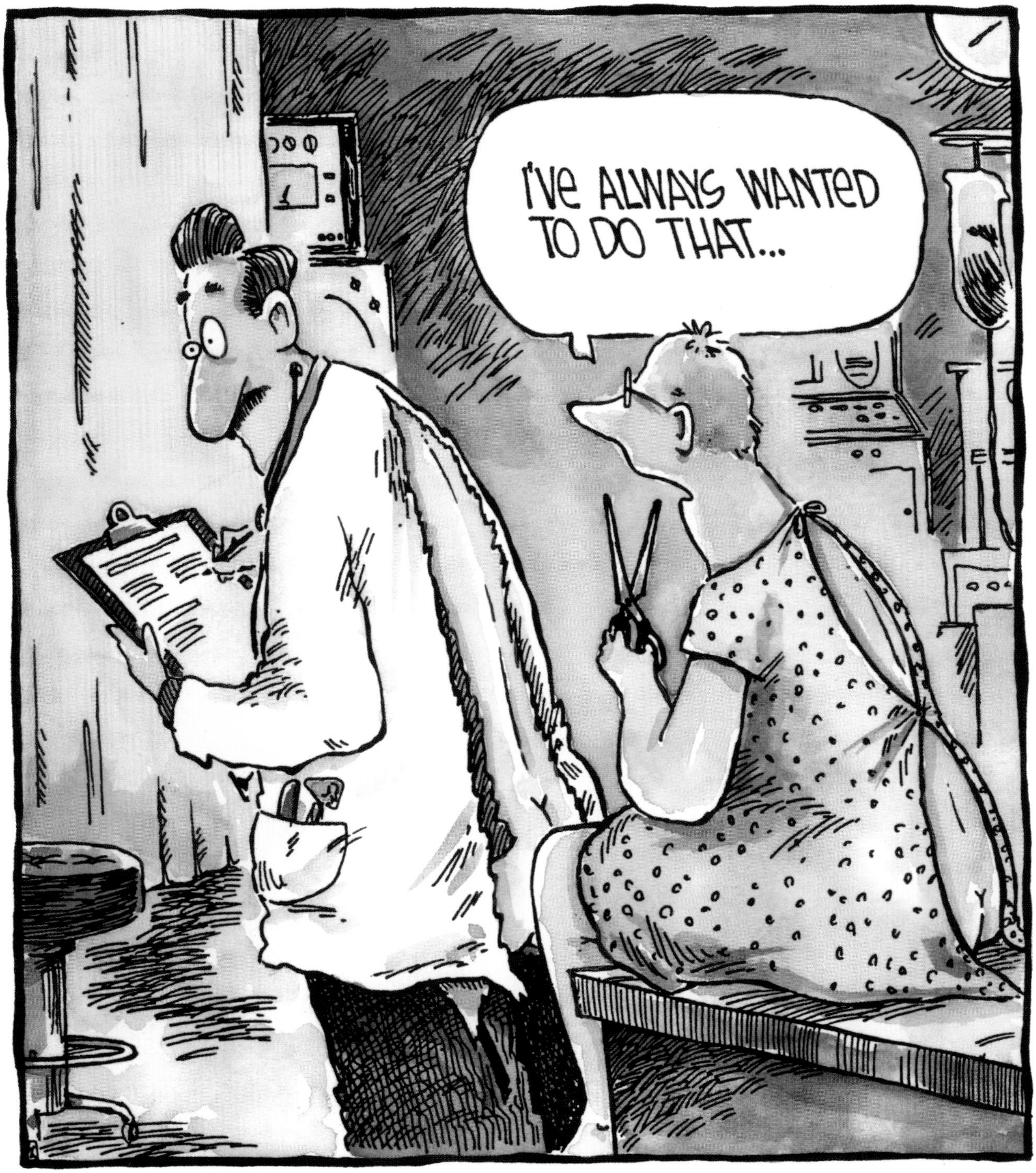
I'VE ALWAYS WANTED TO DO THAT...

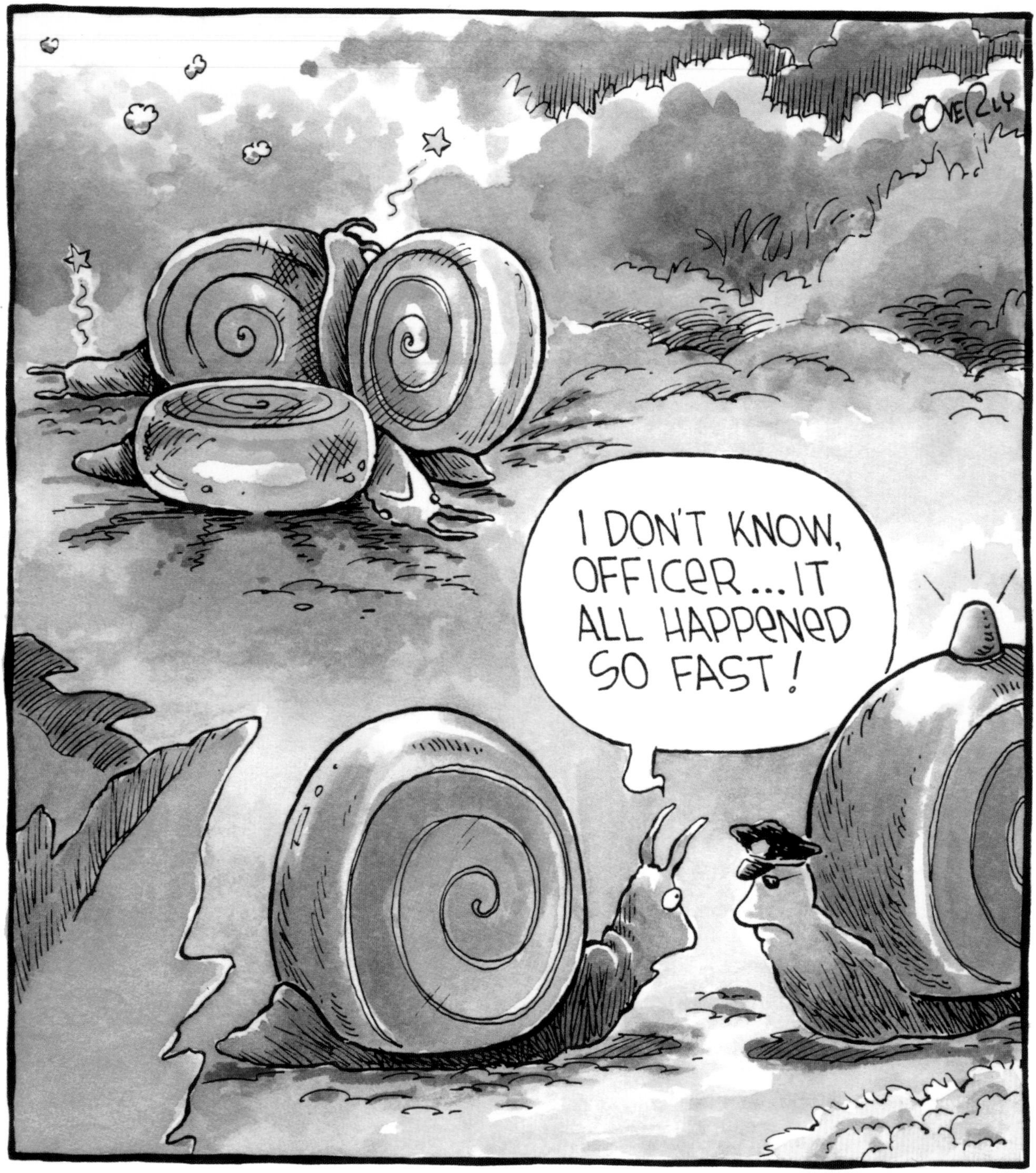
COVERLY
I DON'T KNOW, OFFICER... IT ALL HAPPENED SO FAST!

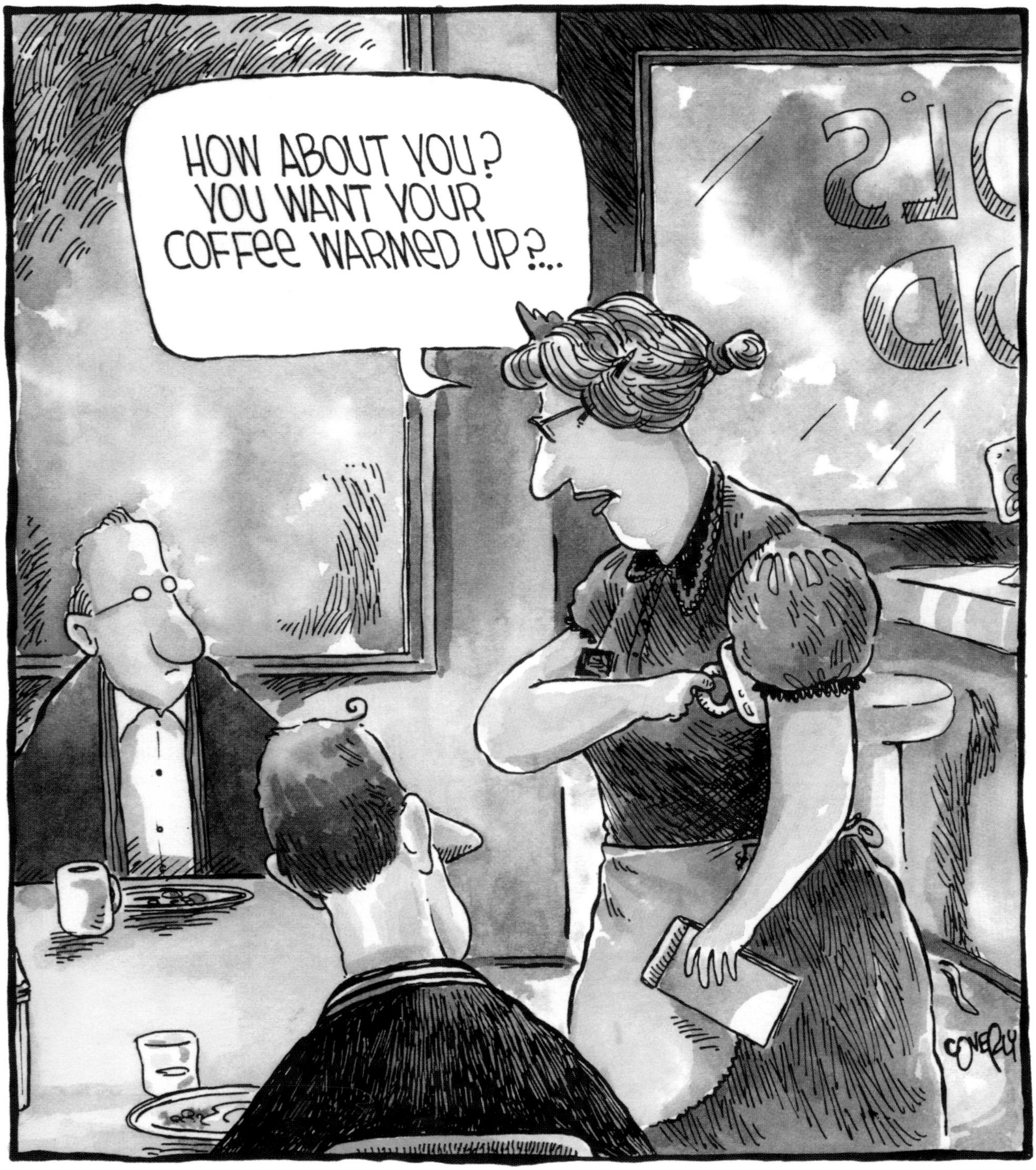
HOW ABOUT YOU? YOU WANT YOUR COFFEE WARMED UP?...
COVERLY

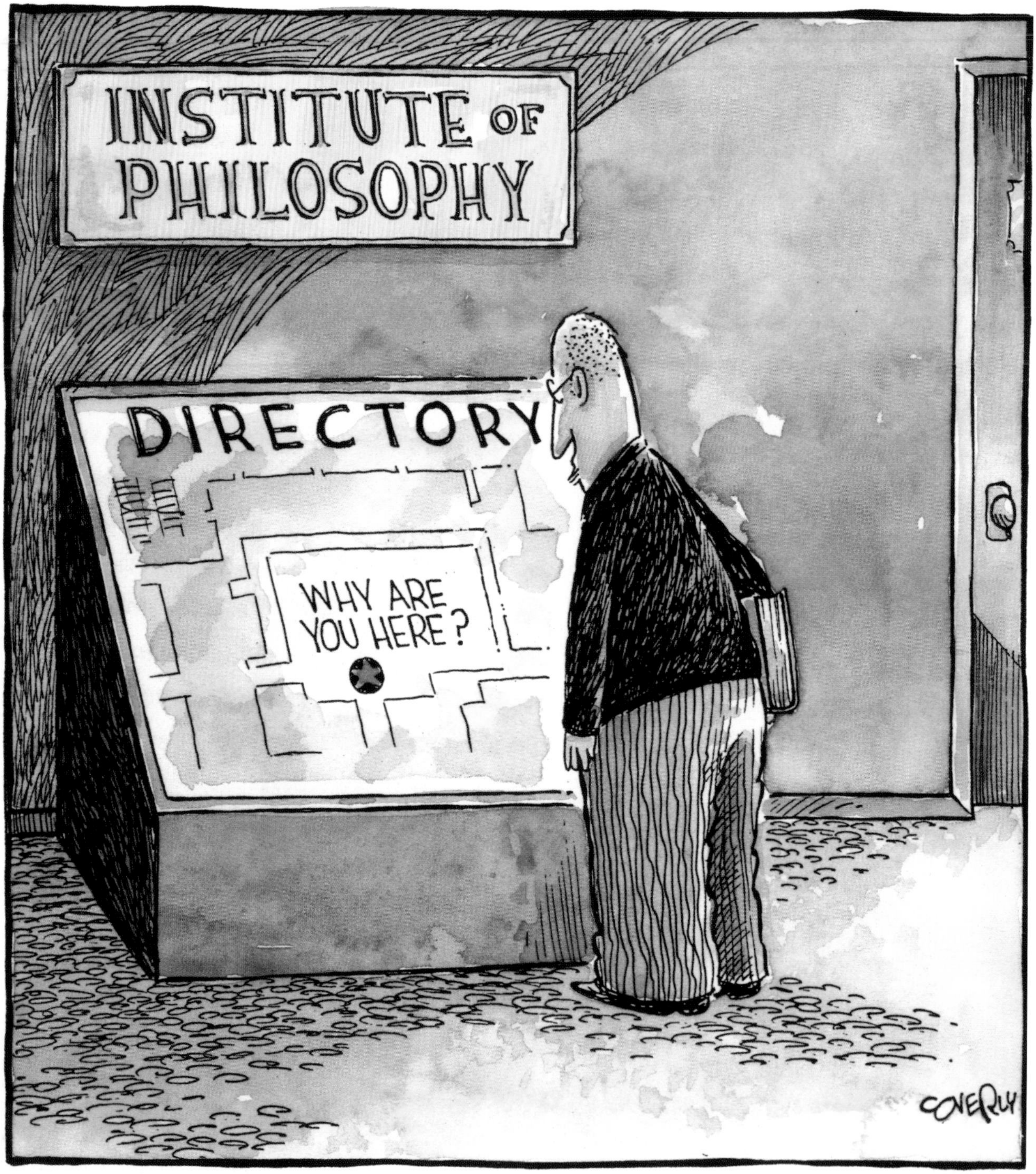
INSTITUTE OF PHILOSOPHY
DIRECTORY
WHY ARE YOU HERE?
COVERLY

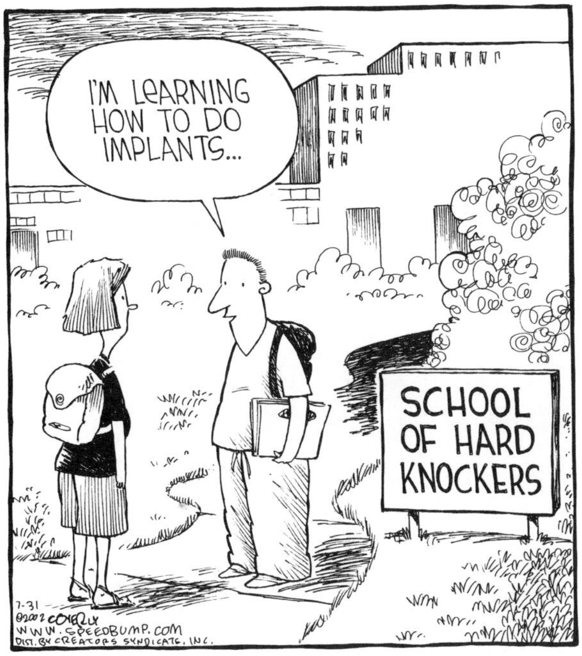
I'M LEARNING HOW TO DO IMPLANTS...
SCHOOL OF HARD KNOCKERS
7-31
©2002 COVERLY
WWW.SPEEDBUMP.COM
DIST. BY CREATORS SYNDICATE, INC.

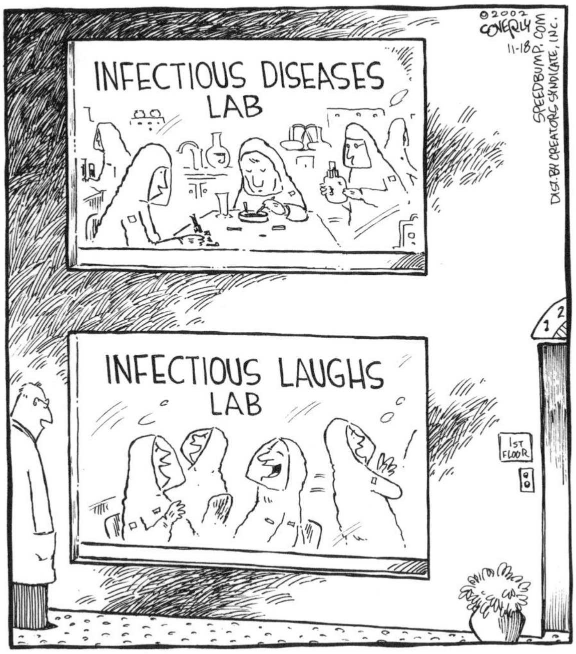
©2002 COVERLY
11-18
SPEEDBUMP.COM
DIST. BY CREATORS SYNDICATE, INC.
INFECTIOUS DISEASES LAB
INFECTIOUS LAUGHS LAB
1ST FLOOR

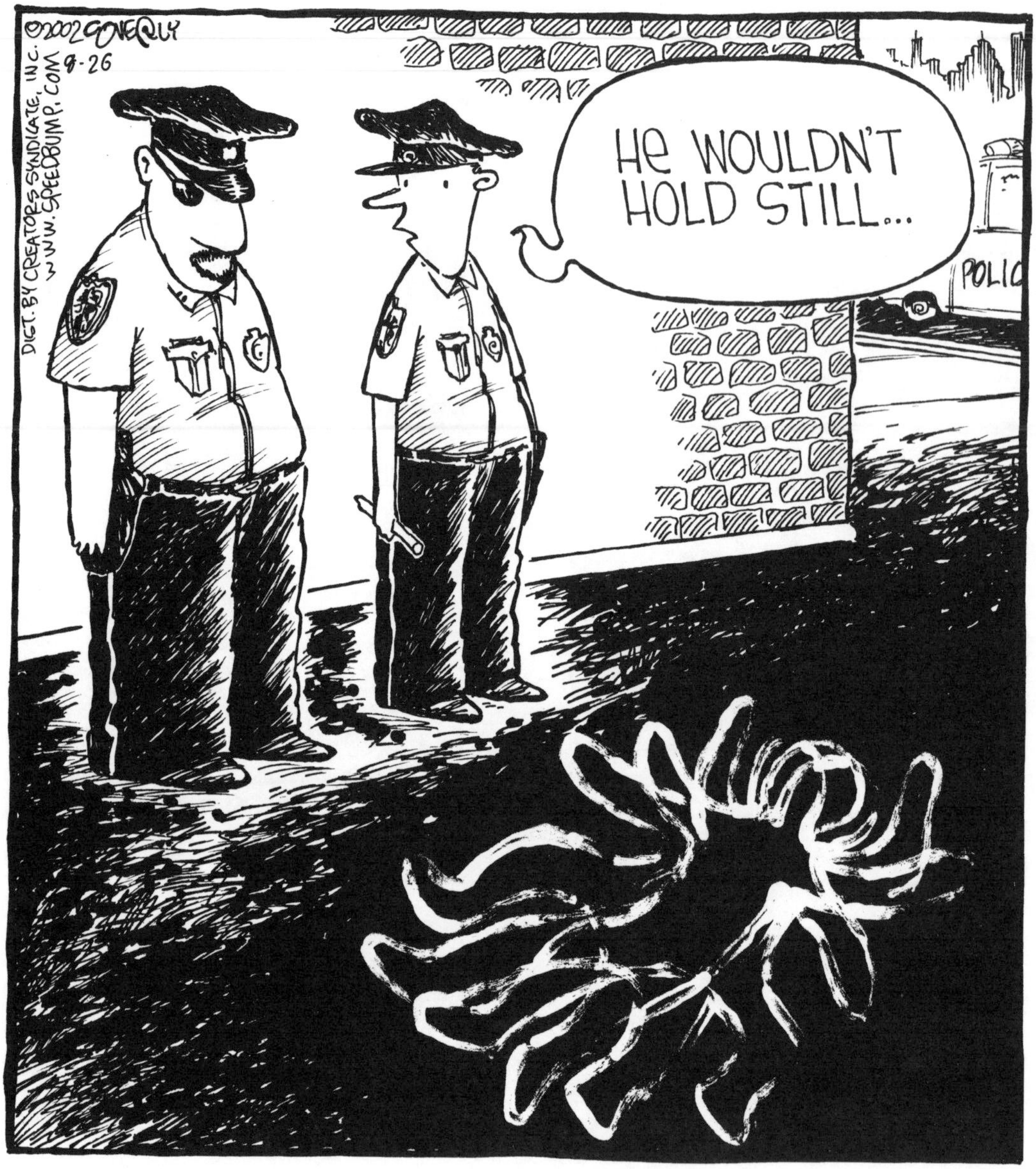

©2002 GOVEQUY
9-26
DIST. BY CREATORS SYNDICATE, INC.
WWW.SPEEDBUMP.COM
HE WOULDN'T HOLD STILL...
POLIC

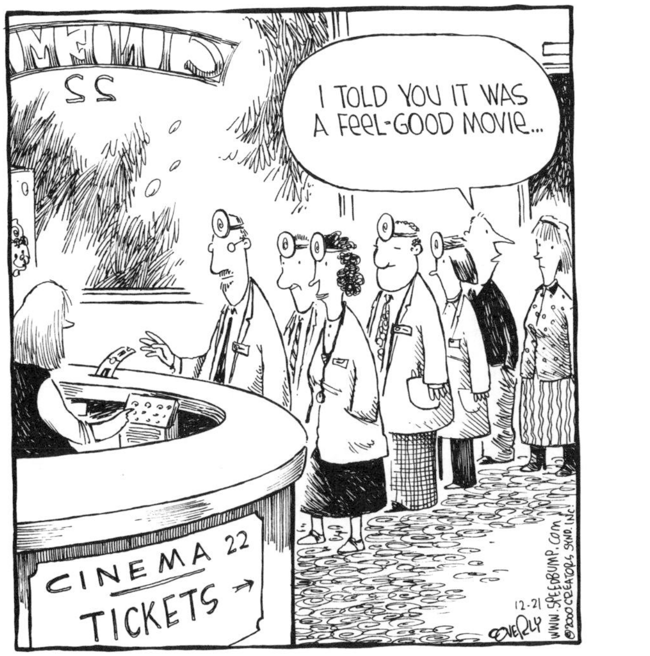
I TOLD YOU IT WAS A FEEL-GOOD MOVIE...
CINEMA 22
TICKETS →
12-21
COVERLY
WWW.SPEEDBUMP.COM
©2000 CREATORS SYND. INC.

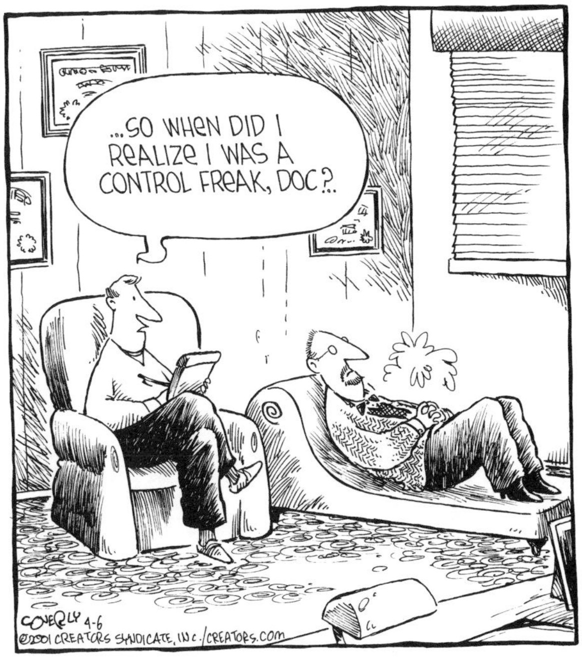
...SO WHEN DID I REALIZE I WAS A CONTROL FREAK, DOC?..
COVERLY 4-6
©2001 CREATORS SYNDICATE, INC./CREATORS.COM

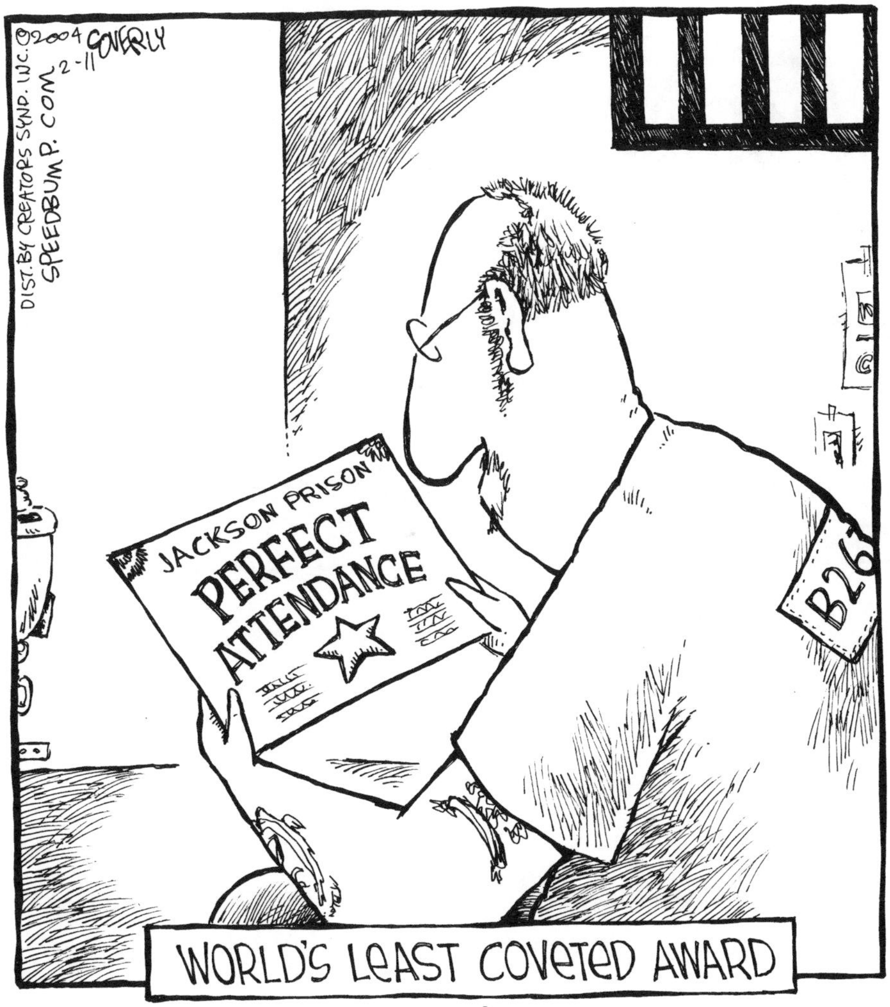
©2004 COVERLY 2-11
DIST. BY CREATORS SYND. INC.
SPEEDBUMP.COM
JACKSON PRISON
PERFECT ATTENDANCE
B26
WORLD'S LEAST COVETED AWARD

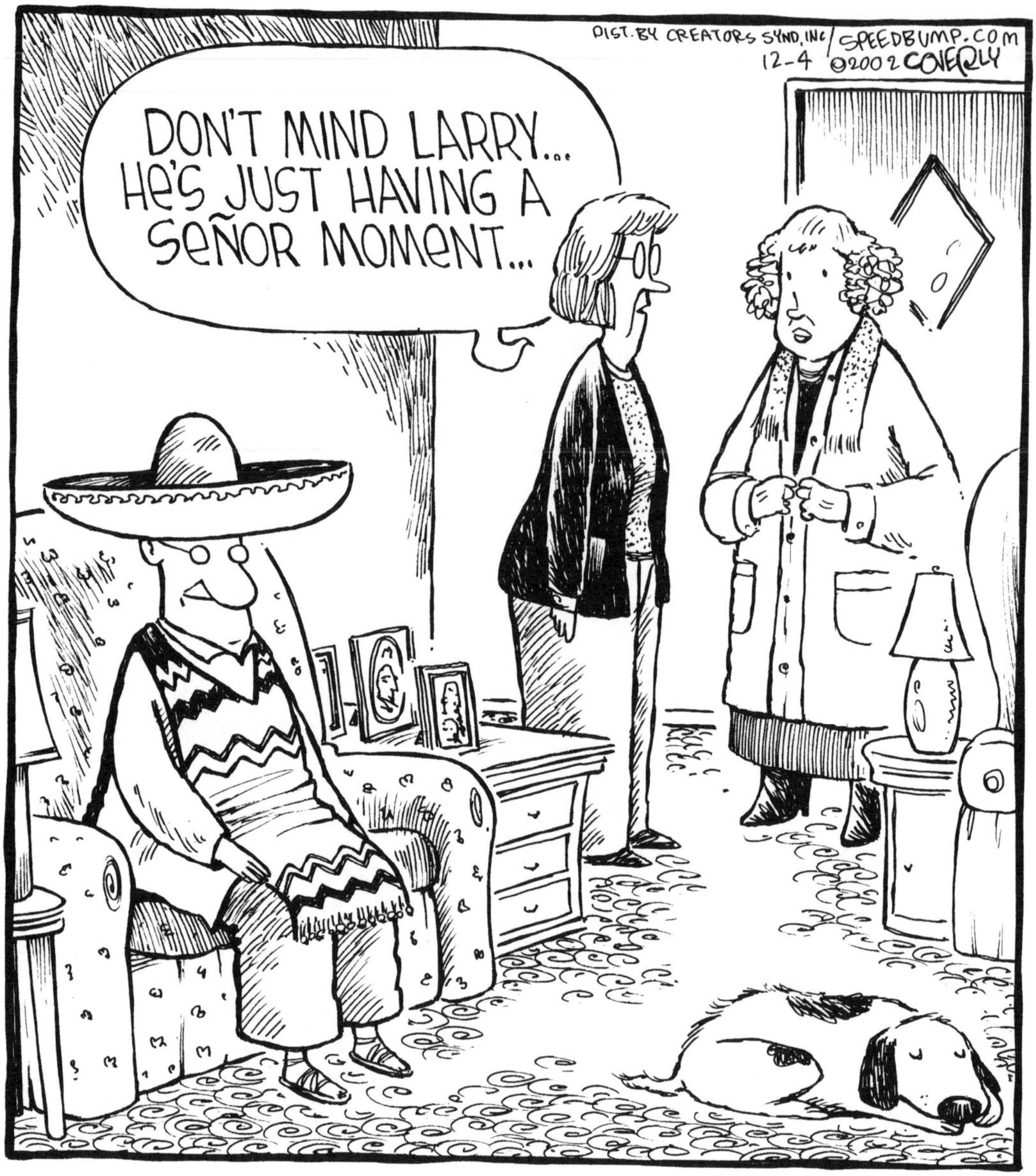
DIST. BY CREATORS SYND, INC / SPEEDBUMP.COM
12-4 ©2002 COVERLY
DON'T MIND LARRY... HE'S JUST HAVING A SEÑOR MOMENT...

Aging

Age does not make us childish, as some say;
it finds us true children.
— Goethe

The older I get, the more difficult it seems to be to come up with ideas. Part of this can be explained by the fact that there's a finite pool of subject matter to choose from.... But the biggest problem, I think, is that I'm moving farther and farther away from that wide-eyed childish outlook that likes to explore all the layers of stuff we adults take for granted. As we get older, we all get more set in our ways and more defensive about them.

For cartoonists, it's a constant battle to try to see the world as fresh and new and to ask in a thousand different ways, "Why is the sky blue?"

Oh, and then there's the neck pain from bending over a drawing table every day, the hand cramps, the inflamed tailbone... have I told you about that bone spur on my elbow . . . ? . . . and the . . .

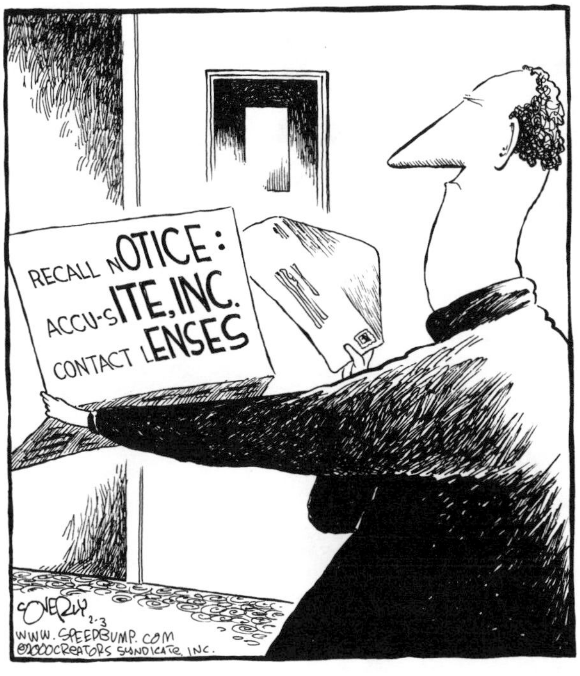
RECALL NOTICE:
ACCU-SITE, INC.
CONTACT LENSES
WWW.SPEEDBUMP.COM

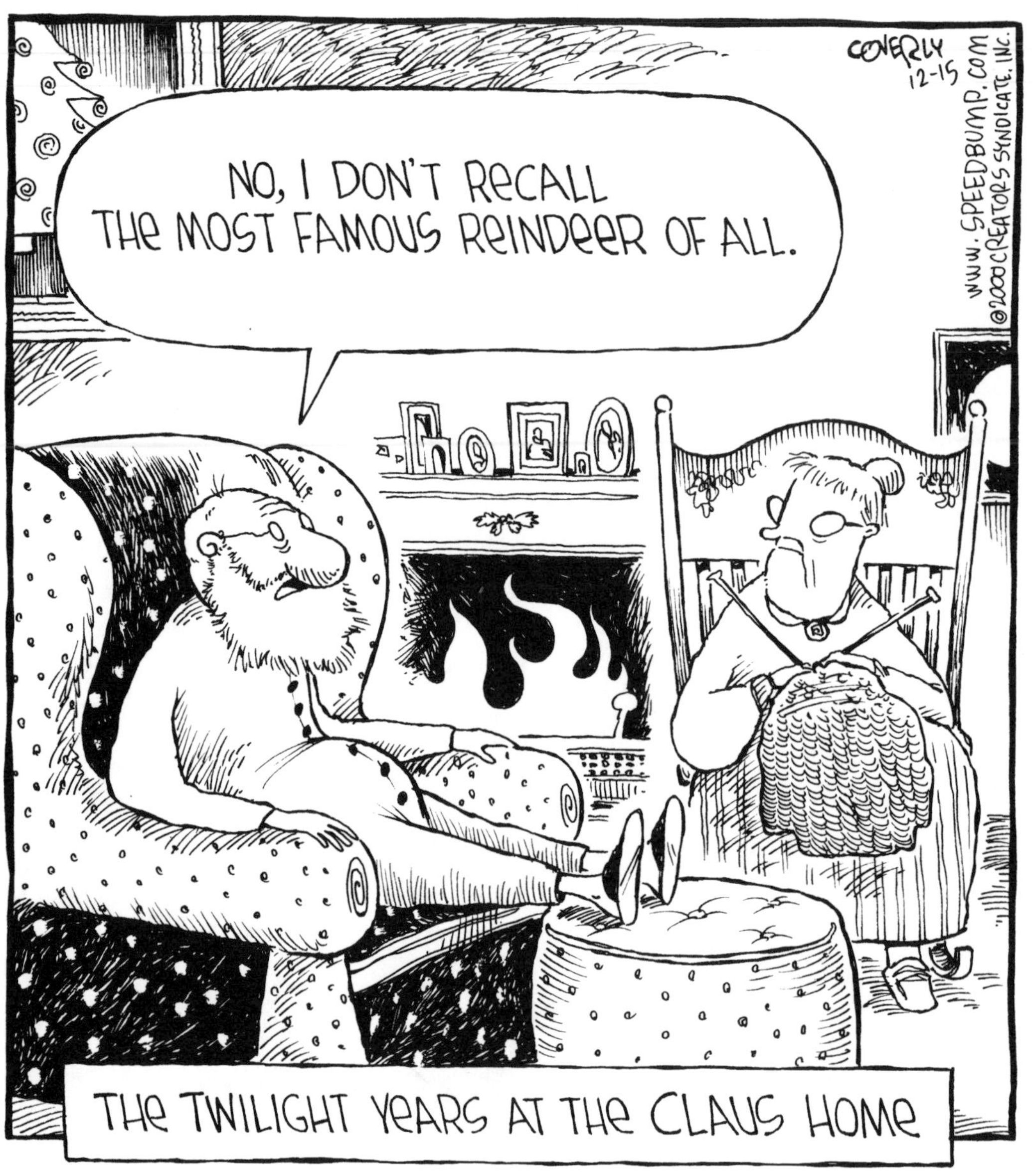
NO, I DON'T RECALL THE MOST FAMOUS REINDEER OF ALL.
COVERLY 12-15
WWW.SPEEDBUMP.COM
©2000 CREATORS SYNDICATE, INC.
THE TWILIGHT YEARS AT THE CLAUS HOME

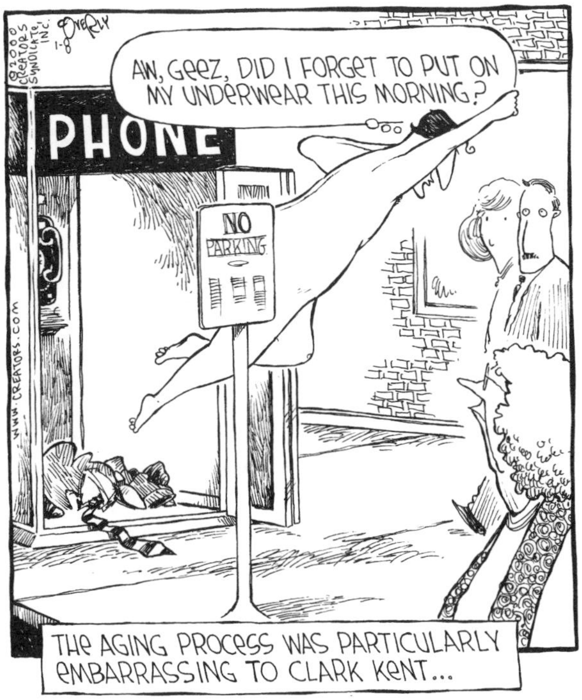
AW, GEEZ, DID I FORGET TO PUT ON MY UNDERWEAR THIS MORNING?
PHONE
NO PARKING
WWW.CREATORS.COM
THE AGING PROCESS WAS PARTICULARLY EMBARRASSING TO CLARK KENT...

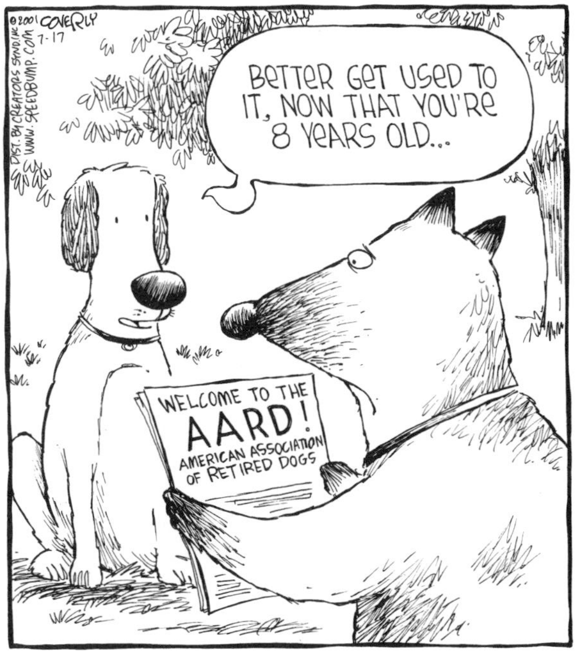
BETTER GET USED TO IT, NOW THAT YOU'RE 8 YEARS OLD...
WELCOME TO THE AARD! AMERICAN ASSOCIATION OF RETIRED DOGS

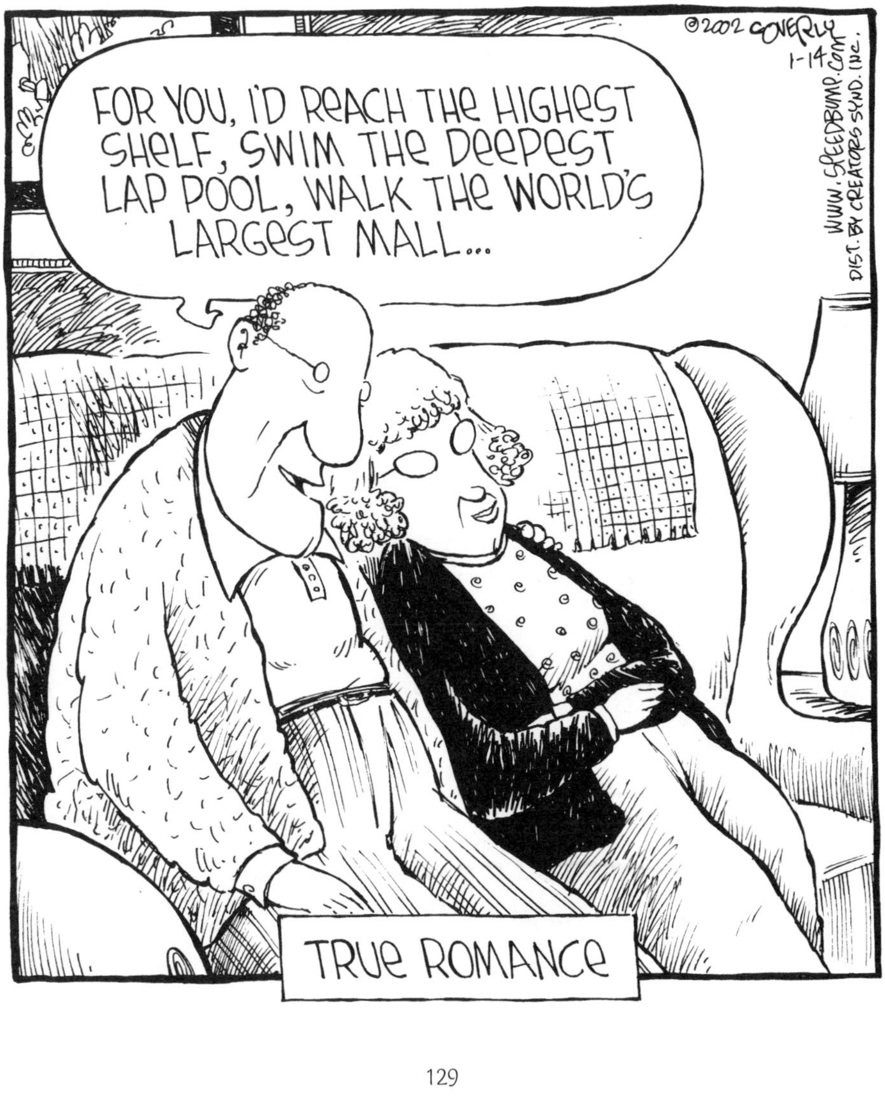
©2002 COVERLY 1-14
WWW.SPEEDBUMP.COM DIST. BY CREATORS SYND. INC.
FOR YOU, I'D REACH THE HIGHEST SHELF, SWIM THE DEEPEST LAP POOL, WALK THE WORLD'S LARGEST MALL...
TRUE ROMANCE

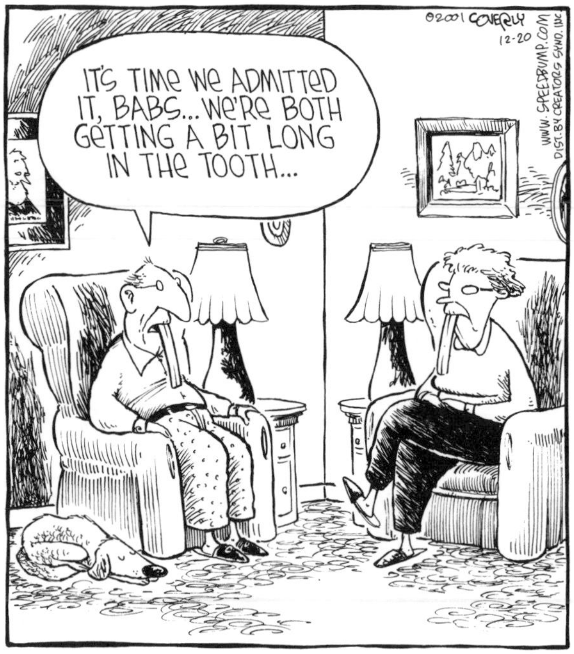
IT'S TIME WE ADMITTED IT, BABS... WE'RE BOTH GETTING A BIT LONG IN THE TOOTH...
©2001 COVERLY 12-20
WWW.SPEEDBUMP.COM DIST. BY CREATORS SYND. INC

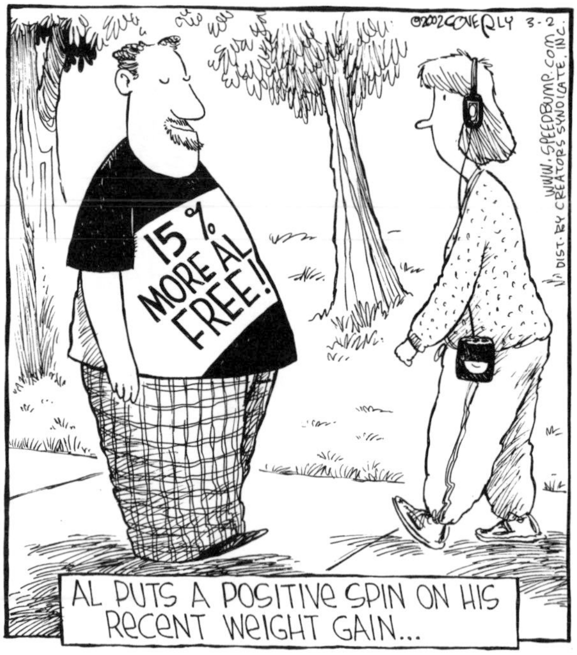
15% MORE AL FREE!
©2002 COVERLY 3-2
WWW.SPEEDBUMP.COM DIST. BY CREATORS SYNDICATE, INC.
AL PUTS A POSITIVE SPIN ON HIS RECENT WEIGHT GAIN...

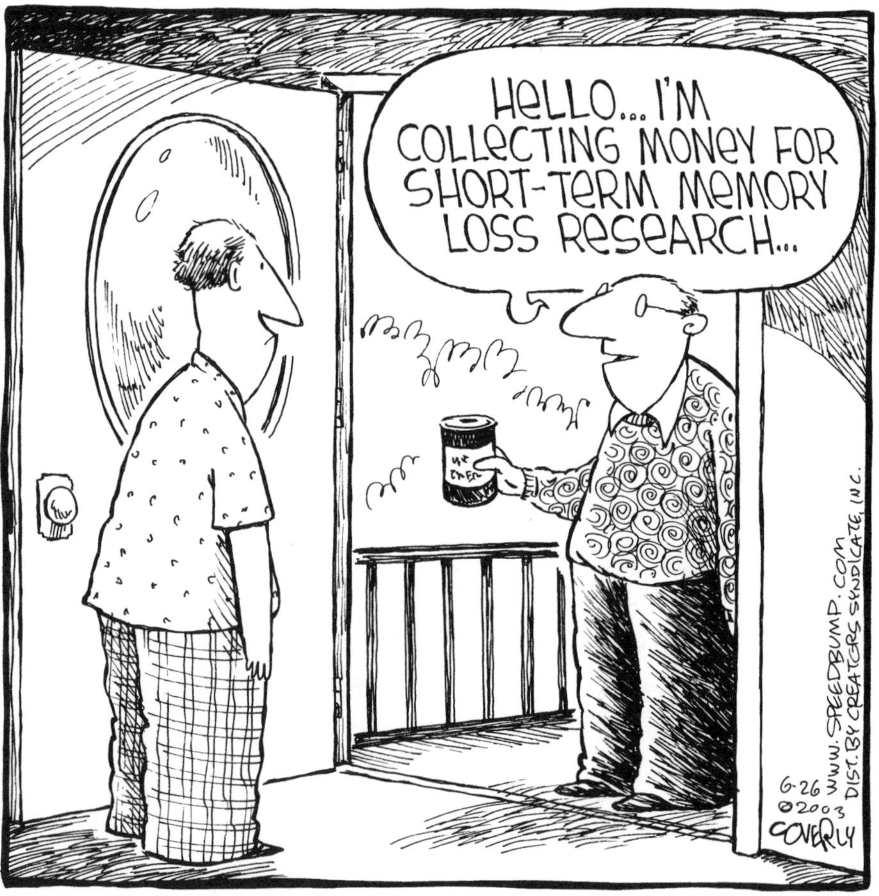
HELLO... I'M COLLECTING MONEY FOR SHORT-TERM MEMORY LOSS RESEARCH...
WWW.SPEEDBUMP.COM DIST. BY CREATORS SYNDICATE, INC.
6-26 ©2003 COVERLY

BY THE FIFTH VISIT, ROGER DECIDED HE'D GIVEN THIS GUY ENOUGH FOR THE DAY.

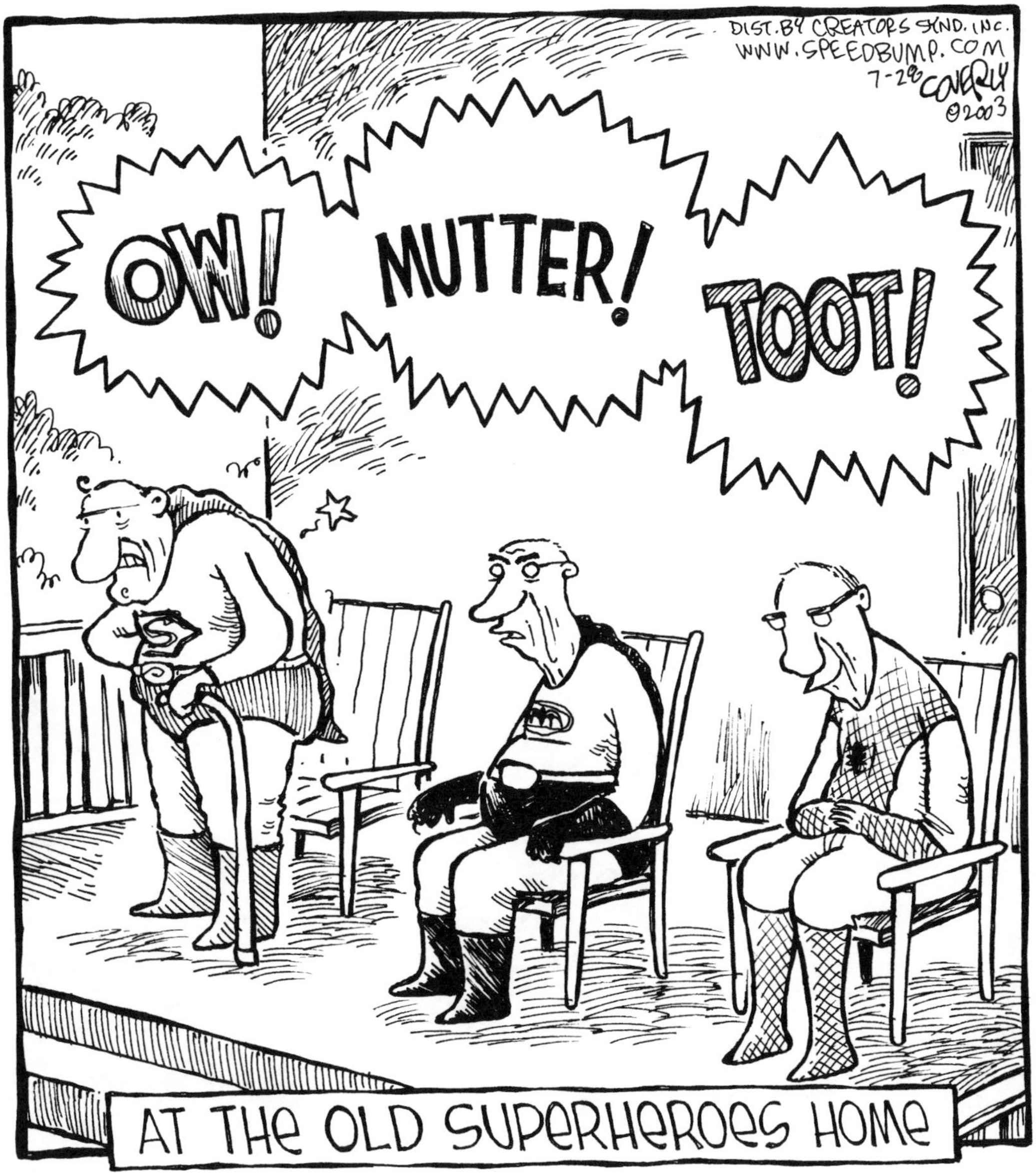
DIST. BY CREATORS SYND. INC.
WWW.SPEEDBUMP.COM
7-28 COVERLY ©2003
OW!
MUTTER!
TOOT!
AT THE OLD SUPERHEROES HOME

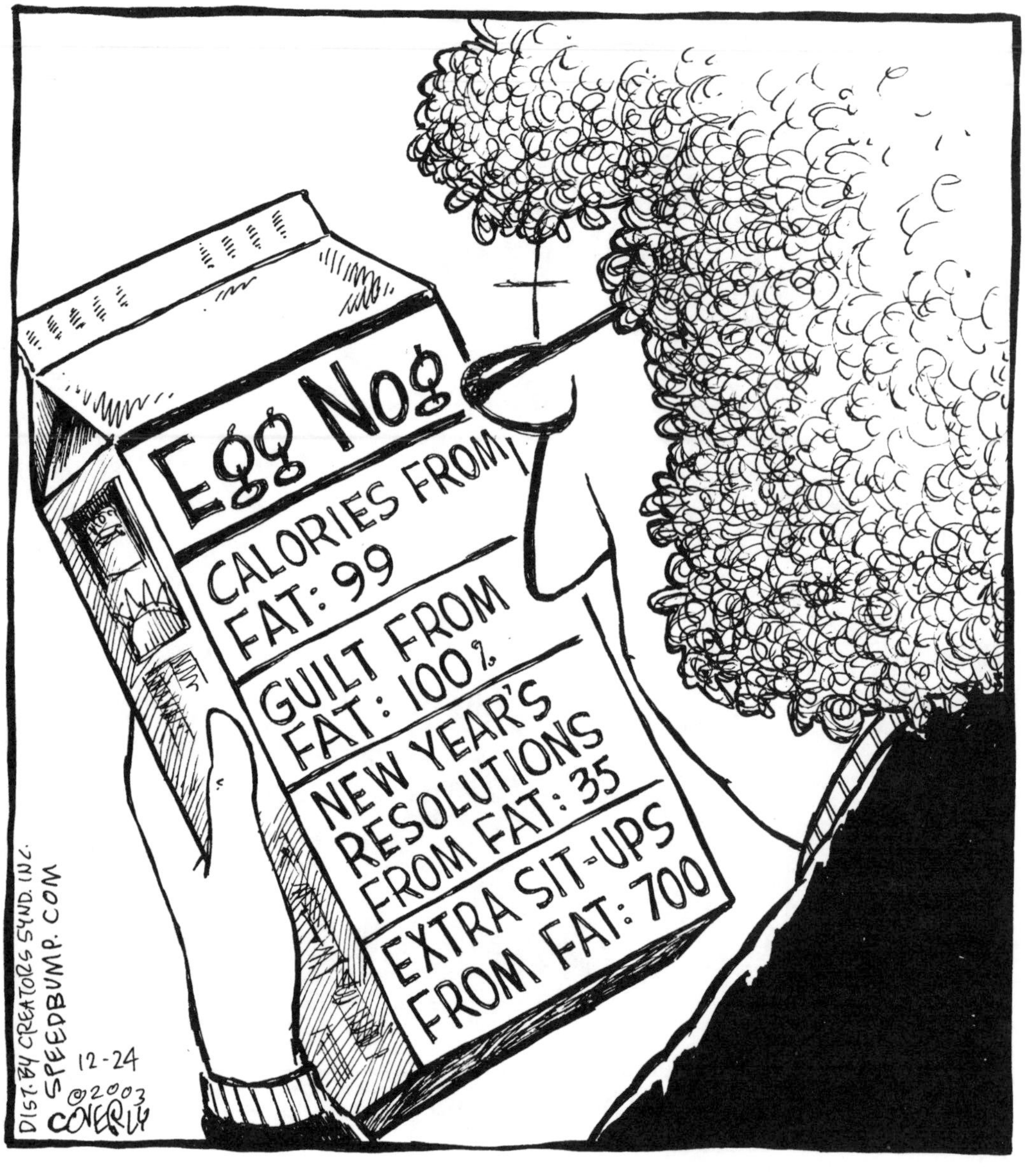
Egg Nog
CALORIES FROM FAT: 99
GUILT FROM FAT: 100%
NEW YEAR'S RESOLUTIONS FROM FAT: 35
EXTRA SIT-UPS FROM FAT: 700
DIST. BY CREATORS SYND. INC.
SPEEDBUMP.COM
12-24
©2003
COVERLY

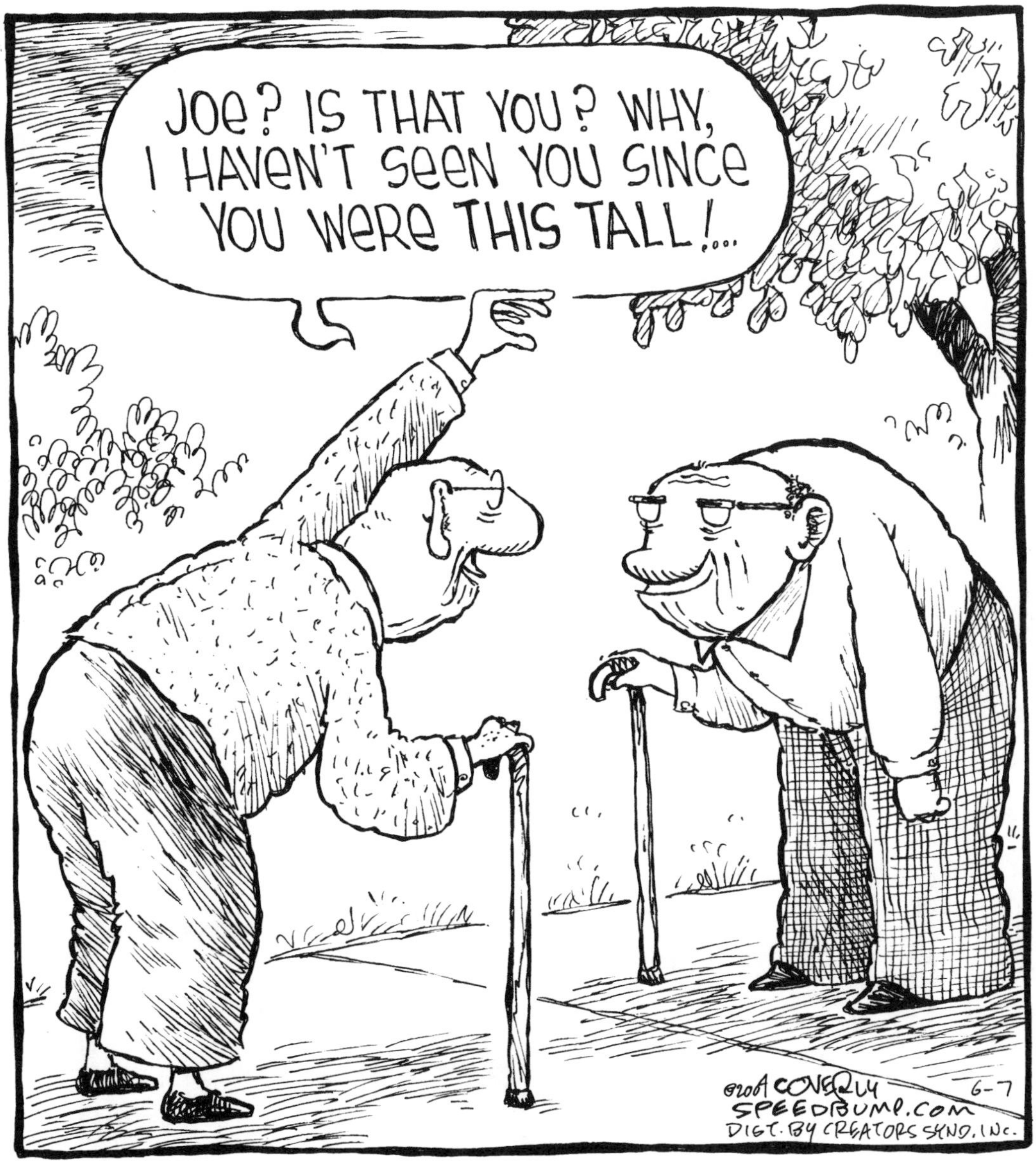
JOE? IS THAT YOU? WHY, I HAVEN'T SEEN YOU SINCE YOU WERE THIS TALL!...
©2006 COVERLY 6-7
SPEEDBUMP.COM
DIST. BY CREATORS SYND. INC.

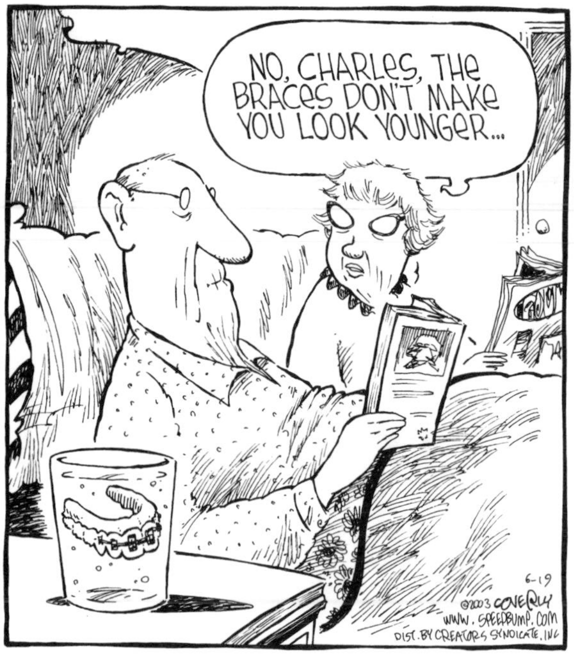
NO, CHARLES, THE BRACES DON'T MAKE YOU LOOK YOUNGER...
6-19
©2003 COVERLY
WWW.SPEEDBUMP.COM
DIST. BY CREATORS SYNDICATE, INC

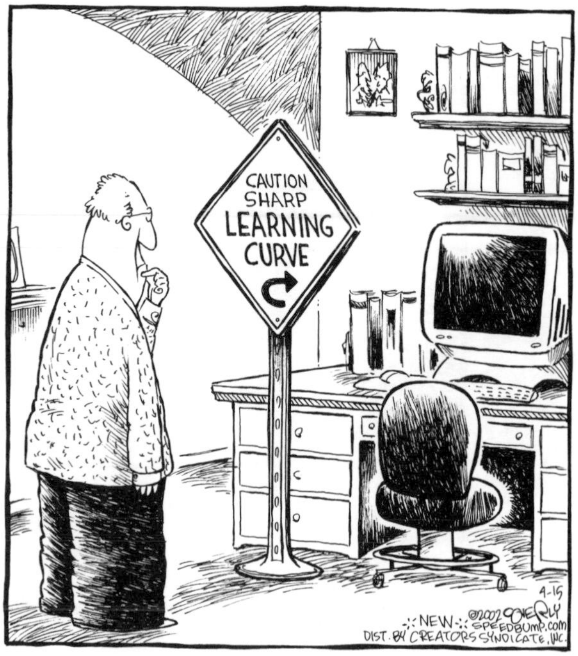
CAUTION SHARP LEARNING CURVE
4-15
NEW ©2002 COVERLY SPEEDBUMP.COM
DIST. BY CREATORS SYNDICATE, INC

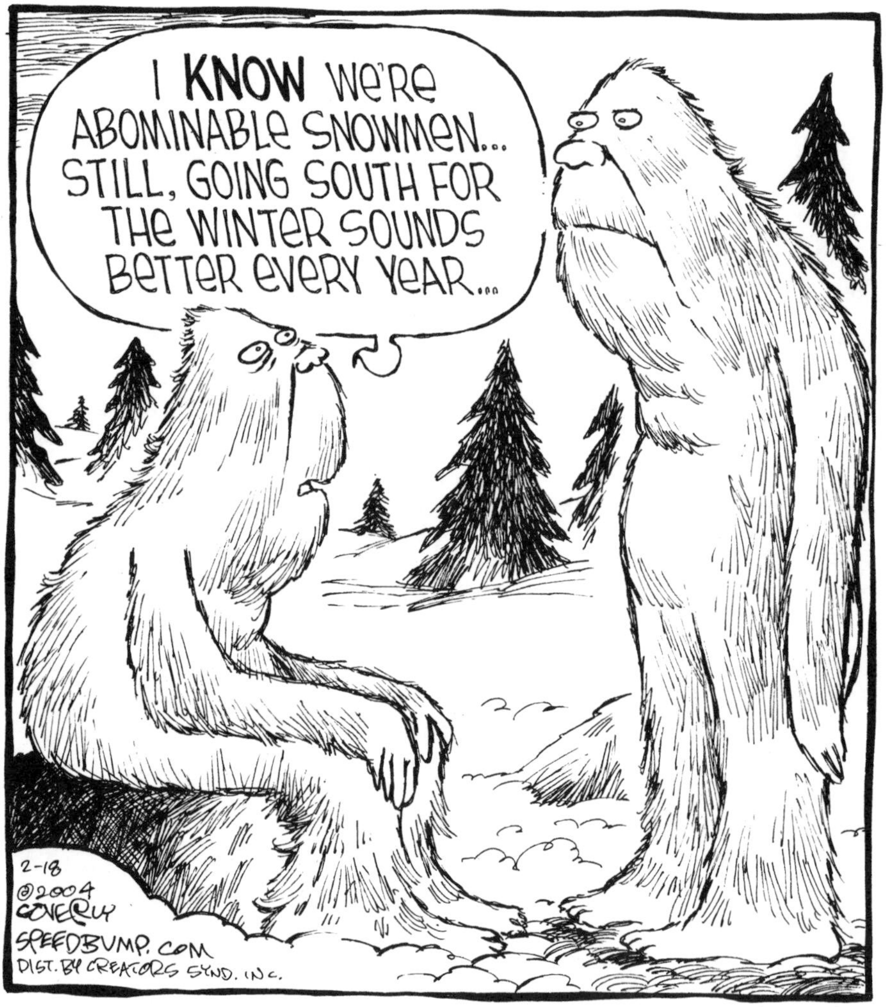
I **KNOW** WE'RE ABOMINABLE SNOWMEN... STILL, GOING SOUTH FOR THE WINTER SOUNDS BETTER EVERY YEAR...
2-18
©2004 COVERLY
SPEEDBUMP.COM
DIST. BY CREATORS SYND. INC.

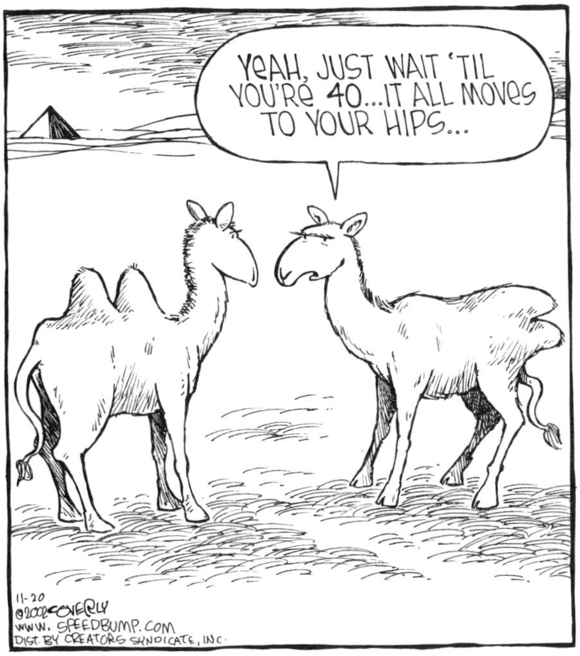
YEAH, JUST WAIT 'TIL YOU'RE 40...IT ALL MOVES TO YOUR HIPS...
11-20
©2002 COVERLY
www.SPEEDBUMP.COM
DIST. BY CREATORS SYNDICATE, INC.

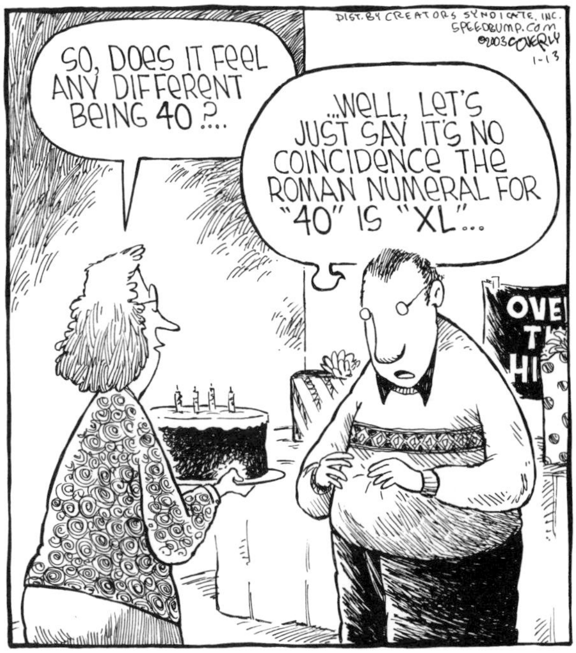
DIST. BY CREATORS SYNDICATE, INC.
SPEEDBUMP.COM
©2003 COVERLY
1-13
SO, DOES IT FEEL ANY DIFFERENT BEING 40 ?...
...WELL, LET'S JUST SAY IT'S NO COINCIDENCE THE ROMAN NUMERAL FOR "40" IS "XL"...

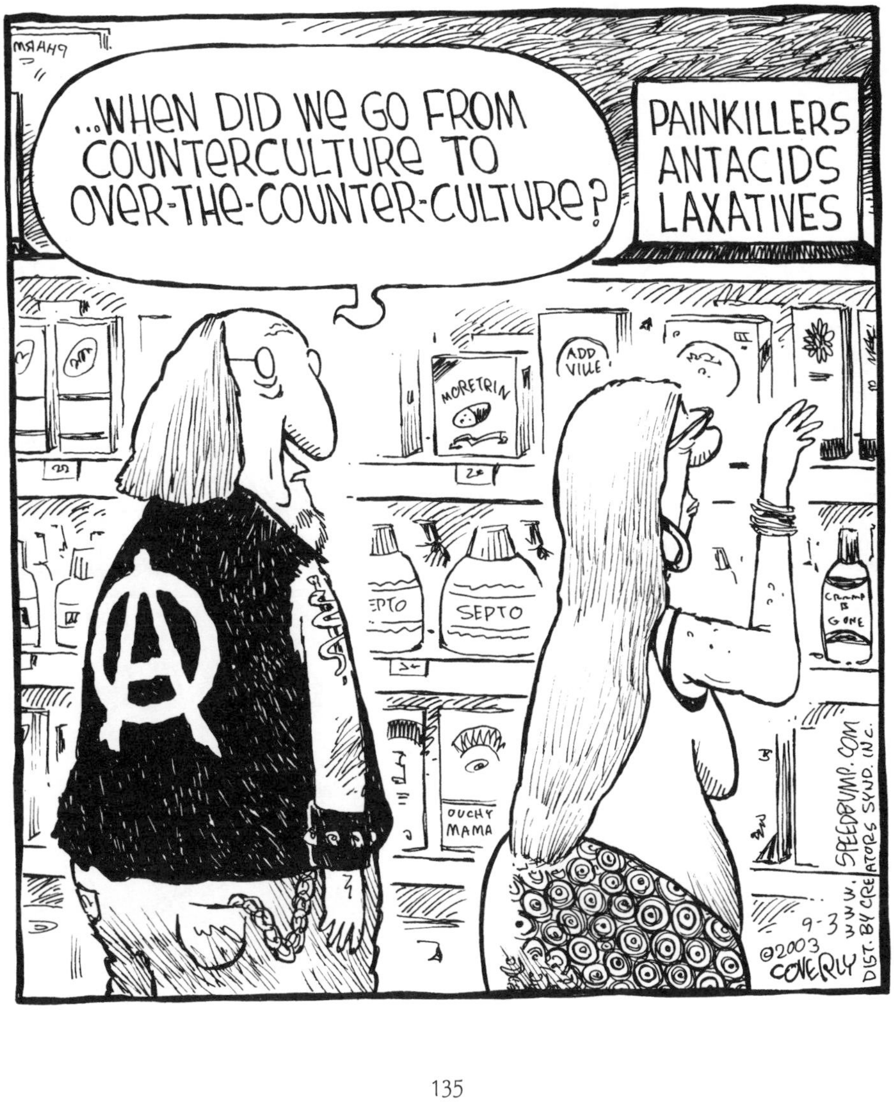
...WHEN DID WE GO FROM COUNTERCULTURE TO OVER-THE-COUNTER-CULTURE?
PAINKILLERS
ANTACIDS
LAXATIVES
MORETRIN
ADD VILLE
SEPTO
CRAMP B GONE
OUCHY MAMA
www.SPEEDBUMP.COM
DIST. BY CREATORS SYND. INC.
9-3
©2003
COVERLY

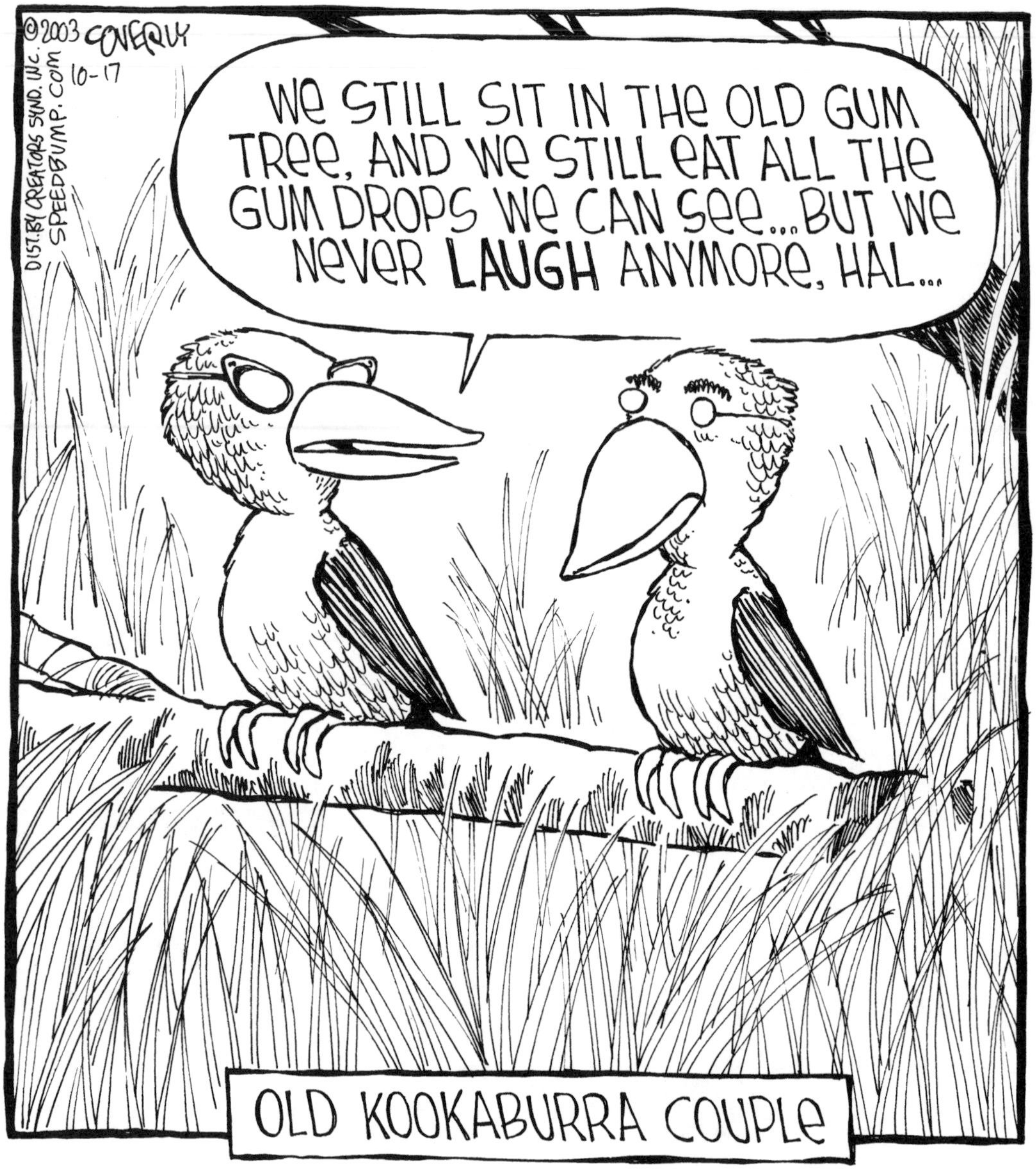
©2003 COVERLY 10-17
DIST. BY CREATORS SYND. INC.
SPEEDBUMP.COM
WE STILL SIT IN THE OLD GUM TREE, AND WE STILL EAT ALL THE GUM DROPS WE CAN SEE...BUT WE NEVER LAUGH ANYMORE, HAL...
OLD KOOKABURRA COUPLE

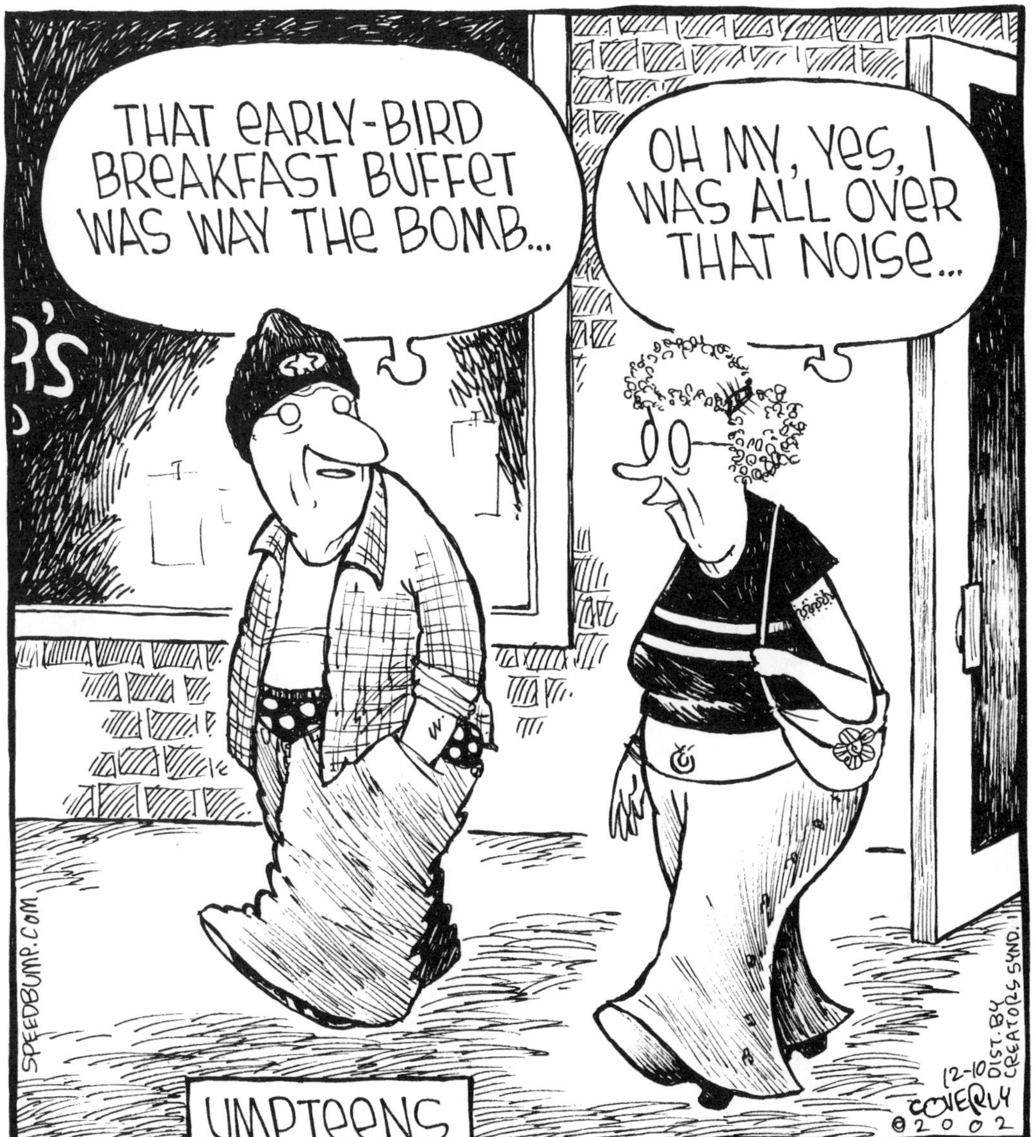
THAT EARLY-BIRD BREAKFAST BUFFET WAS WAY THE BOMB...
OH MY, YES, I WAS ALL OVER THAT NOISE...
UMPTEENS
SPEEDBUMP.COM
12-10
DIST. BY CREATORS SYND.
COVERLY ©2002

Life After Afterlife

I had a near-death experience.

It started out innocently enough. I was standing on our front lawn in my handmade "Mutts" robe, holding a cup of coffee and staring into an early morning Michigan summer sky, just waiting for an idea to hit me. A car approached and slowed down behind me; then came a low, whistling sound, a dull impact to the back of my head, and blackness . . .

I felt a tug and looked up. The sky was gone, and I felt myself being pulled toward a bright light. Well, it wasn't that bright. You'd think it would be like the brightest thing ever if it was the door to the next world. It was more in the 150 watt range. But it was urging me up, and I knew, if I let it, I would not be coming back. I hovered between the light and my body and looked down. Apparently I'd been knocked cold by *The New York Times*. My god, that paper was huge! It occurred to me, though, that if the *Times* actually carried a comics section, the damage to my skull would have been much worse.

What to do? It was a beautiful, if annoyingly dim, light, but there were so many things in my young life I had yet to try, so many afternoons unnapped, so many cold beers sitting in my refrigerator. Well, 10, at last count. I began resisting the light. My head was getting foggy. Emotions, images, old jokes began piling up in my brain, demanding attention . . . and then it came to me:

> What if there were, like, these two angels up in heaven, and one of them was holding his wing that had fallen off, and the other one . . . the other one . . . the other one was saying something like,"*Well, there's your problem . . . You lost a wing nut.*" Yes . . . Yes, that just . . . might . . . work . . .

I sank back into my body like a shot glass of whiskey dropped into a beer and slowly sat up in the unmowed grass.

My head was pounding . . . there was warm coffee splashed across the front of my robe . . . but I had my cartoon idea for the day.

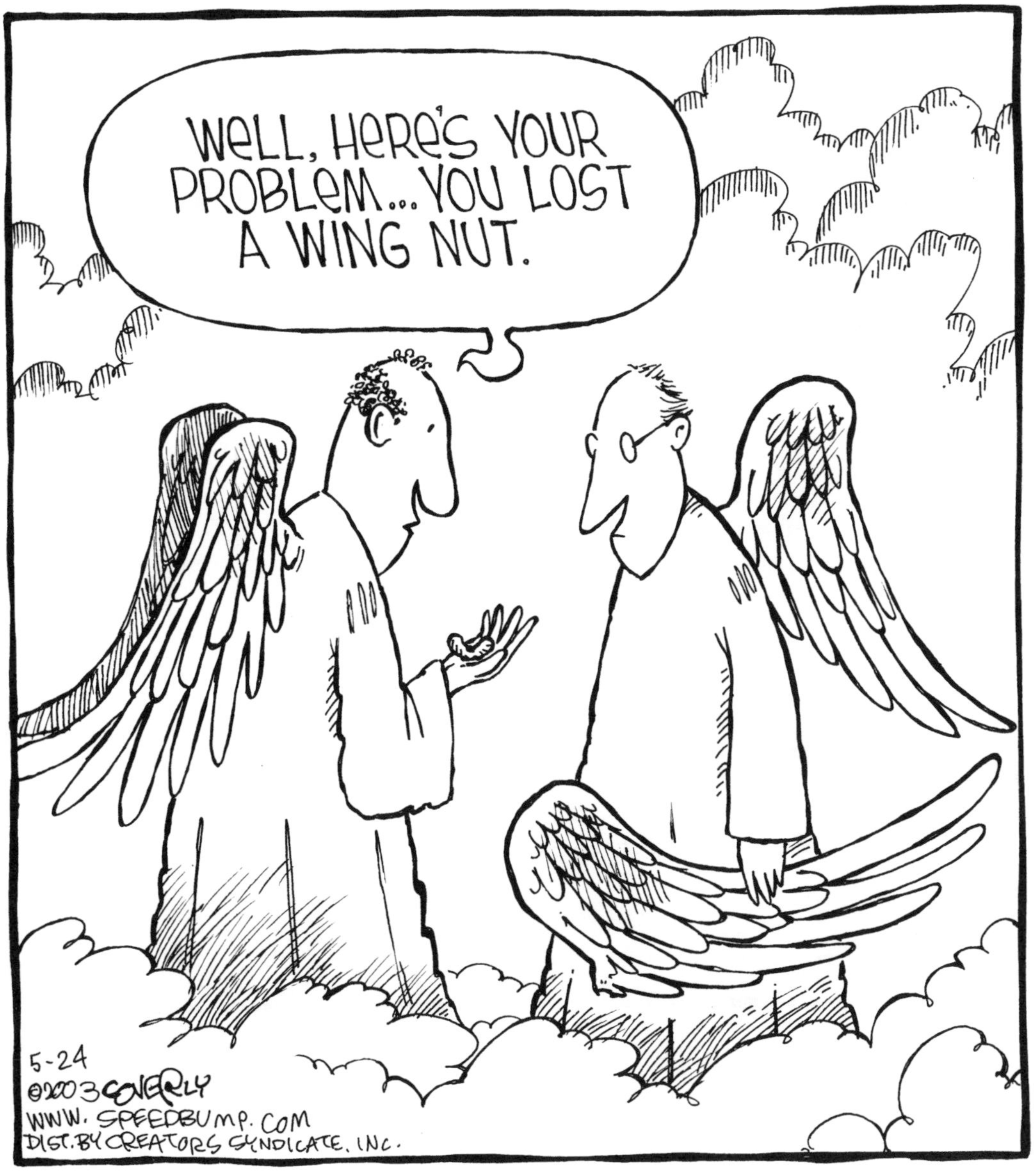
WELL, HERE'S YOUR PROBLEM... YOU LOST A WING NUT.
5-24
©2003 COVERLY
WWW. SPEEDBUMP. COM
DIST. BY CREATORS SYNDICATE, INC.

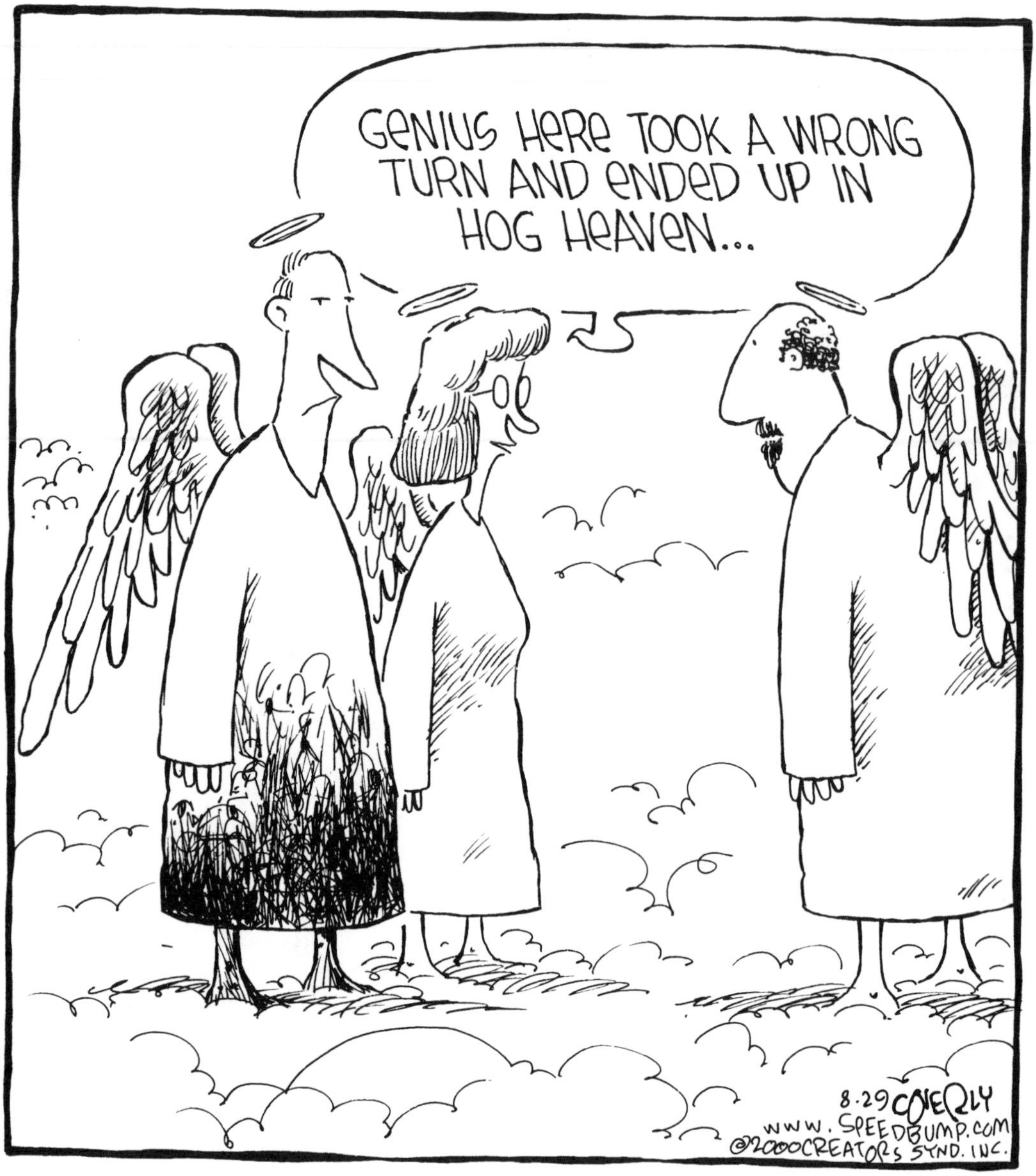
GENIUS HERE TOOK A WRONG TURN AND ENDED UP IN HOG HEAVEN...
8.29 COVERLY
WWW.SPEEDBUMP.COM
©2000 CREATORS SYND. INC.

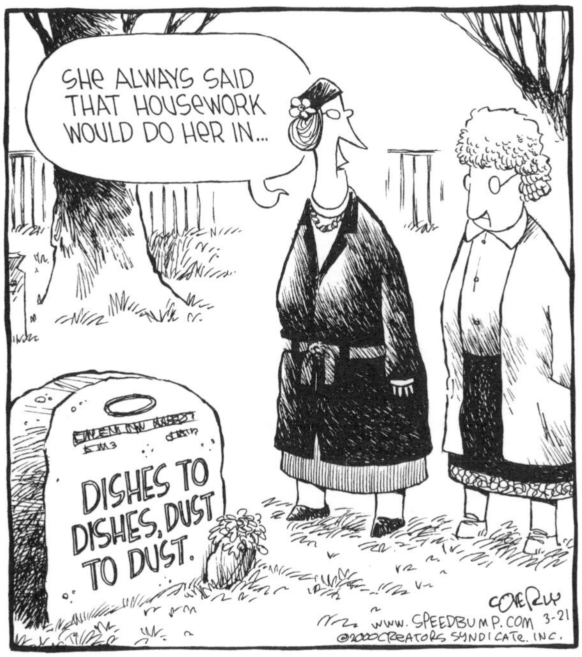
SHE ALWAYS SAID THAT HOUSEWORK WOULD DO HER IN...
DISHES TO DISHES, DUST TO DUST.
COVERLY
WWW.SPEEDBUMP.COM 3-21
©2000 CREATORS SYNDICATE, INC.

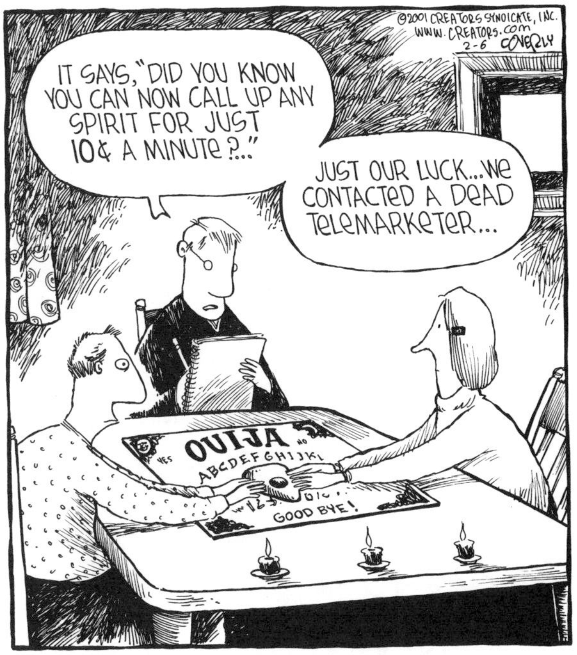
©2001 CREATORS SYNDICATE, INC.
WWW.CREATORS.COM
2-6 COVERLY
IT SAYS, "DID YOU KNOW YOU CAN NOW CALL UP ANY SPIRIT FOR JUST 10¢ A MINUTE ?..."
JUST OUR LUCK...WE CONTACTED A DEAD TELEMARKETER...
OUIJA
GOOD BYE!

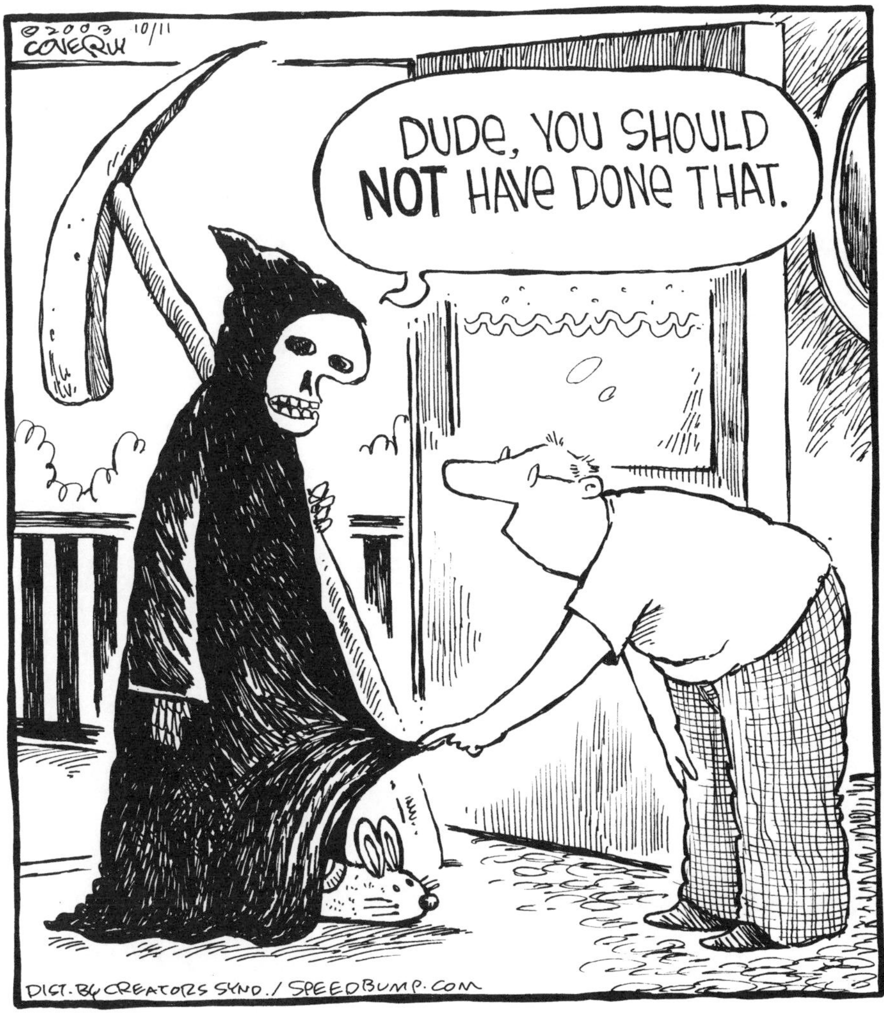
©2003 COVERLY 10/11
DUDE, YOU SHOULD NOT HAVE DONE THAT.
DIST. BY CREATORS SYND. / SPEEDBUMP.COM

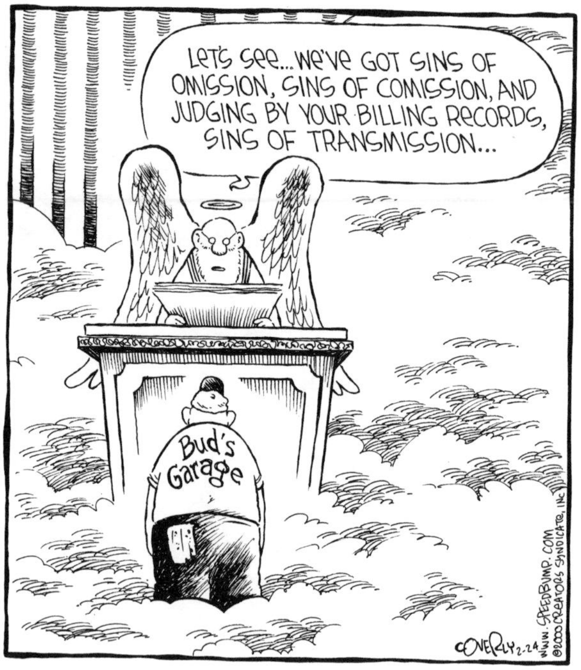
LET'S SEE... WE'VE GOT SINS OF OMISSION, SINS OF COMISSION, AND JUDGING BY YOUR BILLING RECORDS, SINS OF TRANSMISSION...
Bud's Garage

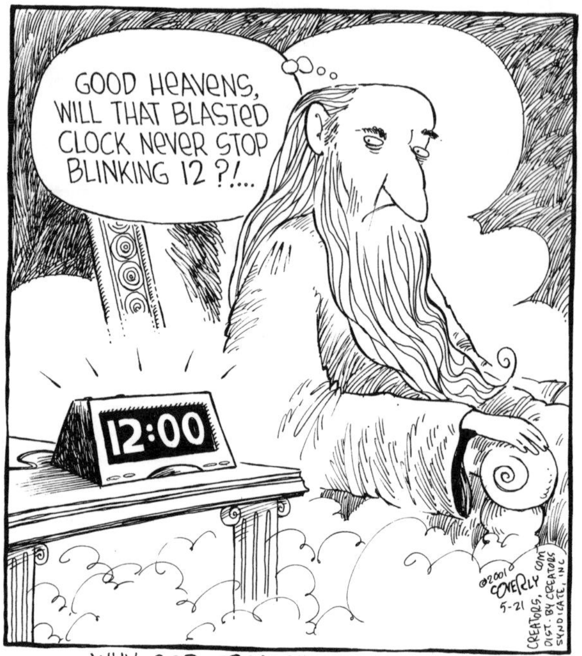
GOOD HEAVENS, WILL THAT BLASTED CLOCK NEVER STOP BLINKING 12 ?!...
12:00

WHY GOD CREATED THE FIRST DAY...

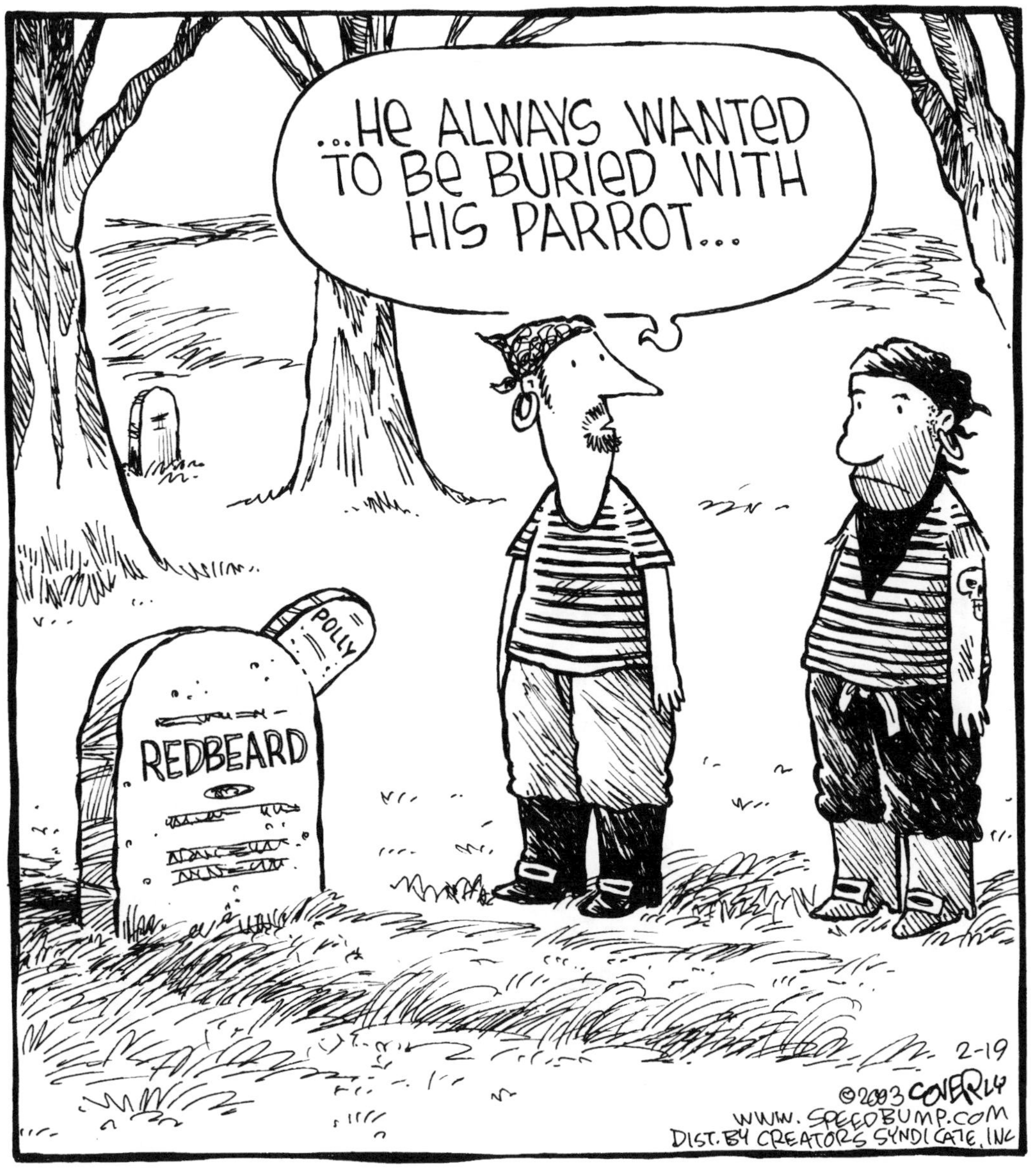
...HE ALWAYS WANTED TO BE BURIED WITH HIS PARROT...
POLLY
REDBEARD
2-19
©2003 COVERLY
WWW.SPEEDBUMP.COM
DIST. BY CREATORS SYNDICATE, INC

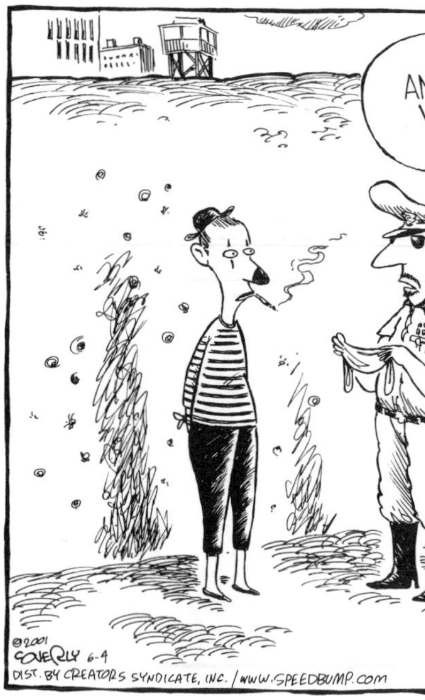
ANY LAST WORDS?...
©2001 COVERLY 6-4
DIST. BY CREATORS SYNDICATE, INC. / WWW.SPEEDBUMP.COM

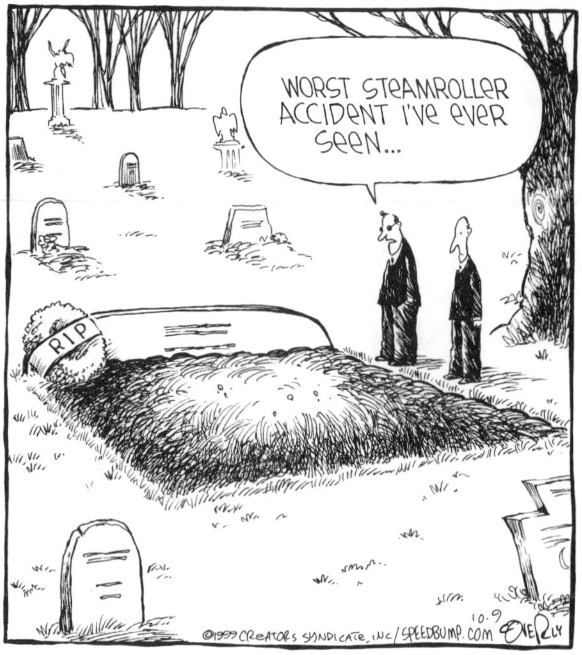
WORST STEAMROLLER ACCIDENT I'VE EVER SEEN...
RIP
©1999 CREATORS SYNDICATE, INC/SPEEDBUMP.COM 10-9 COVERLY

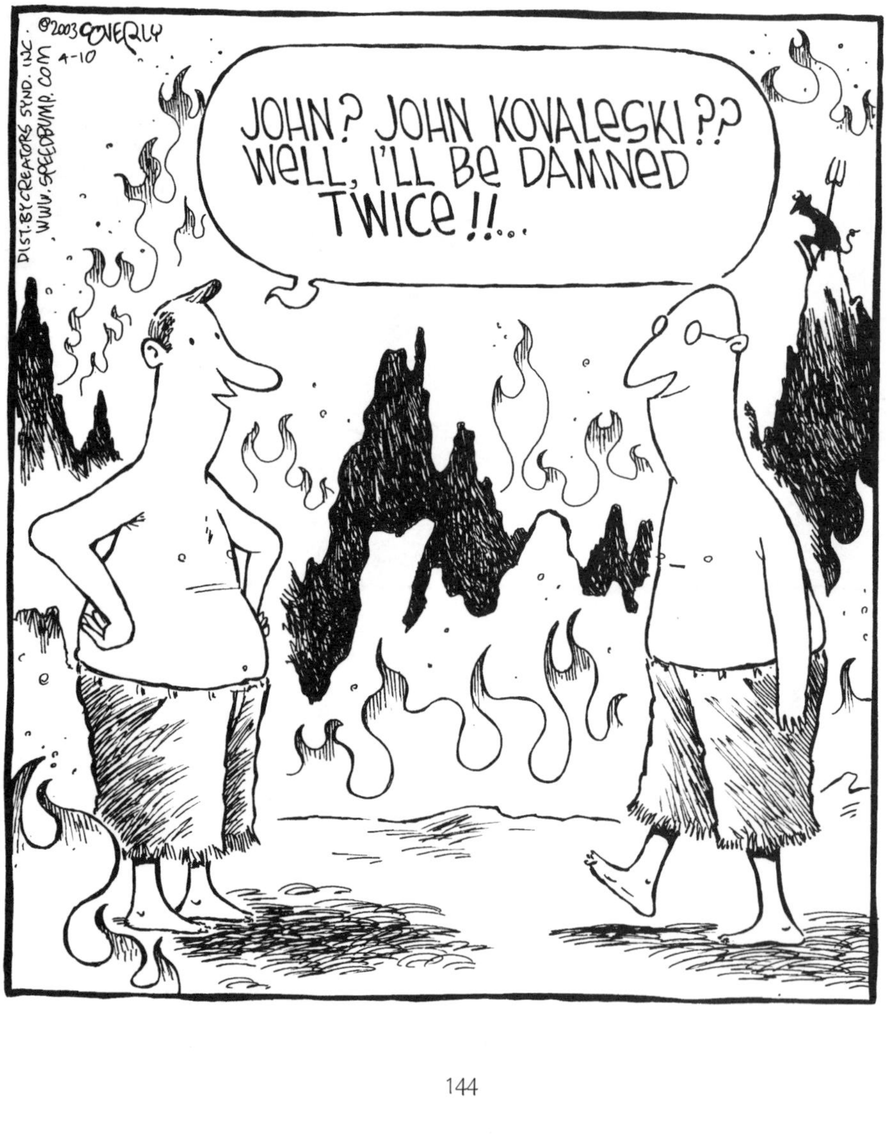
©2003 COVERLY 4-10
DIST. BY CREATORS SYND. INC. WWW.SPEEDBUMP.COM
JOHN? JOHN KOVALESKI?? WELL, I'LL BE DAMNED TWICE!!...

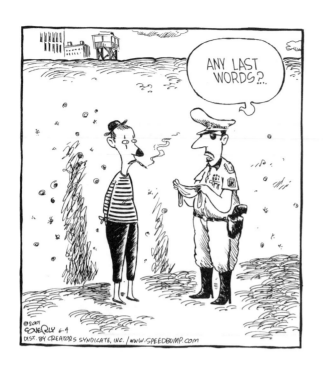

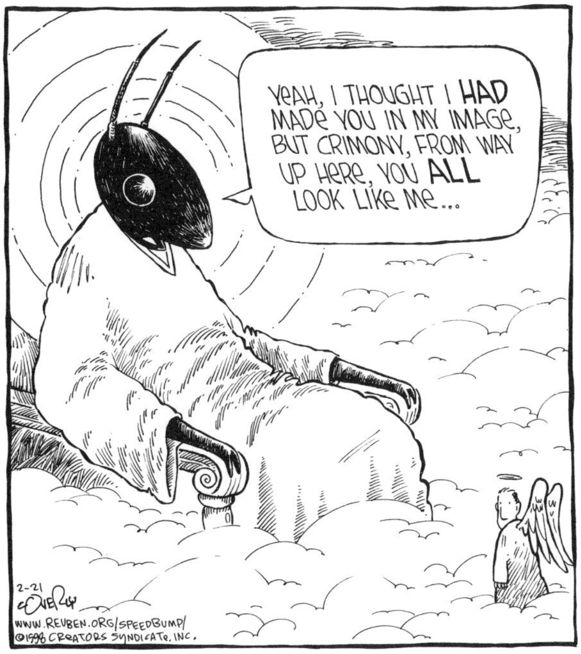
YEAH, I THOUGHT I HAD MADE YOU IN MY IMAGE, BUT CRIMONY, FROM WAY UP HERE, YOU ALL LOOK LIKE ME...

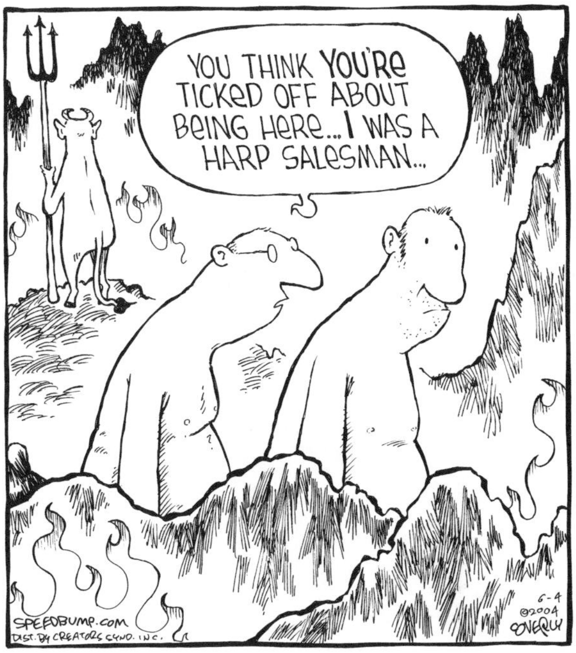
YOU THINK YOU'RE TICKED OFF ABOUT BEING HERE... I WAS A HARP SALESMAN...

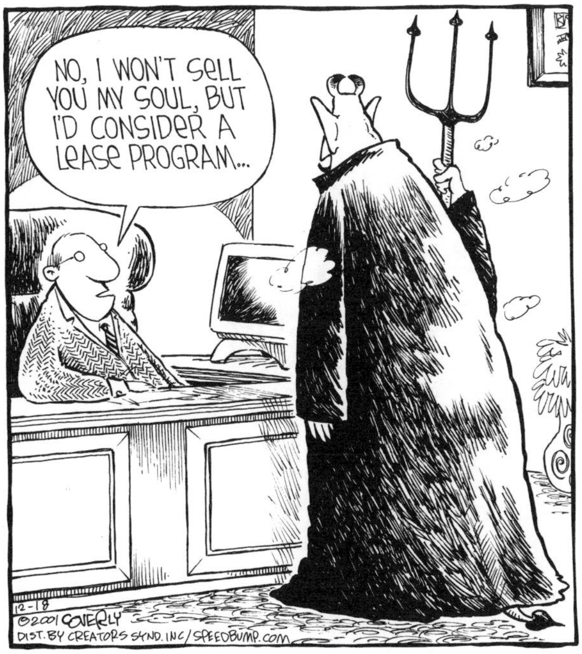
NO, I WON'T SELL YOU MY SOUL, BUT I'D CONSIDER A LEASE PROGRAM...

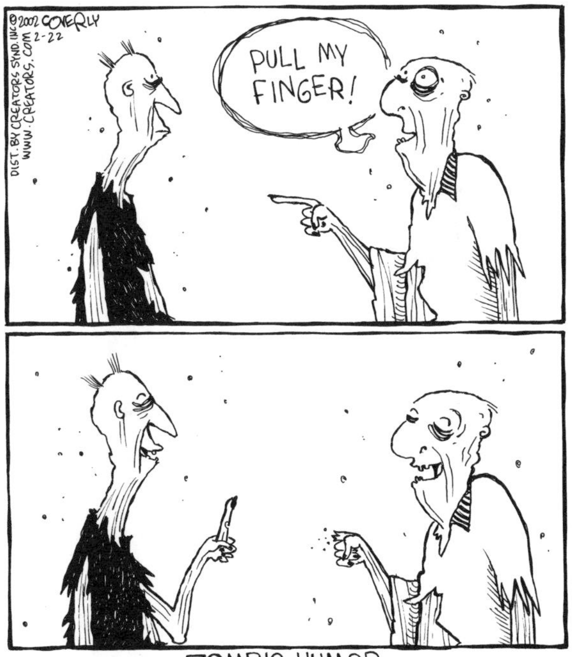
PULL MY FINGER!

ZOMBIE HUMOR

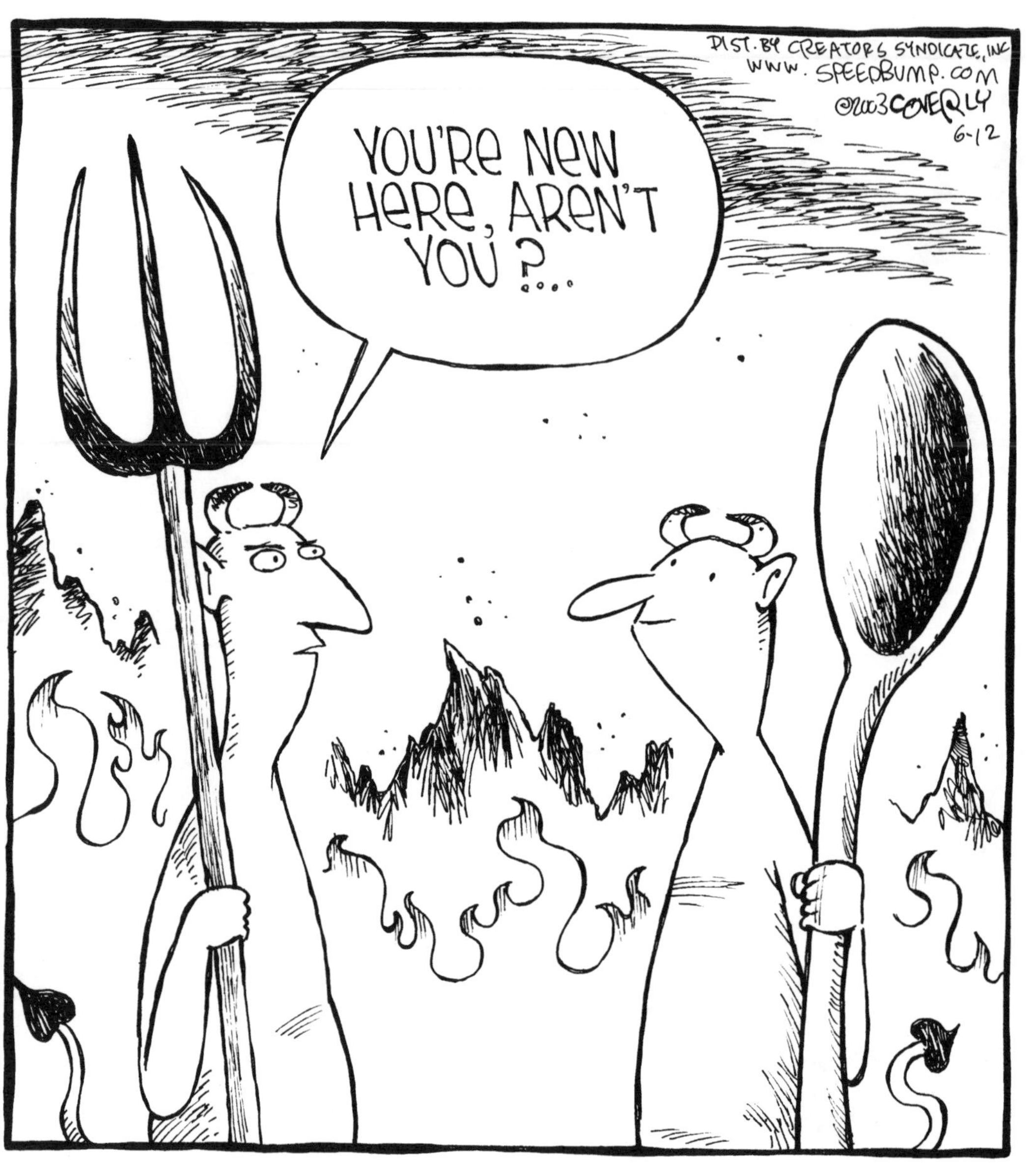
DIST. BY CREATORS SYNDICATE, INC
WWW. SPEEDBUMP.COM
©2003 COVERLY
6-12
YOU'RE NEW HERE, AREN'T YOU?....

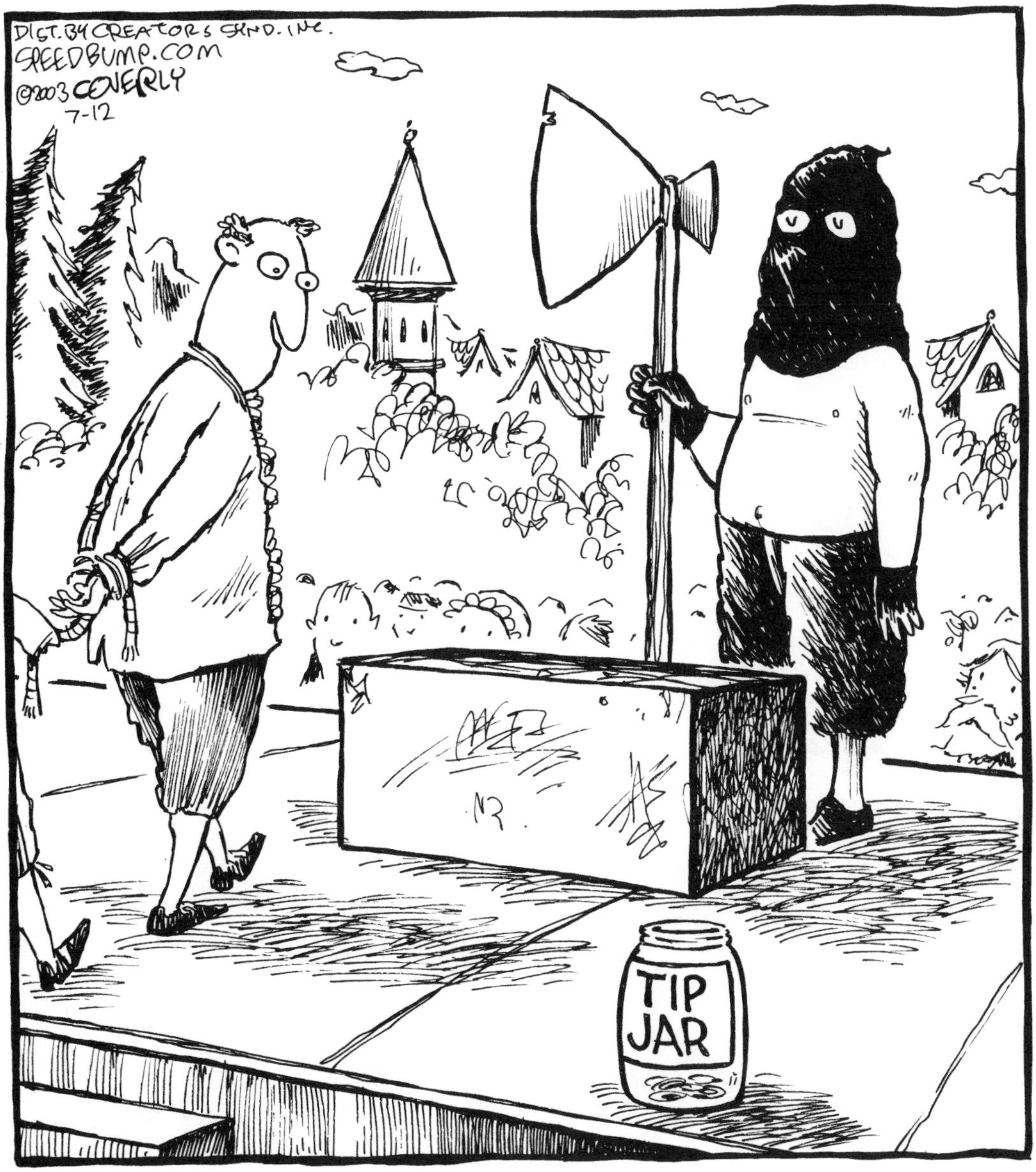
DIST. BY CREATORS SYND. INC.
SPEEDBUMP.COM
©2003 COVERLY
7-12
TIP
JAR

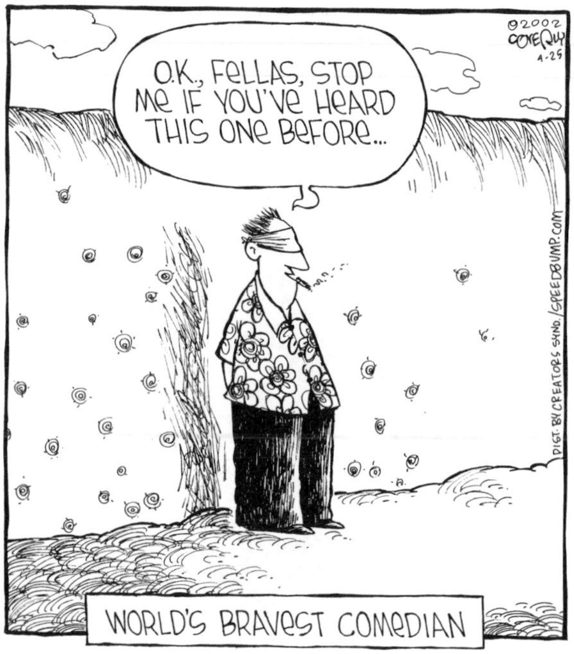
O.K., FELLAS, STOP ME IF YOU'VE HEARD THIS ONE BEFORE...
WORLD'S BRAVEST COMEDIAN

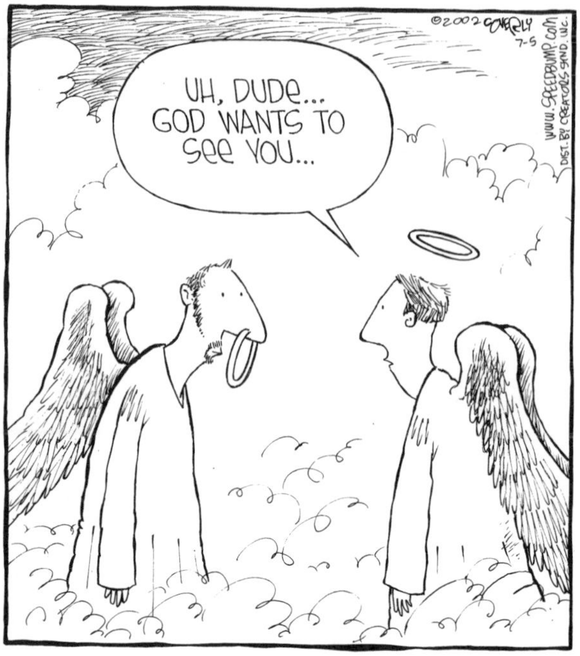
UH, DUDE... GOD WANTS TO SEE YOU...

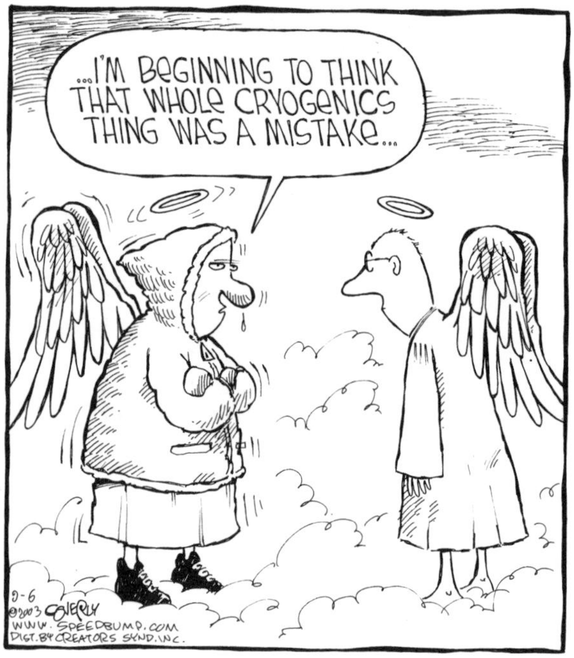
...I'M BEGINNING TO THINK THAT WHOLE CRYOGENICS THING WAS A MISTAKE...

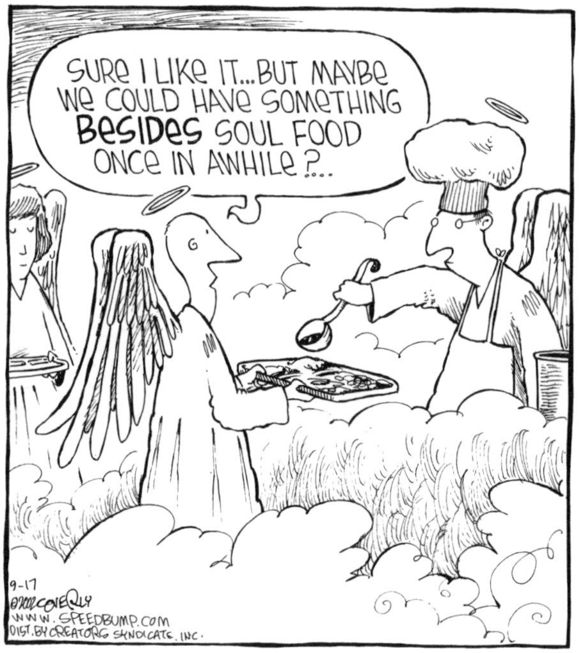
SURE I LIKE IT...BUT MAYBE WE COULD HAVE SOMETHING BESIDES SOUL FOOD ONCE IN AWHILE?...

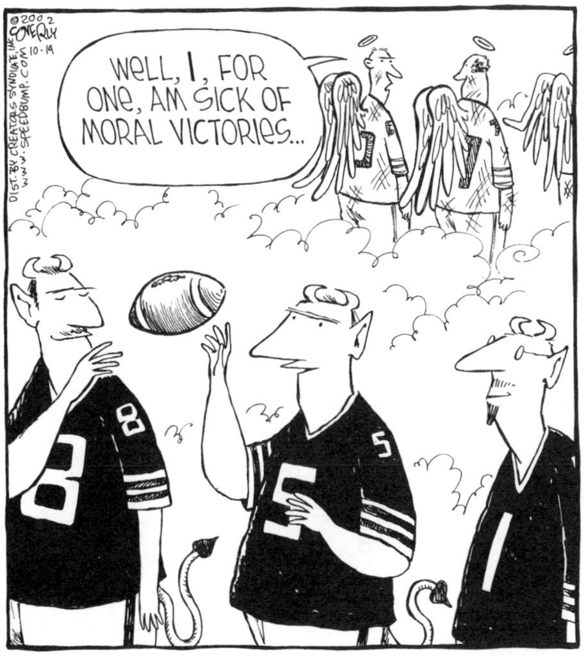
©2002 COVERLY 10-14
DIST. BY CREATORS SYNDICATE INC. WWW.SPEEDBUMP.COM
WELL, I, FOR ONE, AM SICK OF MORAL VICTORIES...

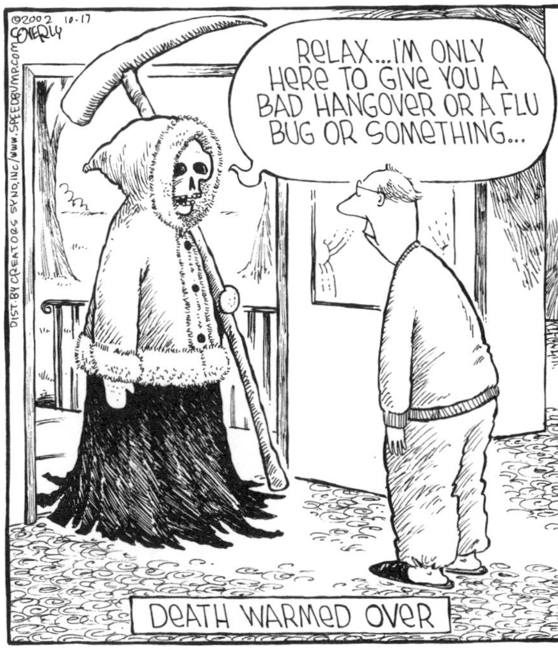
©2002 COVERLY 10-17
DIST. BY CREATORS SYND. INC/WWW.SPEEDBUMP.COM
RELAX...I'M ONLY HERE TO GIVE YOU A BAD HANGOVER OR A FLU BUG OR SOMETHING...
DEATH WARMED OVER

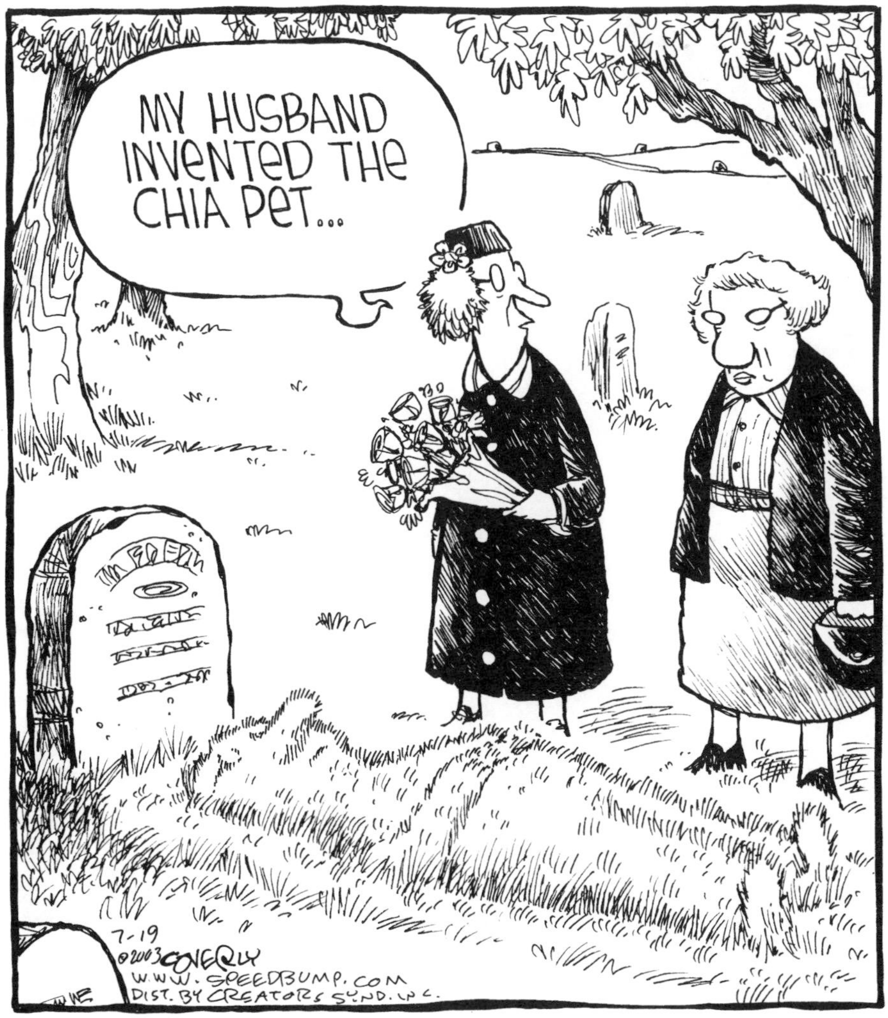
MY HUSBAND INVENTED THE CHIA PET...
7-19
©2003 COVERLY
WWW.SPEEDBUMP.COM
DIST. BY CREATORS SYND. INC.

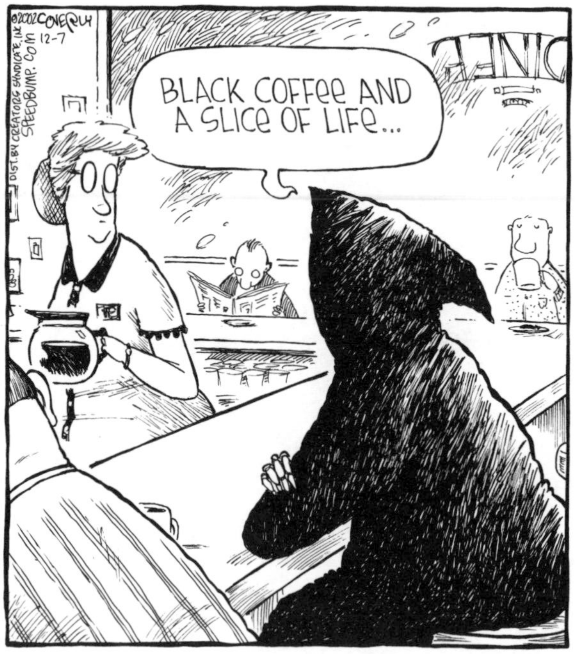
BLACK COFFEE AND A SLICE OF LIFE...

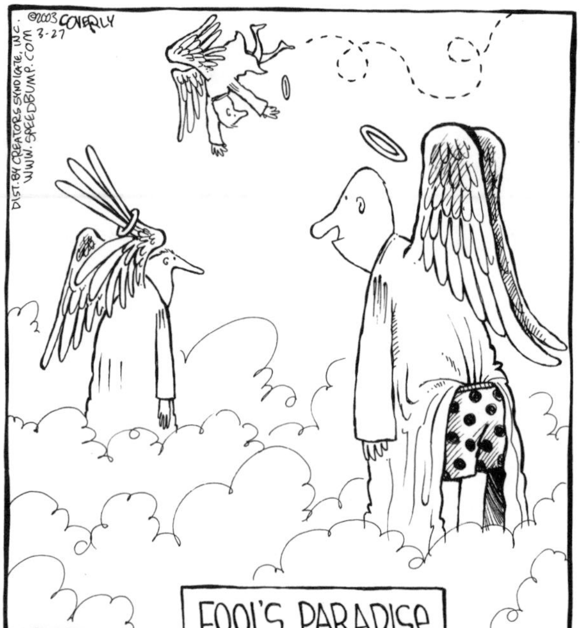

FOOL'S PARADISE

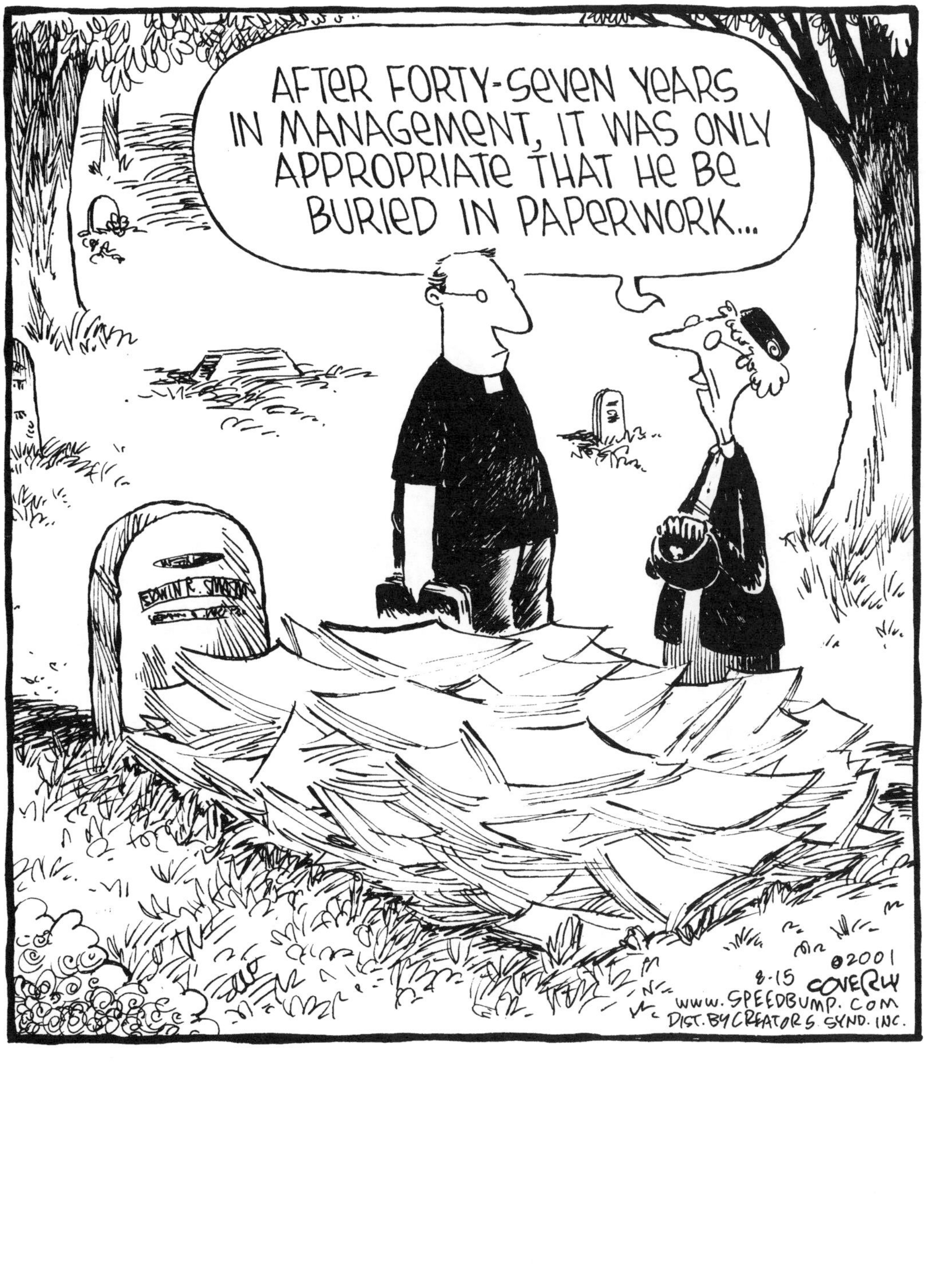
AFTER FORTY-SEVEN YEARS IN MANAGEMENT, IT WAS ONLY APPROPRIATE THAT HE BE BURIED IN PAPERWORK...
8-15 ©2001 COVERLY
WWW.SPEEDBUMP.COM
DIST. BY CREATORS SYND. INC.

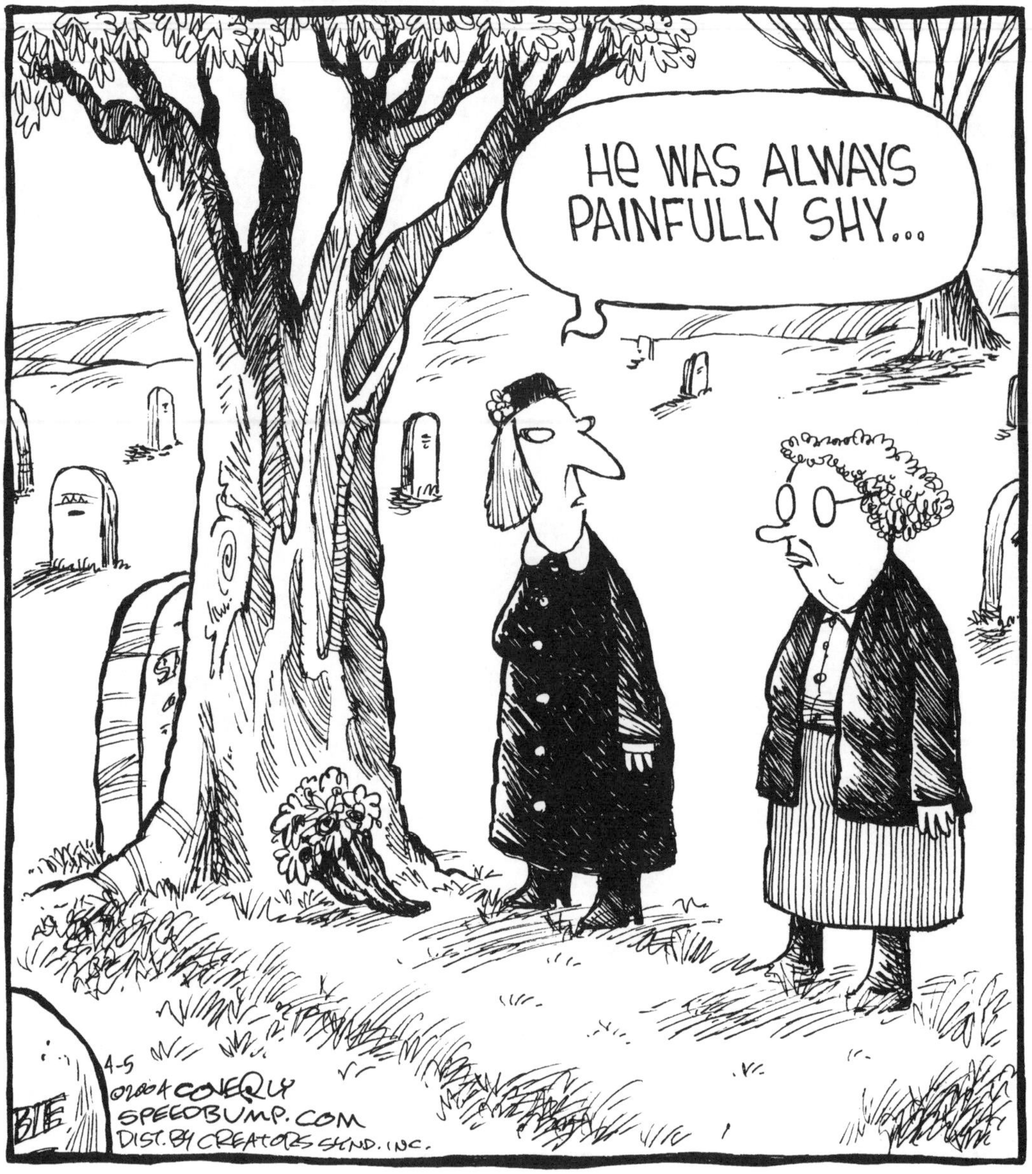
HE WAS ALWAYS PAINFULLY SHY...
4-5
©2004 COVERLY
SPEEDBUMP.COM
DIST. BY CREATORS SYND. INC.

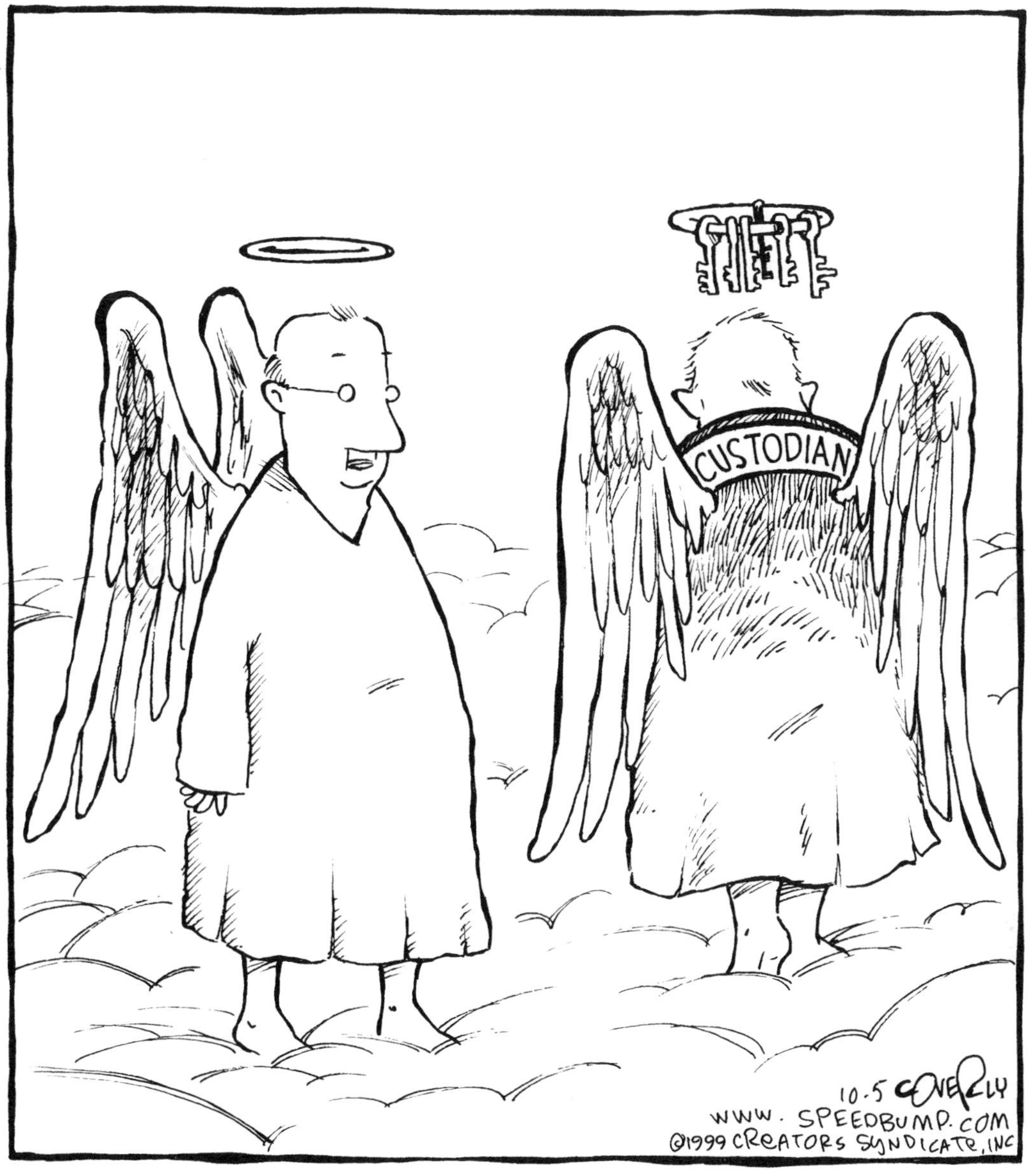
CUSTODIAN
10-5 COVERLY
WWW. SPEEDBUMP.COM
©1999 CREATORS SYNDICATE, INC

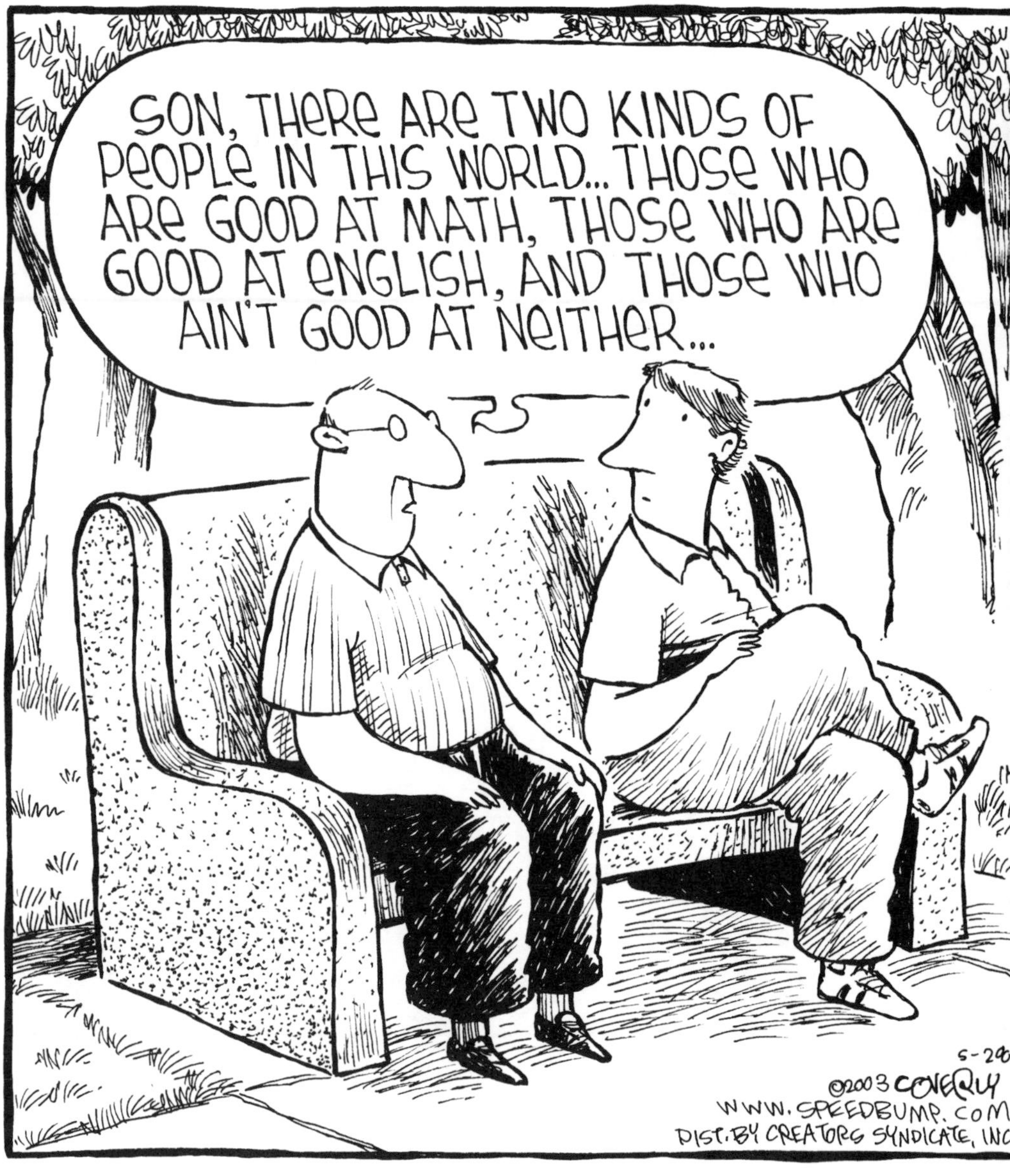
SON, THERE ARE TWO KINDS OF PEOPLE IN THIS WORLD... THOSE WHO ARE GOOD AT MATH, THOSE WHO ARE GOOD AT ENGLISH, AND THOSE WHO AIN'T GOOD AT NEITHER...
5-29
©2003 COVERLY
WWW.SPEEDBUMP.COM
DIST. BY CREATORS SYNDICATE, INC

Not~So~Deep Thoughts

We've all taken ourselves too seriously at some point in our lives, and I'm no exception. After a brief fling considering a career as A Journalist, I decided I would become A Philosopher, and then A Writer. The writing didn't go so well, though, when it became apparent that I could only come up with good ideas for stories . . . but I couldn't actually write good stories. It was painful and tedious for me to turn the idea into something that flowed naturally and ended smoothly. It's for this very reason that I don't draw a comic strip that maintains interesting characters and occasionally tells a story — I have no knack, and even less patience for it.

So now I stick with what comes easiest to me: churning out ideas and getting them onto paper as quickly as possible.

The following cartoons are an attempt to justify my B.S. in philosophy and master's in creative writing (Eastern Michigan University and Indiana University, respectively, for the academically curious). In retrospect, both degrees helped my cartooning. Philosophy trained my thought process in the art of conceptualizing, and the writing aspect of cartooning is self-evident.

These next few cartoons are also me, laughing at myself.

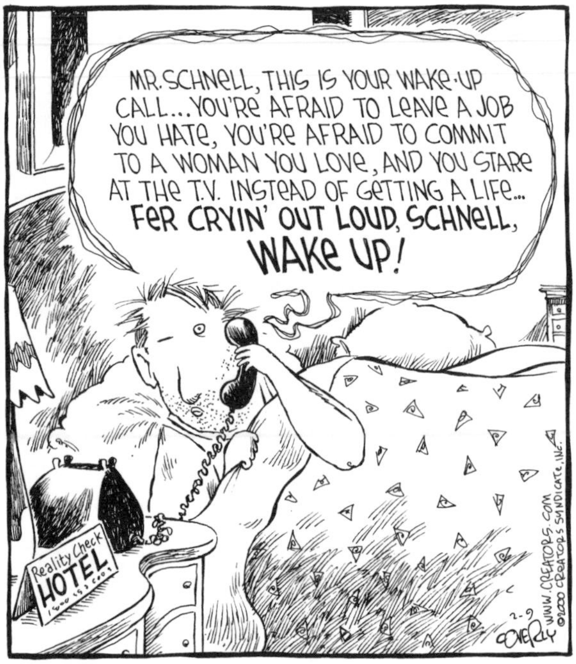
MR. SCHNELL, THIS IS YOUR WAKE-UP CALL... YOU'RE AFRAID TO LEAVE A JOB YOU HATE, YOU'RE AFRAID TO COMMIT TO A WOMAN YOU LOVE, AND YOU STARE AT THE T.V. INSTEAD OF GETTING A LIFE... FER CRYIN' OUT LOUD, SCHNELL, WAKE UP!
Reality Check HOTEL
WWW.CREATORS.COM ©2000 CREATORS SYNDICATE, INC.
2-9
COVERLY

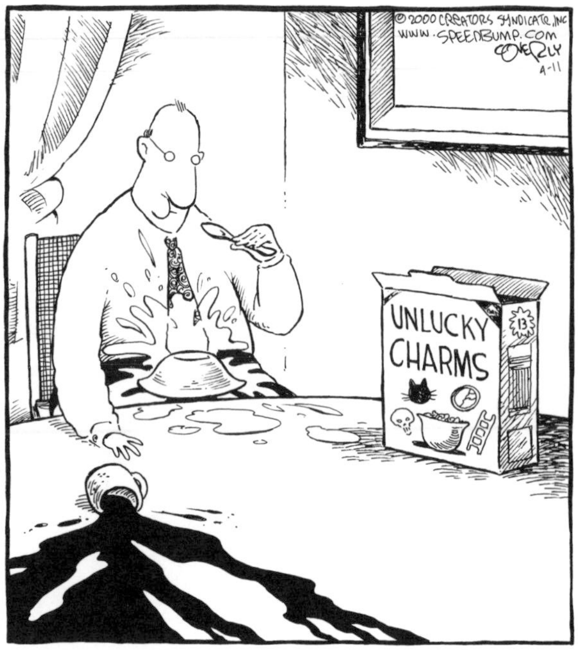
© 2000 CREATORS SYNDICATE, INC
WWW.SPEEDBUMP.COM
COVERLY
4-11
UNLUCKY CHARMS
13

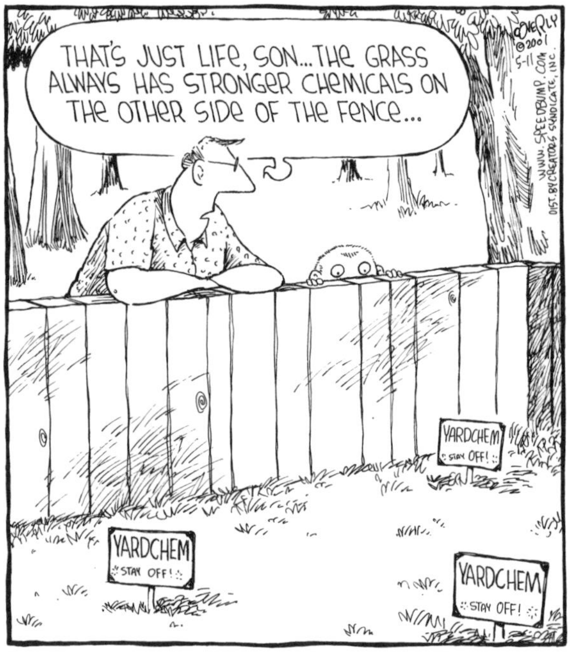
THAT'S JUST LIFE, SON... THE GRASS ALWAYS HAS STRONGER CHEMICALS ON THE OTHER SIDE OF THE FENCE...
COVERLY ©2001 5-11
WWW.SPEEDBUMP.COM
DIST. BY CREATORS SYNDICATE, INC.
YARDCHEM STAY OFF!
YARDCHEM STAY OFF!
YARDCHEM STAY OFF!

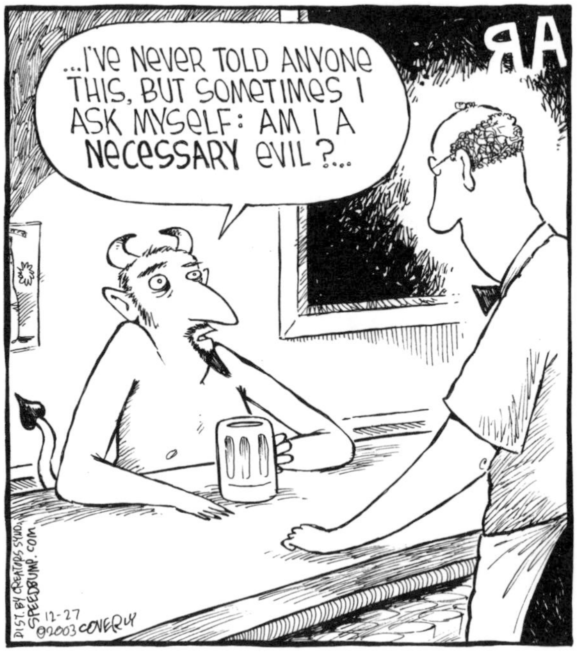
...I'VE NEVER TOLD ANYONE THIS, BUT SOMETIMES I ASK MYSELF: AM I A NECESSARY EVIL?...
DIST. BY CREATORS SYND.
SPEEDBUMP.COM
12-27
©2003 COVERLY

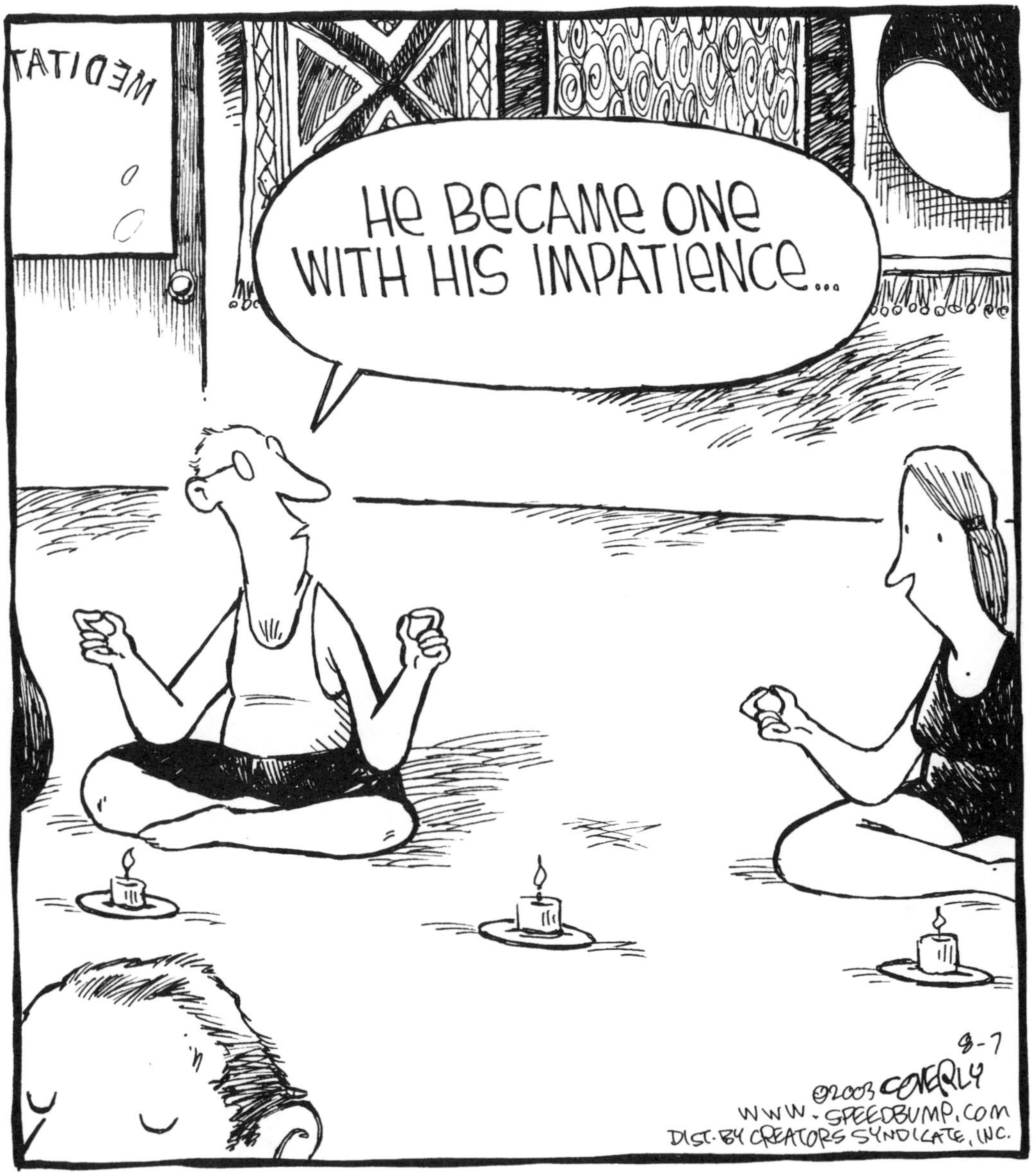

MEDITAT
HE BECAME ONE WITH HIS IMPATIENCE...
8-7
©2003 COVERLY
WWW.SPEEDBUMP.COM
DIST. BY CREATORS SYNDICATE, INC.

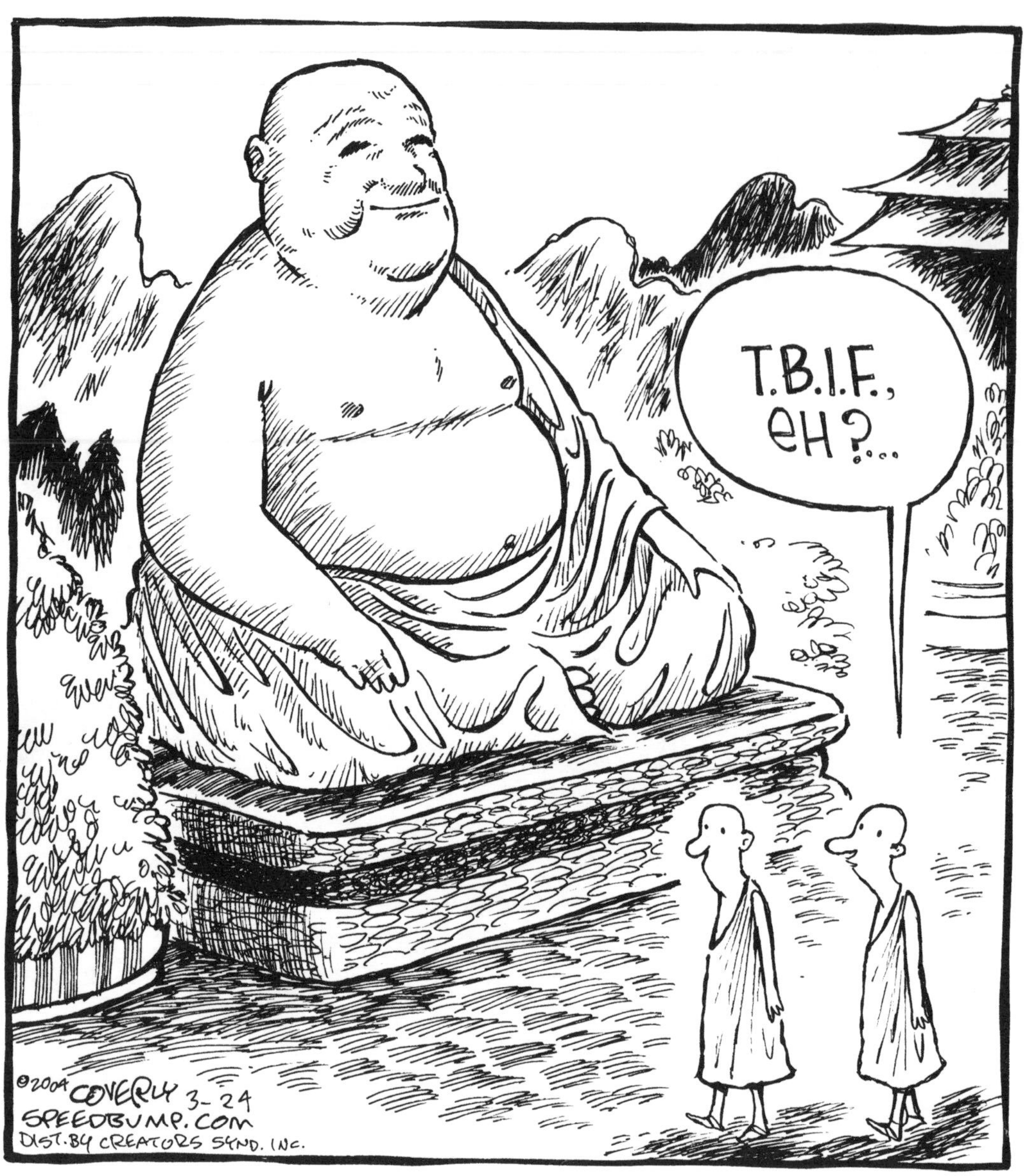
T.B.I.F., eH?...
©2004 COVERLY 3-24
SPEEDBUMP.COM
DIST. BY CREATORS SYND. INC.

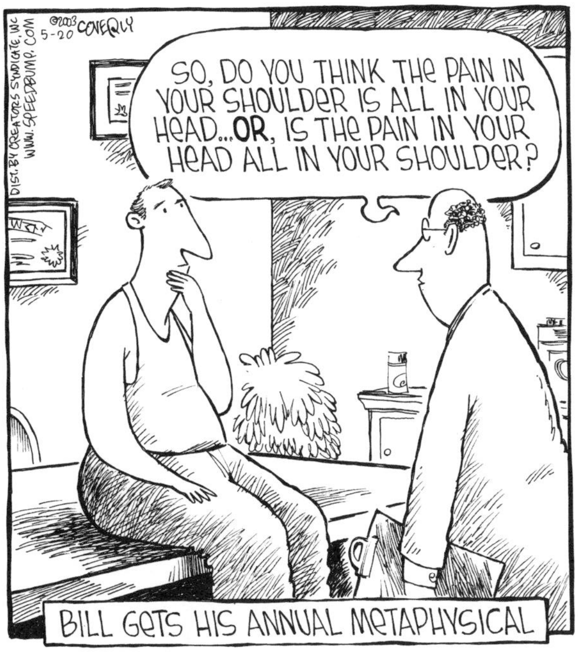
©2003 COVERLY
5-20
DIST. BY CREATORS SYNDICATE, INC
WWW.SPEEDBUMP.COM
SO, DO YOU THINK THE PAIN IN YOUR SHOULDER IS ALL IN YOUR HEAD...**OR**, IS THE PAIN IN YOUR HEAD ALL IN YOUR SHOULDER?
BILL GETS HIS ANNUAL METAPHYSICAL

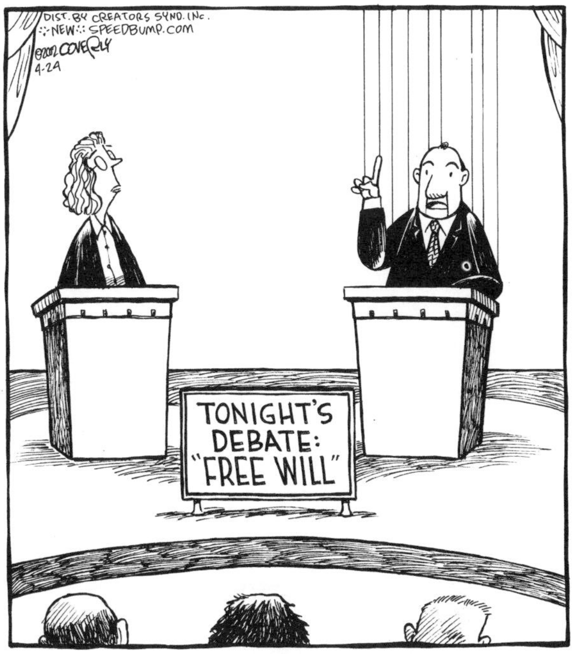
DIST. BY CREATORS SYND. INC.
NEW SPEEDBUMP.COM
©2002 COVERLY
4-24
TONIGHT'S DEBATE: "FREE WILL"

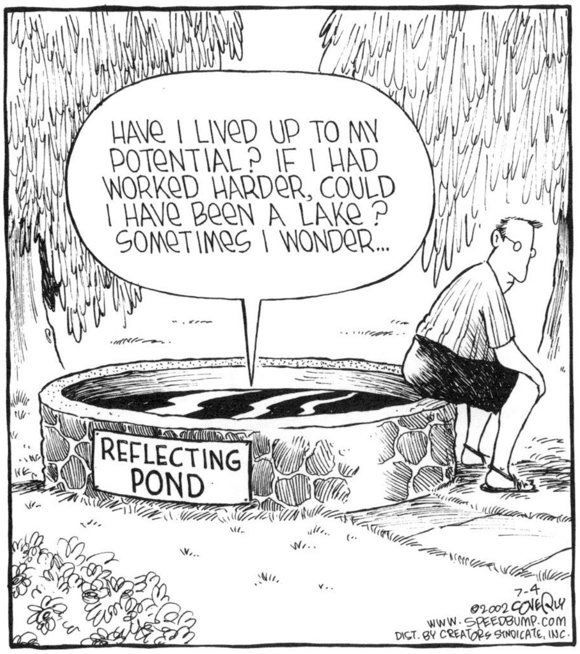
HAVE I LIVED UP TO MY POTENTIAL? IF I HAD WORKED HARDER, COULD I HAVE BEEN A LAKE? SOMETIMES I WONDER...
REFLECTING POND
7-4
©2002 COVERLY
WWW.SPEEDBUMP.COM
DIST. BY CREATORS SYNDICATE, INC.

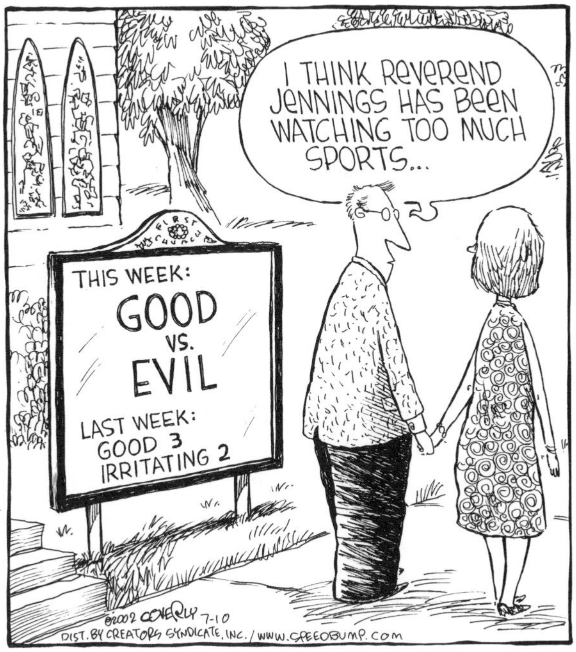
I THINK REVEREND JENNINGS HAS BEEN WATCHING TOO MUCH SPORTS...
THIS WEEK:
GOOD VS. EVIL
LAST WEEK:
GOOD 3
IRRITATING 2
©2002 COVERLY 7-10
DIST. BY CREATORS SYNDICATE, INC. / WWW.SPEEDBUMP.COM

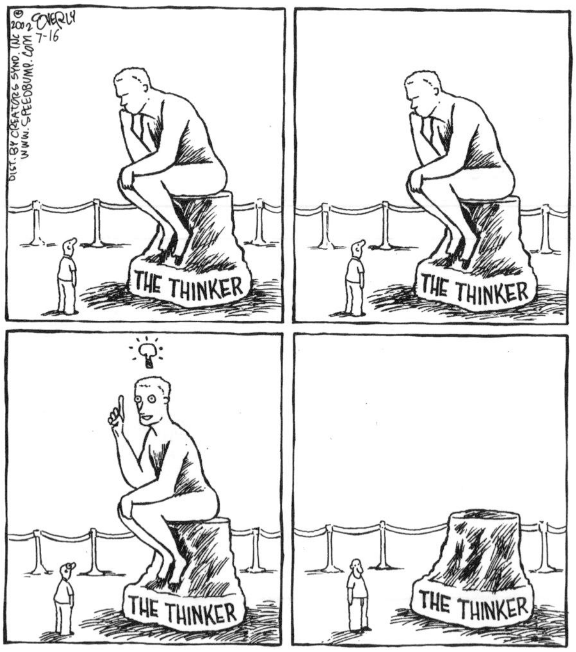
DIST. BY CREATORS SYND. INC
WWW.SPEEDBUMP.COM
©2002 COVERLY 7-16
THE THINKER
THE THINKER
THE THINKER
THE THINKER

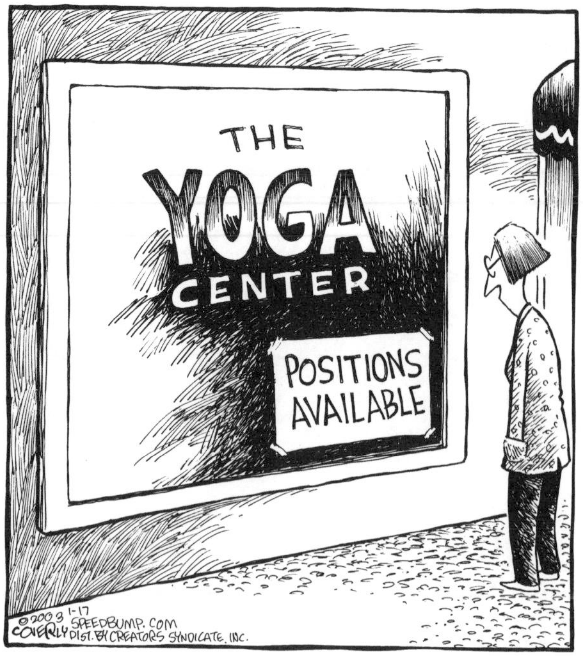
THE YOGA CENTER
POSITIONS AVAILABLE
©2003 COVERLY 1-17
SPEEDBUMP.COM
DIST. BY CREATORS SYNDICATE, INC.

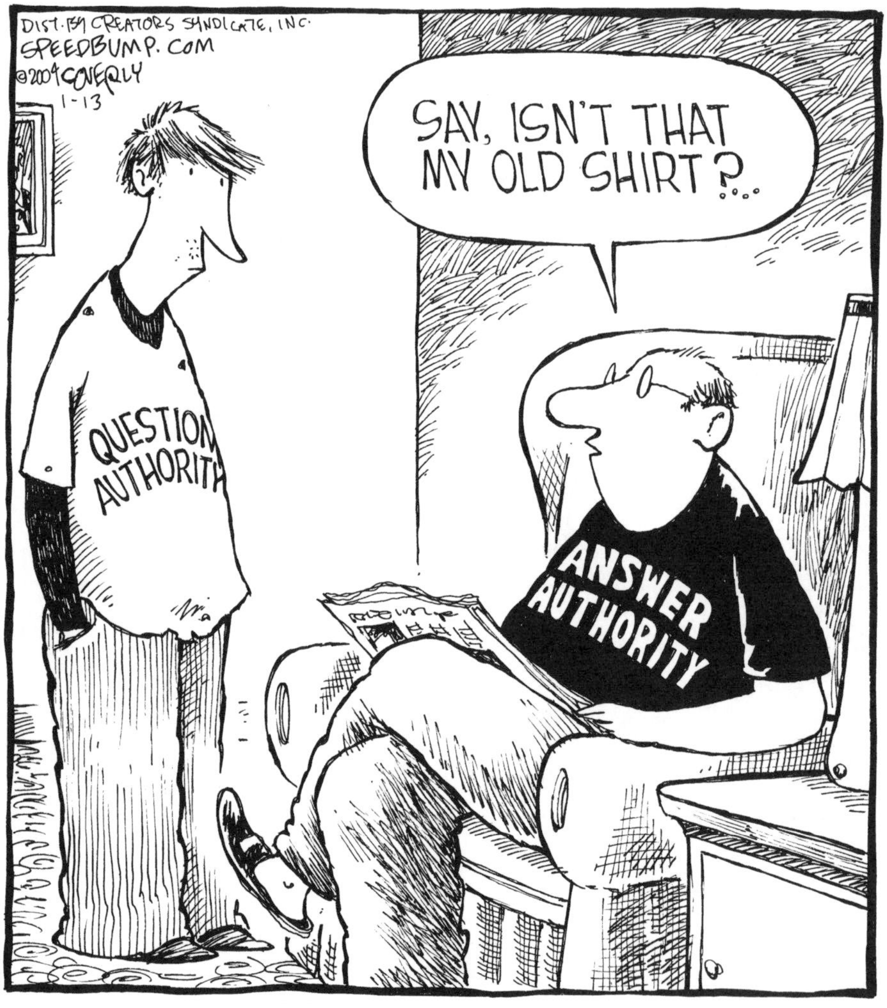
DIST. BY CREATORS SYNDICATE, INC.
SPEEDBUMP.COM
©2004 COVERLY 1-13
SAY, ISN'T THAT MY OLD SHIRT?...
QUESTION AUTHORITY
ANSWER AUTHORITY

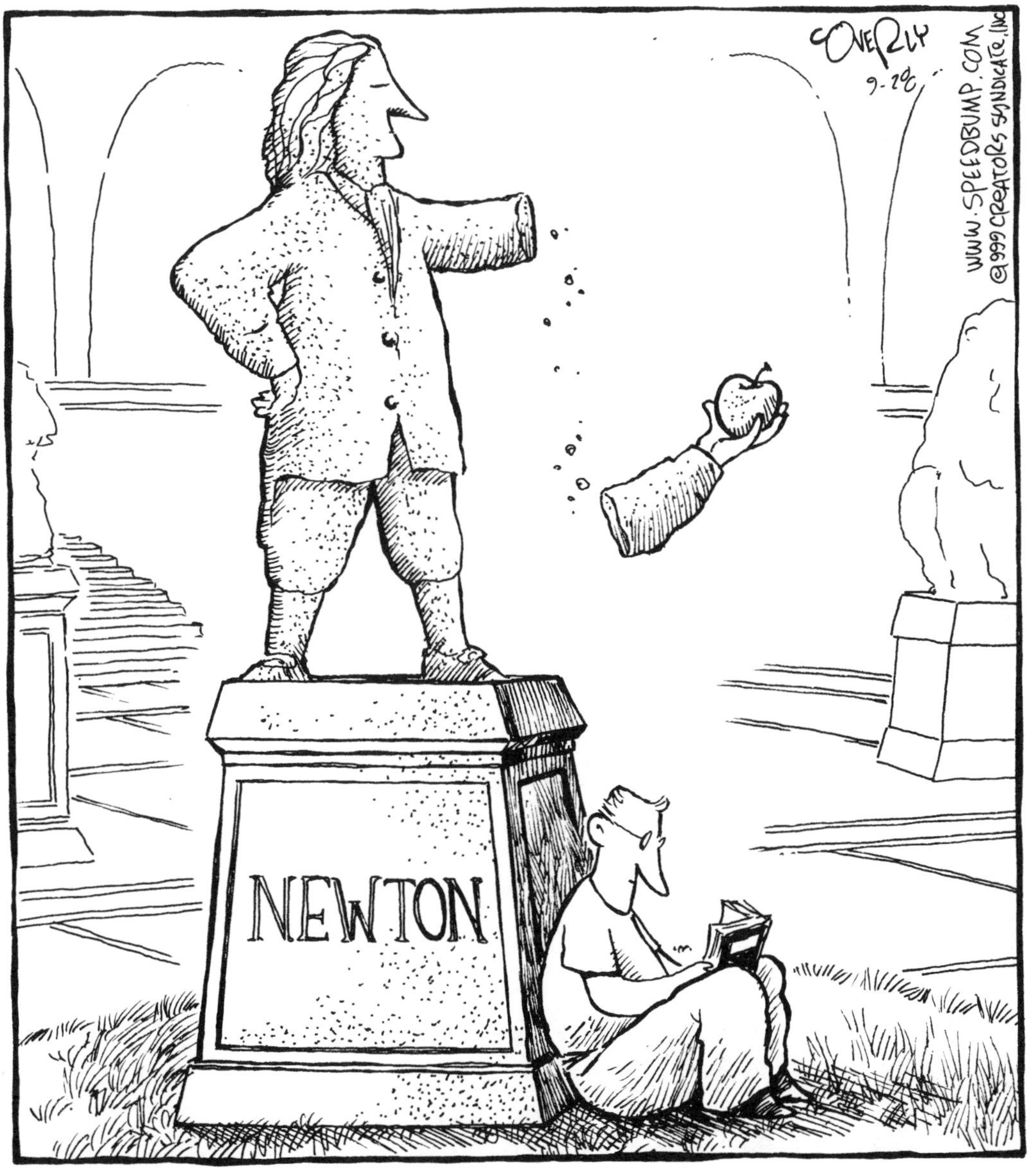
NEWTON
WWW.SPEEDBUMP.COM
©1999 CREATORS SYNDICATE, INC

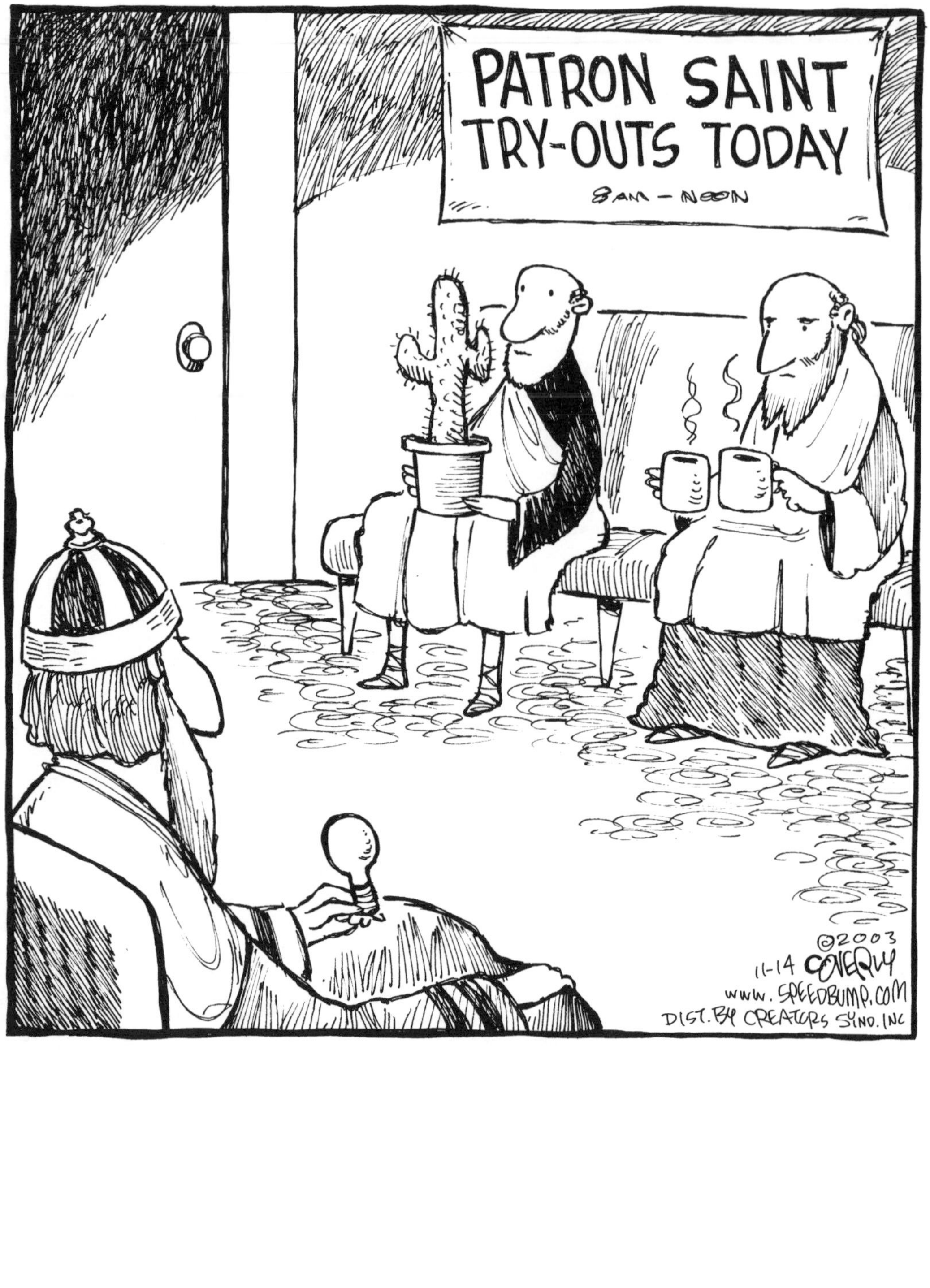
PATRON SAINT
TRY-OUTS TODAY
8AM – NOON
©2003
11-14 COVERLY
www.SPEEDBUMP.COM
DIST. BY CREATORS SYND. INC

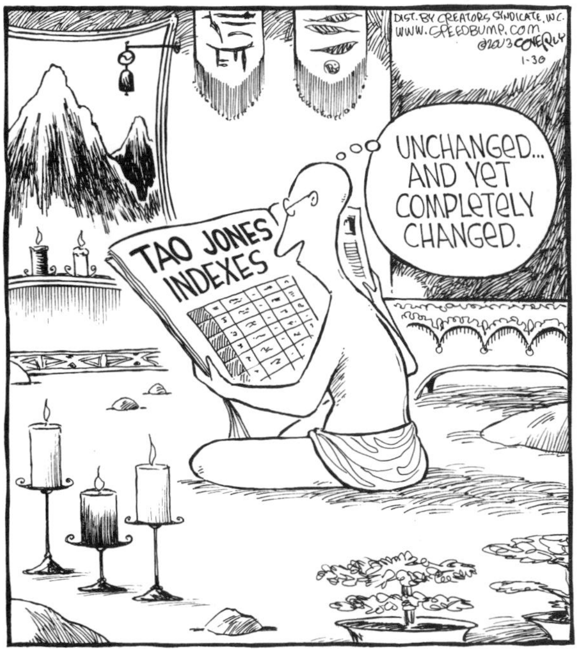
DIST. BY CREATORS SYNDICATE, INC.
WWW.SPEEDBUMP.COM
©2003 COVERLY
1-30
TAO JONES INDEXES
UNCHANGED... AND YET COMPLETELY CHANGED.

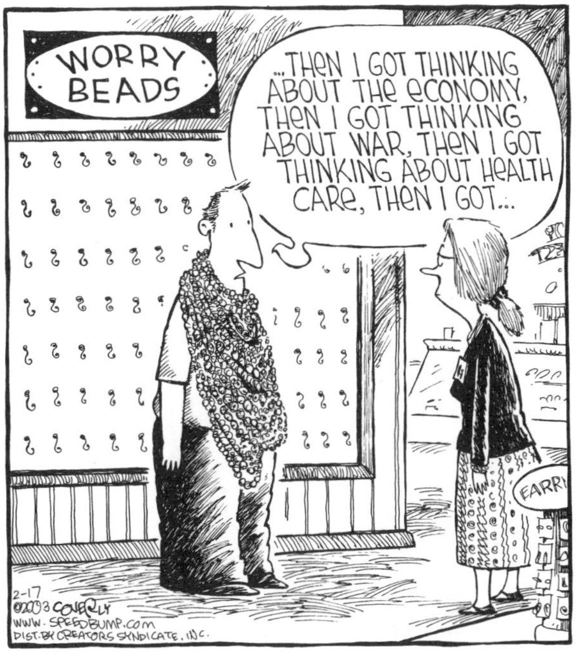
WORRY BEADS
...THEN I GOT THINKING ABOUT THE ECONOMY, THEN I GOT THINKING ABOUT WAR, THEN I GOT THINKING ABOUT HEALTH CARE, THEN I GOT...
2-17
©2003 COVERLY
WWW.SPEEDBUMP.COM
DIST. BY CREATORS SYNDICATE, INC.

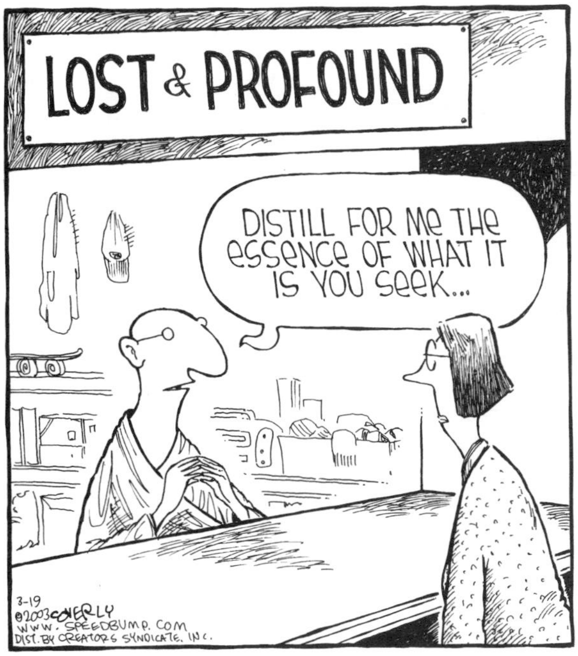
LOST & PROFOUND
DISTILL FOR ME THE ESSENCE OF WHAT IT IS YOU SEEK...
3-19
©2003 COVERLY
WWW.SPEEDBUMP.COM
DIST. BY CREATORS SYNDICATE, INC.

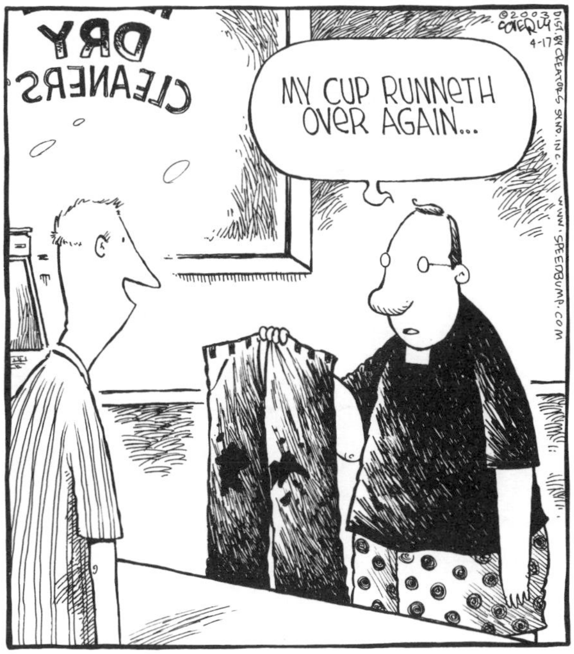
DRY CLEANERS
MY CUP RUNNETH OVER AGAIN...
©2003 COVERLY
4-17
DIST. BY CREATORS SYND. INC.
WWW.SPEEDBUMP.COM

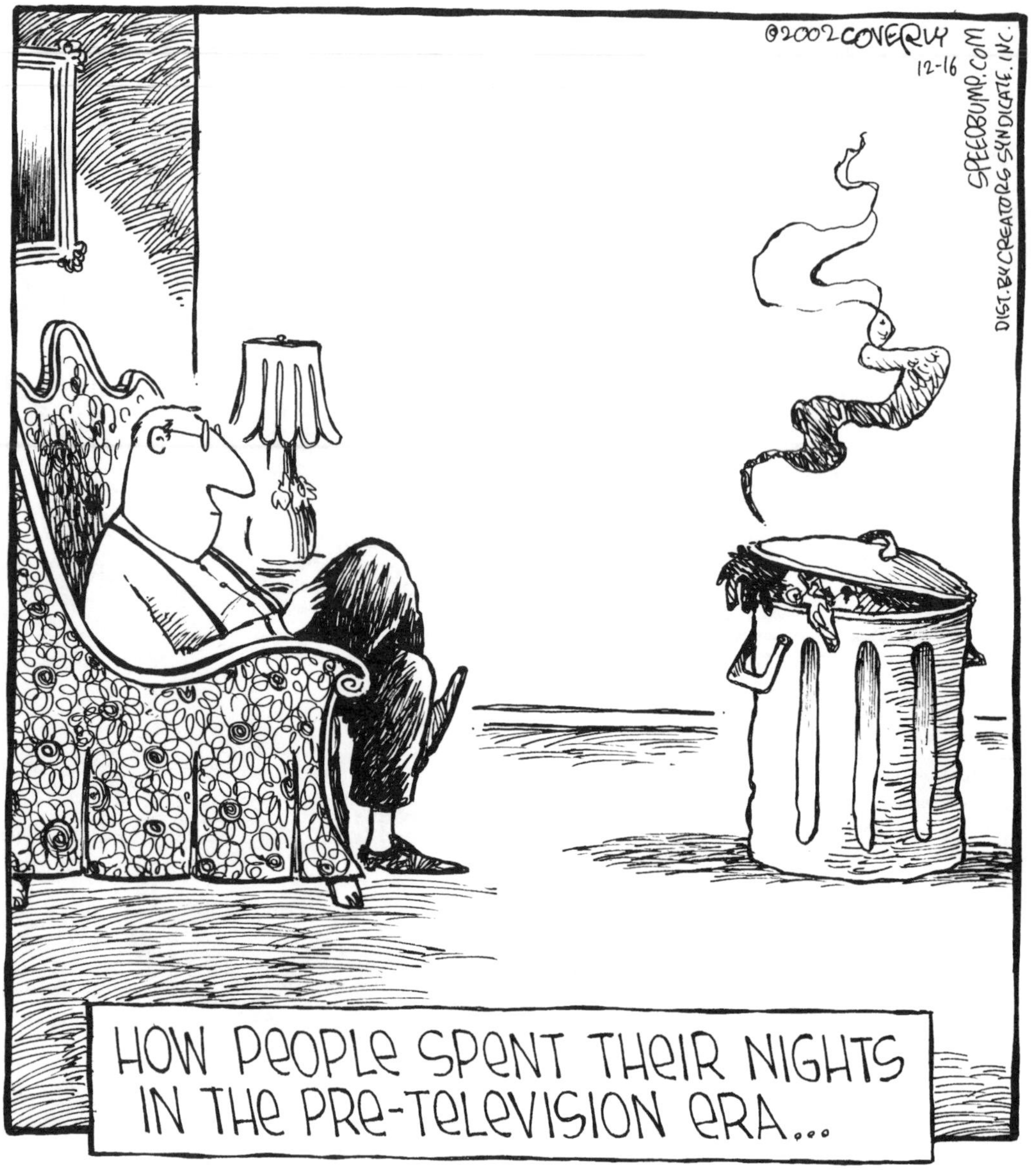
©2002 COVERLY
12-16
SPEEDBUMP.COM
DIST. BY CREATORS SYNDICATE, INC.
HOW PEOPLE SPENT THEIR NIGHTS IN THE PRE-TELEVISION ERA...

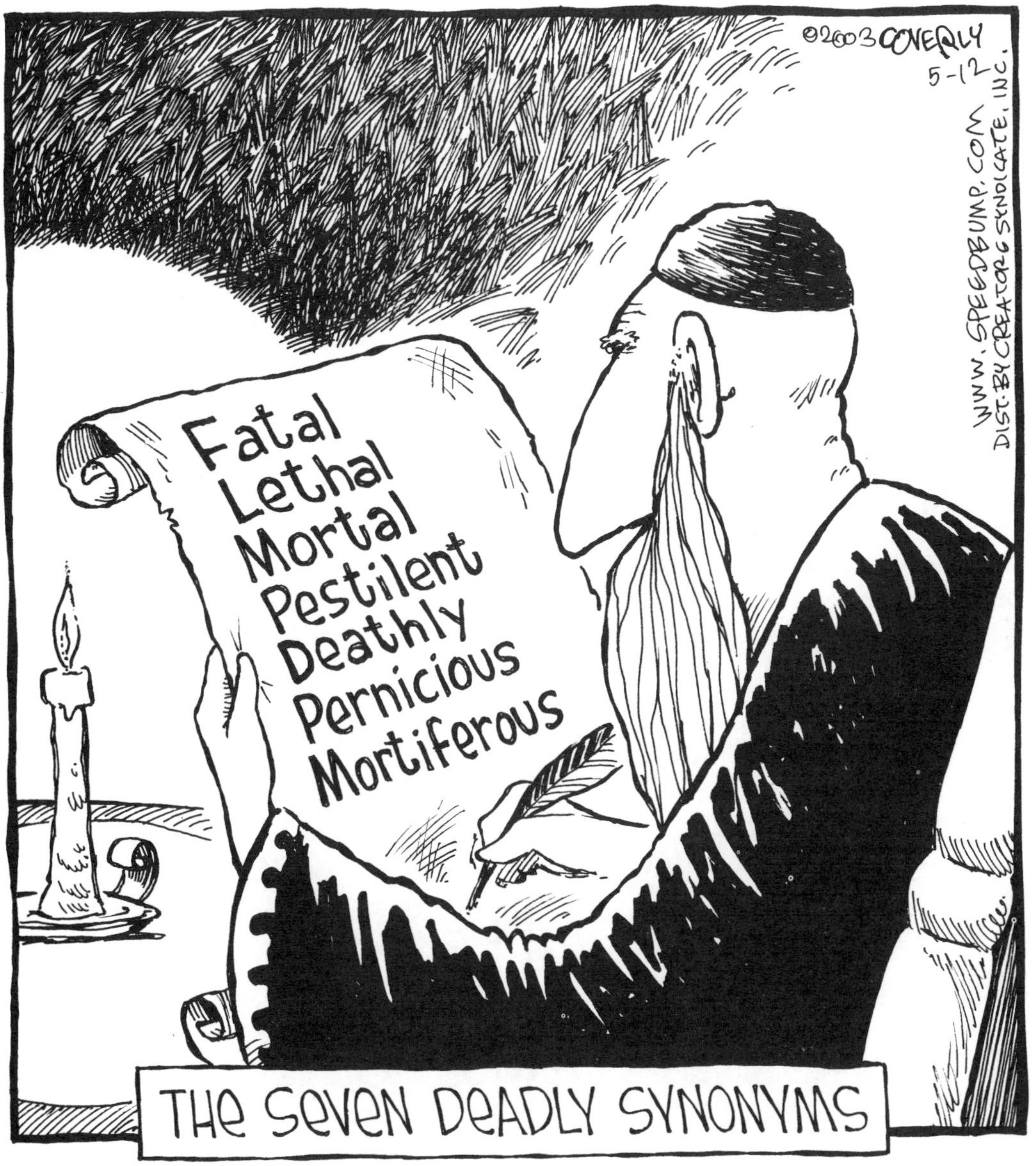
©2003 COVERLY
5-12
WWW.SPEEDBUMP.COM
DIST. BY CREATORS SYNDICATE, INC.
Fatal
Lethal
Mortal
Pestilent
Deathly
Pernicious
Mortiferous
THE SEVEN DEADLY SYNONYMS

HEY, LOOK AT ME! I'M GOING TO BE THE MIGHTIEST OAK IN ALL THE FOREST!
©1999 CREATORS SYNDICATE, INC.
WWW.CREATORS.COM
3-1
COVERLY
I COULD BE A HAPPY SMALLISH OAK...
SMALLISH IS GOOD.

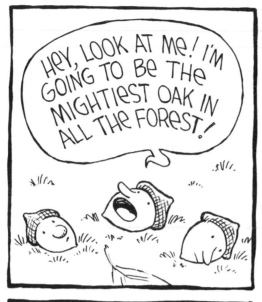

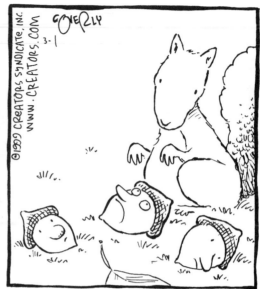

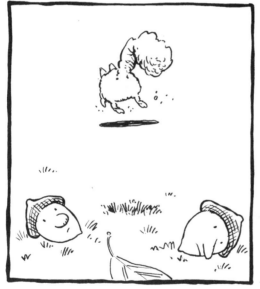

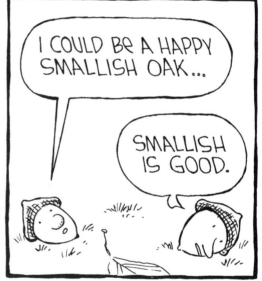

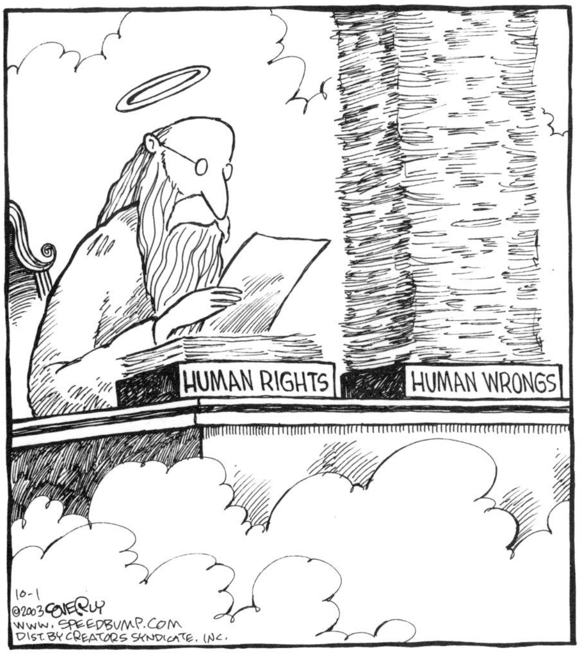
HUMAN RIGHTS
HUMAN WRONGS
10-1
©2003 COVERLY
WWW.SPEEDBUMP.COM
DIST. BY CREATORS SYNDICATE, INC.

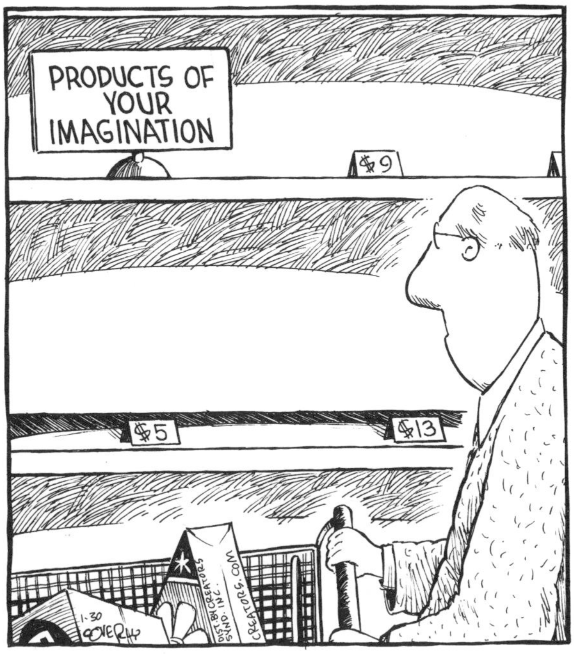
PRODUCTS OF YOUR IMAGINATION
$9
$5
$13
1-30
COVERLY
DIST. BY CREATORS SYND. INC.
CREATORS.COM

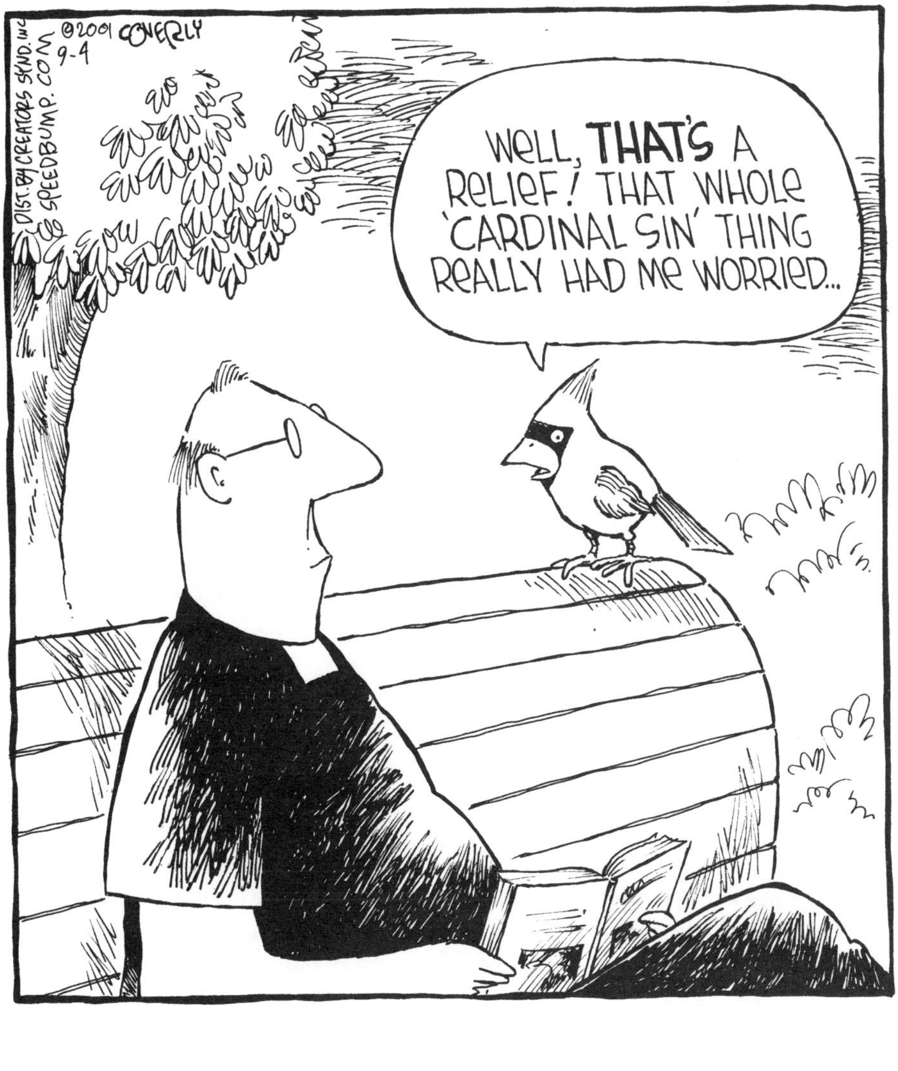
©2001 COVERLY
9-4
DIST. BY CREATORS SYND. INC.
SPEEDBUMP.COM
WELL, **THAT'S** A RELIEF! THAT WHOLE 'CARDINAL SIN' THING REALLY HAD ME WORRIED...

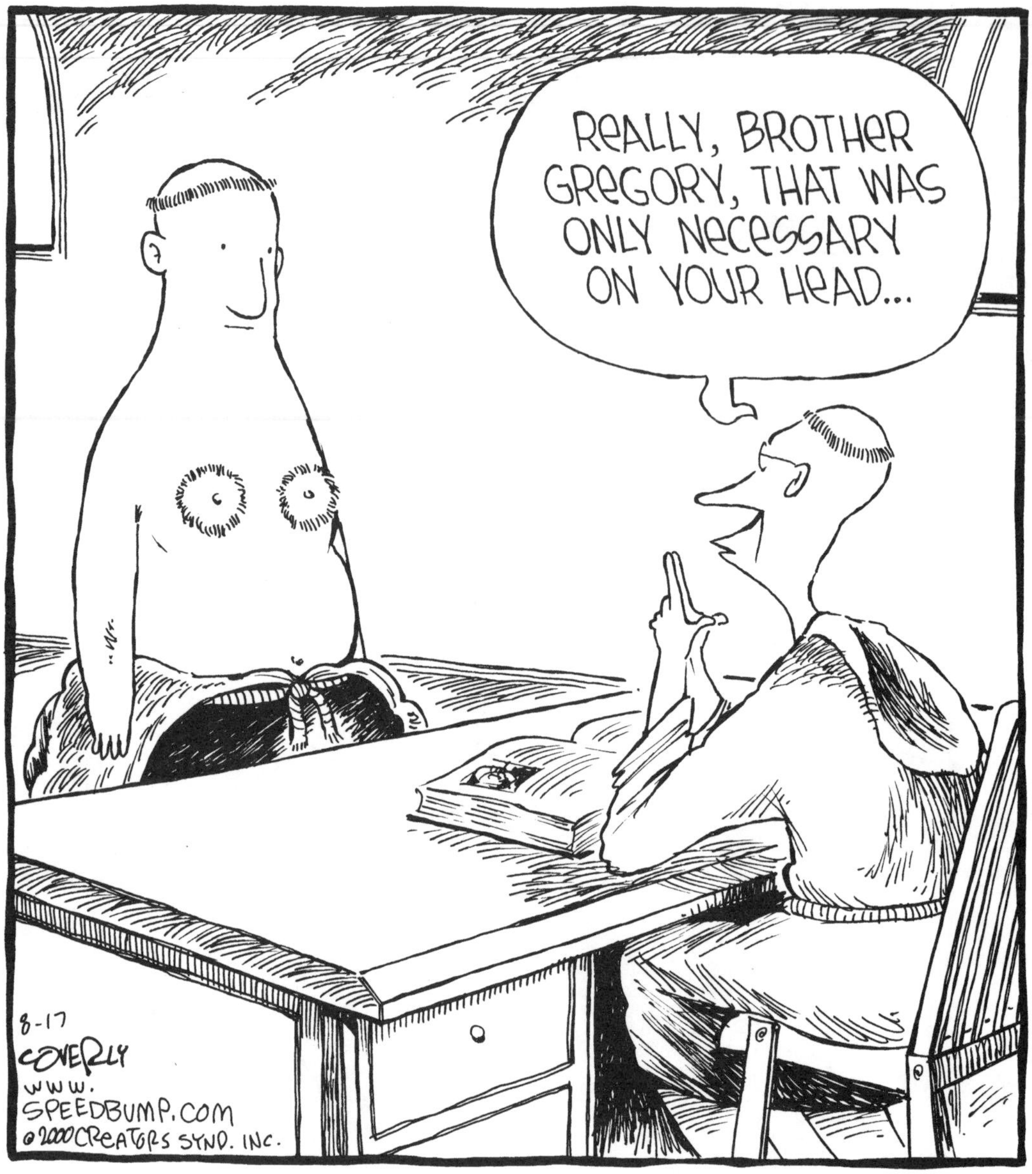
REALLY, BROTHER GREGORY, THAT WAS ONLY NECESSARY ON YOUR HEAD...
8-17
COVERLY
WWW.
SPEEDBUMP.COM
© 2000 CREATORS SYND. INC.

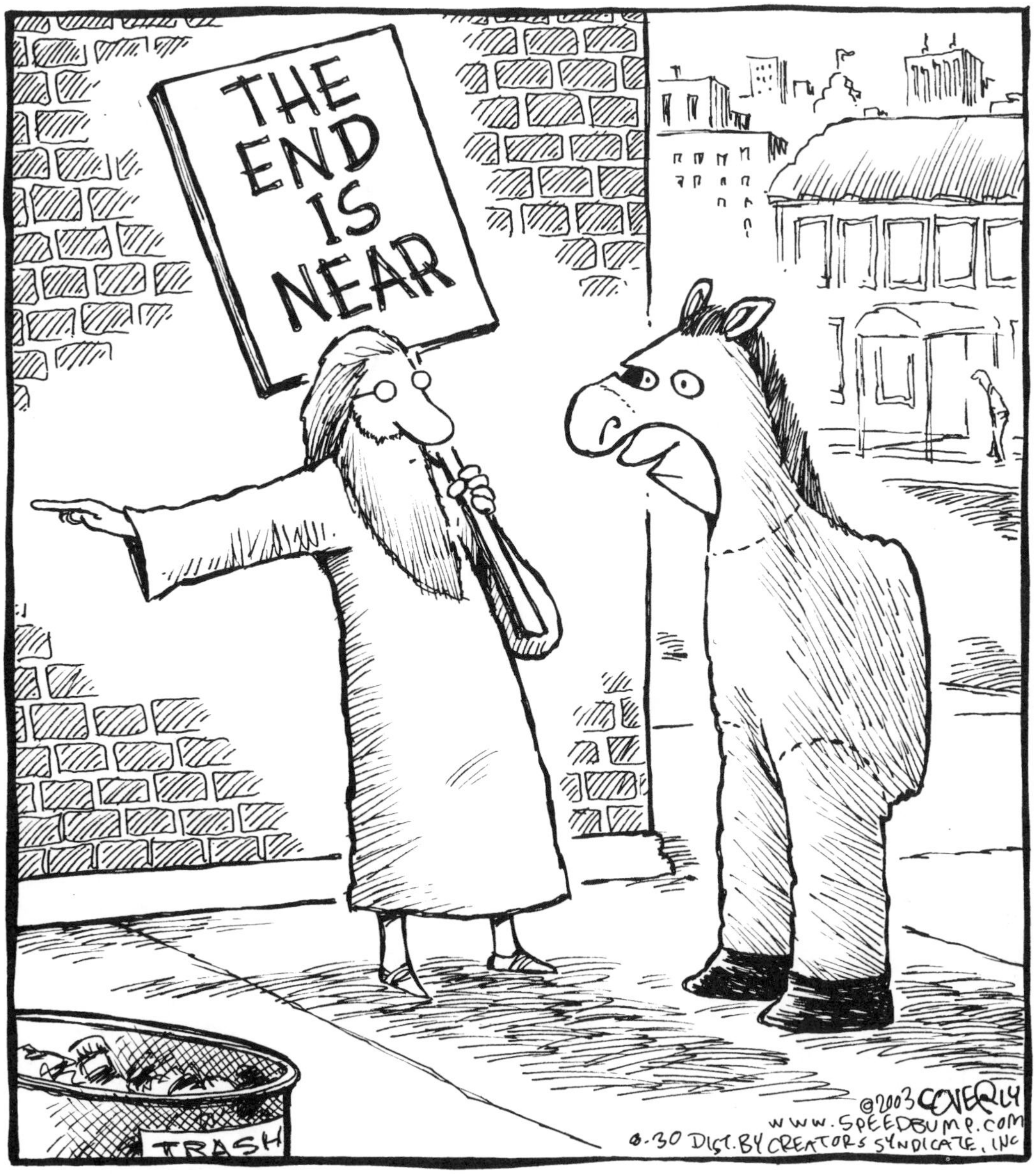
THE END IS NEAR
TRASH
©2003 COVERLY
www.SPEEDBUMP.com
8-30 DIST. BY CREATORS SYNDICATE, INC

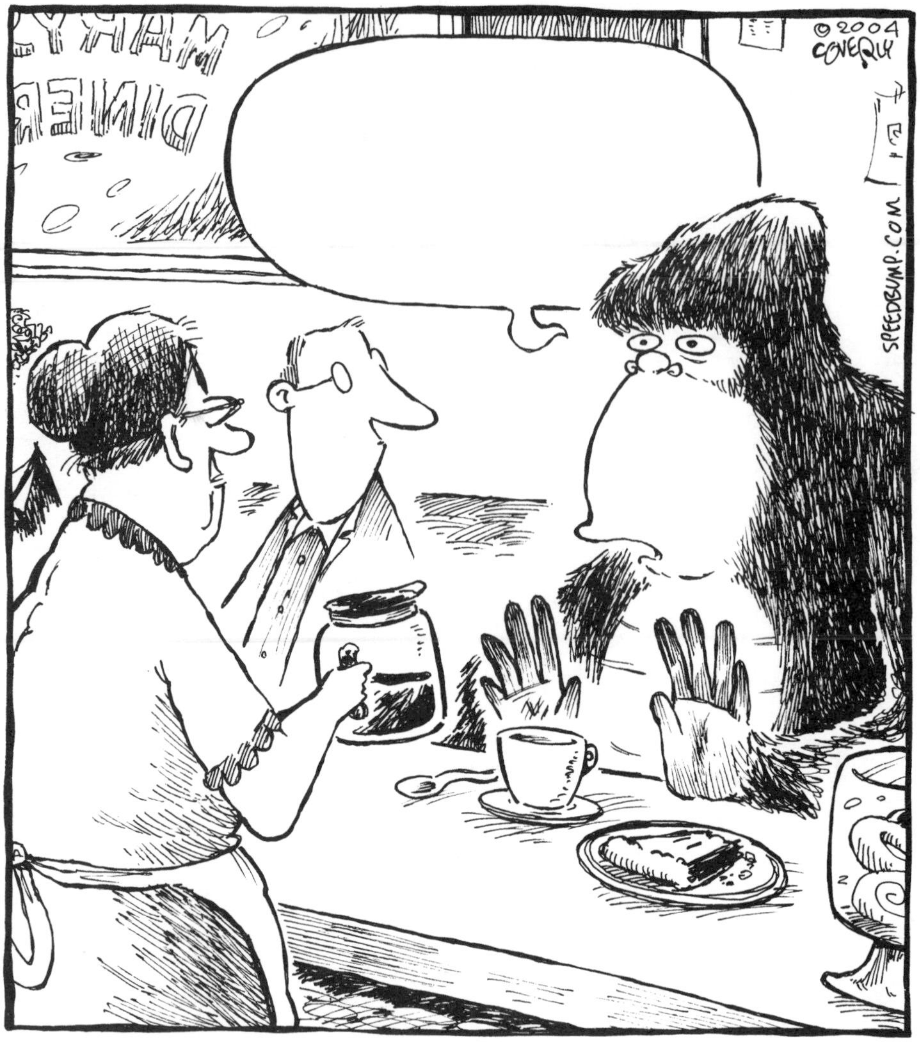
©2004 COVERLY
SPEEDBUMP.COM

Always wanted to be a cartoonist? Never wanted to be a cartoonist but have some time to kill? Hey, here's your chance to finally put your funny bone to good use. Just turn this drawing into a cartoon by filling in the word balloon — and feel free to add a caption at the bottom if you want, though it's not necessary. You may photocopy your entry, or simply include a written note with the words you'd like in the balloon (and in a caption, if you so choose). You may send your entry to the crack "Speed Bump" staff up here in the belfry in one of the following ways:

By email: **speedbump@reuben.org** (put Caption Contest in the subject line)

By post: **Speed Bump Caption Contest**
c/o Creators Syndicate
5777 W. Century Blvd., Suite 700
Los Angeles, CA 90045

For more info, visit **www.speedbump.com**. Deadline is February 6, 2005.

The winning entry will receive three personally inscribed books (you know, to use as gifts . . .), the autographed original artwork, and maybe a used fondue set or something. In addition, the winning entry will appear as a daily "Speed Bump" in many fine newspapers, with the winner's name included inside the cartoon.